Sex
in Modern Era
&
it's Solution
in Islam

By

Dr. MUFTI ALLIE HAROUN SHEIK

ADAM PUBLISHERS & DISTRIBUTORS
New Delhi-110002

© AUTHOR

Adam Publishers & Distributors
(Exporters & Importers)
1542, Pataudi House, Darya Ganj,
New Delhi-110002
Ph. : 23282550, 23284740,
Fax.: 23267510
E-mail : apd@bol.net.in,
        syedsajid_ali@rediffmail.com
website: www.adambooks.in

Edition-2008
ISBN : 81-7435-394-1
Price :

Printed & Bound in India
Published by :
S. Sajid Ali, for,
Adam Publishers & Distributors
1542, Pataudi House, Darya Ganj,
New Delhi-110002, India

TABLE OF CONTENTS

I

FOREWORD

Religion without morals bears no fruit,
Morals without religion have no roots.

We are living in times of extensive scientific, technological and engineering achievements, which in its wake has corroded the entire religious and moral structure that has been so meticulously laid down for us from the day the first human being set foot on this planet. The true teachings of the great Messengers of Allâh Ta'âlâ, which encompasses man's moral and ethical guidance are spurned and rejected publicly and privately. Great efforts are made to indoctrinate, inculcate and groom the younger generation with uninhibited immorality which fosters degeneration and breeds hatred, animosity and prejudice on the basis of race, colour, language and materialistic status.

The word "morality" comes from the word *mores*, which means behaviour and conduct. Love of Allâh Ta'âlâ and love of the whole creation are the two cardinal points of the three allied precepts: religion, morality and science. They are inseparable in Islâm and are indispensably necessary for the establishment of world peace and social harmony. Islâm is a way of life and is deeply connected with social life and human emotions. In Islâm, human life is an indivisible whole and cannot be symbolised by the terms "private" and "public". A true moral life means a complete harmonious life. A moral man is at peace with himself, with his Creator and with the entire world outside him. That is why, basically, in Islâm, a monastic life, divorced from the hurly - burly routines, detached from society and away from humanity, is discouraged. Such escapism is another form of failure and is unacceptable in Islâm.

Islâm lays down a comprehensive code of morality embracing every facet of life and it inculcates belief in life after death wherein reward and punishment will be held out to man. Religion can elevate conduct, behaviour and everyday practicalities if it is integrated with social life. Divorced from social life, religion languishes in churches, monasteries, temples, mosques and isolated areas. Clearly then, Islâm is a way of life where the chamber of the mosque and table of the laboratory go hand in hand.

Human nature is charged with emotions, passions and impulses. Any ethical or moral code which calls for their repudiation is inhuman and unnatural. What is required is their co-ordination and consolidation and their ultimate aim is the possible perfection of man and the strengthening of solidarity amongst all human beings in their everyday life. Unless religion accomplishes all this it will betray itself and will be bereft of all the influences that will enable us to live happily and usefully. Our prayers and worship will be empty and meaningless. That is why Islâm lays great emphasis on two facets. One, creations of Allâh Ta'âlâ which is nature and the other, revelation, which is The Word of Almighty, The Holy Qur'ân - the sum total of all the books revealed to the Messengers of Allâh Ta'âlâ. The latter leads us to investigate the former.

Muftî Allie Haroun, President of the E.I.C., is the founder publisher of OÂSMÎ PUBLICATIONS, which incorporates a scientific and cultural research academy, and is also Honorary Executive Member of the famous Imaamah and Da'wah Institute of Ladysmith. He is an outstanding research scholar, prolific writer and dynamic lecturer, and his Iftâ, arbitrative activities and his academic leadership and potential are well known internationally. In his approach to moral problems, he has adequately dealt with the burning issues of sexual morality in Islâm, highlighting the extent to which Islâmic value systems serve as a protective mechanism against the promiscuous modern western society. Undoubtedly his efforts are of a pioneering spirit and are of an exhaustive nature. His wife Fareeaa Begum is also a prominent educationist, who has, through her enthusiasm and inspiration, been greatly instrumental in influencing the author to accomplish a task of such magnitude.

Thus, the widely read Muftî Allie must be commended for the systematic and methodical manner in which he has thoroughly researched this book. He has thrown light in previously unchatered spheres by providing professional and authentic perceptions on highly sensitive issues, which serves as a guiding beacon not only to Muslims but to anyone wishing to shape his moral awareness. May Almighty Allâh inspire this eminent scholar to produce other outstanding work such as is accessible in this presentation.

SHEIKH ISMA'ÎL 'ABDUR-RAZACK
RECTOR - DARUL QUR'ÂN INTERNATIONAL, LADYSMITH
EX - SENIOR LECTURER : AL - AZHAR UNIVERSITY (CAIRO)

CHAPTER ONE
Introduction
MORALITY IN ISLÂM

MORALITY IN ISLÂM

1.1 INTRODUCTION

Islâm subjects human passions and desires in the service of noble goals such as obedience to Almighty Allâh Ta'âlâ which generates, in life, values of love, virtue, truth and integrity. Those steeped in sensual pleasures and who are slaves to their blind passions, are doomed to a life of deprivation and restlessness, for carnal desires, once rampant, become insatiable. The appetite increases with every effort to satisfy it resulting in a craze for the maximization of sensual pleasure. Such an attitude to life is not conducive to progress either materially or spiritually. Humanity cannot approach higher levels of nobility and virtue unless it is free from the dominance of blind carnal appetite.

Man and woman have a perpetual appeal to each other. They have been endowed with a powerful urge for sexual love, with an unlimited capacity to sexually attract each other. Their physical constitution, its proportions and shape, its complexion, even its contact and touch, have a strange spell on the opposite sex. Their voice, their gait, their manner and appearance, each has a magnetic power. Moreover, the world around them abounds in factors that perpetually arouse their sexual impulse and make one inclined towards the other. The soft murmuring breeze, the running water, the natural hues of vegetation, the sweet smell of flowers, the chirping of birds, the dark clouds, the charms of the moon-lit night, in short, all the beauty and all the grace of nature, stimulate directly or indirectly the sexual urge between the opposite sexes.

This is a clear indication of the design of nature that the great measure in which sexual urge and appeal has been placed in man is not meant to enable him to perform the sexual act more often than animals, but it is meant to unite man and woman in a lifelong companionship. That is why the human species has been endowed, besides sexual desire and appeal, with modesty and resistance.

Modesty or *hayâ*, purity of mind, body and soul are of fundamental importance to the lofty moral culture of Islâm. When *hayâ* is displaced, immorality, with all its accompaniment of evil and other disastrous consequences, becomes the order of the day. The displacement of modesty in a community opens the door to the worst kind of vice which ruins the moral, spiritual and physical fibre of the human being. Man's natural barrier against immorality is the noble attribute which Allâh Ta'âlâ has endowed to people in various degrees. The importance of *hayâ* can be gauged from the fact that the Prophet Muhammad ﷺ equates *hayâ* with Îmân (faith), according it the same pedestal as can be deduced from the following hadîth:

"Hayâ is a branch of Îmân". [1]

Its necessity in the Islâmic moral framework is of such vital importance that the Prophet ﷺ described modesty as an inseparable constituent of Islâm - when *hayâ* disappears, Îmân follows suit. In one instance the Prophet ﷺ mentioned:

" If you don't feel ashamed, then do whatever you like ". [2]

Immorality will certainly fill the vacuum left by the elimination of *hayâ*. The Qur'ân cautions believers:

" Do not follow in the footsteps of Shaitân, for verily, he is for you an open enemy. He commands you with evil and immorality." [3]

For the benefit of the human race and for the healthy development of society, Islâm has decreed the separation of the sexes and has strictly forbidden any unlawful association between them. Even a cursory study of the *Hijâb* (purdah) laws of Islâm will indicate that all such restrictions and advice have been designed to protect the lofty and pure morality which Islâm considers vital for the healthy spiritual development of the believer. While the emphasis of Islâm is on moral and sexual purity, the culture of modern civilization strongly advocates the denial of this purity to make way for the immoral and carnal desires of the *nafs*. Thus self expression of bestial desires is an accepted norm of life in such a society. In view of the utter destruction and total elimination of sexual morality and modesty, western society considers immoral exhibitions such as promiscuous intermingling of sexes, fornication by mutual consent, wife swapping, strip-tease, homosexuality, lesbianism, bestiality, prostitution, pornography and a host of other immoral vices acceptable to the intelligence of man. Such evils are no longer frowned upon. In fact, these shameless deeds of moral destruction are now regarded as healthy acts of pleasure to be cultivated and indulged in without restraint. Those who practice such immorality actually have the gall to campaign for their "rights" to be enshrined in the constitution of countries throughout the world.

Permissiveness has never been so common as it is today. Immorality and obscenity is widely accepted as natural forms of behaviour. Modern man puts forward the argument that he is an animal like any other animal and has certain urges and desires like any other animal. He has a few moments to fulfil these urges and desires after which he will disappear behind the curtain of non existence. Whatever he desires may only be achieved in this short lifespan. Therefore, instead of suppressing his desires, he should accelerate their fulfilment so that he may enjoy the maximum pleasure from life, and should not leave this world with his desires and aspirations unfulfilled.

Most religious codes and moral attitudes have made fornication so distasteful that it presents a picture of sinfulness; but this analysis of fornication shows only that in the need to satisfy his natural desires and urges, man has not observed the limits which have been artificially raised around him. However, universal condemnation of fornication has not gone far enough in opposing this distasteful act. Ironically, according to those who promote such indecent acts, it is no crime to oppose these restrictions and it is nothing for which one may be regarded as sinful. Just as it is absurd to question how an animal satisfies its desires, likewise to say what restrictions man should or should not observe in the fulfilment of his desires, is also absurd. Moreover, according to proponents of fornication, what needs to be examined is whether or not this act does any damage to anyone. If this act is harmful to any individual or society, it should certainly be forbidden otherwise there is no reason not to make it lawful.

This philosophy has proven that beastly qualities are inherent in man and are part of his nature. Arguments have been presented to justify man's slavery to desires, so that conscience, which hinders any sin, may be obliterated, and his heart may indulge in sexual pleasures as if he were doing good. A plan has been prepared for this: if people see, they see pornography; if people hear, they hear sensual music; there is also free mixing of men and women; immoral literature and education; nudity in magazines and newspapers; obscene films and intoxicating drugs and alcohol. In short, is there any instrument which sparks the fire of licentiousness, sensuousness and lust that modern man has not used?

Its consequences are heart rendering; teenage girls in secular schools are sexually active and an alarmingly large portion of school leaving girls have any sense of modesty and still retain their chastity. Thousands of women wander about in the parks, pubs, recreation centres, subway stations and other such places to hunt for their prey, for fun or for money, or for both, and enjoy the pleasures of life without any regret. Nude and gay clubs, centres of fornication, obscenity and immorality are found in almost every big city. Their poisonous tentacles are slowly infiltrating the minds and hearts of unsuspecting Muslims throughout the globe. Therefore, mankind today, is afflicted with a sort of moral leprosy which is eating fast into its vitals and filling the whole world with its stench.

1.2 METHODOLOGY OF THE RESEARCH

The writing of this thesis has been governed by a policy of accuracy, clarity and fairness, so that each aspect is described in a way, which reflects as sincerely as possible its moral development and present character. The aim is to provide reliable information for those who are unfamiliar with most or even all aspects of sexual morality among the various denominations, in a way which does justice to the experience of adherents themselves within each tradition. It involves two main strategies. Firstly, the enquirer set aside or suspended his personal judgements in order to be able to appreciate the subject on its own terms. Secondly, the enquirer then attempted to achieve as much empathy with the subject as possible, trying to develop a feeling for the culture in question that is as close as possible to the experience of those who are members of that ethical denomination. It follows that there is no attempt in this thesis to promote any of the religions at the expense of others, or to advocate anything other than a sensitive understanding of them all.

1.3 CHAPTERIZATION

In this thesis, the issues pertaining to the pre-Islâmic era, the social system of Islâm, divine laws concerning modesty and chastity, sexual vice and its remedy, unnatural sexual tendencies, sex education, and the Islâmic emphasis on sexual morality are discussed under six chapters.

Chapter one comprises the introduction, methodology of the research and chapterization.

The chapter that follows takes readers on a journey of discovery through the world's main spiritual landscapes. The journey begins with primal societies, some of which existed only in prehistoric times while others have endured till our time and continue to exert a significant influence in parts of the world. Thereafter we turn to the activities of the ancient civilizations that emerged from about 6 000 years ago. Our global journey then moves onward from India, before turning westward to the three Abrahamic faiths. These are the religions that have spiritual links with the patriarch Ibrâhîm ﷺ namely Judaism, Christianity and Islâm. Within the limits of an introductory book it is, of course, impossible to cover everything, so we have selected the main religions world-wide which are specifically relevant here, together with the ancient empires and societies because of their inherent interest and great influence on subsequent developments. Thus this chapter commences with a discussion of the decline of mighty civilizations due to the transgression of women's rights and status during the pre-Islâmic era. Thereafter mention is made of the oppression and tyranny which women underwent which eventually led to the cruel practice of infanticide. This can be gauged by the many Qur'ânic and Ahâdîth quotations given. The various forms of marriage undertaken during the Days of Ignorance, which was a gross violation of the Divine Decree and of nature itself, is a topic also discussed. This is followed by a thorough investigation into the slandering of the dignity of women amongst various nations. These evils which resulted in world wide gloom brings this chapter to an end.

Chapter three discusses the social system of Islâm, viz. the purpose of creation and the status of men and women; condemnation of infanticide and the treatment of female offspring; fundamental principals of prohibited relations; man as provider and the woman's sphere of activity and the woman's economic, social and educational rights. A distinction and comparison is drawn between the western concept of morality and the social system of Islâm. Thereafter celibacy and its detrimental effects and securing the safety of chastity through marriage is discussed. This is followed by a complete condemnation of *mut'âh* (temporary marriage). Clandestine affairs and secret liaisons which leads many marriages to divorce courts are also discussed. This chapter concludes by mentioning the abhorrence of divorce in Islâm and the formula that _Sharî'ât_ has prescribed to prevent such a separation.

Chapter four analyses the social vice that emanate from sexual gratification out of wedlock via the agencies of fornication, prostitution, rape and bestiality which is directly linked to

8

pornography. Degrading sexual objectification, which is the common denominator to all pornography, is thereafter elaborated upon. A penetrating discussion ensues regarding the harmful effects and the perpetrators of this vice. This chapter ends by providing Islâmic solutions in curtailing and combating these illicit sexual encounters.

Chapter five revolves around the most common and most prevalent forms of sexual deviation wherein the preference for sexual relations with a person of the same sex such as homosexuality and lesbianism, has been highlighted. This is followed by the question of whether homosexuality is a choice or whether it is found in the genetic and hormonal compound of the human race. Homosexual linked behaviour patterns and gay marriages are also discussed followed by a focus on these unnatural tendencies thriving in the prisons and army. Qur'ânic and Ahâdîth quotations are then given depicting the severe chastisement that was meted out to Sodomites in the past which served as a grim warning to would be offenders. This chapter concludes by outlining the hazards of the deadly Aids, the carrier of which is plagued with the agonising loss of life.

Chapter six exposes the devastating effects that early immoral sexual education, as taught in modern secular schools, has created in the minds and character of school going children, who are taught all the intimate details of genital relationships, even graphically. Such education is currently being spread by large organizations and international associations that promote contraception, abortion and sterilization and who want to impose a false lifestyle against the truth of human sexuality. A call is then made to parents and guardians to reject the promotion of so called 'safe sex', a dangerous and immoral policy based on the deluded theory that the condom can provide adequate protection against Aids and to insist on continence outside marriage, and to accept that fidelity in marriage as the only true and secure education for the preservation of sexual morality.

CHAPTER TWO
The Pre-Islâmic Era
MORALITY IN ISLÂM

THE PRE - ISLÂMIC ERA

2.1 INTRODUCTION

The age before Islâm was steeped in ignorance whereby the mind and the spirit of man had become corrupted while the high standards and values of life had been debased. It was an age of tyranny and slavery in which the very roots of humanity were being corroded by a criminally luxurious and wasteful life on the one hand, and hopelessness, frustration and despair on the other. In addition to this, clouds of infidelity were hovering overhead and the religions of the world were helpless in dispelling them. Religions that called themselves heavenly had already fallen victims to disintegration. They had lost prestige and had become a body devoid of all spirituality and vitality thus reducing them to a mere depository of rituals and symbols.

The Greeks, Romans and Persians who enjoyed the status of leadership throughout the world, had sunk to a state of complete moral depravity. Their empires had become store-houses of vice and mischief. The governing classes, intoxicated with power, indulged in reckless sensuality. The middle classes took extreme pleasure in aping them. As for the common people, they lived in grinding poverty, toiling and sweating like beasts so that the others could live in extreme luxury.

2.2 THE GREEKS

Initially, the Greek ideal of a woman was a lofty one. Greek poetry offered a wealth of impressive and imperishable types of womanhood both in the physical and the spiritual sense eg. Helena, Penelope, Cassandra etc. In fact the capable woman, especially in Hellenistic Asia Minor and also in Greece, occupied a surprisingly independent and influential role even in public life.

Marriage was the rule except in so far as freer forms of sexual intercourse replaced it. In practice, Greek marriage was strictly monogamous in the later period. The mutual relations of married couples were often affectionate, especially in middle class circles. Thus the wife of an officer who for reasons of service was left alone at nights assured him that she had no more pleasure than in food or drink. Divorces were not common. They occurred by common consent, or by the unilateral action of the husband.[1]

But as they progressed, the Greeks, the established intellectual leaders of ancient times, began to hold women in disgrace and cared little for their sexual morality and chastity. Women were regarded as an inferior creation. If a woman gave birth to a child in an unnatural manner e.g. premature birth, she was sent to the gallows. In Sparta, the unfortunate woman who was found incapable of giving the country a soldier for its defence was put to death. When a woman had delivered her child she was, in the interest of the nation, taken from her husband temporarily and given to someone for insemination and propagation of a race of fighting men for the defence of the country. According to the Greek mythology, Pandora was the source of all human ills and misfortunes, like the Eve of Jewish mythology. These misconceptions adversely affected law, social customs, moral as well as general attitude towards life. The Greeks regarded the woman as a sub-human creature whose rank in society was in every way inferior to that of man, for whom alone was reserved the pedestals of dignity.[2]

The Greeks gradually became overwhelmed by sexual excitement to the extent that the corrupt female gained such prominence the likes of which has no parallel in history. The brothels, massage parlours and escort agencies became the focus of attention of all classes of the Greek society, and attracted their philosophers, poets, historians and professional artists. She not only patronized literary functions but also important political affairs. It may seem strange, but the counsel of one who did not remain faithfully attached to one man even for two consecutive nights was eagerly sought and respected in matters which depended on the life and death of the entire nation. Their good taste and worship of beauty aroused in the Greek people a thirst for sensual pleasure and an increase in sexual appetite.

They degenerated to such an extent that even their philosophers and educators did not regard adultery and permissiveness as worthy of censure.

The common man looked upon matrimony as an unnecessary restriction and considered fornication as perfectly lawful. Eventually, these became a part of their religion, and the worship of Aphrodite, the goddess of love and beauty, spread throughout Greece. According to their mythology, this goddess, who was the legal wife of one god, had developed illicit relations with three other gods as well as with a mortal. The result of this last illicit relationship was the birth of another god, Cupid, the god of love. Thus, houses of prostitution became places of worship and whores were considered as pious women dedicated to service of the temples, while fornication was raised to the status of piety and invested with full religious sanctity.

The prevalence of the unnatural act among the Greeks, which was welcomed and encouraged by religion and morality, was also another typical example of their sexual perversion. Nudity and indulgence in the sexual pleasures became known as art and exhibition. Artists displayed this craving in statues and paintings. Moral law makers described it as an extension of the *"bond of friendship"* between two persons. Harmodius and Aristogiton were the first two Greeks who won their countrymen's approval and high acclaim on account of their unnatural relationship with each other and were epitomized in statues to be glorified for ages to come.[3] The Greeks also believed that Zeus, in order to punish human beings, invented women *"a lovely tempter of innocent mankind"* and named her Pandora. *"She, being vain, frivolous and curious, was responsible for causing the spread of old age, disease, insanity, passion, envy, spite, revenge, cruelty, and every other plague that brings mischief and misery to man in this world."*[4]

After this ancient period of pride and grandeur had elapsed, Greece was never afforded another opportunity to retrace its steps to the pinnacle of splendour.

15

2.3   THE RISE AND DECLINE OF THE ROMANS

Among the Romans, the status of the housewife was esteemed. The husband had only a mild superiority which constantly diminished. Corporal chastisement was sometimes recommended but rarely practised. In the conduct of the household the woman had equality. Even among the Roman Stoics there were exertions on behalf of equal education. All sexual intercourse either outside or prior to marriage was frowned upon. In marriage the physical union was for the purpose of producing good citizens. It was to be sustained, however, by the spiritual communion of the partners, who were fully equal. Grounds of divorce were the rise of the husband to a higher social class, childlessness, poisoning of the children or merely the desire for another marriage. The woman had almost incalculable influence, especially when she had sons and when she could act skilfully.[5]

With the advancement on the road to civilization, the status of the woman underwent a drastic change. Divorce became easy and wedlock was ended on flimsy grounds. Seneca, the famous Roman philosopher and statesman from the classical period, had severely criticized his countrymen for the high incidence of divorce among them. He says:

> *"Now divorce is not regarded as something*
> *shameful in Rome. Women calculate their*
> *age by the number of husbands they have*
> *taken."*[6]

The Romans as a nation led a bawdy and sensual life. Visits to prostitutes were considered part of the education of young men in Pompeii. In this city there were about a dozen brothels and a Sin street to cater for the needs of a population of 20 000 souls. In these brothels were found many of the famous obscene frescoes of Pompeii. These works are so outrageous that today female tourists are not allowed to see them.[7] The Roman Emperor Commodus valued nothing in sovereign power except the unbounded license of indulging in his sexual appetites. His hours were spent in the company of three hundred beautiful women and as many boys, of every rank and of every province; and wherever the arts of seduction proved ineffectual, the brutal lover had recourse to violence.

16

The victims died in torment. Some were nailed on crosses; others sewn up in the skins of wild beasts and exposed to the fury of wild dogs; others again, smeared over with combustile materials, were used as torches to illuminate the darkness of the night.[8]

As soon as public morality declined, the flood of nudity and sexual licentiousness burst upon Rome. Dwelling places were decorated with nude and immoral paintings; theatres became the scenes of moral perversion and prostitution became rife. Flora became a popular Roman sport in which naked women competed in race contests. Males and females bathed together publicly. Roman literature was brimming with immodest themes and episodes. When the Romans were completely overtaken by, amongst other factors, carnal desires, they faded into oblivion, leaving not a trace of their glorious past.

2.4   THE PERSIAN EMPIRE

Persia, then practicing the dualistic religious system taught by Zoroaster, and now referred to as Irân, was equal to Rome in the administration of the civilized world. Its moral structures had never been sound. It was an old hotbed of vice and folly. Sexual relationships which were considered criminal in other parts of the world were not unlawful or undesirable in the opinion of the Persians. It is mentioned that Yazdegard 11, who ruled during the middle of the fifth century, married his own daughter and afterwards killed her; and that Bahram Chobin, in the sixth century had marital relations with his own sister. They found nothing sinful in incestuous relationships.[9]

Under royal encouragement, the teachings of Mazdak who proclaimed that wealth and women should be freely and equally available to all men, spread instantly, thus catapulting Persia into sexual lawlessness. According to Tabarî, pleasure-loving people rejoiced at this opportunity and even the common people were caught in this tempest. This movement exerted such great influence that everyone could step into any person's home and take possession of his wife and property. Things accelerated at such a rapid pace that parents could not recognize their children, nor children their parents. The empire was overtaken by corruption and confusion.[10] A flood of sexual immorality and licentiousness swept over Persia. Sensual enjoyment became the chief objective in life. They began competing with other nations, especially Rome, in blind self indulgence, luxury and extravagance.

Assessing the utter moral and social darkness that had enveloped the world during this period, <u>Sh</u>âh Waliullâh Mu<u>h</u>addi<u>th</u> Dehlawî in his famous *Hujjatullâh al-Bâli<u>gh</u>ah* remarks:

> *"Centuries of undisputed mastery over large parts of the world, irreligiousness and wholesale surrender to devilish temptations had created among the Persians and Romans great selectiveness of taste regarding comforts of life. They strove hard to outdo one another in the display of crude sensualism."* [11]

2.5   INDIA

The notorious subordination of the Hindu woman is believed by many authorities to be entirely due to the lawgivers. To some scholars it is inconceivable that the healthy-minded Aryans who entered the Indian peninsula would have subjected their women to the fate they later suffered under the legalistic dispensation, or indeed the Aryan women would have allowed themselves to suffer the general insulting treatment in which they came to be held.

In the Vedic period most religious rites and ceremonies were open to women, who had privileges of participation and observance with their menfolk. They took an active part in the sacrifices and executed ritual acts. The Vedic Age produced a score of eminent female scholars, poets and teachers, but by the time of the lawgivers, the literate woman had become the accursed and detested person. Manu decreed that women had no right to study. Not only did literacy become a rare quality in women, but it was even regarded as disreputable. Girls were once given the same kind of basic education as boys, but the lawgivers declared women to be inherently impure and hence u:.fit to receive sacred education. Women were lumped together with sinners, slaves and outcasts. A man could not eat with his wife but it was meritorious if she ate his left overs. She was not supposed to walk side by side with her husband, but must remain a few paces behind him. Sterility in woman was the supreme curse. Said M.K. Gandhi:

> *"Hindu culture has erred on the side of*
> *excessive subordination of the wife to the*
> *husband. This has resulted in the husband*
> *usurping and exercising authority that*
> *reduces him to the level of the brute."* [12]

Female infanticide was practised on a wide scale from earliest times. The casting away of the children of unmarried mothers, of unwanted girl babies, and the destruction of the foetus are mentioned in Vedic texts. Among the Rajputs, parents used to kill their children by refusing proper nourishment or sometimes even poisoning the nipples of the mother's breast.[13]

2.5.1   THE STATUS OF WOMEN AND SEXUAL LAWLESSNESS

India, which was once the cradle of great religion and a mighty civilization, now absorbed all the evils of moral degeneration that had overtaken the neighbouring countries. The position of women in Hindu society was deplorable. She was regarded as sub-human and worshipped her husband as a god and on his death was forced to burn herself with her dead husband. It was common practice in ancient India to have a family bride, or a common wife of several brothers. All of them had sexual intercourse with her and she bore children from them all.[14]

"*Nyog*" is when a childless woman could have children at will by the younger brother of the husband or some other relative with the permission of the father-in-law or some other authority. This was rife among Brahmans. Similarly, if the husband was very troublesome, the wife could leave him and have children for her husband from some other man. Dayanand mentions:

> *"When the husband is incapable of*
> *begetting offspring, he should permit his*

19

> *wife, saying, 'O you dutiful wife, desirous*
> *of offspring, find for yourself a husband*
> *other than myself, for I shall not be able*
> *to give you children'. Then the wife should*
> *have children by some other man, but*
> *should not be unmindful of the service of*
> *a high-minded husband, she should allow*
> *the husband to get children from some*
> *other women through Nyog.*[15]

There are many other ways mentioned in which people could resort to sexual intercourse through *nyog*. However, the status of women in ancient Indian society is further illustrated by the following:

> *"Fate, storm, death, heil, poison, the*
> *venomous serpent - none of these is so evil*
> *as the woman ... The woman in her*
> *childhood is under the control of the father,*
> *in youth under her husband, and after him,*
> *controlled by her sons, and in their*
> *absence by her relatives, since no woman*
> *is capable of living her life*
> *independently."*[6]

On the death of their husbands, women were condemned to a state of everlasting misery. They were not allowed to remarry and lived as slaves to the brothers of their husbands or their descendants. If a Hindu man's wife died, he was free to find another beautiful woman whenever he wanted, but if the Hindu woman's husband died, not only was she prohibited to re-marry, but she would be cremated alive along with her dead husband (*sati*). Brahman theologians propagated the theory that a woman who did not burn herself would never become free of being born as a woman again.

The *Times of India* reported:

> *"Jaipur - In what happened to be a revival*
> *of a centuries-old custom of "Sati", a*

> *young woman belonging to a warrior caste*
> *of Rajasthan climbed into the funeral pyre*
> *of her husband, police said. Eighteen-year*
> *old Roop Kanwar's husband, Mansingh,*
> *had died in hospital. His body was later*
> *taken to his home village for cremation.*
> *Roop Kanwar sat on the funeral pyre while*
> *it was lit. Hundreds of villagers who knew*
> *of her 'sati' well in advance gathered at*
> *the spot shouting slogans in praise of the*
> *burning widow."*

The paper continued that the most revealing statement came from a village teacher who said:

> *"The society treats a widow as an evil*
> *omen, and an economic liability. She has*
> *to remain barefoot, sleep on the floor and*
> *is not allowed to venture out of the house.*
> *She is slandered if seen talking to any*
> *male. It was better that she died, than live*
> *such a life."* [17]

A police report established conclusively that Roop Kanwar was forced onto the funeral pyre against her will and she did try to escape before it was lit. She was unable to do so as logs of wood were stacked up to her neck. She cried piteously as she died with the flames engulfing her. What a gruesome death for a sixteen-year old widow!

According to Mahabarata the position of women degenerated to such an extent that they were found to be humiliated and helpless in the hands of men, rishis and so-called gods of heaven.

In the episode of Parashar and Satyavati we find the helpless position of a woman who sacrificed her virginity to meet the sexual desire of the great rishi Parashar. He was greatly captivated by her beauty and satisfied his sexual desire in a most heinous way. Such action violated all moral codes of life. All her appeals to save her maidenhood went in vain. The sages in those days were looked upon with awe and terror for their yogic power.

In the episode of Kunti and the "Sun-god" we find a helpless woman in the hand of a so-called god. Kunti in her maiden state received glad tidings that she might have a child if she would worship the desired god. Out of childish curiosity she worshipped the Sun-god. The "god" came before her and wanted to enjoy her. All her appeals for the sake of humanity and morality went in vain.

In the case of King Dusyanta and Shakunala we notice the same wretchedness of women. The King Dusyanta married her and after fulfilling his carnal desires returned to the capital but did not venture to bring her with him. Pregnant, she came to the royal court to meet her husband, but the king immediately refused her petition. It is the sacred duty of a husband to protect his wife against all odds of life, but instead of doing just that, this so-called virtuous king, not only abused her chastity but also began falsely proclaiming her to be a harlot.

Puloma, who was the legal wife of rishi Bhrigu, was pregnant. One demon came to abduct her on the plea that she was his formerly proposed wife. For this purpose he obtained the decree of the "fire-god" in his favour. What a mind boggling incident - how can one's married wife become the property of another person, and that too, by the verdict of a god. What an unvirtuous act! Here, molestation of Puloma means molestation of womankind in general.

In the episode of Sudarsan and Oghavati we find the same tone. Sudarsan ordered his wife that under no circumstances should she neglect the spirit of hospitality. The guests should be entertained at any cost. She should even surrender herself for the satisfaction of the guest if the need arose. It happened that she was forced to have sexual intercourse with her guests.[18] Here we find the clashing of three human virtues viz, hospitality, obedience of woman to her husband and chastity of woman. The first two virtues were chosen and the third was neglected. Thus chastity was not valued much in those days. In the universal outlook, whatever might be the spirit of hospitality, the murder of morality is a crime - it is the direct insult to woman-kind. The spirit of hospitality is indeed very great and one must maintain it with the best effort. But there must be a limit to such entertainment. It is the most vicious act on the part of the guest to demand the host's wife for sexual gratification.

If this is the attitude of the religion of hospitality - then it is not a religion at all. It reflects greatly on womanhood - the women in general would sneer at it with disgust and hostility, since this attitude would elevate prostitution to the pedestal of chastity.

The horrible characterisation of womankind, whereby their fidelity, chastity and morality seemed to have been usurped, can be observed from the following remarks which are depicted in the *Mahabarata.*

> *"Women are the source of all evils. They can forsake all things for gratification of their evil wishes. They are sexual in the extreme point. The sexuality is the flesh and blood of them. They do not care for the husband's good name and prosperity. They unite with other men whenever they get chances. The virtue of loyalty and modesty is unknown to them. They do not hesitate to co-habit with anyone - and for this purpose they do not consider the age, grace, figure and complexion of the co-habiting partners. They care little whether such partners are hunchbacks, dwarfs, blind, foolish, decrepit and ugly. They are lascivious in nature and extremely sexy. In absence of co-habiting partner they use to make artificial masculine penis for sexual gratification. They are so vicious and dangerous that when they are weighed in the weight - box, all extremely harmful things like death, fire, poisonous snakes, the sharp edge of a sword, will not be collectively equal to a woman."* [19]

Nowhere do obscene subjects and sexual themes occupy such a prominent place in religion as they did in ancient India. It requires no great imagination to picture what indecent practices must have gone on in the name of religion. Even prostitution was an accepted way of life amongst the priests. King Dasharatha, who, in order to have a baby son, delivered his three wives to three priests. These 'holy' men, having fully satisfied their carnal desire returned the ladies to the king. In this way, the king was able to fulfil his desires.[20]

Even in present times, this type of religious prostitution is still being practiced. The *Times of India* confirms that the practice of dedicating Harijan girls (regarded as low caste) at childhood to a goddess, and their initiation into temple prostitution when they attain puberty continues to thrive in Karnataka, Andra Pradesh and other parts of South India. The Devadasi system (religious prostitution) was the result of a conspiracy between the feudal class and the priests (Brahmans).

According to a study made during health camps organised by the World Health Organisation in the Devadasi populated areas, it was revealed that the dedicated girls formed 15 percent of the women involved in prostitution in the country, and as much as 70 to 80 percent of the prostitutes in the border districts of Karnataka and Maharashtra.[21]

Brahminism has also created *Kamasutra* - a set of instructions on how to have sexual intercourse. Some of the postures, detailed in *Kamasutra* are so complex that they can only be preformed with the help of one or more assistants.

There were also reports that police arrested a "miracle man" in Western India for raping a number of women, on the pretext of solving their problems, by making them sit naked before an idol which was supposed to render "divine advice". He would hold a blank sheet of paper over a fire on which written words would appear. He would then convince the women to have sex with him on the strength of the 'miracle'. Police discovered that his "divine advice" was nothing but a simple chemical trick. The words were written on the paper with invisible ink and would become legible when held over a flame.[22]

Parallel to this devotion to the flesh and sensuality, a strong movement of self-denial was also apparent in the country. Between these two movements, the moral fabric of the society had been torn to shreds. While a small section of the population was subjecting itself to useless self-torture, the bulk indulged in vulgar self-indulgence.

2.6   JUDAISM

The classical writings of Judaism, almost exclusively written by men, and encompassing a period of over 2 000 years, naturally depict a variety of views on women. It is impossible therefore, to speak of a single Jewish attitude to women. Opinions were affected by different cultural and social backgrounds, by the special patterns which had been obtained in a given age, and by the personal experiences and individual temperaments of the Jewish teachers. Although ancient society was essentially male-dominated, the Jews preserved a generally favourable view of woman, particularly in the framework of the family but also in the religious life.

Within the Covenant, woman had the same moral responsibility as men. The man or the woman who apostasized would suffer the death penalty (Deut. 17:2,5). The woman's status as a human being was recognized in legislation. Special attention was paid to injury suffered by a pregnant woman during a brawl between men. (Ex. 21:22-25) The difference between man and woman was also recognized eg. in their respective modes of dress (Deut. 22:5). Both parties guilty of adultery, the man and the woman, were subject to the death penalty (Lev. 20:10). Likewise, both faced capital punishment for stepmother - stepson incest and a higher punitive measure for sibling (or half sibling) incest (Lev. 20:11). The regulations pertaining to food were incumbent on women as well as men (Lev. 11). The Law demanded equal respect for the father and the mother. (Ex. 20:12).

Nevertheless, there were certain laws that revealed the inferior status assigned to women in Israelite society. A man could sell his daughter as payment for a debt (Ex. 21:7), but he was forbidden to force her into prostitution (Lev. 19:29). If she were sold into bondage, her master was forbidden to resell her. If he were not satisfied with her, she could be redeemed; if he gave her to his son he was to treat her as a daughter (Ex.

21:7-11).

Apart from the laws of impurity to which both men and women were subjected, a woman was regarded as menstruous both during her menstrual flow and for seven days thereafter (Lev. 15:1). She was also regarded as menstruous for the first seven days after giving birth to a male child and forbidden to touch consecrated objects or visit a sanctuary for the next 33 days; both figures were doubled if the child was a female (Lev. 12:2-5).[23]

Women were also feared as a source of temptation. In Babylon, possibly because of the greater laxity in sexual matters among the general population, it was said that a woman's voice is a sexual enticement as is her hair and her leg (Ber. 24a). The woman was also said to have played a key role in introducing disobedience into the Garden of Eden (Gen. 3). The reason for God creating Eve from Adam's rib is stated that she should not hold up her head too proudly; nor from the eye that she should not be coquette; nor from the ear that she should not be an eavesdropper; nor from the mouth that she should not be too talkative; nor from the heart that she should not be too jealous; nor from the hand that she should not be too acquisitive; nor from the foot that she should not be a gadabout; but from a part of the body which is hidden that she should be modest (Gen. R. 18:2).

The biblical view of woman's origin is expressed in Genesis 2:23-24. Created to serve man as a suitable helper, she was formed from a rib taken from the first man, and her essence as a human being is linked with her function as companion to the male. The primary reason for the two sexes is the need for reproduction (Gen. 1:26-28). The woman's chief function was childbearing and the good wife and mother would enjoy praise from her husband and her children (Prov. 31:28). The marital relationship was to be more intimate than that of parent and child (Gen. 2:24). In Rabbinic writings we occasionally hear praises of a virtuous woman. "Her husband is adorned by her, but she is not adorned by her husband." (Gn.r., 47 on 17:15). Before God, wives have equal, if not greater promise than their husbands. (Ex.r., 21 on 14:15). Particular mention may be made of Rahel as an example of one who manifested and extraordinary piety and readiness for sacrifice in the Jewish sense.

Marriage was a duty for loyal Jews. Not to further propagation of the species was tantamount to shedding blood. Marital intercourse was demanded by the Rabbis though not to excess. It was emphasized that it should not be for reasons of carnal desire. Though the main emphasis in Judaism is on the physical side of marriage, there is no lack of a more spiritual and personal relationship between the partners and an appreciation of this factor. Strict Judaism opposed not only adultery and unnatural license, but also extra marital intercourse.

Within the family, marriages with very close relations were forbidden, because one does not unite with 'the flesh of one's body' (Lv 18:6), affinity being held to create the same bond as consanguinity (Lv 18:17). These bans amount to the prohibition of incest.

The Jews staunchly maintained their singular law of divorce. At bottom, this gave the initiative only to the husband. The distinctive feature was that he could give a bill of divorcement conferring freedom to marry again. Apart from childlessness, the main ground was "something scandalous".[24]

The positive attitude of the rabbis to marriage was maintained in post-talmudic literature and Jewish practice. Asceticism and celibacy continued to be rare. Rabbanic teachings sees celibacy as unnatural. It is not he who marries who sins; the sinner is the unmarried man who "spends all his days in sinful thoughts" (Kid 29b). "Marriage is not only for companionship and procreation: it also fulfils one as a person. He who has no wife is not a proper man" (Yev.63a). Sexual desire is not evil or shameful. When regulated and controlled in marriage, it serves beneficial ends. He who, by denying his legitimate instincts, fails to produce children "is as if he shed blood.... and he will have to account for his actions in the world to come (Shab. 31a). Marriage is so important that a man may sell a Torah scroll in order to marry and a woman will tolerate an unhappy marriage rather than remain alone. (Yev. 113a, Kid 7a).[25]

2.7   CHRISTIANITY

Christianity very effectively put an end to all immoral ways, rescued corrupt women and dancing girls, endeavoured to eradicate prostitution and purify the various areas of life of immorality, and spread moral education among the people.We never hear from the lips of Jesus (Hadrat 'Îsâ, A.S.) a derogatory word concerning woman as such. They seemed to have enjoyed considerable rights and privileges.

The introduction of Christianity broke the continuity of paganism, but the old religious feeling was not destroyed; it soon revived, and took up the struggle once more against its new rival.[26]

2.7.1   THE STATUS OF WOMEN

The concepts of a few preachers regarding women and marital relations were sometimes opposed to human nature. Some even believed that the woman was the mother of sin and the basic cause of all evil and corruption. She was the main factor encouraging man to a life of sin and evil and hence leading him to hell. All human error and evil sprang from her. The mere fact that she was a woman was sufficient to make her hated. It was thought that she ought to be sorry for her beauty and attraction because these things served as instruments of evil temptations. It was, therefore, necessary that she should constantly repent for her inherent sins, as she had been responsible for spreading all human ills and suffering in the world.

Ambrosiaster, a series of biblical commentaries during the ancient era, expresses the view that woman were mainly responsible for sin, the man is at most a half willing partner. Her role in involving the man is much the same as was the devil's role in involving her; but at the Fall she was seduced, the man was merely tricked.

Tertulian (150 A.D.) who was father of the early Christian Church explained the Christian doctrine regarding women in these words:

> *"The sentence God passed on that sex lives*
> *on in the present age; so it must be that*

> *the guilt for the sin lives on as well. You
> are the devil's gateway. You are the
> violator of the tree, you are the first
> deserter of God's law; you are the one who
> duped him whom the devil was not
> powerful enough to assault. You shattered
> so easily God's image, man. And you still
> think of putting adornments over the
> animal skin, that cover you."* [27]

Thus, according to Tertullian, God's curse on Eve lives on in all her daughters, and through her daughters, Eve remains the temptress, still the occasion of sin.

2.7.2   THE CONCEPT OF MONASTICISM

The second doctrine was that the sexual relation between man and woman was in itself an objectionable affair, even if it was established within marriage. This monastic conception of morality had already taken root in Europe. Consequently, celibacy and spinsterhood became the principle of nobility of character, and married life came to be regarded as a necessary evil.

Avoidance of marriage became a symbol of piety and holiness and a sign of sound moral character. To live a clean and pure religious life, therefore, one was either not to marry at all, or was to live apart from one's wife in total abstinence from sexual relations. Rules were passed in religious conferences barring church officials from meeting their wives in seclusion. They could, however, see each other in public in the presence of at least two other persons.

Monceaux's philosophy was that:

> *"Woman is the devil's ally on earth against
> man; her weaknesses, her seductions, and
> her coquetries are nothing but stratagems
> of hell. She cannot hope for her forgiveness
> and her salvation except by renouncing the*

> *graces of her sex. And man, if he wishes to*
> *please God, must separate himself as much*
> *as possible from women."* [28]

This implies that for her salvation a woman must emulate angelic likeness, because immortal flesh neither marries, nor has sex, nor wears jewels or adornments.

To Demetrias, an aristocratic lady who had chosen virginity, St Jerome wrote a letter of praise in which he said:

> *"You must act against nature or rather*
> *above nature if you are to forswear your*
> *natural functions, to cut off your own root,*
> *to cull no fruit but that of virginity, to*
> *abjure the marriage bed, to shun*
> *intercourse with men and, while in the*
> *body, to live as though out of it."* [29]

This unnaturalness could include defying the wills of their fathers, abandoning the responsibilities of their households - the supervision of wealth, estates and servants, and even turning their backs on their children to seek the "higher life". In this narrative on Paula, Jerome described admiringly how she left behind her house, children, servants and property in Rome, to the great outcry of the worldly society. As her ship departed from the dock her infant son, stretched forth his hands and her older daughter sobbed silently on the pier, but "overcoming her love for the children with her love for God", and turning her eyes heavenward, she sailed out to sea, with never a backward glance, into the virginal lands to join St. Jerome in monastic rigors in the East. Jerome even regarded an occasional outburst of grief on the death of parents or children, as backsliding into that 'lower female nature'.

Seeing virginity as the shortest route to heaven, it was not surprising that the Fathers were diligent in their urging for the superiority of virginity to marriage. Jerome was the most zealous champion of this task. Scarcely was a mother or daughter deprived of her husband than Jerome had pen in hand to spell out the horrors of marriage, the disgust of childbearing, and the glories of the new continence of widowhood, that was now within their grasp. They had lost, to be sure, the first glory of virginity, but the second glory of widowhood was now open to them. If a mother decided to dedicate her daughter to virginity, Jerome was prepared to prescribe an entire course for the newborn girl. She should be trained in vigils and fasts, and by 'cold chastity' put out the flames of lust. Squalid dress and neglect of hygiene will spoil her natural good looks and keep her from becoming an object of desire.[30]

Marriage in itself was considered a form of 'mastering' or 'taming' women by man, unmarried women being referred to as 'untamed', while a wife was referred to as 'mastered'. In a number of Roman wedding-songs, women were shown as experiencing this mastery as rape, a violation that was not only symbolic but actual, since a man was expected either forcibly to deflower his wife on her wedding night or, sparing her feelings, to sodomize her.[31]

The torch bearers of Christianity kept away from sexual relations, just as people protect their garments while passing through dirt. It is a well known fact that when the well known leader of monasticism, Sewis, became an invalid, his students and colleagues, seeing his extreme old age, wished that he could leave the jungle and take up residence in some more civilized habitation. He agreed to this request, but with the condition that it should be habitation in which there was no possibility of meeting any woman. Such a habitation could not be found, so he stayed in the jungle and died there.

St. Beesle had forbidden himself the sight of a woman, except in extreme compulsion. St. John did not see the face of a woman for forty eight years. At last, his wife was forced to send a message to him that if he did not come to see her, then she would kill herself. Hearing this he sent a message that he would come to see her at night when she would be in her bedroom. His promise was fulfilled - his wife saw him in a dream that night. Queen Zanubia agreed never to have intercourse with her husband except when it became necessary to have an heir to the throne. Though Hapasha was married, she remained a maiden all her life and never let her husband have intercourse with her.

Hatred and disgust for the opposite sex had increased so much that ascetics ran away even from their mothers and sisters, whose company had always been considered a means of respect and pride, but even their nearness was a punishment for them. Once an ascetic was travelling in the company of his mother. On their way, there was a stream over which there was no bridge. Hastily he began to wrap tightly all his body and arm with cloth. His mother asked him in amazement the reason for his action. He replied he had to lift her across the stream and was afraid that if his body touched her body, the entire work of his life would be lost.

It is narrated that St.Pemin suddenly left his family along with six of his brothers and went to the jungle. Having lost her seven sons in this way, his mother became desperate and followed him into the jungle. She reached the place at a time when they were coming out of their cells and going to the church. Seeing the face of their mother, they all turned back to their cells in panic. Their mother followed them, but old age could not compete with their youthful speed and before she could reach the monastery, her sons closed the door of the cell from inside. Now the old woman, with her heart shattered by the grief of separation from her seven sons, cried desperately, which moved the creatures of the jungle. St. Pemin came to the door and enquired the reason for this hue and cry. The mother, sobbing, began her speech in this way:

> "All this shock is through not seeing you.
> Don't you know I am your mother? Did I
> not suckle you? Did I not bring you up to
> adulthood? Is this the reward for all my
> kindness and beneficience? Have you
> forgotten all my rights? But all these words
> proved ineffective. The only answer she got
> from her pious sons was that she would
> see them only after her death. The
> wretched mother therefore went back
> disappointed." [32]

The greatest drawbacks of these philosophies of monasticism is that it does not suggest a remedy for the excesses of sexual desires but only teach rebellion against them, even though the natural feelings of man cannot be suppressed. History testifies that those who tried to build artificial barriers against sexual desire were forced to satisfy it by unnatural and illegal ways.

If one stops the natural flow of water, it will obviously create dirt and stagnate in the byways. Even if man can save himself from these sins through unnatural efforts, his nature cannot accept this struggle. This is because the very constitution and nature of man is such that sexual feelings and desires would keep on awakening with greater intensity. It is only the satisfaction of these feelings and desires that can give him rest and peace. Without this, it would be difficult for his feelings to remain in balance and moderation. Sometimes it has such an intense reaction on man that it renders his entire intellectual and physical system stagnant.

A British team of experts on mental diseases examined the background of eleven thousand mental patients, and reached the conclusion that if one wants peace of mind and protection from various mental diseases, one must get married. Representatives of seventeen countries, investigated and looked through the registers of population census of various countries and found the type of people who usually have a long life. This research showed that married people have longer lives than bachelors and widowers. The figures of all these countries showed that the average life span of married men is 57 years while of unmarried men it is only 39 years. And the longest average age is that of married women.[33]

Jesus ('Îsâ) never married. But he was not a pessimist in relation to it. He did not go into houses to warn against it. He attended weddings. He felt a deep joy for children. He knew the legitimacy, meaning and glory of marriage. He saw in marriage the original form of human fellowship. It has its lessons in God's act of creation. Once a marriage is contracted, it must be carried out in full both physically and spiritually. Only in one passage in the early Christian treatment does the principle of celibacy find a place, namely, in the picture given in Revelation of those who followed the Lamb (Rev. 14:4).[34]

The damage and harm done by abstention from sexual relations is not confined to the individual, but it shatters man's social relations, resulting in the decline of civilization. Behind the shadow of magnificent buildings and palaces and other expressions of civilization, is also the desire of man that around him should be an atmosphere that should increase his sexual pleasure. Suppression of this desire means destroying a very effective agent in the progress of civilization. The most important disadvantage of this celibacy is that it is hostile to the human race. Nature has created an attraction between the sexes so that they may create other beings to take their place when they die. Therefore this sexual attraction is not only for those who are now present, but it is an instrument for the survival of mankind.

2.8 STATUS OF WOMEN IN AFRICA

Among certain tribes of Africa the woman had no importance at all other than as an object of satisfying human lust. She used to move about scantily clad merely concealing her private parts. Even now, in certain remote areas, girls who have reached the age of puberty are kept naked before their marriage with only a few string of beads hanging over their private parts.

In many parts of Africa, men and women may usually have sexual relations before their marriage in order to test the fertility of the woman. Zulus considered adultery a serious offence punishable by thrusting cacti into the vagina of the adulteress.

Among the Swazi tribe the husband is regarded as the owner of his wife and the head of the family.

Among the Lozi tribe, divorce is very common and women have no right to say anything in this regard. If a man wishes to divorce his wife he merely sends her home without giving any reason.

Among the Tallensi of West Africa, men were prohibited from marrying certain classes of women but intercourse with them was not regarded as incestuous.

Among the Mayombe tribe, a woman is considered an outsider and stranger in her husband's village. As such she is not given any place of importance there for being a new member of the family.

Among the Nguni tribe of South Africa a woman is prohibited from drinking the milk of her husband's kraal until the birth of a child which constitutes a symbol that she is no longer a stranger in her husband's family.

In Uganda the kings of Banyoro had been marrying their own sisters. Women of the Ankilo tribe strictly guard their virginity, but as soon as they are married, they are free to entertain the friends and visitors of the husband by sleeping with them. [35]

2.9 PRE-ISLÂMIC ARABIA

The pre-Islâmic era is commonly referred to as *"Jâhilîyah"* or *"The Age of Ignorance"* because of the religious, social and moral disorder that prevailed before Islâm. Centuries of isolation in the peninsula and a sickly insistence on the faith of their forefathers had severely undermined the Arab's moral and spiritual well-being. The sixth century found them plunged into immoral sexual licentiousness, dark idolatry and indulgence in all the characteristics of primitive times.

2.9.1 SOCIAL CONDITIONS AND THE STATUS OF WOMEN

The moral and social conditions of Arabs deteriorated daily. Alcohol meant more to them than life itself. Due to this addiction, and in their state of drunkenness, shameless acts of vice were indulged in by the whole assembly. Ancient Arabic literature was drenched in wine and contained a treasure of expressions for it. Gambling was the favourite past time of all, and a famous gambling locality would attract people from distant countries. Usury was also a widely accepted practice.

Poetry was perfected by them. In the recital of the *Qasîdah*, a kind of descriptive poem, they used to mention, by name, the daughters, wives and sisters of noble and wealthy personages, and openly attribute to them immoralities of every description. There was very little fear of a bloody ending to the poetic contest. Adultery, fornication and incest were practised unblushingly, and were shamelessly published and boasted of in all sorts of immoral poetry.

The position of women in general was very low, as she was regarded as a special creation between the human being and the beast, having no rights and no social or moral respect. Women were deprived of the right of inheritance. A man was free to marry any number of wives and could divorce as he wished. Besides polygamy a man could have unlawful relations with a number of women. Married women were allowed by their husbands to conjugate with others for the sake of offsprings. Teenage girls were allowed unrestricted sexual freedom.

> *"Girls of coquetting disposition often used to go to the outskirts of the city where they allowed the menfolk to take full liberty with them."* [36]

An Arab woman, on seeing a handsome and healthy man, would not hesitate in soliciting sexual intercourse with him.

There was a common tradition of marrying step - mothers and sometimes sisters too. It was common practice for the eldest son to take as wives his father's widows (that is, step mothers), inherited as property with the rest of the estate. The step-son, or in his absence, any close and near relative, used to cast a sheet over the head of the widow, and he who threw the cloth was obliged to marry her. Fathers were forbidden to marry the wives, either of their real or adopted sons, and the violation of this latter custom was considered a crime.

Thus the fairer sex was wretched and degraded. A man had the liberty to marry as many women as he pleased. Although there was no established law to determine which women it was lawful for him to marry, and which were unlawful, a custom not to marry a woman of close relationship prevailed, and it was believed that the issue of such a woman generally proved to be of weak constitution and deficient in physical strength.

Just as the law of marriage was observed and the payment of dowry recognized, similarly divorce was also practised. A man could take his wife back again after having divorced her once, and could do this a thousand times over, as no limit to the number of divorces was fixed. However, a regular term was fixed after the divorce within which period the woman was interdicted from marrying another person, and within which period the parties, becoming reconciled, might marry again. The male very cruelly and inhumanly took advantage of this custom. He married a woman, divorced her on some pretext, and the poor woman had to wait for the fixed period without marrying anyone; when, however, the time was about to expire, her former husband again reconciled her to himself and renewed the marriage, but after a very short time he would once more divorce her, and again marry her at the close of the appointed term, and this he would repeat any number of times. The Arab practised this merciless custom, because every person considered it a reproach when the woman who had been once his wife should marry another man.

There was another kind of divorce, which was called *Zihâr*. It constituted a person's abstaining from touching a part of his wife's body. This practice was solemnised by the party's declaring that that part of his wife's body was as unlawful for him to touch as the corresponding part of his mother's, or of any other close female relative, with whom it was unlawful to marry.

Women were accustomed to quit their homes and mix in the public scantily dressed, and considered it as neither indecent nor immoral to expose any part of their bodies to the public gaze. They also wore false hair, and it was customary to have their bodies tattooed with indigo.

All the male representatives of a family used to avoid the company of all their female relatives during their menstruation, and the latter were forbidden to mix with the rest of the family.[37]

Female slaves, called *Kainad*, were instructed in singing and dancing, and were allowed to sell their favours, the price of which being snatched by the owners.

The Qu'rân refers to the evil practice of the forced prostitution of women in ancient times and forbade it in these words:

> *"But force not your maids to prostitution*
> *when they desire chastity, in order that you*
> *may make a gain in the goods of this life."*[38]

The status of women in Arabia was so low and degrading that they could even be mortgaged in return for a loan. It is narrated by Muḥammad ibn Maslamah 🌼:

> *"When I went to Ka'ab ibn Ashraf and asked him to give me some grain as a loan, he was saying to his men, give your women as a mortgage to me."*

but the men replied:

> *"How can we trust women to you as a mortgage when we know full well that you are the most handsome man in the Arabian Peninsula."* [39]

2.9.2 VARIOUS FORMS OF MARRIAGES

The nature and form of marriage (*nikâḥ*) in pre-Islâmic Arabia will further illustrate the depth of degradation in which women were held during the period of ignorance (*Jâhilîyah*).

(1) Open prostitution: This was carried out entirely by slave girls. The husband would tell his slave wife to go to a specified person after the menses and the person would enjoy the pleasure of sexual intercourse with her. The husband himself would then not have intercourse with his wife until her pregnancy ended. In this way people tried to get sons of high birth or noble qualities. This type of marriage was called *nikâḥ al-istibdâ*, indicating insemination. This practice was also common among the ancient Greeks.

(2) Several men would go to one woman and enjoy sexual pleasure with her. When she had a child, she would send messengers to all her lovers to call on her. They were compelled to come to her and none dare refuse. She would then inform them all of her plight. She would then name the father of the child and ask him to name his child (even if in reality he was not the biological father). The child would go to the person she had named as the father and he could

not refuse to accept it.

(3)   Young and beautiful slave girls would be made to stay in brothels. They were known as *qaliqiyat* and their houses were known as *mawâkhir*. All the prominent men of the time owned and maintained such houses of prostitutes to earn money and also to entertain their noble guests. Whenever a child was born to any of these prostitutes, all her lovers would gather and call a physiognomist, who would, on the strength of his knowledge, identify the father of the child, and no one so named could refuse to accept the responsibility of its maintainence.

(4)   Another form of marriage was that which is now in practice among Muslims all over the world.

Islâm recognized only this fourth form of marriage as legal. A woman had only one husband, to whom she had been legally married in a ceremony in the presence of witnesses and given a dowry. All other form of sexual relationships were declared adulterous and made punishable in a court of law. The *Sharî'ah* announced that earnings made from adultery were unlawful, impure and forbidden, calling it a product of the worst profession and a most filthy form of income.

Ibn Kathîr mentions the incident of 'Abdullah ibn Ubay who owned a brothel in Madînah. One of the prostitutes, named Muadhah, accepted *Tauhîd* (that is, the Oneness of Allâh) and repented for her past sins, but 'Abdullâh ibn Ubay subjected her to torture. When this case was brought to the Prophet 變, he ordered that the woman be taken away from the cruel man.[40]

The decision of the Prophet 變 in the case of Muadhah, clearly establishes that an owner who forces his subordinate into prostitution loses his rights of jurisdiction over her.

This gives some idea as to the depth of degradation into which woman had been thrown during the Days of Ignorance. It also shows the extreme sinfulness into which people had sunk before the advent of Islâm.

39

2.9.3 FEMALE INFANTICIDE

The pre-Islâmic Arabs were embarrassed at the birth of daughters and sometimes a father buried his daughter alive in spite of her soul-harrowing cries. This customary practice was either in fear of becoming impoverished by providing for them, since they were not regarded as a source of future income; or suffering disgrace on their account. Thus poverty and pride both were responsible for this heinous crime. The Qur'ân describes the state of mind of a man who hears of the birth of a daughter in these words:

> *"When news is brought to one of them (of the birth of a female child) his face darkens, and he is filled with inward grief! With shame does he hide himself from his people, because of the bad news he has had! Shall he retain it on sufferance and contempt, or bury it in the dust? Ah! what an evil choice they decide on."* [41]

Sometimes *"kind hearted"* tribal chiefs often bought girls to save their lives. Sa`sa`a says that before the dawn of Islâm he had rescued as many as three hundred girls from the terrible fate by paying compensatory money to their fathers. Sometimes a young girl who had escaped being killed at birth or during childhood due to her father being away from home or for some other reason would be treacherously taken to a lonely spot by her father and killed. [42]

Although the Arabs referred to angels as the "daughters of God" yet they disliked a female child being born to them as the Qur'ân mentions:

> *"When news is brought to one of them of (the birth of) what he sets up as the likeness to the Lord, his face darkens, and he is filled with inward grief.* [43]

It is said that once an Arab was burying his infant daughter alive. While digging her grave, his beard was smeared with dust. The affectionate daughter seeing this dust on her father's beard, could not resist her loving impulse, and at once wiped the dust from her father's beard. The Arab was so moved that tears rolled down his eyes but nevertheless, he buried his loving daughter alive.

The Qur'ân also warns of the dire consequences of killing babies in these words concerning the Day of Judgement:

> *"And when the female infant buried alive*
> *is questioned - for what crime she was*
> *killed".*[44]

In this world of sin and sorrow there is much unjust suffering, and innocent lives sacrificed, without a trace, by which offenders can be brought to justice. The crime was committed and no questions were asked; but in the spiritual world of justice, questions will be asked, and the victim herself, dumb here, will be able to give evidence, for she had committed no crime herself. The proof will be drawn from the very means of concealment. Even today infanticide is not unknown in many countries.

In India, the practice continued until as late as the middle of the nineteenth century. Among all the races of India, there is none more noble than the Rajput: and among the Rajputs, the first rank belongs to the Chuhâns. These people are numerous in the United Provinces. In the district of Manipuri there are more than 30,000 of them and not fifty years ago it was discovered that among them was not a single girl. Every daughter that was born was killed. The higher the rank of the family, the more constant and systematic was the crime. When special inquiries were instituted, it was found that this practice of infanticide, although specially prevalent among the Rajputs, was by no means confined to them, and it was common not only in the North-Western Provinces, but also in Punjab and parts of the Bombay Presidency. A number of villages were visited where there was not a single girl and where there had never been one in living memory. As a matter of fact, whenever polyandry (a woman having more than one husband) is in existence, baby girls are killed in large numbers.[45]

In short, the Arabs, before the dawn of Islâm, were a people quite uncivilized and cruel. They were extremely immoral, voluptuous and lacking in civil sense. Sexual licentiousness was rife. There was gross inequality between man and man, and women were treated as pawns.

41

2.10   CONCLUSION

The pre-Islâmic society was steeped in vice, barbarism, superstition and immoral sexual licentiousness. Woman had lost her true status as well as her natural role in society. The basic object and function of the marital relation was completely forgotten. The feelings of love, compassion and mercy which join two individuals into a single unit and which develop mutual affection, co-operation and a team spirit had totally disappeared.

In fact, no healthy feature of this noble, loving and intimate relationship was left. A woman's honour, respect and modesty, the soul of conjugal relationships, went unrecognized. The form of this relationship was visible everywhere but it was without its true spirit. The woman was the victim of the tyranny and oppression of man.

Women were bought and sold like chattels - the ordinary things of daily life in the market. Men, not only used them as a means of sexual gratification, but also became richer by means of forced prostitution. These practices were not confined to any one society or country, but were common in all countries at that time.

In such circumstances there was need of a system to shake the human race in general and wean it away from its waywardness. The system may be simple, natural and principled. It may galvanise the suffering humanity. Man has always needed some sort of divine direction in his life.

CHAPTER THREE

Social System of Islâm

MORALITY IN ISLÂM

SOCIAL SYSTEM OF ISLÂM

3.1 INTRODUCTION

Islâm brought men back to the natural practice of moderation, thus exterminating extremism. Rights were restored to the people only if it were lawfully theirs. The cause of the oppressed weaker (woman) was championed by Islâm with extreme vigour. The issue of the value of the dignity of woman was revived, and no compromise was allowed. All possible avenues of corruption and debasement were closed. The sexual urge was confined to moderation and certain regulations, by providing a comprehensive code of conduct in connection with conjugal relations, and healthy methods of propagation of the human species were enforced. The family life was moulded to be more pleasant and stable. The woman, instead of being a symbol of condemnation, came to be regarded as a model of dignity, peace and tranquility. Discouraging the practice of celibacy, the value of marital life was emphasized and made obligatory.

3.2 THE CONCEPT OF SOCIETY

Society is a collection of human individuals who have grown interlinked through special arrangements, manners, laws, beliefs and aspirations and have a collective life.[1] That man's life is social, means that he has a social identity. On the one hand, needs, benefits, and undertakings have a social identity and are unmanageable except by division of labour, division of benefits and division of need-fulfilment within a series of norms and arrangements. On the other hand, some kinds of thoughts, ideas, and temperaments govern the population and unify its members.

Social system or organization is the pattern of individual and group relations. Many people refer to social organization as "the social fabric", a metaphor which suggests that human relations are closely interwoven and that strains on one part may weaken the whole fabric in unanticipated ways. This figure of speech emphasizes the harmonious, the interdependent and the consistent tendency. Therefore social system emphasizes that individual and group relations are mostly adaptive outcomes of social processes emerging out of day-to-day interaction, and out of problem solving, co-operation, and accommodation.

Under the influence of what factors has man's social life come into being? Was man created social? That is, was he created as a part of the whole by nature, and is there a tendency inborn in man to join with his "whole"? Or was he not created social, but did external necessity compel the imposition of social existence upon him? That is, does man by his first nature incline to be free and to reject all the bonds and impositions that social life entails, and has he learned through experience that he is incapable of continuing his life in solitude and of necessity submitted to the limitations of social life? Did man, through his primordial reason *(fitra)* and evaluative power, conclude that he might better avail himself of the gifts of creation through co-operation and social life and so choose to share? So the question can be set as follows. Is man's social life natural, necessitated, or elective?

According to the first assumption, that social life is natural, it is like the domestic life of husband and wife, wherein each marital partner has been created as a 'part' of a 'whole' by natural disposition, and each has within a tendency to join with his or her whole. Here the primary factor is the inborn nature of man and sociality is a universal end to which his nature courses. According to the second assumption, that social life is necessitated, it is like the co-operation and alliance of two nations that see themselves as incapable of confronting a common enemy alone and so of necessity establish a kind of association. Here the important factor is some occurrence external to man's being which is accidental and adventitious. According to the third theory, that social life is elective, it is like the partnership of two capitalists who bring a single commercial, agricultural, or industrial entity into being for the sake of greater profits. Here the main factor is the human rational and evaluative faculty, which is an intellectual, and not a natural end.

The Qur'ân teaches us that man's sociality has been embedded within his natural inclination:

> "O people! We created you from a male

46

*and a female and made you into nations
and tribes, so that you might know one
another".*[2]

Having first considered the classification of humanity according to sex
(masculinity and feminity) as natural, the verse at once addresses the
grouping of humanity as nations and tribes. This suggests that the grouping
of the people as nations and tribes is natural and divinely ordained, like
their classification as men or women. Here, in the course of a moral
commandment, the social aspect of the special creation of man is referred
to: It is explained that man has been created so as to emerge in the form
of various national and tribal groupings. Through this appointment to
nations and tribes, the mutual recognition happens that is the inseparable
condition of social life. If these lines of descent, which constitute from
one standpoint the shared feature of individuals and from another the
feature dividing individuals, did not exist, this recognition would be
impossible. Consequently, social life, based on the mutual relationships
of human beings, would be impossible. These and like occurrences, such
as divergencies in stature, shape, and colour, give each individual the
basis for his own personal identity. Suppose all individuals were the same
in stature, shape, and colour; suppose no disparity of relationships and
descents governed them, individuals facing one another would then be
just like the uniform products of a factory. Distinguishing each other,
recognizing each other, and basing their social life on the relationships
and transactions of thought, work, and goods would be impossible.
Therefore, assignation to nations and tribes has a natural wisdom, which
is the differentiation and mutual recognition of individuals, the inseparable
condition of social life.

Another verse also mentions:

*"It is We who portion out among them their
livelihood in the life of this world and We
raise some of them above others in
degrees, so that some might obtain labour
of others".*[3]

Allâh has created people various and dissimilar from the standpoints of physical, spiritual, intellectual, and emotional capacities and possibilities. He has made some superior in one way and others superior in another way. He has thus made all need each other and disposed to cleave to one another by nature. By this means, He has provided the basis for the interconnected life of society.

Social organization also consists of relations that isolate people or groups and that foster disharmony and conflict.[4] The Noble Qur'ân, while upholding for society a nature, character, objective being, obedience and rebellion, explicitly regards the individual as capable of rebellion against the order of corrupt society. In surah *Nisa*, verse 97, Allâh speaks of the section of Meccan society that called themselves the 'oppressed' and 'powerless' and thought their condition excused them for abandoning their inborn responsibilities. They were actually determining and defining themselves in relation to their society. It says that their excuse will by no means be accepted because they could at least have emigrated from that ethos to another one. The Qur'ân elsewhere states:

"O you who believe! You have charge of
your own souls. He who strays cannot
harm you if you are rightly guided".[5]

The teachings of the Qur'ân are founded wholly on responsibility, one's own responsibility and that of society. The narratives of the Qur'ân mostly include the element of an individual's rebellion against a corrupt ethos and environment.

Before we examine the terminology, concept, mission and structure of the Islâmic Society (*Ummah*) it is advisable to look into the concepts and theories of Western secualar philosophies on society and community.

3.2.1   THE SECULAR CONCEPT

The term 'Ummah' can be comprehended and appreciated through an analysis of the secular sociological terms like 'society', 'community', 'nation' and such others. Joseph Bensman considers 'community' as "small, localized political and economic and social unit whose members share values in common,"[6] in a less technical sense. The Islâmic society cannot be categorized as such since it is not a localized entity in a territorial sense nor a professional group in an urban society. The universalistic nature of the Islâmic society is all-pervasive and embodies all professional groups and organizations. The Islâmic society should also not be understood as Ferdinand J.Tonnie's "community of race or society of different races and ethic groups on rational self interest."[7] There is no self-interest in the Islâmic Ummah and it embraces all races and ethnic groups within its Universal Islâmic brotherhood created for the interest of humankind in its true sense, which reflects divine will and not the rational will of the society. Emile Durkhein's distinction of the social group between primitive social groups "on the mechanical solidarity of more undifferentiated individuals" and "the organic solidarity of more differentiated individuals"[8] is also a contradiction to the unity of the Islâmic society. The unity of the Islâmic society relates to the ideological commitment of each individual believer who assigns himself to the collective body of believers on their ideological commitment. Apart, the humane and moral character of the Ummah need not be confused with the materialistic approach of Karl Marx who had classified social system on modes of production and the class system. The meaning and significance of the Islâmic society also differs from the meaning given by the *"Oxford Dictionary"* to community as "the body of those having common or equal rights or rank as distinguished from the priviledged classes, or a body of people organized into a political municipal or social unity; or a religious society." [9] Under the jurisdiction of the Sharî'ah Law to which the Islâmic society is committed, all are equal and there is no common or priviledged class whatsoever, nor is it a mere religious society confined only to the faith and private aspects of life. Apart, none of the definitions given by the *Websters Dictionary* can reflect the essence of the Islâmic Ummah as it describes community as "a society of people having common rights and privileges or common interest, or living in the same district, city, etc. under the same laws and regulations".[10] No doubt the Islâmic society enjoys common rights and privileges under the Sharî'ah laws, but the Sharî'ah laws and regulations should not be confused with the modern perspective of civil and political rights under the Secular Law. Furthermore, it is not a localized or nationalistic body of people, but rather a universal body which surpasses all geographical and national boundaries.[11] Therefore the Islâmic Ummah is in a sense a society by virtue of its common purpose, but it is not a limited society of a small number of people nor is its purpose limited as political, social, cultural, recreational - but a Divine purpose - to witness the 'truth' to humankind. Consequently, if society has a real existence, it must necessarily have laws and traditions peculiar to itself.

3.3   SEX AND THE PROMISCUOUS SOCIETY

3.3.1   SIGNIFICANCE OF SEX

Sexual appetite and sexual union are ingrained in human nature. After puberty, it finds expression and gradually flares up, becoming a pressing demand at a certain stage. Man finds it an over-whelming passion, whether sleeping or walking or going about one's duties in day time, it is there like an obsession. There is a constant struggle between his passion and his good sense of judgement. The carnal urge incites him to go ahead with the means of its gratification, totally oblivious of the limits of the approved and the forbidden, but his better sense prevails upon him and puts checks on his urge. In this never-ending struggle, his good sense of judgement and his passion prevail on each other.
The real significance of sex is clearly illustrated by this Qur'ânic verse:

"All things We made in pairs." [12]

This verse makes a reference to the universality of the sex-law and the Master Engineer of the universe Himself divulges the secret of His creation. He says that the universe has been designed on the relationship of pairs, and all that one can see in this world is indeed the result of the mutual interaction of these pairs.

Three basic principles of sex-law can be deduced from this verse:

(1)   The principle according to which Allâh Ta'âlâ has created this world and the way according to which He is running its great system cannot be vile and unholy. It indeed is sacred and ought to be holy. Though the opponents of this scheme may hold sex dirty and despicable and so shun it, the Creator of the universe cannot desire that His Factory should cease to function. He will naturally want that all the parts of His Machine should continue working in order to fulfil

the purpose for which they have been designed.

(2)   The existence of both the active and the passive partners is equally important. Neither the 'activity' of the active partner is in any way exalted nor the 'passivity' of the passive partner in any way debased. Only the foolish, inexperienced people can think of replacing the active partners in it by the passive partners, and vice versa.

(3)   'Activity' in itself is naturally superior to 'passivity' and feminity. This superiority is not due to any merit in masculinity against any demerit in feminity. It is rather due to the fact of possessing natural qualities of dominance, power and authority. For if both partners are equally powerful and neither is dominant, there will be no question of submission, and the act will not take place at all. If the cloth is as hard as the needle, sewing cannot take place. In contrast to this, the passive partner should naturally be soft, tender, womanly, for these qualities alone can help her perform her role successfully.

Man and woman are not only physical entities but they are living organisms also. Let us analyze the natural object of their being a sexual pair. The Qur'ân mentions:

>   *   *"He has made for you pairs from among yourselves, and pairs among cattle."*[13]   42:11

>   *   *"Your wives are your farms."*[14]   2:223

In the first verse, mention has been made of the pairs of man and animal together, and of the common object intended thereof, that is, the propagation of the species as a result of their sex relationship. In the second verse, man has been considered separately from the other animal species, and it has been indicated that the relation between the partners of a human pair is that of a cultivator and his farm which is a biological fact.

The mystery of sex has not only its physical aspects, but its moral and spiritual aspects, and therefore mankind is in this respect differentiated from the lower animals, and among mankind the grade and qualities are suggested by the phrase "from among yourselves".

These verses furnish us with three more principles:

(1)   Allâh Ta'âlâ has created human beings also as male and female, like all other animals, for the purpose of perpetuating the human race. This is a clear demand of man's animal nature and cannot be overlooked. Allâh has not created the human species to allow only a handful of individuals to nourish and tend themselves on the earth and disappear. He indeed wants it to survive till an appointed time. He has placed sex urge in the animal nature of man so that human beings join as pairs and procreate to keep His earth humming with life. Therefore, a law given by Allâh cannot be such as will crush and suppress the sexual urge, and inculcate its hatred and teach total abstinence from it. On the contrary, such law will also fully provide for the satisfaction of this urge of human nature.

(2)   By comparing man and woman to the cultivator and the farm, it has been indicated that the natural relationship of the partners of the human pair is different from that of the other animal pairs. Just as it is not enough for a cultivator to only sow seeds but also to water his field, fertilize it and look after it, so too is woman also not such a farm that a man would by the way cast a seed in her, and then let her grow it into a tree. But in fact when she becomes pregnant she stands in need of being carefully looked after and cared for by her 'cultivator'.

(3)   The sex attraction in a human pair is biologically of the same nature as is found in the other animal species. The powerful urge of procreation placed in them by nature causes all those members of the opposite sexes who possess the ability to procreate to be mutually attracted.

3.3.2   EVILS OF THE PROMISCUOUS SOCIETY

There seems to be four main types of sexual relations, of which we either have a society of pure homosexuals and lesbians, an entirely promiscuous society, a society in which no sexual relation exists except between husband and wife, or a '*laissez-faire*' society in which all these are tolerated.

If men continued to be moral, then a society of pure homosexuals is a self defeating one, since it severs the enjoyments of sex for its reproductive function. An entirely promiscuous society seems, to many, to be the best, and in the long run the inevitable form of sexual relations. In such a society, sex, it is thought, ceases to be a problem, since here they shall for the first time, combine complete freedom with the deepest enjoyment as well as the procreation of children. This, however, is a mere illusion in which one does not see the facts as they are but as one wants them to be. Here are some of the difficulties that beset such a society.

Far from being the natural or ultimately the inevitable, and even if man is viewed as a mere animal, this is a dream which shall never be realized. This is so because the human being is basically and biologically a pair-forming species. As the emotional relationship develops between a pair of potential mates it is aided by the sexual intimacies they share. The pair-formation function of sexual behaviour is so important for our species that nowhere outside the paining phase do sexual activities reach such a high intensity.

The facts are therefore against those who argue that man is basically promiscuous. A promiscuous society is one where everybody chooses whoever he likes at whatever time he prefers. As a reality it is a society in which sexual deprivation becomes the main problem. The young and the beautiful are universally more attractive than the plain or the ugly, and the old. And then there are personal tastes such as tone of voice, physique, culture, gesture, dress, etc. If a person fails to find the mate of his or her liking, then even if he or she is physically satisfied, he or she is most likely emotionally deprived.

In such a society people are sure to be obsessed with sex; the search for the younger, the more attractive, and such like, becomes a full-time occupation. If time is a valuable asset, then much of it is unnecessarily wasted in such a society. This leads inevitably and naturally to the commercialization of this human need - a commercialization which through advertisements, pictures, magazines, the employment of sexually attractive girls and occasionally boys and men, and a hundred other cunning devices, yet increase the obsession with sex.

The natural outcome of this is a distortion of human values. In such a society a person's worth will depend on the accident of her or his being a certain age or having good looks or a beautiful body. Girls are rewarded socially and materially, and even 'crowned' not for anything they achieved but for something they possess at their hour of birth. By implication the less beautiful girls are punished for no fault of theirs. How unjust or even cruel an arrangement, one might say. The fact is that a promiscuous society is definitely a cruel one. Even in a normal society, the feeling that one is getting older - and hence less attractive and less wanted therefore is somewhat annoying, but how much worse it must be in a society where the worth of a person is determined, above all, by the degree of his or her physical attraction, almost to the exclusion of other considerations.

If many criminal tendencies among both the young and the old are said to have their origins in broken homes and unstable families, what is going to be the fate of the army of parentless children which a promiscuous society produces? Contemplating them, some might say: *"Well, no one ever seriously advocated this kind of society. All we stand for is a society where every individual or group of individuals shall have the freedom to lead the kind of sexual life they prefer. In such a society, married people will live side by side with promiscuous individuals, each appreciating and respecting the ideas and choices of the others."*

But, on even a little reflection, one will realize that this will do neither. Firstly, because the evil consequences of promiscuity, will not be eradicated by having those who practise them living among married people. All the complications, though on a narrow scale, will be there. Secondly, if the consequences are admitted to be harmful, then why encourage, and not reduce, the factors responsible for them. The unfortunate fact is that tolerating promiscuity means encouraging it and pushing more and more people to practising promiscuity inasmuch as tolerance leads others to experiment, and in due course to practise it. The inevitable result will be that the society will become more and more licentious and it is married people who will come to be looked upon as 'abnormal'.

Therefore, sexual anarchy has been found under different terms in human civilization. Sometimes it has been called a social and cultural need; sometimes it has been labelled a demand of nature; and sometimes it adopt a religious colour. However, it is merely an excuse to give expression to base human desire.

Sexual pleasure is more attractive and intoxicating than many other joys and delights of life. Man can only keep away from it through the ideals of modesty, chastity and piety. When these ideals are declared out-of-date, the sexual urge so overpowers the faculties of thought, mind and action of man that he does not see anything other than sexual pleasure. All his powers and abilities are spent in seeking this gratification. Regarding this, Dr Alaksus writes:

> *"The present society has completely ignored the moral feeling and totally suppressed its manifestations from all sides. An attitude of irresponsibility is common. People who are virtuous and distinguish between good and bad, work hard and are wise and prudent, are helpless and despised by others. If any woman, having a number of children, gives attention to them instead of looking for a personal career, she is considered as having a low I.Q. Homosexuality, fornication and adultery is widespread and very popular and sexual morality is completely forgotten."* [15]

The great flood of sex has engulfed us from every direction. It has infiltrated every department of our civilization and every facet of our social life. Even political life has come within the ambit of the waves of sexuality and sexual bribery. Sexual extortion have become a common occurrence. Sexual maniacs and their supporters are in ambassadorial posts and pleasure-seeking people are municipal officers, ministers and leaders of political parties.

Sexual anarchists have entered the public services in large numbers and are involved both in natural and unnatural types of voluptuousness. An increase in the number of divorces and sexual crimes, sexual filth on radio and television, and in literature and commercial advertisements - an emphasis on sex in every field of life is a prelude to the destruction of the West. Presently the environment is so full of nudity, that even commercial advertisements are based on sexual themes. Sex has so permeated culture and civilization that it is visible in every aspect of Western life.

If one examines the physical and psychological state of a licentious and voluptuous person, one will find he is nourishing deadly viruses within himself

The first effect of voluptuousness appears in one's physical strength and power. Nature has bestowed powers upon men and these powers are unlimited. Lavish use of these powers will definitely diminish them.

Sexual power is a powerful form of human strength. It is such a powerful source that it can produce many new persons. If any person wastes this energy, he casts away from himself such a great power with the ability of creating many lives like him.

This gives one some idea of how the abuse of sexual pleasure destroys the physical powers of a person. For many ages it has been authentically proven and recognized that every kind of physical disturbance and disruption is the consequence of this action.

3.4   WESTERN CONCEPT OF MORALITY

It is extremely interesting to know how the question of women's rights and their claim for complete freedom resulted in the destruction of morality.

An American writer, Mary R. Beard, gives three different views on the subject of women's place in society. She mentions that women's problems can only be solved by complete equality with man, and that this equality can only be established under communism. A second view is that woman must find her greatest happiness and can contribute most to the state by limiting her ambitions to domesticity and still more narrowly to child-bearing, in order that population rate may be high enough to keep a given nation secure against crowded societies on its borders, and strong enough within for aggressive action, when desired, against neighbours or more distant communities; this is the ideology of Fascism. The third view is that a woman must have the right to choose her way of life, even to the point of the self-centred interests; this is the only reference in her ideologies to democracy.[16]

The concept of liberty and freedom gained prime value during 18th and 19th century Europe. All other values and ideals were forgotten, even the respect for order and discipline, without which real freedom cannot be practiced, were completely forgotten.

It is an established fact that when any strong concept takes hold of any civilization, it pervades every area of human life. The same thing was experienced with the concept of liberty which entered into the social field and took the form of a demand for a complete readjustment of sex relations.

France, which was the centre of all revolutionary ideas, the romantic school of literature and poetry, first made an organized drive to popularize the ideal of sexual equality. D. George Sands, who headed this school, was a woman of loose sexual morality. She proved unfaithful to her husband, who was driven to separation. Thereafter, she led the life of a libertine forming promiscuous sexual relations with a number of men. She severely criticised the institution of marriage and advocated free love. She was followed by another group of poets, novelists and dramatists who emphasized the natural birthright of men and women to indulge in free sexual relations without the encumbrance of marriage. They questioned chastity and they objected to the restrictions of piety on youth.

In one of her novels, D. Sands presents the character of an ideal husband. The wife of the hero establishes illicit relations with another man, but the husband is too large-hearted to censure and hate her. Accounting for this liberal attitude, he says that he has no right to trample underfoot a rose which desires to spread its sweet smell to others, besides him. At another place she expresses the following ideas:

> *"I have not changed my opinion, I have not made peace with society, and marriage is always according to my judgement one of the most barbarous institutions ever imagined. I have no doubt that it will be abolished, if the human race makes any progress towards justice and reason; a bond more human, and not less sacred, will replace it, and will secure the existence of the offspring who will be born of a man and a woman, without ever fettering the liberty of either. But men are too gross and women too cowardly to demand a nobler law than that which rules them: heavy chains must bind beings who lack conscience and virtue."*[17]

This was then the personal character of the woman who deeply influenced the new French generation by her charming and romantic works for as long as thirty years.

Similarly Paul Adams and many other writers spent all their art and skill on imbuing youth with blind courage and dash, so as to remove all shadows of hesitation caused in the mind by the outmoded moral ideals. He writes:

> *"It is a great evil among the Latin races that lovers refuse to admit plainly and*

> *candidly their relish for voluptuousness,*
> *and for the joyous companionship of the*
> *sexes ... Then be refined and sensuous*
> *savants, not building a temple to the*
> *servants of your pleasures nor lazily*
> *falling asleep at their feet, but choosing a*
> *new guest for each moment of pleasure.*"[18]

Pierre Louys went even further. He emphasized the ideas that moral restrictions in fact hindered the proper growth of man's intellectual, scientific and spiritual development. He tried to establish the idea that civilization was at its peak in Athens, Alexandria, Babylon, Rome, Venice and other centres at the time when sensuality, moral lawlessness and sexual licentiousness flourished unchecked. But as soon as moral and legal restrictions were imposed on human urges, the human soul was also doomed to destruction. He made every possible effort to establish that nudity and promiscuous intermingling of the sexes were perfectly justified by stating:

> *"The time when naked humanity, the most*
> *perfect form that we can know or even*
> *conceive, can unveil itself under the*
> *lineaments of a consecrated courtesan*
> *before the twenty thousand pilgrims; where*
> *the most sensual love from which we were*
> *born, was without defilement, without*
> *shame, without sin ..."* [19]

Under the stress of these social changes and intellectual movements, family ties loosened and domesticity lost its importance for women, who were forced into the economic field by circumstances beyond their control. The ideal of sex equality came nearer fulfilment than ever before. During the Second World War, millions of American women were taken into the armed forces, placed in uniform, disciplined by officers of their own sex working under naval and military authorities.

To release men to fight, thousands of uniformed women worked as secretaries, clerks and officials. With skill and courage, women served as doctors and nurses in the battle areas and in hospitals at home, and many were killed at the fronts while working near or under fire. At the end of the war, American men and women alike, in general, hoped for a return to civilian life, and this meant a heated debate over the public policies to be adopted with regard to "equality of rights" in the distribution of employment and in the competition for places and rewards in the economy and society. The old debate over women's place in society was re-opened with added intensity. When the War Department of the United States issued its booklets for the education of soldiers at Round-Table Forums, it included one manual inviting a pointed question: *"Do you want your wife to work after the war?"*

In this discussion, one side argued that times had changed, that it is good and fitting for women to work, that they are competent in all kinds of jobs, hanker after economic independence, and are likely to hang on to cash for dear life. On the other side were those who argued that women's place is in the home, that her function is child-bearing and child-rearing, and that men will not stand her competition with returned veterans.

The status of women in the United Kingdom and other parts of the globe was similar, during the war. In general, experience had revealed that the periods of degeneration of nations in the world have been those when woman left their household duties and went outside the home. The departure of woman from the duties of domesticity becomes a means of decline of nations because of two factors. Firstly, it leaves a great part of life in abeyance and many problems are left unsolved because these can only be dealt with properly by the expert hand of woman, and man is totally unable to deal with them. Secondly, it changes the nature of the relationship between man and woman and the direction of their pursuits, and experience bears testimony that people following this way of life have never been successful.

3.5   ISLÂMIC CONCEPT OF MORALITY

Morality and ethics go hand in hand. Ethical actions are generally moral actions. Ethics which is derived from the Greek word *ethos*, is the philosophy which deals with human actions relating to its goodness and rightness. It also refers to the characteristic spirit or tone of a community. And moral actions are which reveal the virtues. Morality, which has a Latin origin *mos, morales* refers to the degree of conformity to moral principles. So moral actions and ethical actions are inter-related.

Being a human being and a member of society, man has some duties to perform and obligations to fulfil. But the spirit of duty and sense of obligation are not inborn. He has to acquire them by dint of proper culture. This culture must be processed through some prescribed principles and orders. Man has instincts, both good and bad. By habitual culture he may develop the good instincts and give up the bad ones. Good morals is the backbone of society without which no good social order can be formed. A congregation of mentally decrepit men can increase the bulk of society, but it fails to make it enlightened. To build up one's character as a virtuous one, good conduct is an important factor. Good manners and morals are the stepping stones to the formation of a noble, lofty character. Good character is the crowning jewel - it is the diamond which scratches all but is never scratched by others. It is the balancing wheel round which the good actions of mankind revolve.

All sins which man commit under the impulse of his lustful nature, run counter to the purpose of his creation according to Islâm. Obviously, when they are committed under the impulse of his carnal desires, there must be in human nature itself something which prevents man from persuing these sins. It is *hayâ*. Literally, *hayâ* is usually defined as shyness, modesty or moral dignity, but in Islâm it has a much wider meaning. It is more than chastity, decency, purity, humbleness, virtue and virginity. It definitely does not refer to timidity, coyness, sheepishness, and such aspect of Western characters. Islâmically it implies that shame and modesty which a wrongdoer feels before his own nature and before Allâh. This modesty is the force which prevents man from indulging in indecency and obscenity. If, however, he commits a sin under the impulse of his animal nature, the same shyness makes him feel the pangs of conscience. The moral teachings of Islâm aim at awakening this dormant feeling of shyness in human nature and try to develop it as part of man's mental make-up, so that it may serve as a strong moral deterrent against all evil inclinations.

The feeling of *hayâ* is inherent in man though in a crude form. It abhors all sins by nature, but it lacks knowledge. Therefore, it does not know why it abhors a particular sin. This lack of knowledge gradually weakens its feeling of abhorrence with the result that man begins committing sin under the impulse of his animality, and the repeated commission of sins at last destroys his sense of modesty altogether. The moral teachings of Islâm aim to educate *hayâ*. It not only acquaints it with open sins, but also lays bare before it all the evils of desire and intention hidden in the innermost heart of man. Thus, it warns it of all possible mischiefs of the evil spirit, so that it may detest them consciously and with conviction. Then the moral training further sharpens the sensitivity of this *hayâ* to such an extent that it does not let go unwarned, even the most minor lapse on the part of one's intention and desire.

3.6   THE STATUS OF WOMEN IN ISLÂM

Man and woman are members of the same species, proceeding from the same stock, being born from the same parents. The first Qur'ânic advice in connection with the rights of women that was declared announced:

> *"O Mankind! revere your Guardian Lord,*
> *Who created you from a single soul,*
> *created of like nature, his mate, and from*
> *two of them scattered (like seeds) countless*
> *men and women, revere Allâh, through*
> *Whom you demand your mutual rights, and*
> *revere the wombs that bore you, for Allâh*
> *ever watches over you."* [20]

4:1

Among the most wonderful mysteries of our nature is that of sex. The unregenerate male is apt, in the pride of his physical strength, to forget the all-important part which the female plays in his very existence, and in all the social relationships that arise in our collective human lives. The mother that bore us must ever have our reverence. The wife, through whom we enter parentage, must have our reverence. Sex, which governs so much of our physical life, and has so much influence on our emotional and higher nature, deserves - not our fear, or our contempt, or our amused indulgence, but - our reverence in the highest sense of the term. With this fitting introduction we enter into a discussion on women and family relationships.

Man and woman are members of humankind and the Qur'ân has invariably called them spouses and companions of each other. As human beings, man and woman are equal having the same human rights and obligations. Man is the father and bread-winner of the family, while woman is the mother and mistress of the house, managing the house and bringing up the children. Man and woman are two complementary parts of humanity and in the absence of one of them, humanity is incomplete. The roles of man and woman are neither opposed to each other nor inferior or superior to each other.

Woman enjoys a very high status of respect and honour in an Islâmic society. As a wife she is the queen and mistress of the house. She manages the house and brings up and teaches the children. She enjoys full and complete social, religious, cultural, legal and economic rights. She is entitled to receive dower and maintenance from her husband. To protect the woman's economic interest, various rules are prescribed for dower in marriage.

She can own and manage her property and can also purchase or sell the property without the intervention of her husband. She can sue and be sued and she can enter into contracts independently of her husband. In case of differences with her husband, she can nominate an arbitrator or can take the matter to an Islâmic court. She can even seek the dissolution of marriage in extreme cases.

The notion that a woman is a sub-human creature or at least treated as such is totally wrong. Woman is not a separate creation but belongs as much to the human race as man. How can there be any difference of origin between them? Rather each should pride in close proximity of the other and consider the position as something honourable. It would be correct to say that the Qur'ânic verse:

> *"O Mankind! We created you from a single*
> *(pair) of a male and female, and made you*
> *into nations and tribes, that you may know*
> *each other (not that you may despise each*
> *other) ..."* [21]

points to the fact (amongst other things), that there is no man on earth who is not indebted to a woman for his birth. Is there a man who can claim to have been born entirely from a man without the agency of a woman? What right has he then to ascribe all honour and glory to his own sex and regard the other sex as lowly and despicable? In the physical make-up of human beings, the feminine elements go with the male elements. Rather, the medical researches have shown that the female elements dominate in their physical make-up. Just think how the woman carries the foetus about in her womb, then delivers it, brings it up, suckles it. Does man take part in any of these strenuous selfless services? Our entity took shape in the mother's womb. It was there that we were nurtured with her life blood. And this woman, our benefactor, may become a source of disgrace and shame to us! Whatever our attitude towards her, it was the woman who undertook our training and upbringing when we could neither walk nor speak and tell others our needs or our troubles. It was she who taught us to walk, taught us speech and took care of us up to the age of self-consciousness. And with all that, the woman became low and despicable! Disgusting is that intellect, which takes this line of thought, damned be that tongue which dares express such ideas, and accursed be the one who nurtures such evil-inclinations in his mind.

In the position of a mother, the woman enjoys a unique status of honour and esteem. She is the focus of attention for all the members of the family. In a Muslim home, her opinions carry a lot of weight in all family matters. When the Qur'ân enjoins upon the believers to obey their parents, it especially mentions the services rendered by the mother.

> *"And we have enjoined on man (to be*
> *good) to his parents. In travail upon travail*
> *did his mother bear him, and in years twain*
> *was his weaning (hear the command),*

> *'Show gratitude to Me and to thy*
> *parents: to Me is (thy final) goal.'"* [22]

Prophet Muḥammad (ﷺ) declared in unambiguous words that the best person for one's association and obedience is one's mother. Paradise lies under her feet. The Qur'ân also forbids us to show by word or deed, the slightest displeasure or frown in our dealings with the parents, even if they become a little irritable in their behaviour in old age; and to show respect to a mother in outward form as well as a deep seated feeling of love and recognition of her unsurpassed loving care and sacrifices in our up-bringing. Regarding this the Qur'ân declares:

> *"Your Lord has decreed that you worship*
> *none but Him, and that you be kind to*
> *parents. Whether one or both of them*
> *attain old age in your life, say not to them*
> *a word of contempt, nor repel them, but*
> *address them in terms of honour."* [23]

The Muslim mother has consequently a great feeling of security about the type of care and consideration she can expect from her children when she reaches old age. Thankfulness to parents is linked with gratitude to Allâh, and a failure in either of these respects is indeed a major failure in one's religious duties.

Islâm has conferred the same religious, social, economic, legal and political rights and obligations on woman as those which have been bestowed upon man. Like man she is obliged to discharge all the duties placed upon her by the Islâmic faith, such as worship of Allâh, belief in Allâh and His Messengers, prayer (ṣalât), charity (zakât), fasting and pilgrimage. However, on account of her physical constitution, she has been given certain concessions in the fulfilment of certain religious obligations in some situations. She is exempt from jihâd (holy war) and Jumu'ah (Friday) prayer in congregation in the mosque. During menstruation she is exempt from prayers, fasting and certain rituals in ḥaj. Otherwise a man and a woman are equal in the performance of religious duties.

Women in Islâm enjoys very wide legal rights. She has rights of getting married as much as a man has. She has full liberty to choose her partner in life. No marriage under Muslim Law can be solemnised without her consent. If she is forced into marriage, she can sue in a court of Islâmic law for its dissolution. If she is married as a minor, she can exercise her option after attaining puberty and can repudiate the marriage. She is entitled to maintenance from her husband like food, clothing and lodgement. She enjoys absolute and unrestricted rights regarding dower or bridal gift which she is entitled to receive from her husband. It is interesting to note that the husband has no such right to receive any obligatory gift from his wife. She can also seek divorce or the dissolution of marriage in certain extreme cases.

3.6.1   THE ECONOMIC ASPECT AND INHERITANCE

In communities which base their civil rights on brute strength, the weaker go to the wall and public opinion expects nothing else. Even in modern democracies of the saner sort, we are often told that it is the fate of the weaker sex to suffer: strength here becomes the passport to power and privilege. Islâm , while upholding sane manly views in general, enjoins the most solicitous care for the weak in every way - in rights of property, in social rights, and in the rights to opportunities of development. Time and again is it impressed on the community of Muslims to be just in their dealings with women.

Thus, a woman enjoys rights of property in Islâm. She can acquire, own, possess and dispose of her property independently of her father or husband. According to Islâmic law, woman's right to her money, real estate or other properties is fully acknowledged. This right undergoes no change whether she is single or married. She retains her full rights to buy, sell, mortgage or lease any or all her properties. Nowhere is it suggested that a woman is a minor, simply because she is a female. Islâm has bestowed upon her rights of inheritance in her various capacities like wife, mother, daughter and sister after the death of her close relatives.

Probably for the first time in the history of the world, Islâm granted the women an opportunity to live an independent life, if she so wished, with the assets that were her own, and she need not necessarily be dependent on a man.

The daughters who had been denied their share in the inheritance so far, were now made sharers in the property left by the deceased. Regarding this, the Qur'ân mentions:

> *"Allâh thus directs you as regards your*
> *children's (inheritance), to the male, a*
> *portion equal to that of two females; if only*
> *daughters, two or more, their share is two*
> *thirds of the inheritance; if only one, her*
> *share is half."* [24]

People were really amazed when it was first known in those early days of the revelation of the Qur'ân, that females were to get a share of the inheritance and a fair share for that matter, when they are unable to take part in the battles to protect life and property against the enemy. But Islâm had come to restore the rights of those who had been denied those rights by the tyrants whose oppression and tyranny were soon put down by force - though after a long period of arguing and reasoning with them. It was made evident to one and all that ownership and proprietary rights were not the privilege of men alone but women were the shareholders in this form of economic authority and power. The Qur'ân re-enforces this ideology by mentioning:

> *"From what is left by parents and those*
> *nearest related, there is a share for men*
> *and share for women, whether the property*
> *be small or large, - a fair and just share."* [25]

Woman, in whatever capacity she may be, cannot be denied her right to the property because of her sex. Regarding this the Qur'ân mentions:

> *"For the parents a sixth share of the*
> *inheritance to each, if the deceased left*
> *children; if no children, and the parents*
> *are the (only) heirs, the mother has a third;*
> *if the deceased left brother (or sisters), the*

mother has a sixth." [26]

In the verse quoted above where the father has been made the inheritor in the bequest, the mother has also been given the right of inheritance. It may be one third or one sixth but nowhere has her sex stood in the way of her obtaining the due share of the bequest.

After having examined the share a woman receives as a daughter and as a mother, we would now look to her position as a wife. Here too she has not been denied her share of the bequest. The Qur'ân mentions:

> *"In what your wives leave, your share is half, if they leave no child; but if they leave a child, you get a forth; after payment of legacies and debts. In what you leave, their share is a forth, if you leave no child; but if you leave a child, they get an eighth, after payment of legacies and debts."* [27]

This clearly illustrates that just as the husband has been made the inheritor of the bequest of the wife, so has she been made the inheritor in the husband's inheritance. None dare deprive her of her share of the property of the husband.

The method of division of inheritance has clearly been laid down by the Qur'ân and the general rule is that women are entitled to inherit half the share given to a man. This may, if taken in isolation from other legislation, appear to be unfair; however, it must be remembered that in accordance with Qur'ânic injunctions, men are charged with the maintenance of all the women and children in their family, and therefore their necessary obligations of expenditure are far higher than those of women. The half-share that a woman inherits may therefore be considered a generous one, since it is for her alone. Any such money or property which a woman owns or any business which she runs is entirely her own and her husband has no right to any of it. From this point of view, even fifty per cent share out of the inheritance is enough for her. An examination of the inheritance law within the overall framework of the Islâmic Law reveals not only justice but also an abundance of compassion for woman.

3.6.2   SOCIAL AND POLITICAL RIGHTS

In the social and political field also, a woman enjoys many rights. She can participate in the social, educational and religious festivals and events after observing the rules of decency, modesty and proper dress. She can adopt a legitimate source of earning income within the Islâmic framework and can participate in the family welfare. Although it should first be stated that Islâm regards her role in society as a mother and a wife as the most sacred and essential one. Neither maids nor babysitters can possibly take the mother's place as the educator of an upright, complex-free and carefully-reared children. Such a noble and vital role, which largely shapes the future of nations, cannot be regarded as "idleness". She has as much right to an education as a man has although within the parameters of *Sharî'ah*. In the political life of the Muslim Ummah she also enjoys rights and obligations. Female citizens of an Islâmic state have also got rights of mutual consultation and of being consulted as the male citizens have. Islâmic history bears evidence that the Prophet 𝕤 and the pious <u>Kh</u>alîfs used to consult the women in many matters. Enjoining good and forbidding wrong is an important political function of an Islâmic state and the woman have also been enjoined to discharge this duty along with men. The Qur'ân mentions:

> *"The believers, men and women, are protectors, one of another; they enjoin what is just, and forbid what is evil ..."* [28]

3.6.3   FEMALE LEADERSHIP

Is it permissible for a woman to become head of state or to govern a country? Scholars of Islâm maintain conflicting views on this fragile issue. Those who oppose the above proposition and contend that a woman is not permitted by Islâm to become the head of state produce the following arguments from the Qur'ân and Ḥâdî<u>th</u>:

(1)   It was Âdam 🙶, the man and not the woman whom Allâh placed as viceroy on earth.

> *"Behold, your Lord said to the angels:*
> *'I will create a vicegerent on earth'.*
> *They said, 'Will Thou place therein one*
> *who will make mischief and shed blood?*
> *- whilst we do celebrate Thy praises and*
> *glorify Thy Holy Name.' He said: "I*
> *know what you know not."* [29]

Since man has been made viceroy, how can a woman rule? - is the argument.

(2) It was Âdam ﷺ, the man before whom the angels prostrated at the command of Allâh.

> *"And behold, We said to the angels, "Bow*
> *down to Âdam", and they bowed down,*
> *except Iblîs, he refused and was haughty*
> *and he was among those who rejected*
> *faith."* [30]

So it is argued that the angels prostrated before the man, how then can a woman rule over him?

(3) Though the women have similar rights as men, yet the men are a degree above them.

> *"And women shall have rights similar to*
> *the rights against them, according to what*
> *is equitable; but men have a degree (of*
> *advantage) over them. And Allâh Ta'âlâ*
> *is Exalted in Power."* [31]

Hence, the argument is, since man is superior to woman, she cannot rule over him.

(4) Evidence of two women is equal to the evidence of one man.

> *"And get two witnesses, out of your own*

> *men, and if there are not two men, then*
> *a man and two women, such as you*
> *choose, for witnesses, so that if one of*
> *them errs, the other can remind her."* [32]

Therefore, the argument is that the testimony of a woman is equal to half that of a man, how then can she rule over him?

(5) Men have been declared as qawwâm (in charge) of women and, according to some who translate the word qawwâm as ruler, they are rulers of women.

> *"Men are the protectors and maintainers*
> *of women, because Allâh Ta'âlâ has given*
> *the one more (strength) than the other, and*
> *because they support them from their*
> *means. Therefore the righteous women are*
> *devoutly obedient, and guard in (the*
> *husband's) absence what Allâh would have*
> *them guard."* [33]

The man is the head of the family while a woman enjoys a secondary position. So it is argued that a woman who cannot become even head of the family in the presence of a man, how can she become head of the state or the nation?

(6) Allâh Ta'âlâ has sent only men as prophets for guidance of humanity.

> *"Before you, also the apostles We sent were*
> *but men, to whom We granted inspiration,*
> *if you realise this not, ask of those who*
> *possess the message."* [34]

Since a woman has not been made a prophet, she cannot be ruler either.

(7) The womenfolk have been instructed to stay in their homes.

> *"And stay quietly in your homes, and make*
> *not a dazzling display, like that of the*
> *former Times of Ignorance ..."* [35]

One who cannot come out of her house except in the case of very essential need, how then can she be permitted to assume the responsibilities of the head of state which require full time engagements out of her home.

(8)   Women have been directed to observe *purdah* when they come out of their houses.

> *"O Prophet! Tell your wives and*
> *daughters, and the believing women, that*
> *they should cast their outer garments over*
> *their persons (when abroad); that is most*
> *convenient, that they should be known (as*
> *such) and not molested; And Allâh is Most*
> *Forgiving, Most Merciful."* [36]

When a woman cannot come out of her house before strangers without observing *purdah*, how can she hold political offices, specially the office of the head of state which requires frequent meetings with men, not only from one's own country but also with foreigners.

(9)   Women, who are generally brought up in ornaments and trinkets, cannot present logical reasoning in disputes.

> *"Is then one brought up among trinkets,*
> *and unable to give a clear account in a*
> *dispute ..."* [37]

From this they argue that a woman is weak by nature. She is very delicate and is brought up in fineries and ornaments and lacks logical reasoning and sound argumentation. Therefore, she renders herself to be incapable of ruling.

(10) When Prophet Muhammad ﷺ heard that the Persians, had made the daughter of Kisrâ ruler over them, said: *"Never shall a people prosper who make a woman their ruler."* [38]

In another hâdîth narrated in Bukhârî it is mentioned:

> *"Once the Rasûl of Allâh ﷺ went out to the mussalâ (to offer the prayer) of 'Îd al Adhâ or 'Îd al Fitr. Then he passed by the women and said, "O Women! Give alms, as I have seen that the majority of the dwellers of hell-fire were you (women)."*

They asked, *"Why is it so, O Rasûl of Allâh ﷺ?*
He replied, *"You curse frequently and are ungrateful to your husbands. I have not seen anyone more deficient in intelligence and dîn (religion) than you. A cautious sensible man could be led astray by some of you."* The woman asked, *"O Rasûl of Allâh ﷺ! What is deficient in our intelligence and dîn?"* He said, *"Is not the evidence of two women equal to the witness of one man?"* They replied in the affirmative. He said, *"This is the deficiency in your intelligence. Isn't it true then women can neither pray nor fast during her menses?"* The women replied in the affirmative. He said, *"This is the deficiency in your dîn."* [39]

Those who advocate the concept that woman can rule advance the following arguments:

(1) The Qur'ân has not explicitly prohibited the rule of woman anywhere. When the Qur'ân has not overlooked even minor issues while laying down the rules and regulations governing the conduct of an individual in the family and society, how could it overlook such an important and vital issue like the rule of woman if it is *harâm* and adversely effects the progress and welfare of humanity. The silence of the Qur'ân on this crucial issue means that the Muslim community has been left to decide it according to the circumstances and according to their best interest, they contend.

(2)   Similarly, advocates of woman's rule, advance the episode of a woman ruler, the Queen of Shêbâ, which has been related in chapter twenty seven of the Qur'ân. These were the deductions which they made:

(a)   Her rule was not that of an autocrat. She had very good rapport when consulting others on all important affairs of the State (a quality which was lacking in most of the male rulers of her times).

(b)   She was a very wise woman and her sound opinion could not be ignored. She convinced her chieftains to come to terms with Prophet Sulaimân ﷺ.

(c)   Like a true statesman, she was against war and loved peace. Instead of agreeing with her war lords, she advanced very sound arguments against the war. Thus a decision was taken to start negotiations rather than going to war.

(d)   Prophet Sulaimân tested her judgement by miraculously producing her throne and presenting it to her in a disguised form. She immediately recognized it.

(e)   In spite of all that she accepted Islâm when she met the Prophet and saw the light despite the fact that she was the ruler of a disbelieving nation and had lived all her life among the sun-worshippers and idolaters.

The Qur'ân has not spoken of the rule of the Queen of Shêbâ with disapproval and condemnation or denunciation. Rather her habit of consulting others before taking decisions on vital issues, her peace-loving temperament, her wisdom and sound judgement and her readiness to accept Islâm at once rather than persisting in disbelief, have found special mention in the Qur'ân.

(3)   To support their contention, they also argue that Hadrat 'Âishah, the wife of the Prophet ﷺ, commanded the troops and participated in the 'Battle of the Camel' in order to get *qisâs* of the murder of Hadrat

'Uthmân ⚛, the third righteous Khalîf.

(4) The supporters of the women's rule do not accept the hâdîth pertaining to the daughter of Kisrâ as authentic since its reporter Abû Bakrâ was found guilty of false evidence and was punished by Hadrat 'Umar ⚛.

(5) Proponents of woman's rule also cite the fatwâ (Islâmic verdict) of Maulânâ Ashraf 'Alî Thanwî who gave a decree in favour of the rule of Shâhjahân Begum, the Queen of Bhopal. He stated that if the government was democratic and the affairs of the state were being conducted by the ruler with the help of elected representatives and in consultation with them, then there was no bar against the woman becoming the head of State or government. He mentioned that in such a situation the woman ruler was in fact one of the counsels and the woman was eligible for counselship because the Prophet of Islâm consulted Umme Salamah at Hudeybiyah and acted upon her advice.[40]

If a critical examination of the arguments advanced by both parties is made, that is, those who oppose women's rule and those who support it, it would be noticed that none of them has been able to carry their point conclusively. Arguments given in favour of the proposition and arguments given against it are by and large indirect and generally not relevant. These arguments simply bring home the fact that man and woman are equal in some matters while in others they are not, as nature has intended different fields of activity for them.

A common conclusion erroneously reached by proponents of female leadership is the story of the Queen of Shêbâ. This is a grave misconception, for it should be realized that she ruled before submitting to the will of Allâh Ta'âlâ and accepting Islâm. This fact alone cuts through the backbone of the arguments for female leadership.

So ridiculous is this proof that it is like using the actions of the pre-Islâmic idolaters as proof for an Islâmic practice. Queen Shêba's leadership was in the state of kufr (disbelief). Muslims follow the dîn as expounded by Muhammad ⚛, that is, Islâm, as opposed to Bilkîs, in her state of kufr.

Also, once Muhammad ﷺ had proclaimed a law contrary to an existing one, then that proclamation would be adhered to. Moreover, Bilkîs submitted to Sulaiman's law and he took over her kingdom by taking control of her throne. Critics have taken the leadership aspect out of context. In context, one has to admit that had Bilkîs even been a Muslim (which she was not) at the time of her rule she was overthrown by a Prophet. This point lends greater weight against female leadership than for it. Similarly, after accepting Islâm, she did not reclaim her throne implies that even Bilkîs agreed to be ruled by a male. The arguments in favour of female leadership using this story is therefore baseless.

Similarly ʿÂishâh's commanding of the army in the Battle of the Camel has been repeatedly misquoted as "proof" for leadership rather than against it. She did not go to engage in a battle, nor to claim *khilâfat* or leadership, but to find a peaceful solution in flushing out and punishing the murderers of ʿUthmân ﷺ. Moreover, she totally regretted her involvement and her coming out of the house to such an extent that whenever she remembered this incident she wept so profusely that her headcover would become wet. Therefore the incident described cannot be used to prove the right of women to take up leadership in Islâm. None of her sayings or advice she gave to the thousands who sought it, contains encouragement towards female leadership. One isolated episode with the initial hesitation and later deep regret could not and cannot be used as proof for female leadership. In fact it is a clear proof to the contrary.

A woman is not only physically weak and mentally emotional, tender, sensitive and delicate, but is also under great strain for a few days every month during menstruation. Then she has periods of physiological as well as psychological strain during pregnancy, birth and suckling. She is naturally most suited for the job of childbearing, and their nursing, training and education. The chief office of the state needs qualifications and qualities quite opposed to the natural endowments of a woman. Islâm has therefore advised against entrusting the chief executive post of leadership (*imâmat*) of the nation to a woman for these very reasons, and not because of any feeling of hatred or contempt for her. Muslim scholars have summed up the qualifications necessary for a candidate for leadership in these words: he has independent judgement (of a *mujtahid*) in the fundamentals and details of *Dîn* (Islâmic religious science), so as to satisfy people of every opinion; he has a deep and penetrating vision of human problems and is fully acquainted with the strategies of war and peace, as otherwise, he will not be able to solve the various problems facing *Dîn* and *Millat* (creed); and he should be a man of great determination and courage, so that no power can obstruct him in the fulfilment of his duties.

Obviously these qualities are more often found in men than in women; and even then in very few men.

Even in modern times, and in the most developed countries, it is rare to find a woman in the position of a head of state acting as more than a figure head, a woman commander of the armed services, or even a proportionate number of women representatives in parliaments, or similar bodies. One cannot possibly ascribe this to backwardness of various nations or to any constitutional limitation on woman's rights to be in such a position as a head of state or a member of parliament. It is more logical to explain the present situation in terms of the natural and indisputable differences between man and woman, a difference which does not imply any "supremacy" of one over the other. The difference implies rather the "complementary" roles of both the sexes in life.[41]

3.6.4 EDUCATION OF WOMEN

In the early period of Islâm, the wives of the Prophet 🕮 and other women companions played a great role in the spread of learning and knowledge of the Qur'ân and Sunnah. Whenever the companions of Prophet Muhammad 🕮 found any difficulty in respect of any hadîth and enquired about it from 'Âishah (R.A.), they found that she certainly had knowledge about it. Hâfiz ibn Hajar mentions regarding the knowledge of 'Âishah:

> "`Âishah learned many things from the Prophet 🕮 and lived for about fifty years after him. People gained a great deal from her and reported many commands and manner of the Prophet 🕮 from her; so much so, it is said, that about one fourth of the commands were transmitted by her."[42]

In Islâm therefore, both men and women are credited with the capacity for learning, understanding and teaching, and one of the aims of acquiring knowledge is that of becoming more conscious of Allâh Ta'âlâ.

It goes to the credit of Islâm that it was the first religion that impressed upon women that they could not achieve perfection without knowledge. Acquisition of knowledge was as great a duty of woman as man, for Islâm wanted the womenfolk to develop their rational faculties along with their physical ones and thus ascend to higher plains of spiritual existence whilst on the other hand, Europe did not recognize any such right for women till very recently and did in the end grant it to her only when compelled by the pressure of economic circumstances.

Therefore in Islâm women have educational rights higher than those of their western counterparts. If these rights are not realized, or remain only potential in her hands, that would indicate the bankruptcy of her feminity, and these cannot be replaced by law or by constitutional voting rights.

The most suitable area to concentrate on women's education would be the principles of religion, home making, child-bearing and what is necessary concerning health, worship and human relations. For she who helps her husband in his domestic life is better than she who demands voting rights and equal participation with men in governing the country. By God she is not fit for that.[43]

Muḥammad 'Abdul Raûf of the Islâmic Centre in Washington writing from an Islâmic perspective in the U.S. mentions:

> *"Advantage should not be taken of the woman's body and her flesh should not be put on public display ... toleration of an evil leads to other evils. First we condone public exposure; next, dating and easy mixing; next, pre-marital relations; next, the elevation of homosexuality to an acceptable normal status; and next, anti-sex marriages. Where, and when, shall we*

stop?" [44]

Jane Smith states:

> *"What is the need for a girl to study science and arts etc ... when she does not know how to take care of the house and the family?"* [45]

A contemporary author warns about the evils of educating women to be equal to men:

> *"Girls are to be educated in areas that belong to them and not to men. We do not want at all to educate women to be secretaries or managers of offices of government."* [46]

And again:

> *"You who persist in educating women, strengthen yourself before you begin your task, make religion her banner waving over her head, and her crown shining over her forehead ... or you would lose her character ... and would find her education a path to evil and a way of corruption."* [47]

Let us also hear what Madame Truman has to say on moral degradation:

> *"These girls are neither street florets nor the victims of traffic in flesh. They are young and mostly simple, innocent girls between fifteen and twenty years of age and students of schools and colleges ... At the moment the American Government and the American nation are faced with the serious problem of the offspring of*

anonymous fathers. Last year the number of children born to unmarried mothers was hundred and twenty five thousand. And a hundred thousand of these were college students. It has also been investigated by the Investigation Commission of Education and Training that the fathers of these one hundred thousand children are also the 'promising' students of colleges ... The reason behind this scandalous state is that the American families have allowed their girls perfect freedom, with the result that a young girl who is normally starved of love and care in her own family circle, on her entry into a college, meets some student among the boys who becomes a friend and she soon finds herself involved in an experimental love affair, culminating in free sexual relations. "[48]

This is sufficient evidence to demonstrate that a woman is so volatile, that encouraging her to enrol in such institutions for 'higher education', which are the breeding grounds for immorality, could also arouse in her a feeling of abandoning all sense of modesty. Muslims should therefore tread such slippery paths with extreme caution.

3.6.5 KIND TREATMENT TO FEMALE OFFSPRINGS AND PROHIBITION OF INFANTICIDE

In Islâm the child has a right to life. Neither the father nor the mother have the right to take the life of the child, whether a boy or a girl, by killing it or burying it alive. Allâh Ta'âlâ mentions:

"And do not kill your children out of fear of poverty; We shall provide for them and for you. Truly, their slaying is a great sin." [49]

> *"When the female child who was buried*
> *alive is asked for what crime she was*
> *killed."* [50]

Whatever the motive for this crime may be, whether economic, such as fear of poverty and lack of provision; or non-economic, such as fear of disgrace in the case of a daughter, Islâm absolutely prohibits this savage act which is nothing but premeditated murder and the oppression of a feeble, helpless human being.

The Prophet ﷺ took an oath of allegiance from both men and women at the time of their accepting Islâm. This oath of allegiance included the condition that they would not kill their children and would consider it an absolutely prohibited crime:

> *" ... That they will not steal nor commit*
> *zinâ (adultery) nor kill their children ... "* [51]

The history of human civilization bears evidence that the woman was regarded as an embodiment of shame and sin in the world. The birth of a daughter so embarrassed a father that he could not raise his head for shame. The in-law relations were looked upon as base, mean and disgraceful. For this reason, the inhuman custom of disposing of daughters by killing them had become common among many nations.

It is Islâm which revolutionized this state of affairs not only legally and practically but also intellectually. Islâm has indeed changed the mentalities of both the man and the woman. The concept of giving the woman her rights and a place of honour in society has in fact been created in man's mind by Islâm.[52]

Whenever there was an occasion for it the Prophet ﷺ induced people to treat their daughters and other girls kindly. The Prophet ﷺ said:

> *"Whoever brings up two girls until they*
> *attain adulthood, he will be with me on the*
> *Day of Reckoning, and so close to me as*
> *these two (adjacent fingers) of mine, and*

> he pointed to his two fingers joined
> together." [53]

'Âishah (R.A.) narrates:

> "One day a woman came to me with two
> of her daughters. She was poor and
> helpless and she begged for something to
> eat. All that I had was a single date fruit
> at that time, and I gave it to her. She
> divided the date into two halves and gave
> one half to each of her two daughters, not
> taking anything herself. Then she got up
> and left the place.

When the Prophet 🕌 came to me, I related the incident to him. On hearing it he remarked:

> "Whosoever puts up with hardship for his
> or her daughters, and treats them kindly,
> for him or her, those daughters will become
> a shield against hell-fire." [54]

These are the evidence that prove that the Prophet 🕌 was not there only to champion the cause of menfolk alone, but took equal, rather, greater pains to redeem the women from the dishonour to which they were subjected.

3.6.6 RETAINING MAIDEN NAME

A Muslim woman is privileged in the sense that she must retain her full identity, that is, her maiden name. Suppose a Maryam Muḥammad marries a Fârûq Mûsâ, she never changes her surname and becomes a Mûsâ. Her doing so is regarded as un-Islâmic. The wife retains her identity while she is with her husband, and when he passes away or divorces her and she marries another man, there is no such inconvenience of changing of names for the third or fourth time. Her first maiden (father's) name is used till she passes away.

In contrast we find that nearly all Christian women lose their maiden names soon after marriage as she has to sign her maiden name for the last time in the Church register after the wedding ceremonies.[55] It was only Lucy Stone, one of the famous speakers on the movement to emancipate women, who retained her maiden name as a protest against the unequal laws applicable to married women. She became known as Mrs Stone and not as Mrs Blackwell.[56]

3.7 WESTERN CONCEPT OF SEXUAL EQUALITY AND FEMINISM

In Western society, (a society which does not respect divine and secular laws - Muslims are also included) equality between the sexes, was taken to mean that man and woman were not only equal in moral status and human rights, but that the woman was also free to undertake the same sort of jobs as were done by the man, and that moral restrictions on her needed to be slackened as they were for him. This wrong concept of equality led woman astray and made them unmindful of their natural functions on the performance of which depends the very existence of the human race and civilization. She became wholly absorbed in her economic, political and social pursuits. Her electioneering campaigns, service in offices and factories, competition with men for commercial and industrial vocations, sports and physical exercises, social entertainments, and her absorption in the club, stage and musical concerts, besides several other engagements, so overwhelmed her that she became utterly indifferent to the responsibilities of married life. Besides this, she developed a hatred for her natural duties, affecting ultimately the family system which is the basis of civilization.[57]

The most radical movement in recent times which is changing the entire social structure of human relationships is the feminist movement, popularly referred to as the drive for Women's Liberation. This movement is not a unique product of modern age. Its roots reach back into ancient times. Plato advocated the abolition of the family and social role determined by sex. In 1884 Engels publicly proclaimed marriage as a "dreary mutation of slavery", urged its abolition and suggested public responsibility for the rearing of children. In the early 1960's the beginning of Feminist confrontation in the form of marches, pickets and sit-ins occurred. College and university girls began to participate in these political activities.

In contrast to the women who assembled at the Seneca Falls Convention in 1848 and merely protested against the ill-treatment and abuse of American women by drunken husbands and achievement of their legitimate rights in marriage, control of property and earnings, and equal pay with men for the same job, the demands of their modern successors were far more radical. In the largest feminist demonstration ever held, on August 26, 1970, hundreds of women marched down Fifth Avenue, New York City, carrying placards which read:

HOUSEWIVES ARE UNPAID SLAVES! STATE PAY FOR HOUSEWORK! OPPRESSED WOMEN! DON'T COOK DINNER! STARVE YOUR HUSBAND TONIGHT! END HUMAN SACRIFICE! DON'T GET MARRIED! WASHING DIAPERS IS NOT FULFILLING! LEGALIZE ABORTION! DEPENDENCY IS NOT A HEALTHY STATE OF BEING!

Today's feminists are totally opposed to any social roles being determined by sex. They advocate the absolute equality of men and women, notwithstanding anatomical differences. They deny that there is any biological distinction between men and women on the basis of sex. They demand the abolition of the institution of marriage, home and family, assert complete female sexual freedom and that the upbringing of children should be a public responsibility. They insist that all women be given the right to complete control over their reproductive lives. They are demanding that all restrictions must be lifted from the laws governing contraception so that devices can be publicly advertised and made easily available to any woman regardless of her age or marital status. Pornography, prostitution and fornication should be allowed uncensored. Abortion should not only be available on demand but should be supplied free by the state to any woman who wants one at any stage of her pregnancy so that the "poor woman" can take full advantage of this facility. In schools, all courses must be equally co-educational - home-economics must not be exclusively female or shop mechanics only for boys. Segregation must be broken down in gymnasiums and physical education. Girls should be allowed to compete in all sports and physical exercises with boys at all ages. All mass-media must be radically changed to eliminate sex-stereotyping roles and portray women as equal to men in all fields of work and production. Children's books are criticized by feminists because they do not show in their stories more single-parent families, unmarried mothers and divorced women as models for the children. Girls should be given mechanical toys to play with and boys should be given dolls. Radical feminists propose men and women living in large communes where the welfare and rearing of the children would be a public responsibility. They are demanding that child-care centres are made available to parents on a 24-hour basis provided to the public free on demand just as parks, libraries and recreational facilities are taken for granted in most American communities.

Women must be financially independent and no profession or occupation should be barred to her on account of her sex.[58]

> *"A lot of women who may say that they just want to play the traditional roles are simply fearful - or unable to imagine other ways of being. Old roles can seem to offer a certain security. Freedom can seem frightening, especially if one has learned how to achieve a certain degree of power inside prison. Perhaps they are just afraid of choices. We don't seek to impose anything on women but merely to open up all possible alternatives. We do seek choice as one of the functions which makes people human beings. We want to be full people, crippled neither by low custom nor our own chained minds. If there is no room in that in nature, then nature must be changed."* [59]

One of the 'alternative choices' for women the feminists seek to make socially acceptable is lesbianism.

> *"The women's liberation movement has members who were lesbians before its*

*existence and those who have become
lesbians since their involvement with the
movement. For some of the latter,
lesbianism is a form of political protest.
Say the radical feminists:
"Lesbianism is one road to freedom -
freedom from oppression by men."* [60]

The lesbian minority in America, which may run as high as ten million women, is a woman, who is drawn erotically to women rather than to men. Perhaps the most logical and least hysterical of all statements about homosexuality is the following by Drs. J. Fort and J. Adams, psychiatrist and psychologist respectively:

*"Homosexuals like heterosexuals should
be treated as individual human beings and
not as a special group either by law or
social agencies or employers. Laws
governing sexual behaviour should be
reformed to deal only with clearly anti-
social behaviour involving violence or
youth. The sexual behaviour of individual
adults by mutual consent in private should
not be a matter of public concern."* [61]

Feminism is an unnatural, artificial and abnormal product of modern day social disintegration which in turn is the inevitable result of the rejection of all moral and spiritual values. We are convinced of the abnormality of the feminist movement because all human cultures we know of make a clear-cut distinction between "masculinity" and "feminity" and structure the social roles of men and women accordingly. The disintegration of the home and family, the loss of the authority of the father and sexual promiscuity have been directly responsible for the decline and fall of every nation in which these evils become rampant.

Some may argue that if this is so, why is Western civilization so extraordinarily vigorous and dynamic and despite its moral corruption, still unchallenged in its world-domination? These claims are nothing but mere deceptions and illusions, for the following points prove to be contrary:

When moral depravity, self-worship and sensual indulgence have touched extremes; when men and women, young and old have become lost in sexual craze; when men have been completely perverted by sexual excitements; the natural consequences leading a nation to total collapse will inevitably follow. People who witness the progress and prosperity of such declining nations, which indeed stand on the very brink of an abyss of fire, are led to conclude that their self-indulgence is not impeding their progress but accelerating it. They think that a nation is at the peak of its prosperity when its people are highly self-indulgent. But this is a sad conclusion. When the constructive and destructive forces are both working side by side and the constructive aspect on the whole seems to have an edge over the destructive aspect, it is wrong to count the latter among the factors leading to the former.

Take, for instance, the case of a clever merchant who is earning high profits by dint of his intelligence, hard work and experience. But at the same time, if he is given to drink, gambling and leads a care-free life, will it not be misleading to regard that side of his life as contributing to his well-being and prosperity? As a matter of fact, the first set of qualities is helping him to prosper whereas the second set is pulling him down. If on account of the positive qualities, he is flourishing, it does not mean that the negative forces are ineffective. It may be that the evil of gambling would bring his whole future to naught in a moment and it may be that the evil of drinking leads him to commit a fatal mistake rendering him bankrupt and it may be that the evil of sexual indulgence leads him to commit murder, suicide or leads him to some other calamity. One cannot imagine how prosperous and triumphant he would have been had he not fallen a prey to these evils.

Similarly is the case with a nation. In the beginning it receives an impetus from constructive forces but then, due to lack of proper guidance, it begins to gather round it the means of its own destruction. For a while the constructive forces drag it along under the momentum already gained. But the destructive forces that are working simultaneously weaken it so much that one stray shock can send it sprawling to its doom.[62]

Susan Faludi argues that the Women's Liberation Movement has run into increased opposition. Women have been told by politicians, business leaders and advertisers, amongst others, that women have won the war for women's rights, and now enjoy 'equality' with men. However, they are warned at the same time that the rights they have won have been at considerable cost. She says:

"Behind this celebration of women's victory, behind the news cheerfully and endlessly repeated, that the struggle for women's rights is won, another message flashes. You may be free and equal now, but you have never been more miserable".[63]

In America for example, magazines and newspapers have mentioned that professional career women are prone to infertility and health problems such as alcoholism and hair loss, while women without children and women who do not get married are prone to depression or hysteria and the root cause of these problems is said to be feminism.

None can deny the fact that as human beings man and woman are equal. Both make up the human race together as its equal constituent parts. Both are equal partners in building up community life, creating and bringing about civilization, and thus serving humanity. Both stand in need of mental and intellectual training and education so that they may duly contribute to the happiness and welfare of society. In view of these facts the claim for equality is absolutely justified, and every good civilization is duty bound to afford its women also the opportunities along with men of developing this natural abilities. They should also be provided the facilities for educational advancement; they should also be given social and economic rights like men; and they should also be granted an honourable place in society so that they may also develop self- respect and dignity. The nations which have denied their womenfolk this kind of equality, which have kept them illiterate and ignorant and which have deprived them of social rights, have ultimately themselves been doomed. For to debase and corrupt one half of humanity is to debase and corrupt the whole of humanity. How can wretched, uncultured, ignorant and illiterate mothers rear and bring up children who would turn out to be proud, cultured and enlightened human beings?

The other aspects of equality is that man and woman should have the same sphere of activity, they should have to shoulder equal responsibilities in all spheres of life, and that they should have identical positions in society. Let us firstly analyze these demands from the physiological, biological and psychological perspective.

It has been established by biological research that woman is different from man not only in her appearance and external physical organs, but also in the protein molecules of tissue cells. From the time that sex formation of the foetus starts, the physiological structures of the two sexes begin to develop differently. The female physical system is evolved in order to bear and bring up children. As soon as a girl attains maturity, menstruation starts affecting the functioning of all her physical organs. The investigations made by famous biologists and physiologists show that during menstruation, the following changes take place in the female organism.

(1) The power of resistance in the body decreases with the result that heat is lost unduly, resulting in fall of temperature.

(2) Pulse weakens, blood pressure falls below normal and corpuscles decrease.

(3) Tonsils, endocrines and lymphatic glands undergo changes.

(4) The process of protein metabolism suffers a setback.

(5) The release of phosphates and chlorides slows down and the process of gaseous metabolism deteriorates.

(6) Digestion becomes difficult, and protein and fats are not easily assimilated by the body.

(7) Respiration slows down and the vocal organs suffer changes.

(8) Muscles become lethargic and feel cold.

(9) The ability to concentrate weakens.

These changes render an otherwise healthy woman sick. Less than 23 per cent of women have painless discharge of the menses. Once one thousand and twenty women were taken at random and subjected to investigation. It was found that 84 percent among them suffered from pain and other problems during menstruation.[64]

Many women, who are normally healthy and cheerful, become depressed and moody during the "low" period, and are generally nervous and excitable. Irritably, hypersensitiveness and a tendency to quarrel easily are symptomatic of these phases. Due to this she begins bungling in matter of daily habit. A lady motor driver, for instance, would drive slowly as if under strain, and become nervous at everything. A lady magistrate's comprehension and ability to take decisions would both be adversely affected. A female dentist would find it difficult to locate the required instruments. In short, a woman's mental and nervous system becomes lethargic and disorderly during menstruation. Thus, she begins behaving as if under duress. She loses freedom of action, and is thus rendered unfit to undertake any work of responsibility. Some authorities on the subject have been led to conclude that most crimes and suicide by women are committed during this period.

The period of pregnancy for women is even more disturbing than menstruation. A pregnant woman cannot undertake any work of mental and physical exertion which she could easily undertake at other times. According to experts even a healthy woman remains subject to extreme mental derangement during pregnancy. She becomes fickle, mentally disturbed and unwell, with the result that her capacity to understand and think is seriously impaired.

After delivery has taken place a woman remains exposed to various troubles. Her internal wounds may easily become septic. Her muscles begin to contract and return to the pre-pregnancy state, and this upsets her whole system. Thus, after impregnation a woman remains sick or nearly sick for about a year, and during this period her general efficiency is reduced to half, or even less than normal.

Then comes the two year period of suckling when she does not live for herself but for the trust that nature has placed in her care. The best of her body is turned into milk for the baby. Substitutes like artificial feeding and bottle is no solution at all since all specialists agree that for the proper development of the child there is no better nutrition than the mother's own milk. Then, for a long time to come she has to pay the fullest attention to the bringing up and training of the child. Nurseries and nursing homes cannot provide and make up for motherly love. The affection, kindly regards and good wishes so badly needed by a child in early childhood cannot be evoked from the hearts of hired nurses, since the best place where a child can be naturally nourished and brought up is on the mother's lap.

In view of these facts, let us now consider the demands of justice and fairplay. The question is: Will it be just and fair to demand that a woman perform all these natural functions in which man is not, and cannot be, her partner, and also shoulder those social responsibilities equally with him for the carrying out of which he has been absolved from all other natural duties? Will it be fair to require her to undergo all sorts of hardships set for her sex by nature and also to earn her living in the economic field? Will it be proper and right to make her take equal part with man in defending the country, promoting the cause of industry and commerce, agriculture and administration of justice? Above all, will it be just and moral to require her to allure men's hearts also by her presence in mixed gatherings and provide them with means of entertainment and pleasure? It is not justice, but sheer injustice; it is not equality, but sheer inequality. Justice and fairplay would demand that the one who has already been burdened by nature should be given light duties in society, and the one who has no such natural duty should be required to shoulder all the important and heavy social responsibilities including the duties of supporting and protecting the family.

Therefore to prepare woman for manly jobs is utterly against the will and design of nature. It neither helps humanity nor the women herself. Imagine for a while the plight of a land or naval force which wholly consists of women. It is quite possible that right in the midst of war, a fair number of them might be down with menstrual discharge, a good number of delivery cases forced to stay in bed, and a fair percentage of pregnant ones fuming and sulking uselessly. One may say that the military service is rather too strenuous for women. But one may ask: Which is the service among the police, judicial, administrative, construction, railway, industrial and commercial services does not require steadfast, dependable capacity to work? Therefore the people who want women to undertake manly duties perhaps want to 'defeminize' them all and finish off the human race, or perhaps they want to lower the general standards of efficiency in all affairs of life. To drag the woman into these fields of activity, is to abuse her as well as the fields of activity themselves. This will bring about the woman's downfall and not her advancement in life. Advancement is not curbing one's natural endowments and creating instead such qualities artificially as do not form part of one's nature. Real advancement consists in developing the natural gifts, polishing and refining them, and providing for them better and ever increasing opportunities for action.[65]

For this very reason, man's life and civilization on earth stand as much in need of aggressiveness and coarseness as of tenderness and softness. Good statesmen, good generals and good administrators are as necessary as good mothers, good wives, and good house-keepers. To ignore or discard any of these aspects is tantamount to harming and corrupting man's social life.

Man, on the other hand, has to discharge a quite different duty for which he is equipped aptly but differently from woman. He has to engage in the struggle of life going on in the outside world, be it in the form of subduing wild beasts in the jungle, or contending against the forces of nature, or the forming of a government, or legislating about national economy. He has to tackle all these problems to scratch a living, and safeguard his person, his wife as well as his children against oppression.

This should explain the various differences found in the respective physical constitutions of man and woman: Why is it that man joyfully pursues the professions where he has mostly to draw on his physical and intellectual faculties whereas in emotional life he is just as lively as a child; and why is it that a woman is adjusted in her natural sphere of emotional activities only and derives so great a pleasure out of these viz., nursing, fostering and teaching etc? Although these activities are mere off-shoots, they cannot in themselves satisfy her natural urge for a husband, a home, a family and children.

This does not, however, mean that man and woman are fundamentally and irreconcilably different from each other. Nor does it imply that all the members of a sex lack all the potentialities necessary for the functions which the members of the opposite sex alone by nature are fit to perform.

If you find a woman who is capable of ruling, dispensing justice, lifting heavy burdens and fighting in wars ... and if you come across a man who can cook, do household chores or who has got very tender motherly feelings for children or is very fickle emotionally and is visited by shifting moods, then you must remember that it is all natural; there is nothing unnatural about it. It is the legal result of the fact that each sex has in itself the germs of both sexes. But this does not at all prove what these misguided modernists and the discordant Easterners would have us believe. The real problem stated briefly rather is: Can all these extra functions that a woman is called upon to perform substitute for her real and natural function? Does she in the presence of these no longer feel the desire for a home, children and family? Above all, does she no longer feel the need for a male partner for the satisfaction of her sexual instinct?

3.8   THE INSTITUTION OF MARRIAGE

The institution of marriage has existed in one form or the other throughout human civilization. Various customs and rituals have come to be associated with marriage. Among the warlike tribes of the antiquity there was a custom of wife capture whereby a woman was captured forcibly and made wife against her and her family's will. Much social and military honour was attached to this form of marriage. The system of wife purchase was prevalent in many societies and it survives even today. This system also helped the development of polygyny among the affluent classes. In some societies, like the Hindus, substantial amount of *jahez* or dowry is given by the family of the bride to the bridegroom. Since the Hindu customary law deprives the daughters from inheritance, they are given huge dowries at the time of their marriage. Among some nations, marital arrangements provide for the exchange of women without payment. One man gives his sister into marriage to another person who in turn gives his sister to him. In some ancient societies, incestuous marital relationships had existed.

In many communities of the world a system of arranged marriages exist in which choice of the bride and bridegroom does not matter, neither the consent of the bride is taken. In some cases even the groom and the bride have not seen each other before marriage and they meet each other for the first time at the ceremony. In almost all societies, marriage has become a publicly celebrated ceremony involving many socio-religious customs, formalities and rituals. The economic burden of such rituals generally falls more heavily on the family of the bride who provides not only rich feasts to the groom and his party, but also gives a large dowry to the bride which she takes to her husband's house. Thus we see that in most of the rituals, ceremonies and forms of marriage, the females are generally at a disadvantage.

Islâm abolished all these evil customs and rituals connected with marriage thereby redeeming the position of the woman. In Islâm, *nikâh*, or lawful marriage, is the union of two souls for love, and two bodies of procreation and legalizing of children. Family and tribal life depend upon it. If this lawful method is abandoned, social orders, civilizations and cultures the world over would crumble.

Marriage creates a family consisting of children and wife. Families create society and the progress of a family means the progress of society. Marriage creates a new company of kith and kin, because sons and daughters go to create new families. Hospitalities, fellow feeling, kindness and mutual help become binding among these relations. Marriage therefore gives impetus to what is called 'social virtues'.

Therefore the husband and wife are the principles of family formation. Their relationship in marriage is described in the Qur'ân as being made up of two major attributes: love (passion, friendship, companionship) on the one hand, and mercy (understanding, reconciliation, tolerance, forgiveness) on the other, within the overall objective of tranquillity. The Qur'ân says:

> "And among His signs is this, that He
> created for you mates from among
> yourselves, that you may dwell in
> tranquility with them, and He has put

94

love and mercy between your hearts." [66]

Procreation is also one of the paramount advantages of marriage, namely, to contribute through legitimate means to the continuity and preservation of the human race. The sexual urge serves the function of bringing the mates together for the fulfilment of this basic objective. The Qur'ân states:

> *"And Allâh Ta'âlâ has made mates for you of your own nature, and made for you out of them sons and daughters, and grandchildren, and provide for you sustenance of the best."* [67]

Almighty Allâh Ta'âlâ in providing the male with intricate fertilizing organs and the female with a receptive fertile womb, is telling us most eloquently of the purpose of these provisions. To let them be idle is to ignore the divine wisdom written on these God-given instruments.[68] Procreation through marriage is also a means of seeking the pleasure of the Prophet Muhammad ﷺ who has called upon his nation.

> *"Marry so your number increases."* [69]

The practice of marriage is an answer to his call.

A Muslim marriage is a civil contract based on mutual consent of the bride and bridegroom, as distinguished from the sacramental form of marriage. Most of the incidents of contract are consequently applicable to such a marriage, for example, consideration of marriage in the form of dower, breach of the contract by divorce, giving of legal rights and obligations on the contractual parties and bestowing no greater power on the husband than what the contract provides in a lawful manner. A woman has absolute right in her acquired properties before and after her marriage.

Although marriage is the natural law, it may be delayed for two reasons - if a suitable partner cannot be found or if a person does'nt possess the financial resources to maintain a wife. No sooner are these obstacles removed, Allâh's direction is then to contract a marriage.

'Abdullâh ibn Mas ûd ﷺ narrated: *"We were with the Prophet ﷺ while we were young and had no wealth whatsoever.* The Prophet ﷺ said: *'O assembly of youths; whoever amongst you possesses the physical and financial resources to marry, should do so, because it helps him guard his modesty, and whoever is unable to marry should fast, as fasting diminishes his sexual power.'"* [70]

From all these narrations it can be deduced that marriage in Islâm is multidimensional. It is a form of worship, thus being an act of piety; a means of emotional and sexual gratification, thus curbing illicit sexual relations; a bond of mutual affection between the spouses; and finally, it is a means of legitimate procreation.

The argument that the temporary pleasure sought by a man and a woman in a private place, through illicit relationship out of wedlock, without accepting the responsibilities of parenthood, does not at all affect society, is baseless. Such an act not only harms the society to which they belong, but also harms the whole of humanity.

These are some of the social crimes that emanate from sexual gratification out of marriage. Firstly, free sexual relationships lays the foundation for both consenting partners exposing themselves to the danger of contracting those contagious diseases connected with illicit encounters viz., gonorrhoea, syphilis and the deadly Aids. These diseases are not only carried by the patient himself, causing the destruction of the victim's physical energies, but it also infects his progeny, children as well as his grandchildren. The incidence of blindness, dumbness, deafness and weak-mindedness in children is mostly the fruit of a few moments of pleasure-seeking, so madly craved by a reckless, cruel man. Secondly, every adulterer may not contact venereal diseases but he cannot escape the vices that go with fornication. Deceit, shamelessness, immorality and selfishness are some of the vices that afflict a fornicator who carries them along into all his dealings with society. A society which abounds in people with such vices cannot prosper for long. Thirdly, holding fornication as permissible clearly implies that prostitution should thrive uncurbed in society. Fourthly, the product of free sexual relationship can yield only illegitimate children which is indeed a most heinous crime both against the child and society, because illegitimate impregnation takes place at a time when both partners mate under the impulse of their lustful passion, being devoid of all human feelings. Thus an illegitimate child can possibly inherit only the animal instincts of its parents. Being inferior in status, resourceless, helpless and wretched, there exists a strong possibility that he will not become a useful citizen on the basis that his status may result in his developing a complex. A famous orientalist declares:

> *"The pleasure that a Muslim derives from kissing his child is not imaginable to many Westerners, because in the civilized world of today, few men are positive that their children are really their own."*
> He adds: *"I do not think that the Westerners can bear to see the Easterners enjoying this privilege. Perhaps they will take it away from them soon."* [71]

The fact is that, there has been no period of civilization in which the importance of married life has not been realized. The *Al-Ahrâm* Daily issued an article about a university woman-professor who advised her students to marry first. In front of hundreds of her students she stood in a party to give a speech on the occasion of her retirement. She said:

> *"Here I am, in my sixtieth year at one of the highest position. I have succeeded in every year of my life. I have accomplished a lot. Every minute of my life was profitable. I've got fame, a lot of money, and had the chance to voyage all over the world. But am I happy after all this? I have forgotten what is more important than all that: marriage and children. I've forgotten to settle in a home of my own. I've only thought of this when I decided to resign my post. At that moment I realized that I had done nothing in my life. All the hardwork I have done is lost. For I am going to resign and one or two years will*

pass and then everybody will forget me in the course of their busy life. Had I married and had a family of my own I should have left a better and greater effect in this life.

I advise every girl-student listening to me to put this job into her consideration and after that she could think of work and fame. In fact a woman would lose if she left marriage, something that no fame, honour, position, or money would compensate. She would lose a quiet happy nest. This experience of sixty years is in front of everybody to consider." [72]

We should also bear in mind that along with other objects already mentioned, the greatest aim of marital ties is the protection of the priceless jewel of chastity and morality.

3.9   POLYGAMY

Since times immemorial, polygamy has been a recognized and established institution in almost all human societies. Its practice was common among the royalty but sometimes it was also practised by the common people. Among the Hindus in India, polygamy prevailed from the earliest times. There was apparently no restriction on the number of wives a man might have. There are many instances in the Hindu Scriptures mentioning the multiple wives of Hindu kings and heroes. A high caste Brahmin, even in modern times, is privileged to marry as many wives as he chooses. Medes, Assyrians, Babylonians, Persians, Athenians, Phoenicians, Thracians, Lydians and the Pelasgians all practised polygamy. [73]

Polygamy was common in Biblical and Talmudic times. Ḥaḍrat Ibrâhîm (Abraham) had two wives, Ḥaḍrat Y'aqûb (Jacob) and Ḥaḍrat Mûsâ (Moses) had four each, Ḥaḍrat Dâwûd (David) had nine wives and Ḥaḍrat Sulaimân (Solomon) had seven hundred wives and three hundred slave girls.

Mosaic Law did not impose any restriction on the number of wives a Hebrew husband could have. In latter times, the *Talmûd* of Jerusalem restricted the number to the ability of the husband to maintain the wives properly.

Even in Christianity which has become synonymous with monogamy, Jesus (Hadrat 'Îsâ) himself never uttered a word against polygamy. Rather some famous Christian theologians like Luther, Bucer, etc, do not hesitate to deduce the legality of polygamy from the parable of the ten virgins, spoken of in the Gospel of Matthew (25:1-2), for Jesus envisages there the possibility of the marriage of one man with as many as ten girls simultaneously.[74]

Though Islâmic Law permits polygamy yet the reforms introduced by Islâm in this institution are praise-worthy. It restricted the number of wives to four and tied it up with the condition of justice and equal treatment for all wives. Regarding this the Qur'ân mentions:

> *"If you fear that you will not be able to deal justly with the orphans, marry women of your choice, two, or three, or four, but if you fear that you will not be able to deal justly (with them), then only one, or (a captive) that your right hand possess. That will be more suitable, to prevent you from doing injustice."*[75]

The unrestricted number of wives of the *Times of Ignorance* was now strictly limited to a maximum of four, provided you could treat them with perfect equality. If injustice was anticipated then the recommendation would be towards monogamy. After the battle of *Uhud*, when male members were killed, the widows were large in numbers. Polygamy was therefore introduced in order to give protection to the helpless widows. This measure also saved immorality of the society that would have possibly been created by the existence of a large number of young widows.

Also, the permission of polygamy is a door kept open for those who cannot contain themselves within the sphere of monogamy. It does not mean that every Muslim has been ordered to marry four wives. Islâm does not compel any one to have more than one wife nor does it impose polygamy as a universal practice. One should therefore regard monogamy as the norm and polygamy as the exception, in case of genuine need, and that too with the condition of justice and equality attached. The husband must try his very best to maintain balance and accord his wives equal treatment in the things on which he has control like food, clothing and lodging. Regarding this the Prophet 鑿 warned:

> *"When a person has two wives and he does not observe equality and deal justly with them, he will come before the throne of the Justice of Allâh Ta'âlâ with only half his body."*[76]

Of the things on which he has no control like love and affection,even there he should not display by his outward behaviour that he loves one wife and hates the other one. The husband should not incline towards his favourite one altogether and neglect the other one completely. The Qur'ân mentions:

> *"But turn not altogether away (from one), leaving her as (hanging) in suspense. If you come to friendly understanding and practise self-restraint, Allâh Ta'âlâ is Most Forgiving, Most Merciful."*[77]

In this material world there are two principal causes of division between man and wife, money and "the other woman" or "the other man". Here is the case of "the other woman". Legally more than one wife (up to four) are permissible on condition that the man can be perfectly fair and just to all. But this is a condition almost impossible to fulfil. If in the hope that he might be able to fulfil it, a man puts himself in that impossible position, it is only right to insist that he should not discard one but at least fulfil all the outward duties that are incumbent on him in respect of her.

And in the matter of voluntary justice too, according to Maulânâ 'Abdul

Majîd Daryâbâdî:

> *"It is not necessary that equality be observed in everything numerically. An African wife will be used to things quite different from those of an American wife, and the needs, tastes and interests of an old or middle-aged woman will be quite different from those of a young woman. What is desired is not stereotyped treatment of all of them without discrimination on natural grounds, but to keep everyone satisfied according to the capacity, tastes and the circumstances of a particular wife. Our jurists have declared justice among wives as obligatory but have defined justice as abstaining from injustice so that no one wife may have to suffer."* [78]

One may observe that, although it has been abused in some times and some places, polygamy has under certain circumstances a valuable function and in other instances it may even be a positively beneficial arrangement.

The most obvious example of this occurs in times of war when there are inevitably large numbers of widows whose husbands have been killed in the fighting. One has only to recall the figures of the dead in the first and second world wars to be aware that literally millions of women lost their husbands and were left alone without any income or care or protection for themselves or their children. If it is still maintained that under these circumstances a man may marry only one wife, what options are left to the millions of other women who have no hope of getting a husband? Their choice, bluntly stated, is between a chaste and childless old maidenhood, or becoming somebody's mistress, that is an unofficial second wife with no legal rights for herself or for her children. Most women would not welcome either of these since most of them have always wanted and still do want the security of a legal husband and family.

The compromise therefore is for women under these circumstances to face the fact that if given the alternative many of them would rather share a husband than have none at all. And there is no doubt that it is easier to share a husband when it is an established and publicly recognised practice than when it is carried out secretly with attempts to deceive the first wife.

It is no secret that polygamy in some form is widely practised in Europe and America. The difference is that while the Western man has no legal obligations to his second, third or fourth mistresses and their children, the Muslim husband has completely legal obligations towards his second, third or fourth wives and their children. The situation is no better with some of the woman secretaries and actresses, especially if the boss is sexually demanding. Many a secretary has caused calamities to many families. They have made husbands deprive their families of their property. Some of them have even gone further, as they have caused the divorce of poor, innocent wives.

If polygamy is not permitted to support the widows and bring the unmarried women into marriage bond, it would lead not only to economic misery of many families but also to immoral practices like prostitution, adultery, sexual anarchy etc. It is not strange, then, to hear that some of the fairer and weaker sex who cannot get married try to find some sort of satisfaction with their pet animals, such as dogs, if they cannot obtain sexual release from their male servants. Such a social disintegration can be averted only if a man is permitted by law to have more than one wife.

This is the testimony of an English lady appearing in a Lagos Weekly quoting an article from the London newspaper 'Truth':

> "The number of vagabond girls has increased, and it has caused a nuisance in our society. Being a woman I look at these poor girls with pity. But will my pity and sympathy do anything to change things or help cure such illness? ... the only medicine is to allow man to marry more than one wife, through which the calamity will be

erased; as the girls will then be housewives. The European tribulation is: 'One husband one wife', what is the culmination for married men to one wife with illegitimate children who are a burden upon the society. Had polygamy been permitted, no such thing would have happened." [79]

The above article was written almost a century ago before the tragedy of the two world wars, and when there were between 800 000 and 1 000 000 prostitutes in London alone. Had the lady who wrote the above article been living today what would she have said?

Mrs Birdsell, President of *Young Woman's Christian Association*, during her address to the Booking Committee said:

"There are over twelve million young girls over the age of fourteen in the U.S.A., who are all unmarried. And against this number there are only nine million young men. So three million girls will never be able to have husbands, since the war has badly upset the balance of male and female population of the country." [80]

If polygamy is not allowed, which earthly power can save chastity and morality from being destroyed. And if after all it can be saved, who is going to take upon himself the responsibility of this oppression, against these three million souls who will suffer for no fault of theirs, but due to the wrong concepts of society.

Polygamy is also portrayed as an infringement of the rights of women but practically monogamists go on practising clandestine and underhand polygamy by defiling secretly the wives, daughters and sisters of other people. Polygamy is considered an evil but left-handed wives are kept without any scruples. No eye brows are lifted on sexual promiscuity where enticement is provided by semi-nude dresses, free intermingling of strangers of opposite sex, posters depicting nude women, sex symbols and obscenity in cinemas and videos where physical contours move in rhythm with seduction and vulgar music.

There may be other circumstances unrelated to war; individual circumstances, where marriage to more than one wife may be preferable to other available alternatives - for example, where the first wife is chronically sick or disabled and cannot satisfy the sexual urge of the husband. There are, of course, some husbands who can manage this situation, but no one would deny its potential hazards. A second marriage in some cases could be a solution acceptable to all three parties. 'Allâmah 'Abdul 'Azîz Shâwesh Miṣrî has narrated an eye opening experience:

> *"In London I happened to meet a Spaniard.
> We exchanged views about many issues
> relating to Islâm. And as soon as polygamy
> came up for discussion, he said, 'My wife
> is mentally deranged and several years
> have passed since her illness began and
> due to this difficulty I have to seek
> mistresses to satiate my sexual appetite,
> since I cannot take to myself another wife.
> If I had another lawful wife, I would have
> had lawful offsprings and heirs to my vast
> property, and would have been a source of
> solace to me and stood by me in the hour
> of my need.'"* [81]

There are instances in which a wife is sterile and the natural desire for progeny may lead the husband to contract another marriage, without divorcing the first wife yet wanting to have children. Under Western law a man must either accept his wife's childlessness if he can, or if he cannot he must find a means of divorce in order to marry again. This could have been avoided if the parties agreed on a second marriage.

Some men, may, by nature, be sexually very strong, so they cannot remain content with one wife. A woman is disabled on account of menses for almost a week in every month and besides that, pregnancy, delivery and weaning of the child is spread over almost a period of more than two years. During these periods, she is unable to meet the husband's biological needs.

There are even instances, where a marriage has not been very successful and the husband loves another woman. This situation is so familiar that it is known as the '*eternal triangle*'. Under Western law the husband cannot marry the second woman without divorcing the first one. But the first wife may not wish to be divorced. She may no longer love her husband, but she may still respect him and wish to stay with him for the security of marriage, for herself and their children. Similarly the second woman may not wish to break up the man's first family. There are cases such as this where both women could accept a polygamous marriage rather than face divorce on the one hand or an extra-marital affair on the other.[82]

These examples were mentioned, because to the majority of Westerners, polygamy is only thought of in the context of a harem of glamorous young girls, not as a possible solution to some of the problems of Western society itself. But then again, to some "sceptical and enlightened" westerner this question arises: If one concedes the arguments given in support of a man having more than one wife in certain circumstances, would the same arguments be extended to the situation of a woman in relation to her husband/husbands? To be more precise, if a woman becomes invalid and sexually incapacitated and because of that the husband is allowed to have a second wife, why the same should not hold good in respect of women. If a husband becomes invalid, would it be permitted for the wife to have a second husband?

The question of a woman having more than one husband raises a number of problems. One of them is the question of inheritance. If a woman has more than one husband, there is no certainty of the paternity of the child, and this is something which will be very disturbing to men, not to be sure that a certain child is their own, that it might be the child of another husband. From a sexo-sociological viewpoint, it is possible for a man to have sexual relations with all his wives, if he has more than one, and impregnate them. But if a wife has more than one husband, she can, even in that case, be impregnated only by one.

This should also be considered that once a woman is pregnant she is not available for sexual relations for some of the time resulting in forced monogamy which is unnatural. If the possibilities of a properly married second wife are denied, the dangers of illicit sex become very real. If this is the situation in a "one-husband-one wife" equation, what would be the predicament in a "many-husband-one-wife" polygon? [83]

Islâm has forbidden polyandry not for any partiality towards man, but for the good of man and woman both and of the entire human society.

A forced monogamy is responsible for many of the evils of prostitution and leads to hatred and quarrels, to intensify jealousy in women and to an insistence on the more physical relationship which turns purity into corruption. The woman's natural jealousy is not at man's loving another, but at his forsaking her.

Dr Le Bon advocates:

> "A return to polygamy, that natural relationship between the sexes, would remedy many evils, prostitution, venereal disease, abortion, the misery of the illegitimate children, the misfortune of millions of unmarried women, resulting from the disproportion between the sexes, adultery and even jealousy." [84]

To Muslims, monogamy is the ideal and polygamy is the concession granted to human nature.

3.10   THE CONCEPT OF *MUT'AH* (TEMPORARY MARRIAGE)

Literally *mut'ah* means enjoyment, but technically it means a marriage contracted for a fixed period in return for a recompense. During pre-Islâmic days the Arabs used to contract such a marriage which had its origins from the fourth century onwards as mentioned in Fath al Qadîr:

> *"When a man came to a village and he had no acquaintance there (to take care of his house), he would marry a woman for as long as he thought he would stay, so that she would be his partner in bed and take care of his house."*[85]

Similarly Imâm Tirmidhî states:

> *"When a man came to a strange village, where he had no acquaintance, he would marry a woman for as long a period he thought he would stay, so that she would look after him and his property."* [86]

Caetani also concluded that *mut'ah* in the pagan period was religious prostitution that took place during the occasion of pilgrimage.[87]

This practice continued until it was revealed:

> *"And who abstain from sex except with their wives or (the captives) whom their right hands possess."* [88]

Here ibn 'Abbâs is reported to have said that all other forms of sexual indulgences are unlawful except the two forms mentioned in the above quotation.

The main idea or intention or purpose behind marriage should be to retain the woman in wedlock for life and not to enjoy a relationship with lewdness as is the case in fornication. This means there should be no time limit to marriage. In other words, timely marriage, such as *mut'ah* which is prevalent in the Shî'ah community is unlawful.

There has been a great controversy as to its reference in the Qur'ân. While the overwhelming majority maintain that there can be no reference to such a temporary marriage of pleasure in the Qur'ân which stands for moral excellence and deals only with *nikâh* or lawful marriage, the Shî'ahs contend that there is a reference to *mut'ah* in this verse:

> *"Except for these, all others are lawful,*
> *provided you seek them (in marriage) with*
> *your wealth, desiring chastity, not lust, so*
> *give them their recompense for what you*
> *have enjoyed of them in keeping with your*
> *promise."* [89]

Shî'ah commentators claim that *ajr* (compensation) refers to the price of *mut'ah* agreed upon by the two parties. On the contrary the Sunnis state that it refers to the *mahr* (bridal money given to the wife by the husband). Shî'ahs also explain the term *istamta'tum* (what you have enjoyed) as the physical act of consumation. However this is contradicted by the following verse: *"There is no blame upon you if you have divorced women whom you have not touched (i.e. the marriage has not been consummated) or specified for them a mahr. But give them (a gift of) compensation (matti'ûhunna)."* [90]

There are six Qur'ânic verses containing words with the root letters of the word *mut'ah*,[91] such as istamta'tum, matâ'an, etc., which are derivatives, yet none of the verses gives even a hint of the meaning interpreted by the Shî'ahs, neither do they relate any of these verses to their concept of *mut'ah*. One may thus raise the objection that if a word used on six different occasions in the Qur'ân does not refer to temporary marriage, then how can the same word in a single verse refer to it? It is also interesting to note that the Qur'ân continues with this advice: *"So marry them with the permission of their families and give them their dowers according to what is reasonable."* [92] Such a case is only possible in a regular marriage since these conditions are not necessary in *mut'ah*. Although the Shî'ahs present verse twenty four of Sûrah al-Nisâ in support of their belief in *mut'ah*, they completely ignore the above verse quoted above, which follows immediately thereafter. They seem to be very selective in presenting Qur'ânic and Aḥadith quotations that agree with their specific beliefs, yet blatantly sidelining others that utilizes the same terminology and clarifies any ambiguity in interpretation.

To grasp the full meaning of the text one has to understand the difference between temporary marriage and lawful marriage. The object of marriage is to sanction sexual relations between two members of the opposite sex with a view to the preservation of the human species, the fixing of descent, restraining men from immorality, the encouragement of chastity and the promotion of affection and of mutual assistance. Therefore, the institution of marriage cannot be temporary and only to satisfy mere lust. The parties to the marriage inherit each other and the *nikâḥ* settles the paternity of the child.

Contrary to this, *mut'ah* is an open licence for sexual pleasure with as many women as one can financially afford. The women who engage in *mut'ah* are hired women; thus it can be performed with all women irrespective of their age, character, conduct or religion. The only precondition is that the woman agrees to the price and the length of the *mut'ah* and that the man pays her the compensation after having fulfilled his carnal desires with her. One can discern for oneself whether such a practice leads to sexual immorality or promotes chastity. Similarly, in *mut'ah*, it is clearly specified that there is no inheritance between the parties, but there are conflicting statements with regard to the paternity of the child. Some say that the child is ascribed to the man while the others hold the opinion that it is for the woman to whom it is born. Actually it is very difficult to decide the paternity of the child as *mut'ah* is for a limited period, it may be even for a few hours or a day, after which the stranger or traveller who had contracted it, departs. How is it then possible to attribute the child to a stranger who vanishes from the scene, and what about the woman's maintenance until she has delivered, because it is only when the male partner departs that she may come to know about her pregnancy? And will she, in fact, wait and not marry until she delivers, in such circumstances, where every passer-by is a welcomed guest?[93] Further, in *mut'ah* there is neither guardian of the woman, nor are there witnesses to witness it and, as such, it is no better than fornication.[94] Ḥâfiz ibn Ḥajar mentions that according to Baihaqî even Ja'far ibn Muḥammad, (the same

Ja'far al-Ṣādiq - sixth Imâm of the Shî'ahs) held it to be *zinâ* (fornication).[95]
Ibn Taymîyyah mentions that:

> *"No child (born of fornication) can be*
> *attributed to the fornicator."* [96]

There is no divorce in *mut'ah*, the parties to it separate from each other
after the expiry of the contracted period.

Qurṭubî mentions that *mut'ah* is neither *nikâḥ* nor is it applicable to the
captive women, and according to al-Dâr Qutnî, 'Alî ibn Abî Ṭâlib is
reported to have said that *mut'ah* is forbidden by the Prophet ﷺ as it was
for him who could not find (any alternative), and was abrogated when the
revelation came with regard to *nikâḥ* (marriage), *ṭalâq* (divorce), *'iddat*
(waiting period) and *mîrâth* (inheritance).[97] On the authority of Abû
Hurairah ؓ, the Prophet ﷺ said:

> *"Mut'ah is annulled by ṭalâq, 'iddat and*
> *mîrâth."* [98]

3.10.1 OPINIONS EXPRESSED BY ADVOCATES OF *MUT'AH*

One of the strongest and forceful proponents of the Shî'ah ideology that
the believer only attains perfection after he has experienced *mut'ah,* is
expressed by 'Abd al Ḥusain Aḥmad al-Amînî, the author of al-Ghadir,
where he mentions that besides the Shî'ah writers, the validity of *mut'ah*
is established even by the authoritative works of the Sunnî 'Ulamâ. He
proceeds further and deals with the creed of Rawâfiḍ according to whom
there are two kinds of *mut'ah*: minor and major. The one which is common
among them is the union between a male and a female to satisfy mere lust
in return for something material or food. The other, more detestable, is
called *'mut'ah al-dauriyyah'* or circulatory marriage of pleasure whereby
a group of men enjoy the society of a woman, by turns, each for some
hours, and this is considered a religious function rewarded by Allâh Ta'âlâ.

In contradictinction, *mut'ah*, he says, was introduced by the Prophet ﷺ
himself under certain terms fixed and acted upon during his life time and
continued thereafter till it was forbidden by the Khalîf 'Umar. The terms

or conditions are: *al-ajr* (recompense); *al-'ajal* (fixed period); *al-'aqd* (contract comprising offer and acceptance); *al-iftirâq* (separation on the expiry of the fixed period); *'iddat* (waiting period imposed upon the woman before she remarries and *'adm al-mîrâth* (non-inheritance between the parties).

He mentions that these are the terms which cannot be denied by the Sunnî 'Ulamâ as they were acted upon by the companions of the Prophet 🕮 and their successors, thus establishing its validity. He then tries to substantiate his contention in a plausible manner by referring to some of the commentaries and books of the 'Ulamâ Haq. Hereunder, each of his points of argument and the books which he uses for substantiation, is illustrated. He mentions:

(1)   That the above mentioned six conditions of the contract of *mut'ah* cannot be denied by the Sunnis.[99]

(2)   That the Qur'ânic verse already mentioned: *"Except for these, all others are lawful, provided you seek them in marriage with your wealth, desiring chastity, not lust, so give them their recompense for what you have enjoyed of them in keeping with your promise"*, relates to *mut'ah*.[100]

(3)   That *mut'ah* was lawful according to the *Sharî'ah* (Islâmic Law) and the people acted upon it not only in the days of the Prophet 🕮 and Abû Bakr ⁕ but also in the reign of Khalîf 'Umar who was the first person to forbid it in his last days.[101]

(4)   That the companions of the Prophet 🕮 and their successors considered *mut'ah* as valid and not abrogated although it was forbidden by 'Umar ⁕. Among these are the following persons of high dignity and nobility: 'Alî, Ibn 'Abbâs, 'Imrân ibn al-Husain Khaza'î, Jâbir ibn 'Abdullâh al-Ansârî, 'Abdullah ibn Mas'ûd al Hazlî, 'Abdullah ibn 'Umar al-Adawî, Mu'âwiyya ibn Abî Sufyân, Abu Sa'êd al Khudrî al-Ansârî, Salamâ ibn Umayyâ al-Jâmî, M'abad ibn Ummayâ al-Jâmî, al-Zubair ibn al 'Awwâm al Qurshî, al Hakam, Khâlid ibn al Muhâjir al-Makhzûmî, 'Umar ibn Huraith al-Qurshî, Ubay ibn Ka'ab al-Ansârî, Rabî ibn Umayyâ al-Thaqafî, Sa'êd ibn

Jubair, Tâûs al-Yamanî, Atâ Abû Muḥammad al Yamanî, al-Suddî.

(5)   That Ibn Ḥazm has given a great number of the companions of the Prophet ﷺ who assert that *mut'ah* is valid and there are others from amongst their successors and all the jurists of Mecca. Qurṭubî states that the people of Mecca used *mut'ah* very often.[102] Râzî also said that there is a controversy about the abrogation of the Qur'ânic verse (4:24), a large majority of the community holds it as abrogated, while a part of it considers it to be as lawful as it was.[103] And according to Abû Ḥayyân the persons belonging to the Prophet's family and the successors of his companions were convinced of the validity of *mut'ah*.

Thereafter the Shî'ah, al-Amînî, erroneously proceeds to prove that the Khalîf 'Umar had no right to forbid *mut'ah* when it was acted upon not only in the days of the Prophet ﷺ and Abû Bakr ◌ but also in his own period:

(1)   Jâbir ibn 'Abdullâh said: *"We used to contract mut'ah, in return for a handful of dates and flour, in the days of the Prophet ﷺ and Abû Bakr ◌ until 'Umar ◌ forbade it in the case of 'Umar ibn Ḥuraith.*[104]

(2)   Urwâ ibn al-Zubair ◌ has related: *"Khaulah, daughter of Ḥakim, came to 'Umar ibn Khaṭṭâb and said: 'Rabiyya ibn Ummayyâ contracted mut'ah with a woman who became pregnant. Thereupon 'Umar came out drawing up his cloak in great rage and said: 'This is mut'ah and I would have stoned him to death, had I announced it before.*[105]

(3)   'Alî ◌, as reported by al-Ḥakm said: *"None but a wretched would have committed fornication, if 'Umar had not forbidden mut'ah."*[106]

(4)   Atâ ◌ said: *"I have heard ibn 'Abbâs say: 'May Allâh Ta'âlâ bless 'Umar: mut'ah was but a favour from Allâh Ta'âlâ for the followers of Muḥammad and none except few would have been dragged into zinâ (fornication) had he not forbidden mut'ah."*[107]

(5)   As related by Sulaiman, it is said by Umm 'Abdullâh that a man
       came from Syria and asked her to get him a woman so that he may
       practice *mut'ah* with her. Thereupon she pointed out a woman and
       he entered into an agreement with her witnessed by trustworthy
       witnesses. He co-habited with her and went away. Being informed
       of it, 'Umar ibn al-Khattâb sent for her and asked her to inform him
       if the man returned. Accordingly she informed him and he sent for
       the man (who had contracted *mut'ah*) and said: *'What made you
       act like this?'* In reply he said: *I acted upon it in the days of the
       Prophet* 🌟 *who did not prevent me until he expired. I, then,
       continued it in the days of Abû Bakr* 🌟 *who also did not prevent me
       till he passed away, again it was repeated by me in your days and
       you did not say that it was forbidden: 'By Allâh Ta'âlâ, had I
       announced that it was forbidden I would certainly have stoned you
       to death. Let it be declared forbidden so that nikâḥ (lawful marriage)
       is distinguished from fornication.'*[108]

After having cited the various forms of the above statement, al-Amînî
goes on to say that 'Umar was convinced of the fact that in *mut'ah* there
can be no punishment of stoning to death and, therefore, he expressed the
view that it was lawful not to be severe in the case of *mut'ah*, and therefore
the punishment of stoning was merely to threaten the people.' Again he
wrongly refers to Jassas, Qurtubî, Ibn Qayyim and Râzî to prove that 'Umar
🌟 was not right in declaring unlawful what was lawful in the days of the
Prophet 🌟 and that al-Ma'mûn treated *mut'ah* as valid and Imâm Malik
regarded it as lawful. He further adds that 'Umar was very harsh in this
manner and the people listened to him but did not accept the unlawfulness
of *mut'ah*.[109] This is a malicious allegation against one of the most ardent
torch bearers of Islâm. Therefore we now attempt to refute all his
arguments.

3.10.2   THE ABOLITION OF *MUT'AH*

Al-Amînî erroneously attributes the introduction of *mut'ah* to the Prophet
🌟, whereas in reality it was in vogue from the fourth century. It cannot be
denied that loose unions and fornication were common in the Days of
Ignorance. It is no wonder then that such a custom as *mut'ah* which was
already there could not have been eradicated totally at the advent of Islâm,

since Islâm was still a minority force. It was permitted on particular instances such as during war when it is hard for men to keep away from women for a long time.

As it was a transitional period and fornication and adultery (*zinâ*) was rampant in the *Jâhilîyya*, those who were still waverers were apt to commit *zinâ* while the staunch adherents of Islâm, being unable to exercise self-restraint for a long period of time asked the Prophet ﷺ to allow them to be castrated. Such being the case, especially on military expeditions, the Prophet allowed them to marry women for a definite period, in return for a robe or something special.

This temporary marriage, under the pressure of circumstances, seemed to have continued for a short time in the early period of Islâm and then its prohibition was proclaimed in degrees. It may be recalled that the same method was adopted in the prohibition of drinking wine. According to Hadrat 'Alî ؓ it was forbidden by the Prophet ﷺ on the Day of Khaibar. Sabrâ al Juhnî related that he went on military expedition with the Prophet ﷺ who permitted them *mut'ah* on the Day of the Conquest of Mecca and also forbade it before he resumed his onward march saying that Allâh had forbidden it up to the Day of Resurrection. The prohibition was regarded by the companions of the Prophet ﷺ as definite, while Ibn 'Abbâs opposed them and held that *mut'ah* was permissible in the case of necessity. When it became known to Ibn 'Abbâs that people considered it a free license and transgressed the limits, he stopped giving his verdicts and was converted to the opposite view.[110]

Let us refer to the verdict of the Imâm of al-Azhar. He says that *mut'ah* is a lustful union and cannot be called a marriage. There can be no law which allows a woman to marry eleven men in a year and which permits a man to have contracts of marriage with women every day with no such rights and obligations as are attached to marriage. This is far from *Sharî'ah*, which provides for self - restraint and chastity.[111]

The six conditions of *mut'ah* described by al-Amînî are not found in the books which he has referred to except *'ajal* (definite period) and *ajr* (recompense or reward) which are common features of *mut'ah*. Jassas, he says, has admitted all the terms while it is Jassas who accuses the Shî'ahs of discarding the waiting period, or *'iddat* which the wife in a regular marriage observes on the death of her husband and that no parentage of the child is established. According to Jaṣṣaṣ the woman taken in *mut'ah* is not, at all, a wife and this is nothing but fornication. Khâzin does not refer to the terms of the contract of *mut'ah* as having been introduced by Islâm which is the claim advanced by al-Amînî. Similarly, there is no reference to these terms in Ṣaḥ iḥ Muslim, except a remark in its commentary that, according to the 'Ulamâ, *mut'ah* was a contract for a definite period which terminated on the expiry of the stipulated period and the parties did not inherit from each other.[112]

3.10.3   THE QUR'ÂN AND ḤADÎTH REGARDING *MUT'AH*

Al-Amînî has quoted several of the Sunnî commentators of the Holy Qur'ân in asserting that there is a reference to *mut'ah* in the Qur'ânic verse (4:24), intending to prove that not only the Shî'ah 'Ulamâ but also the Sunnî 'Ulamâ have accepted it.

Al Râzî: According to him there is a conflict of opinion as to the abrogation of the Qur'ânic verse (4:24). A large majority held the sanction derived from this verse for *mut'ah* to be abrogated while only a few considered it as lawful as it was before. He concludes by saying that the reasons given by those who want to prove the validity of *mut'ah* do not disprove the fact that the Qur'ânic verse was abrogated later. According to him, it is incorrect to contend that the traditions relating to the abrogation of *mut'ah* must be continuous, for it might be that those who heard about the abrogation forgot it, but when 'Umar reminded them of it in a big gathering they admitted what he said. The contention that it was 'Umar who forbade *mut'ah* for the first time is not acceptable, for if *mut'ah* was valid and 'Umar declared it to be forbidden it would mean his disbelief and the disbelief of all who listened to him but did not oppose him. This leads to the disbelief of 'Ali 🕮 himself who remained silent. All such contention is absolutely baseless, for the declaration of 'Umar that *mut'ah* was forbidden goes back to and is based upon the declaration of the Prophet 🕮 and means nothing except that it was forbidden by the Prophet 🕮.[113] Ṭabarî has stated that the verse refers to lawful marriage and what has been added to it (by Ibn 'Abbâs) is not permissible.[114] Here it should be noted that in his last days, Ibn 'Abbâs ultimately retracted his opinion and converted to the opposite view.

Al Jaṣṣaṣ mentions that the words ' ˌsiring chastity and not lust' are indicative of a regular marriage and not *mut'ah* which is only to satisfy the sexual appetite as is evident from the negation therein of inheritance and of the waiting period on the death of the husband and also there being no regard for the paternity of the child.[115]

Al-Zamakhsharî states that this verse refers to lawful marriage and the obligations of the husband after experiencing valid retirement *(khalwat ṣaḥîhah)*. He proceeds by saying that the verse has come in connection with *mut'ah* which was for three days at the conquest of Mecca and thereafter forbidden.[116]

Al-Qurṭubî: Quoting Sa'îd ibn al-Musayyab, he mentions that *mut'ah* was abrogated by the Qur'ânic verse enjoining inheritance as there is no inheritance in *mut'ah*. Therefore all the jurists, companions of the Prophet ﷺ and their successors are unanimously united that the permission deduced from the Qur'ânic verse is abrogated and *mut'ah* is unlawful.[117]

Ibn Kathîr: *Mut'ah* was permissible in the early days of Islâm and thereafter prohibited. The best explanation is provided in Ṣaḥîḥ Bukhârî and Ṣaḥîḥ Muslim wherein 'Alî is reported to have said that *mut'ah* was forbidden by the Prophet ﷺ on the Day of Khaibar and as reported by Muslim, Sabrâ ibn M'abad said that he was on expedition with the Prophet ﷺ on the Day of the Conquest of Mecca when the Prophet ﷺ said: *'O you people! I had permitted you mut'ah with women but Allâh has forbidden it up to the Day of Resurrection; whoever of you who has married a woman for a period shall give her what he promised and claim nothing of it back.'* [118]

Qâdî Baidâwî mentions that *mut'ah* was permissible for three days when Mecca was conquered and thereafter forbidden and Ibn 'Abbâs is reported to have withdrawn his verdicts.[119]

Al-Âlûsî states that it cannot be denied that *mut'ah* was permitted out of extreme necessity such as on expeditions and it was thereafter forbidden. There is no conflict of opinion, among the 'Ulamâ of Islâm, about the unlawfulness of *mut'ah*, except that the S̲h̲î'ahs hold it permissible. The report that Imâm Mâlik considered it lawful is baseless. As regards the punishment prescribed for *mut'ah*, the predominant view is that there is no capital punishment.[120]

'Abdullâh ibn 'Abbâs declares that it is forbidden by Allâh Ta'âlâ, since it was permitted only to meet the urgent need of the people.[121]

Ibn Taymîyyah who is well known for his deep understanding of S̲h̲arî'ah advises that there is nothing in the Qur'ân to indicate its permissibility. He goes on further to say that the Sunnî follow not only 'Umar ﷺ but all rightly guided K̲h̲alîfs including 'Alî ﷺ; but the S̲h̲î'ahs who follow 'Alî ﷺ oppose him in what he has reported from the Prophet ﷺ.[122]

Ibn Qayyim, his student, declares that *mut'ah* was proved to be forbidden twice but the question is whether the prohibition on the Day of K̲h̲aibar was a definite one or of the nature of prohibition which may be waived off in the case of necessity. This is why ibn 'Abbâs allowed it to meet the necessity but when people transgressed the limits he held back his verdicts and was converted to the opposite view.[123]

S̲h̲aukânî announces that it is incumbent upon all to obey what has reached them about the prohibition of *mut'ah* and particularly when its prohibition is authenticated and definite.[124]

Al-Nawawî concludes that the statements that *mut'ah* was acted upon not only in the days of the Prophet ﷺ but also by Abû Bakr and 'Umar, applies to those whom the news of the prohibition of *mut'ah* had not reached till 'Umar prevented them from it.[125]

Finally, extracts from the commentaries of the Holy Qur'ân and passages from the Aḥâdîth have been given, which Al-Amînî, overall spokesman of the S̲h̲î'ah community, has referred to, but there is nothing to support his claim that *mut'ah* is permissible by the text of the Qur'ân and the sunnah of the Prophet ﷺ. On the contrary, his claim is rejected and the fact is established that it is the lawful marriage which Islâm has prescribed, and *mut'ah* has been described by the learned as nothing but hiring woman to satisfy sexual appetite, currently labelled as 'legalized prostitution'.

The references given disclose his bold attempt to misrepresent the facts.

3.10.4 *SHÎ'AH* BELIEFS AND PRACTICES ATTRIBUTED TO THEIR OWN SOURCES

These statements extracted from the most authentic Shî'ah books, need to be examined in order to determine whether *mut'ah* promotes morality, as Islâm advocates, or if it, instead leads to adultering human lineage by way of legalized religious prostitution.

The method of contracting *mut'ah*: When Hishâm Sâlim asked how one should contract *mut'ah*, Imâm J'afar aṣ-Ṣâdiq answered that one should say, "I am marrying you for this period of time for this amount of money. When the prescribed period is over, there will be annulment, and there will be no *'iddah* after this." [126]

No divorce, inheritance or witnesses: The narrator asked Imâm Bâqir about the women of *mut'ah*. The imâm said, "She is not among those four (women classified as wives) because she neither needs a divorce, nor is (a child born of her) entitled to any inheritance. She is like a hired woman!" [127]

There is no need for witnesses or any open declaration in mut'ah: [128] The minimum compensation that could be paid to the woman for sexual relations is one dirham. [129]

An open license with all women: Mut'ah is allowed with all types of women. She may be a virgin, married, widowed or may belong to any sect, group or religion. If one desires, he may have *mut'ah* with one thousand women since these are like hired women. Abân ibn Tughlag related that he said to Imâm J'afar aṣ-Ṣâdiq, *"Often during my travels I come across a very beautiful woman and am not sure if she has a husband or if she is an adulteress or if she is one of dubious character."* The imâm responded, *"Why should you worry about all of these things? Your duty is to believe what she says. If she says that she has no husband, then you should engage in mut'ah with her."* [130] Imâm J'afar was asked if *mut'ah* was permissible with a virgin girl. He replied, *"There is no harm in it if the girl is not too young. However, a nine-year-old girl is not considered too young."* [131]

Glorifying mut'ah: Imâm J'afar aṣ-Ṣâdiq mentioned that no one can close the door of blessings which Allâh opens for His servants. *Mut'ah* is one of His blessings.[132] If a person contracts *mut'ah* once in his lifetime, Allâh Ta'âlâ will grant him Paradise and he is saved from shirk (associating partners with AllâhTa'âlâ). In a fabricated narration it is mentioned that the Prophet 醐 said, "The man who contracts *mut'ah* once will be saved from Hell. If he does it twice he will be in the company of virtuous men in Paradise and the one who contracts it three times will be my companion in Firdaus (the highest stage in Paradise).[133]

One who engages in mut'ah once gets the status of Imâm al Ḥasan. The one who engages in it twice becomes equal in status to Imâm al Ḥasan. The one who performs it thrice reaches the position of Imâm 'Ali and he who practices it four times acquires the status equal to that of the Prophet 醐.[134] In another fabricated ḥadîth Imâm Bâqir narrated that the Prophet 醐 said:

> *"When I was being taken to Heaven during the M'irâj (ascension), Jibraîl met me and told me, 'O Muhammad, Allâh has promised to forgive all of the sins of those women who practice mut'ah."* [135]

It must be emphasised that these Aḥadîth are forged and must thus not be misconstrued as being an authentic ḥadîth from the sunnah of the Prophet 醐.

I'ârat al-Furûj (the loaning of vaginas): Under this heading the Shî'ah imâms in their books of *fiqh* (jurisprudence) have discussed the various conditions under which a woman can be temporarily given to another person. The books give details as to how a woman can be loaned only for the pleasure of seeing her naked body or for the pleasure of enjoying her kisses or for the pleasure of having sexual intercourse with her. Since most of these descriptions are of an extremely explicit nature they do not deserve being reproduced here. However, the following is of a milder nature.

Imâm Abû 'Abdullâh (J'afar aṣ-Ṣâdiq) said, *"If a person allows another person to kiss his slave girl, then such a kiss is permissible, and the man should be contented with the kisses alone, but if she offers him her vagina, then everything is permitted."*[136] The sayings of the Shî'ah imâms and doctrines are classified as 'ḥadîth'. Technically, Shî'ahs make no distinction between the sayings of the Prophet ﷺ and those of their imâms.[137] These quotations occupy the status of ḥadîth in their eyes and serve as the foundation of the Shî'ah faith and practices.

Now it is left to the discretion of the reader to judge whether this temporary marriage *(mut'ah)* is in harmony with Islâmic sexual morality. Would such a practice create a society based on chastity and virtue, or would it open the doors for lust and lewdness? Furthermore, if the Shî'ahs are allowed to practice their religious beliefs, who would organize the "religious duty" of supplying young girls with whom one could engage in the practice of *mut'ah*? Would the Shî'ah community issue religious licences to a few virtuous women to take up this profession on a full-time basis or would devout Shî'ahs allow their wives, mothers, sisters and daughters to participate in the virtues of *mut'ah* in their spare time? Moreover, how would these girls be religiously different from those prostitutes plying their trade in the escort agencies, brothels and massage parlours? The Shî'ah imâms and their books seems to remain relatively silent on these issues. Therefore such doctrines and practices are in direct contrast to a society based upon the Sunnî interpretation of the Qur'ân and ḥadîth in which *mut'ah* is regarded as legalized prostitution and adultery and is definitely forbidden.

The institution of marriage sanctions sexual relationship between a man and wife for the propagation of the human species and for the promotion of love and union between the parties. Sanctity of marriage is one of the leading features of Islâmic Jurisprudence. This rules out as un-Islâmic all forms of temporary and 'companionate' marriages where lust is the sole motive. Real satisfaction comes not from sexual experience but from a relationship which is lasting and continuous and which is built on feelings of affection, devotion and tenderness.

3.11   REFRAINING FROM MARRIAGE

Islâm on the one hand, is against sexual licence, thereby prohibiting adultery and fornication, and closing all avenues leading to them. On the other hand, Islâm is also against suppressing the sexual urge, prohibiting celibacy and castration. The following verse depicts that there is no monasticism in Islâm:

> *"Then We caused Our messenger to follow in their footsteps, and We caused 'Îsâ (Jesus), son of Mary, to follow, and gave him the Gospel, and placed compassion and mercy in the hearts of those who followed him. But monasticism they invented – We ordained it not for them, only seeking Allâh's pleasure, and they observed it with no right observance..."* [138]

A Muslim is not permitted to refrain from marriage on the grounds that he has dedicated himself to the service or worship of Allâh Ta'âlâ and to a life of renunciation. Islâm does not consider self-imposed permanent celibacy a virtue. The following hadîth proves its prohibition:

> *"Three groups of people came to the residence of the Prophet 🌸 to ask about his mode of worship. When they were told of it, they seemed to have belittled it (they expected more). They then said, 'Where are we compared to the Prophet 🌸? He has already been forgiven by Allâh for anything that he did or would do.' Then one of them said, 'As far as I am concerned, I will pray all night forever.' Another said, 'And I will fast continuously.' Still another one said, 'I will desert woman and will never marry.' When the Prophet 🌸 returned he asked them, 'Are you the ones that said so and so?'*

121

*Then he solemnly stated: 'By Allâh, I am
more God-fearing and devout than you.
Nevertheless I fast and I break my fast, I
pray and I go to sleep, and I marry. He
who deviates from my way is not of me.'* [139]

The institution of marriage sometimes fosters sexual relationship between a man and wife for the propagation of the human species and for the promotion of love and union between the parties. Sanctity of marriage is one of the leading features of Islâmic Jurisprudence. This rules out as un-Islâmic all forms of temporary and 'compassionate' marriages where lust is the sole motive. Real satisfaction comes not from mere sexual experience but from a relationship which is lasting and continuous and which is built on feelings of affection, devotion and tenderness.

3.11.1 THE DETRIMENTAL EFFECT OF ABSTINENCE

The most important evil of celibacy is that it is hostile to the human race. Nature has created an attraction between the sexes so that they may create other beings to take their place when they die, thus securing the survival of mankind. Therefore this system, if practiced globally, would lead to the depletion of humankind which is contrary to the purpose of creation.

Similarly, the wise physician, Galen, mentions that if the seminal fluid is retained in the body for a long time, gives rise to various conditions, leading even to mental derangement and epilepsy. Seminal discharge with temperance, on the other hand, has a pleasant effect on the general health and many diseases are prevented. An excess of it in the seminal reservoir has a damaging effect on the body and hence the inherent demand to discharge it any way in moments of desperation. [140]

Imâm Nawawî writes:

*"The demand of strong passion for sexual
union sometimes becomes so
overwhelming that if it is not met soon
enough, it harms the body, the heart, and
the eye-sight."* [141]

Shâh Walî-ullâh in describing the evils resulting in sexual abstinence from marriage announces:

> *"When the seminal fluid is being produced in abundance, it affects the mind as well, with the result that the young men become unduly interested in the good looks of beautiful women, and their love finds a place in their hearts. This fever affects the sexual organs also, which makes the demand of sexual union very much pressing and the desire for dissipation manifests itself in various forms. In case of remaining unmarried, it prompts him to fornication, his morals become lax, and the day soon arrives when his lust plunges him into great dangers."* [142]

These statements point to the fact that abstinence from marriage not only harms the individual and society but also is in itself unnatural.

3.12 PROHIBITED DEGREES OF MARRIAGE

3.12.1 PERMANENT PROHIBITIONS

Entertaining any sexual thoughts concerning such close relatives as one's mother, sister and daughter is instinctively abhorrent to human nature; there are even certain animals which avoid mating with such closely-related animals. The respect a man feels for his aunt is like the respect he has for his mother, and likewise uncles are regarded as fathers. Since the family must live together in intimacy and privacy but without incestuous relations, the *Sharî'ah* intends to cut at the root of any such sexual attraction among such close relatives. The natural sentiments of love and affection between a man and the above-mentioned female relatives must be kept strong forever. If marriage were permitted between such relatives, it would cause jealousy, dissension, and the disruption of families, destroying the very sentiments of love and affection which give permanence to the family structure. Similarly, the offspring of marriages to such close blood relatives would most probably be defective and weak.[143]

A Muslim is permanently forbidden to marry a woman who belongs to the following categories:

1) The mother, including the maternal and paternal grandmothers.

2) The step mother(s), whether divorced or widowed. This prohibition is out of honour and respect for the father.

3) The daughter(s), including the granddaughters from the son or daughter.

4) The sister(s), including the half and step-sisters.

5) The paternal aunt(s), whether she is the real, half, or step-sister of the father.

6) The maternal aunt(s), whether she is the real, half, or step-sister of the father.

7) The brother's daughter(s), i.e., his niece.

8) The sister's daughter(s), i.e. his niece.

9) The foster mother, who suckled him during his infancy before the time of weaning, i.e. when milk was the primary source of food.

10) Foster sisters: Just as a woman becomes a mother to a child by virtue of suckling, likewise her daughters become his sisters, her sisters his aunts, and so on. The Prophet 🌸 said:

> "What is ḥarâm (forbidden) by genealogy
> is ḥarâm by reason of fosterage." [144]

11) The mother-in-law, irrespective of whether a man and his wife have

engaged in sexual intercourse or not. Nikâḥ is sufficient to bestow upon the mother-in-law the same status as the mother.

12) The step-daughter (his wife's daughter by a previous marriage), on condition that he has consumated the marriage with her mother, i.e. his wife. If he divorces his wife without having intercourse with her, it is permissible for him to marry her daughter by a previous marriage.

13) The daughter-in-law, i.e. the wife of the real son, not that of the adopted son.

3.12.2 TEMPORARY PROHIBITIONS

Temporary prohibitions are those which can be removed by a change of circumstances. They are as follows:

14) Sisters as co-wives: A man cannot marry two sisters at one and the same time because the feeling of love and sisterliness which Islâm wants to maintain would be destroyed. This temporary prohibition becomes nullified as soon as his wife passes away, or he divorces her, and takes her sister in marriage.

15) Married Women: A person cannot marry a married woman who is living with her husband. However, this restriction is lifted immediately on the dissolution of her marriage either by the death of her husband or divorce by completion of her 'iddat (waiting period).

16) Four Wives: A person cannot wed more than four wives simultaneously. He can only do so if one of his wives is divorced or passes away.

17) *Iddah*: Women cannot be married during their 'iddah. As soon as this expires a person can contract *nikâḥ* with her.

18) *Mushrik* women: Men are prohibited from marrying *mushrik* women (those who worship idols or associate partners with Allâh). They

125

are classified as being temporary prohibited because once they accept Islâm, this prohibition is lifted. The Qur'ân mentions:

> *"And do not marry mushrik women until*
> *they believe, for a believing bondmaid is*
> *better than a mushrik woman, even though*
> *you may admire her. And do not marry*
> *(your girls) to mushrik men until they*
> *believe, for a believing bondsman is better*
> *than a mushrik, even though you may*
> *admire him..."* [145]

19) Fornicatresses: Those women who scratch a living through prostitution cannot be legally taken into *nikâh*, since this profession is a crime against her husband and society. She defiles the bed of her husband and casts a doubt on the parentage of their children. Therefore Islâmic Sharî'ah prohibits marriage to a prostitute until she repents and demonstrates she is not pregnant (by continuation of her menstrual period).

3.13 THE LEGALITY OF DIVORCE

It is part of human nature that in spite of all man's achievement, there are times in his life when it becomes impossible to continue with his marital relations in happiness and cordiality, despite attempts at reconciliation and counselling. As a last alternative Sharî'at Islâm has permitted the couple to separate in an amicable manner, rather than dragging on the relationship indefinitely thereby increasing the animosity and frustrations of the imcompatible partners. Prior to discussing and appreciating the Islâmic concept of divorce, it would be relevant to review other systems regarding such a separation.

3.13.1 DIVORCE DURING THE PRE-ISLÂMIC PERIOD

During this period, except for a very few societies; divorce was practised everywhere in the world. It was a common occurrence that when a man became angry with his wife, he would then turn her out of the house, with or without a just cause, and the unfortunate woman had no legal recourse against him, nor any claim to his property, nor even a right to maintenance. When the Greek civilization was at its zenith, unrestrained divorce was allowed amongst her inhabitants. Under Roman law a judge was empowered to annul a marriage even if the two parties had incorporated a condition against separation in their marriage contract. During the ancient Roman era, divorce was an impossibility after the religious rites of marriage had been performed, but at the same time the husband was given unlimited power over his wife, to such an extent that he could even kill her under certain pretexts. Only at a later stage, was divorce incorporated into the civil law of the country.

The ancient Hindus considered marriage as an indissoluble union, continuing even after the death of either spouse. This was the reason that a woman whose husband died during her lifetime had to immolate herself alive together with his corpse during the cremation ceremony.

Despite the restraints prescribed by the Jewish law, men enjoyed immense powers to divorce their wives. If a husband felt that his wife was not beautiful enough, and wished to substitute her for a more glamorous one, he was free to do so. Similarly, the wife's minor defects could be used as a springboard for separation. For instance, if her armpits emit an unpleasant smell; or both her eyes are not equal in size; or if she is hunch-backed, lame or sterile; or if she possesses some moral defects such as lack of fine taste in eating, greed, gluttony or bad temper, etc. Although a husband could divorce his spouse for something which made her unpleasant to him, she in turn could not exercise this right even for legitimate reasons.

In contrast to even Judaism, Christianity is the only religion which prohibited divorce and marriage to divorced men and women. These statements have been attributed to Ḥaḍrat ʿÎsâ (﷽ - Jesus):

> *"Whoever divorces his wife must give her
> a writing of divorce. But I tell you, whoever
> divorces his wife, save for the cause of
> adultery, causes her to commit fornication,
> and whoever marries a divorced woman
> commits adultery."*[146]

The reason for this as given in the words of the Gospels is:

> *"Whatsoever God has joined together let
> no man put asunder."* [147]

This statement is valid in the sense that, since the husband and wife are married by God's permission and legislation, one may say that God has joined them together, although it is the man who enters into the marriage contract. Similarly, since God has permitted and legislated divorce in relation to certain reasons and circumstances, one may say that God has separated them, even though the man implements the divorce. It thus becomes clear that no man puts asunder what God has joined together, and putting asunder is in the hands of Almighty God, and is it not God Himself who puts them asunder due to the reason of sexual immorality?[148]

In spite of the fact that an exception with regard to the prohibition of divorce in the case of sexual immorality has been declared in the New Testament Gospels, orthodox Catholics try to eradicate this exception by declaring, *"The meaning here is not that adultery is an exception in the case of which divorce is permitted, because in Christian law there is no divorce. The phrase, 'Except for unchastity', means that the marriage itself is annulled, since its legality and correctness have been violated; thus while it is seemingly a marriage, in actuality it is adultery. Consequently, in such a case it is permissible for the husband, or rather incumbent upon him, to leave the woman."* [149]

In addition to those reasons mentioned in the text of the Gospels, the Protestant denominations permitted divorce on the grounds of adultery, betrayal of the husband, and other specified reasons but considered it unlawful on any other grounds such as – cruelty, high-mindedness or prolonged quarrels. The orthodox Coptic Church of Egypt has made provision for divorce on the grounds of a wife being barren for three years, chronic illness and prolonged dissension which cannot be resolved.

As a result of this uncompromising stand of Christianity with regard to divorce, people in Western countries were obliged to resort to civil legislation in order to legalize it. Unfortunately, many of them, the Americans, for example, went to an extreme of permissiveness in the matter of divorce so that it is granted for quite trivial reasons. Some Western philosophers warn that this ease at which divorce is made possible, will dilute the sanctity of the marital bond and erode the very foundations of family life. A well-known judge declared that the time is not too far off when, in Western countries, marriage will be replaced by a loose and tenuous relationship between men and women, similar to a commercial transaction, which can be broken for the most trivial reasons. Since there will be no bond of religion or love between such a pair, they will be united only by their lusts and the desire to experience a variety of pleasures, a type of relationship which is against principles of every religion:

> *"This phenomenon of regulating personal affairs through civil law is against the teachings of every religion and is not to be found anywhere in the world except among the people of the West, even Hindus, Buddhists and Zoroastrians observe religious injunctions in the ordering of their personal affairs. Although we may find among them those who have made innovations in the teachings of their religions in matters of public concern, such innovations are not undertaken in personal affairs, that is to say in marriage, divorce, and what pertains to family life."* [150]

Arthur Hess, a barrister, writes in an essay:

> *"Twenty years back there used to be one divorce out of every seven marriages. But*

> *now the figures reveal that in the United*
> *States of America, there is one divorce for*
> *every three marriages — and this rate is*
> *mounting regularly."* [151]

The pagan Arabs divorced their wives during any period, with or without any valid excuse. They also used to revoke the divorce, once given, and then pronounce divorce again and repeat this procedure as many times as would suit their fancy, with the result that the poor woman could not get out of the clutches of the cruel husband. Some husbands divorced their wives as many as a hundred times. They even accused them at pleasure, of adultery, smearing them with such allegations as would deter would be suitors. It is a well established fact that, *'the greatest torment in life is a companion who neither agrees with you nor leaves you alone.'* Even after their spouses were dismissed, no legal punishment could be administered to them in exempting themselves from the responsibilities of maintenance. They knew no rule of humanity in treating their wives.

Such extremism resulted in the decadence of the morals and chastity of the people, ruining their homes and demoralising their sensitive nature of love, affection and mutual attraction. It is against this background that the law of divorce introduced by Islâm in the early seventh century conferring substantial rights on the womenfolk appears to be a great blessing for humanity especially for the weaker sex.

3.13.2 DIVORCE IN ISLÂM

Divorce without lawful necessity and without first exhausting all alternate avenues of resolving the conflict is extremely abhorred in Islâm. The Holy Prophet 鑒 has mentioned:

> *"Among the permitted acts, divorce is the*
> *most hated by Allâh Ta'âlâ."* [152]

Islâm strictly cautioned against hasty and irrational decisions in the matter of divorce, since it involves not only the relations of two individuals and two families but also their dignity and morality. On the other hand, Islâm also recognized that when a marriage becomes impossible to sustain, it is better for the parties to separate amicably, rather than being miserably bound together and groan under tyranny and oppression. Nevertheless, since divorce is the last resort, these are the initial preventative measures a husband should ensure before pronouncing ṭalâq (divorce). If the husband senses that feelings of disobedience and rebelliousness are rising against him in his wife, he should try his best to rectify her attitude by kind words, gentle persuasion, and reasoning with her. If this is not helpful, he should sleep apart from her, trying to awaken her agreeable feminine nature so that serenity may be restored and she may respond to him in a harmonious way. If this approach fails, it is permissible for him to reprimand her lightly with his hands, avoiding her face and other sensitive areas. Under no circumstances should he resort to using a stick or any other instrument which might cause pain or injury. Once, when the Prophet ﷺ was angry with a servant he mentioned that had it not been for the retaliation on the Day of Reckoning, he would have lightly beaten the servant with a *miswâk* (tooth-cleaning stick).

If all these approaches fail, and the rift between the husband and wife widens, the matter then descends on the Islâmiç society for solution. Two individuals of goodwill and sound judgement, one from the wife's and one from the husband's side, should meet with the couple in order to try to resolve their differences. Perhaps the sincerity of their efforts may bear fruit and Allâh may bring about reconciliation between the partners. Allâh Ta'âlâ refers to these various approaches by mentioning:

> " ... *And as for those women on whose part you fear disloyalty and ill-conduct, (first) admonish them, then refuse to share their beds; and (finally) beat them (lightly). Then if they return to obedience, do not seek for a way against them; indeed, Allâh is Most High, Great. And if you fear breach between the two of them, appoint an arbiter from his family and an arbiter from her family. If they desire to set things aright, Allâh will bring about reconciliation between them; indeed Allâh is Knowing, Aware.* " [153]

131

An excellent plan for settling family disputes, without too much publicity or mud-slinging, or resort to the trickery of the law. The Latin countries recognize this plan in their legal systems. It is a pity that Muslims do not resort to it universally, as they should. The arbiters from each family would know the mental constitution of both parties, and would be able, with Allâh Ta'âlâ's help, to effect a real reconciliation.

After having deligently pursued all these avenues, and the husband cannot successfully arrive at any solution, then Islâm allows him the avenue of divorce in resolving his difficulty honourably. But it should be remembered that Islâm has permitted divorce reluctantly, neither liking or encouraging it since it is the most hated among all permissible things in the sight of Allâh, i.e. it is permissible under unavoidable circumstances, when living together becomes a torture, mutual hatred is deep seated, and it becomes difficult for the two parties to observe the limits of Allâh Ta'âlâ and to fulfil their marital responsibilities, as the Qur'ân declares:

> *"But if they separate, Allâh Ta'âlâ will*
> *provide for each of them out of His*
> *abundance..."*[154]

If they must separate, it must be done with dignity and kindness, without injury, mutual abuse, or infringement of rights. Allâh Ta'âlâ says:

> *"...Then (either) retain her in honour or*
> *release her with kindness..."* [155]

3.13.2.1 THE REVOCABLE ṬALÂQ (DIVORCE) AND 'IDDAT (THE PERIOD OF WAITING)

As a deterrent against the divorce taking effect immediately the Sunnah has sanctioned the revocable divorce and greatly abhorred ṭalâq being pronounced thrice simultaneously. A period of waiting has been fixed for a woman prohibiting her to remarry immediately after being divorced. If she is a menstruating woman she will wait for the duration of three cycles. If she is non-menstruating or has attained the age of menopause, she will have to wait for three months. If she is pregnant, her waiting period is the end of the gestation time or delivery of the child. Apart from the considerations of making sure of the pregnancy and the protection of the offspring, if any, in the case of revocable divorce, the husband gets sufficient time to reconsider his predicament, and with her presence in the same house makes it quite probable that the mutual affection and sympathy between them may be rekindled, so the possibility of retracting his pronouncement becomes even greater.

Some people are of the misconception that the power of divorce should be in the hands of the court rather than in the hands of the husband. Such opinion is due to the lack of thought on their part. To hand over such cases to the court and to prove adultery is to jeopardize the lives of both the husband and the wife, since the second marriage of the divorced wife after so much publicity and scandal will become virtually impossible. Islâm by its very nature is against wilful fault-finding and publicity of shameful deeds except where they stand revealed and proved by profession, and an admonitory effect is in view. A little thought over the law will reveal the fact that Islâm has empowered the *Qâḍî* (judge) to annul marriage ties, only in cases, which, if revealed, will do no harm to anyone, rather will benefit some, such as the wife of such a person who has lost manly vigour totally for reasons of physical or physiological impotence, castration or amputation of the penis.[156]

A divorced woman cannot be prevented from marrying anyone she chooses after the expiry of her *'iddat*, provided it is done within the confines of Sharî'ah. The present malady is that divorced men pursue all types of *"uncivilized"* methods into intimidating and preventing their ex-wives from re-marrying, resembling a fiasco worse than the days of Jâhilîyah. Likewise some families or guardians prevent them from returning to their husbands when the possibility of reconciliation is apparent. Regarding this the Qur'ân announces:

> *"And when you divorce women and they complete their 'iddah, do not prevent them from marrying their (former) husbands if they agree among themselves in an honourable manner."* [157]

133

A selfish man, because he has divorced his wife, may, in the probationary period before the divorce becomes absolute, subject her to insulting language or treatment, and while giving her residence and maintenance, may so restrict it as to make her life miserable. This is forbidden. She must be provided on the same scale as he is, according to his status in life. If he uses the law for the injury of the weaker party, his own moral and spiritual nature suffers.

3.13.2.2 DIVORCE AT THE REQUEST OF THE WIFE *(KHUL'A)*

The Qur'ân permits a wife to request her husband for a divorce *(khul'a)* if she fears cruelty or desertion by him. It can be achieved through mutual agreement of the two parties or through the order of the *Qâdî* on payment by the wife to the husband of a certain amount through mutual consent. The Qur'ân mentions:

> *"If a wife fears cruelty or desertion on her husband's part, there is no blame on them, if they arrange an amicable settlement between themselves; and such settlement is best; even though men's souls are swayed by greed. But if you practise self-restraint, Allâh is well acquainted with all that you do."* [158]

There is a precedent of *khul'a* during the prophet's period. The wife of Thâbit ibn Qais came to the Prophet 🕊 and said, *"O Messenger of Allâh, I am not angry with the faith and morals of Thâbit, but I am afraid something may happen to me contrary to Islâm on which account I wish to be separated from him."* The Prophet 🕊 said, *"Will you give Thâbit back the garden which he gave you as your settlement?"* She replied, *"Yes."* Then the Prophet 🕊 said to Thâbit, *"Take your garden and divorce her at once."* [159]

On the other hand, it is forbidden for a man to torment his wife and compel her to seek a divorce so that he could extract the property or part thereof from her. Only if she is proven guilty of definite sexual immorality can a husband demand this right. The Qur'ân mentions:

> *"...Nor should you treat them with*
> *harshness in order that you may take away*
> *part of what you have given them, (for you*
> *may not take it back) unless they are guilty*
> *of open lewdness."*[160]

3.14   INJURIOUS COMPARISON *(ZIHÂR)*

In the Days of Ignorance an Arab would say to his wife, *"You are to me like the back of my mother"*, which was known as *z̧ihâr*. The companionship between the spouses would immediately be terminated at the pronouncement of these words as in the case of a divorce, but the woman was not at liberty to exit the husband's residence, rather she was pinned and dragged on as a deserted wife. Islâm intervened and prohibited this evil practice as is evident in the case of Khaulah, the wife of 'Aus ibn Sâmit, who was treated in a very similar manner. The Qur'ân bears testimony to this incidence by mentioning:

> *"As for those of you who put away their*
> *wives by likening them to the backs of their*
> *mothers, they are not their mothers; their*
> *mothers are no other than those who gave*
> *birth to them; and most surely they utter a*
> *hateful word and falsehood. Allâh is One*
> *that blots out sins and forgives*
> *(repeatedly)."* [161]

The person who resorted to this practice was ordered to free a slave; or if he could not find one, then to fast for two successive months, and if unable to do that, to feed sixty poor people.

When a person utters a false, irrational, indecent word, its retribution is that he should give expiation. These penalties in the alternative are prescribed, that we may show our repentance and our renunciation of iniquity and rude language within the framework of sexual morality.

Since Khaulah loved her husband and pleaded she had little children whom she had no resources to support herself and whom, under *zihâr*, her husband was not bound to support, Islâm abolished this system once and for all.

3.15   ISLÂM FORBIDS THE OATH OF DESERTION *(ILÂ)*

In the pre-Islâmic days the Arabs used to frequently take oaths that they would not indulge in sexual relations with their wives, keeping them in suspense and bondage sometimes throughout their entire lives, thus having neither the status of wives nor that of divorced women free to marry elsewhere. This procedure, which was commonly referred to as *Ilâ*, in reality was meant to inflict pain on a woman by keeping her hanging in the air.[162]

Although it is true that relations between husband and wife do not always remain cordial, yet the Sharî'ah does not sanction that the strained atmosphere should continue indefinitely. A maximum period of four months is extended to them wherein which they legally remain each others spouse but practically lead separate lives without indulging in sexual intercourse. Such a separation is classified as *Ilâ* in Islâm. During this interim period they must either reconcile or separate permanently so that each one could be at liberty to marry the person of his or her choice.[163] Concerning this the Qur'ân declares:

> "For those who take an oath of abstention
> from their wives, a waiting period of four
> months (is ordained); if they return, indeed
> Allâh is Forgiving, Merciful. But if their
> intention is firm for divorce, then, indeed,
> Allâh is Hearing, Knowing." [164]

3.16 INVOKING SELF DAMNATION *(LI'ÂN)*

If one of the married partners accuses the other of unchastity, the accusation partly reflects on the accuser as well. Moreover, the link which unites married people, even where differences supervene, is sure to act as a steadying influence against the concoction of false charges particularly where divorce is allowed (as in Islâm) for reasons other than unchastity. Suppose a husband catches a wife in adultery. In the nature of things four witnesses - or even one outside witness - would be impossible. Yet after such an experience it is against human nature that he can live a normal married life. The matter is then left to the honour of the two spouses.

Thus if a Muslim wife is accused by her husband of adultery and files a case against her in the presence of an Islâmic judge, he would be commanded to present four eye-witnesses to the crime. Failure to do so, would result in him being requested to swear an oath four times that he is sincere in his accusation against his wife, and the fifth time he would announce that if he is falsely implicating her, then the admonition of Ailâh would envelop him. On the other hand, if his wife also declares her chastity and rejects the allegation against her, she will also be compelled to swear an oath four times that her husband is levelling false charges against her purity, and the fifth time she will have to announce that if her husband is really true in his accusation, then the anger of Allâh may descend upon her. When this procedure, which is known as *Li'ân*, is over, then the husband should divorce the wife, and the *Qâdî* will separate both of them. Regarding this Allâh Ta'âlâ mentions:

> *"And for those who launch a charge against their spouses, and have in support no evidence but their own, their solitary evidence can be received if they bear witness four times with an oath by Allâh that they are solemnly telling the truth; and the fifth oath should be that they solemnly invoke the curse of Allâh on themselves if they tell a lie. But it would avert the punishment from the wife, if she bears witness four times with an oath by Allâh*

> *that her husband is telling a lie; and the*
> *fifth oath should be that she solemnly*
> *invokes the wrath of Allâh on herself if her*
> *accuser is telling the truth."* [165]

Since the procedure of *Li'ân* strikes a heavy blow to the affection and confidence of the participating partners, Islâm no longer compels them to be bound together in such a doubtful union of hostility, but rather they are immediately separated, as it is against human nature that the parties can live together happily after such an incident.

3.17 ḤALÂLAH – LEGALIZING A PREVIOUS MARRIAGE

Since it may sometimes occur that a person due to hasty decisions had irrevocably divorced his wife, which makes remarriage unlawful between them, repents and once more desires her as his spouse a solution is provided by the Holy Qur'ân:

> *"So, if a husband divorces his wife*
> *(irrevocably), he cannot, after that,*
> *remarry her until after she has married*
> *another husband and he has divorced her.*
> *In that case, there is no blame on either of*
> *them if they re-unite, provided they feel*
> *that they can keep the limits ordained by*
> *Allâh. Such are the limits ordained by*
> *Allâh, which He makes plain to those who*
> *understand."* [166]

Thus she only becomes ḥalâl (legal) to the first husband, after having remarried and the second husband divorces her after having consumated the marriage. His death will also have the same effect. This, in reality, is referred to as ḥalâlah. It is a grave error to confuse this ḥalâlah with that of the pre-Islâmic times. The formula then was that after being irrevocably divorced she would marry another "friend" of the first husband on the understanding that he would divorce her without having had sexual intercourse. Immediately after the divorce she was then legal for the first husband, who would remarry her.

This sort of sham second marriage to bypass the prohibition against the husband who had nullified the first marriage was a ploy which could not be tolerated in Islâm. It is compulsory, therefore, in Sharî'ah, that the marriage with the second person is a genuine one containing no condition that he will divorce her. It is also impressed that the second husband must not divorce her without sexually using her so that the first husband feels the pinch of jealousy of his former wife lying in the arms of a third person due to his own fault in hastily divorcing her.[167] The abuse of such a procedure to defeat the prohibition of remarriage between the parties who were separated by irrevocable divorce has been strongly condemned by the Holy Prophet 🕊 in these words:

"The curse of Allâh be on the man who commits ḥalâlah and the man for whom ḥalâlah is committed." [168]

Ḥadrat 'Umar ⚭ was of the opinion that such fraudulent scheming was tantamount to adultery.

After our discourse on the issue of divorce, one who is unfamiliar with the Islâmic concept of such a regulation would be curious to be informed as to why such a right is exclusively reserved to the males and not to both the males and females as is practiced in contemporary societies? This line of argument is baseless for the mere fact, that it is not only now, but for the past fifteen centuries the judicial system of Islâm not only elevated their position from mere chattels to refined human beings but also bestowed upon a woman such a privilege that she could approach a *Qadî* and request the dissolution of a marriage on the grounds of insanity, cruelty, lack of maintenance, a husband's absence over an unusually long period, i.e. missing from home, etc. This dissolution can even be extended to incompatibility as was demonstrated in the case of Bint Qais.

Similarly, due to their physiological and psychological make-up, they are usually somewhat impaired during certain periods of every month, even the strongest, healthiest and most determined ones among them. If, then, women were given the power of unilateral divorce, a great possibility exists wherein millions of them would divorce their spouses wreaking havoc in society.

3.18 CONCLUSION

From all the statistics and observations presented thus far, one may notice that modern developments in marriage law and the status of women throughout the world are leaning towards the Islâmic pattern, although unconsciously, in many ways, stressing guidance, tolerance and counselling before divorce, privacy of divorce proceedings and speeding of the process of divorce once it has been established that marriage has irretrievably broken down.

Therefore the law of Islâm elevates the dignity of women and does not compel unhappy couples to stay together, but its procedures help them to find a basis on which they can be reconciled with each other. If reconciliation is impossible the law does not impose any unnecessary delay or obstacle in the way of either partner's remarriage.

CHAPTER FOUR
Sexual Vice and its Remedy
MORALITY IN ISLÂM

SEXUAL VICE AND ITS REMEDY

4.1　INTRODUCTION

Perverted people of the modern era visualize illegal and deviated sexual gratification as natural acts and regard marriage as an unnecessary innovation of civilization. They seem to think that it is perfectly natural that whenever one feels the urge, or finds the opportunity, and whenever two members of the same or opposite sex mutually agree, sexual intercourse should take place, even without the presence of a deeper spiritual bond. They do not consider such conduct to be demeaning to the nature of man. This is indeed a wrong perception of the character of human beings since man has the capacity to form spiritual relationships that transcend beyond the mere physical. Thus the humanity of man is not two independent traits, but have to merge together to constitute his personality. Due to their inter-dependance, it is impossible to reject the demands of one in favour of the other.

4.2　*ZINÂ* (ILLICIT SEXUAL GRATIFICATION)

It is not surprising that all the revealed religions have prohibited fornication and adultery and have fought against these crimes against society. Islâm, the last of the divinely revealed religions, is very strict in prohibiting *zinâ*, for it leads to confusion of lineage, child abuse, the breaking-up of families, bitterness in relationships, the spread of veneral diseases, and a general laxity in morals; moreover, it opens the door to a flood of lust and self-gratification. Therefore, in Islâm, whatever excites passions, opens ways for illicit sexual relations and promotes indecency and obscenity, is prohibited.

Fornication has been defined as the disappearance of the glans penis of a sober and sensible major (adult) person into the vagina of a woman, not his own legally married wife, and this act not being due to any mistake or compulsions.

The Arabic word *zinâ* refers to sexual intercourse between a man and woman not married to each other. It therefore implies both to adultery (which implies that one or both of the parties are married to a person or persons other than the ones concerned) and to fornication, which in its strict signification, implies that both parties are unmarried. The English word *adultery* applies to a married man or woman indulging in illicit sexual intercourse with one who is not the legal wife or husband, while *fornication* implies that both parties are unmarried. Thus *zinâ*, which is a major sin in Islâm, refers to both adultery and fornication.

The following is mentioned in the Old Testament:

;

> *"The Lord gave the following regulations. Do not have sexual intercourse with any of your relatives. Do not disgrace your father by having intercourse with any of his wives. Do not have intercourse with your sister or step-sister, whether or not she was brought up in the same house with you. Do not have intercourse with your grand-daughter that will be a disgrace to you. Do not have intercourse with your aunt, whether she is your father's sister or your mother's sister. Do not have intercourse with your uncle's wife. She is, your aunt too. Do not have intercourse with your daughter-in-law or with your brother's wife. Do not have intercourse with the daughter or grand-daughter of a woman with whom you had intercourse, they may be related to you, and that would be incest. Do not take your wife's sister as one of your wives, as long as your wife is living. Do not have intercourse with a woman during her monthly period. Do not have intercourse with another man's wife..."* [1]

Adultery is not only shameful in itself and inconsistent with any self-respect or respect for others, but it opens the road to many evils. It destroys the basis of the family; it works against the interest of children born or to be born; it may lead to murders and feuds and loss of reputation and property, and also loosen permanently the bonds of society. Not only should it be avoided as a sin, but any approach or temptation to it should be avoided. The Qur'ân mentions:

> *"And approach not adultery, for it is a*
> *shameful deed and an evil, opening the*
> *road to to other evils."* [2]

Compare this austere attitude of Islâm with the sordid morality of the modern-day West where sexual fidelity and discipline are quickly becoming a thing of the past.

Zinâ is a very grievous crime. One should not even draw near it implies that one should not even commit those actions which are done by the preliminary impulses of lewdness as seeing a woman without legitimate authority of <u>Sh</u>arî'ah, kissing a woman, shaking hands with a woman etc, as is customary in western society. This verse forbids even the preliminary motions of lewdness also.

Islâm forbids looking at a member of the opposite sex with desire; for the eye is the key to the feelings, and the look is the messenger of desire, carrying the message of fornication or adultery. A poet of ancient times has said;
> *"All affairs begin with the sight, the raging*
> *fire a spark can ignite,"*

while a contemporary poet declares,
> *"A look, then a smile, then a nod of the*
> *head, then a talk, then a promise, then the*
> *warmth of the bed."* [3]

The Prophet ﷺ considered hungry and lustful looks at a person of the opposite sex as 'the *zinâ* of the eyes', according to his saying,
"The eyes also commit zinâ, and their zina is the lustful look." [4]
He termed "the lustful look" zina because it gives sexual pleasure and

gratification in an unlawful manner. This is also what Hadrat 'Îsâ (Jesus) 觊 is reported to have said in the Gospel of Matthew:
"You have heard that it was said, you shall not commit adultery. But I say to you that everyone who so much as looks at woman with evil desire for her has already committed adultery with her in his heart." (Matt. 5.27 - 28).

Indeed, such hungry and lustful looks are not merely a danger to sexual morality but they also result in agitation of the mind and disturbed thoughts.

The Prophet 鐘 declared that *zinâ* is the greatest crime after <u>*shirk*</u> (associating partners with Allâh Ta'âlâ):

> *"There is no sin after <u>shirk</u> greater in the eyes of Allâh than a drop of semen which a man places in the womb which is not lawful for him."* [5]

Fornication creates disturbance in genealogy and is the cause of many dissensions and strife and in an evil way makes its head in society.

Once a man came to the Holy Prophet 鐘 and asked him to permit him to engage in fornication. The Prophet 鐘 remained silent for a while, while the companions around him rebuked the man at his discourteous and insolent questions to the Prophet. They said to him that he should control his tongue in the presence of the Messenger of Allâh and should not utter such derogatory statements. The Prophet 鐘 called him near and asked him whether he approved of this act being committed to his mother, daughter, sister, paternal or maternal aunt. He said, *'May Allâh sacrifice my life on you, O Messenger of Allâh, never!'* The Prophet replied, *'Similar is the case with others. They will greatly abhor this action being committed to their mothers, daughters, sisters, paternal and maternal aunts.'* Then the Messenger of Allâh prayed to Allâh on his behalf that his heart be purified and his shameful parts made secure. Abû Imâmâ mentions that after this prayer his condition became such that he did not cast an eye on any strange woman.[6]

Islâm strictly abhors adultery and therefore commands the Muslims to refrain from all those satanic temptations that encourages a person to engage in such unlawful encounters. Even to glance at an unknown woman with a passionate, lustful intention is also considered a sin. Similarly, the adultery of the legs is walking towards an unlawful woman with evil temptations, and the adultery of the hands is touching, patting and caressing a strange woman who is prohibited to one.

4.2.1 PUNISHMENT FOR *ZINÂ*

The Qur'ân and Aḥâdîth have clearly defined the punishments to be meted out to those committing *zinâ*. Because the Arabs were steeped in the vice of *zinâ* in the Days of Ignorance, the Qur'ân transformed this unhealthy environment, accommodating the new converts in a gradual process over a length of time. The first injunction was directed towards the women restricting those guilty of *zinâ* to their homes until death. Allâh Ta'âlâ declares:

> *"If any of your women are guilty of adultery, take the evidence of four (reliable) witnesses from amongst you against them; and if they testify, confine them to their houses until death do claim them, or Allâh Ta'âlâ ordains for them some other way."* [7]

Here it must be emphasized that the overwhelming majority of the commentators of the Qur'ân are of the opinion that the word *'fâhishah'* refers to adultery or fornication.

Thereafter divine revelation was directed towards both men and women regarding their punishment:

> *"If two persons among you are guilty of adultery, punish them both. If they repent and amend, leave them alone, for Allâh is Oft-Returning, Most Merciful."* [8]

The third injunction categorically and specifically defined the punishment

147

to be meted out to the offenders:

> *"The woman and the man guilty of adultery*
> *or fornication, flog each one of them with*
> *a hundred stripes; let not compassion move*
> *you in their case, in a matter prescribed*
> *by Allâh, if you believe in Allâh Ta'âlâ and*
> *the Last Day and let a party of believers*
> *witness their punishment."* [9]

If you believe firmly in Allâh Ta'âlâ you should not hesitate a little in the promulgation and execution of His Laws and Commandments. You should not diminish the punishment of the culprit feeling merciful upon him, nor should you withdraw the punishment, nor should you devise a very light form of punishment which may mar its punitive aspect totally. You should understand very well that Allâh Ta'âlâ is All-Wise and is Kinder to His servants than you. His order, whether lenient or severe, is not devoid of wisdom and mercy for the collective creatures of the universe.

The punishment should not be given in solitary confinement, it should be administered before an assembly of Muslims because in that humiliation there is the perfection and publicity of the punishment, and a source of lesson for the on lookers.

Here a misconception may arise that as in the case of fornication, the punishment for adultery too, has also been restricted to a hundred lashes, since the Qur'ân remained silent on *rajm* (stoning to death). This misunderstanding has been clarified by the following hadîth:

> *"Take it from me, accept it from me,*
> *undoubtedly Allâh has now shown a path*
> *for them (adulterers). For unmarried*
> *persons (guilty of fornication), the*
> *punishment is one hundred lashes and an*
> *exile for one year. For married adulterers,*
> *it is one hundred lashes and stoning to*
> *death."* [10]

Hadrat 'Umar ﷺ also predicted anti-rajm sentiments in future generations: Ibn 'Abbas ﷺ has reported:

> *"'Umar said: I am afraid that after a long time has passed, people may say: 'We do not find the verses of rajm (stoning to death) in the Book of Allâh, and consequently they may go astray by leaving an obligation that Allâh Ta'âlâ has revealed. Lo! I confirm that the penalty of rajm be inflicted on him who commits illegal sexual intercourse if he is already married and the crime is proved by witnesses or pregnancy or confession.' "*[11]

Some scholars are of the opinion that an offender who is going to be stoned to death, need not be punished with a hundred lashes, citing the incidence where the Prophet ﷺ stoned two Jewish adulterers and withheld lashing them. Some jurists are of a contrary opinion maintaining that Khalîf 'Alî ﷺ punished a woman with lashes on a Thursday and stoned her on a Friday. His explanation was that she was lashed in accordance with Qur'ânic injunction and stoned in keeping with Prophetic compulsion.

Anyone who has been accused of *zinâ*, has to be proven guilty by one of these four conditions:

1) Four eye witnesses.

2) Self confession.

3) Circumstantial evidence e.g. an unmarried woman becomes pregnant.

4) *Liân* i.e. each of the spouses curses himself/herself in the event of his/her allegation of adultery is incorrect and curses the other if the allegation against him/her is fabricated.

4.2.1.1 FOUR EYE WITNESSES

There should be four eye witnesses who have seen the man and the woman committing *zinâ*. They must have caught or seen them red handed participating in the actual act. All the witnesses must be Muslims; mature; sane; pious and trustworthy; able to converse (not deaf or dumb); have good memory by which they could distinctly remember what had transpired; have actually seen the offender engaged in the sexual act and it is not merely speculation from the circumstances; the witnesses should not be near relatives of the accused; there must be no hatred between the witness and the accused; all the witnesses must be men; all must bear testimony in one sitting and must definitely be impartial.

In case the witnesses cannot establish the crime or tell lies they must be lashed eighty stripes each. Over and above that the slanderer or slanderers are to be deprived of one of their natural rights i.e. that of bearing testimony. They are forbidden from giving any further evidence on any matter throughout their lives, unless and until they repent and reform. Only then are they welcome back and once more bestowed with their right of bearing testimony, and are permitted to mediate as witnesses. Therefore, the most serious notice is taken of people who put forward slanders or scandalous suggestions about women without adequate evidence. If anything is said about a woman's chastity, it should be supported by evidence twice as strong as would ordinarily be required for business transactions. That is, four witnesses would be required instead of two. Failing such preponderating evidence the slanderer should himself be treated as a wicked transgressor and punished with eighty stripes. Not only would he be subjected to this disgraceful form of punishment, but he would be deprived of the citizen's right of giving evidence in all matters all his life, unless he repents and reforms. Regarding this the Qur'ân declares:

> "And those who launch a charge against
> chaste women, and produce not four
> witnesses (to support their allegations),
> flog them with eighty stripes, and reject
> their evidence ever after, for such men are
> wicked transgressors. Unless they repent

> *thereafter and mend their behaviour*
> *then Allâh Ta'âlâ is Oft-Forgiving, Most*
> *Merciful."* [12]

The punishment of lashes is inflicted in any case for unsupported slander. But the depriviation of the civic right of giving evidence can be cancelled by the man's subsequent conduct, if he repents, shows that he is sorry for what he did, and that he would not in future support by his statement anything for which he has not the fullest evidence. Thus his civic right of giving evidence is once more restored to him. Nevertheless, Imâm Abû Hanîfah adopts a more serious opinion and considers that neither the punishment of eighty lashes nor the incompetence of bearing testimony is cancelled by repentance; but it merely obliterates the spiritual stigma of being regarded as a wicked transgressor.

This malicious misrepresentation has been treated by Islâm with such severity that no one even dares to cast scandalous allegations against any chaste woman. At times pious and chaste women tend to be simple-hearted and indiscreet, but due to the evil and selfish motivation of some jealous people, problems could arise. Such good natured women harbour no evil designs and their innocent indiscretion may land them and their associates in extreme difficulties.

This was precisely the situation in which Hadrat 'Âishah (R.A.) found herself when a false allegation was cast against her chastity creating untold miseries, not only to her father but also to the Prophet ﷺ. Had not the Qur'ân exposed the falsehood of this fabricated allegation, Islâm would have suffered a great dent to its pristine purity.

The particular incident occurred on the return from the expedition to the Banû Mustaliq, A.H. 5-6. When the march was ordered, Hadrat 'Âishah was not in her tent, having gone to search for a valuable necklace she had dropped. As her litter was veiled, it was not noticed that she was not in, until the army reached the next halt. Meanwhile, finding the camp had gone, she sat down to rest, hoping that someone would come back to fetch her when her absence was noticed. It was night, and she fell asleep. Next morning she was found by Safwân, a Muhâjir companion of the Prophet, who had been left behind at the camp expressly to pick up anything inadvertently left behind. He put her on his camel and brought her, leading the camel on foot. This gave occasion to enemies to raise a malicious scandal. The ringleader among them was the chief of the Madîna Hypocrites, 'Abdullâh ibn Ubai. He had other sins and enormities to his debit, and he was left to the spiritual punishment of an unrepentant sinner, for he died in that state. The minor tools were given the legal punishment of the law, and after penitence mended their lives.

Allâh Ta'âlâ mentions:

> *"Those who slander chaste women, indiscreet but believing are cursed in this life and in the Hereafter, for them is a grievious penalty on the Day of Judgement, their tongues, their hands, and their feet will bear witness against them as to their actions."* [13]

Our own limbs and faculties are the strongest witnesses against us if we misuse them for evil deeds instead of using them for the good deeds for which they were given to us. According to Imâms Mâlik and Hanbal, even if a person accuses someone merely by implication, it is sufficient to punish him with eighty lashes, but according to Imâm Abû Hanîfah and Shâfi'î, the accused should be asked about his intention and in making the accusation before punishment is awarded to him. If he mentions that he did not deliberately intend slandering the woman then he shall be punished by *ta'zîr* (a punishment prescribed at the discretion of an Islâmic judge or ruler).

Since Islâm safeguards the honour and dignity of every Muslim, it has imposed strict measures against the slanderers so that the punishment for fornication and adultery may have its desired effect. Leaving everyone launching false charges against all and sundry without concrete evidence is the source of all lawlessness. Any innocent person might have false scandalous accusations levelled against him, thus tainting his character with the element of doubt. Every husband or wife becomes doubtful about the chastity and morality of his or her partner. They may even become doubtful about the authenticity of their mariage relationship.

In a society abounding with people of such traits where every male and female accuses everyone else of *zinâ*, it is highly likely that those in whose heart is a disease or those who were hesitant in committing such scandalous remarks, may now publicly and brazenly do so. Therefore to protect the chastity of the pure woman, three types of punishment is directed towards the slanderer viz. corporal punishment (eighty stripes); moral punishment (deprived of witness) and religious punishment whereby they are stigmatised as being impious.

In normal circumstances two witnesses are sufficient but for the allegation of *zinâ* it is compulsory to have four who were eye-witnesses to this offence being committed by the guilty person. The benefit of the slightest doubt in the statement of testimony of the witnesses should go in favour of the accused.

4.2.1.2 SELF CONFESSION

With the absence of four witnesses, it sometimes occur that the guilty ones feel remorseful and voluntarily present themselves to receive the penalty. They may confess that they committed adultery or fornicated. Each of them must be punished in accordance with his or her marital status i.e. flogging a hundred lashes to those who are unmarried and stoning to death to those who have tasted married life. The proof of the guilt of the accused must come in the form of four confessions which he voluntarily makes in one sitting. If he confesses thrice but retracts his confession the fourth time, he should not be stoned.

It is narrated that Mâ'iz ibn Mâlik al-Aslamî came to the Prophet ﷺ while he was in the mosque and confessed of his sin saying:
"O Messenger of Allâh, I require you to cleanse and purify me of this evil."
The Holy Prophet ﷺ turned away from him and sent him away saying,
"Go back and seek forgiveness of Allâh Ta'âlâ and turn to Him penitently."
Mâ'iz retired to a little distance away from the Prophet ﷺ and approached him again saying, *"O Messenger of Allâh, purify me"*. Mâ'iz received the same reply from the Prophet ﷺ until he made this confession for the

fourth time.

The Prophet ﷺ asked him, *"From what shall I purify you?"* He said: *"From adultery."* The Prophet ﷺ asked, *"Is he gone insane?"* He was informed that this person was perfectly normal. Then he enquired, *"Has he drunk wine?"* A man got up and smelt his breath and found that there was no traces of alcohol in it. He asked, *"Have you committed adultery?"* *"Yes,"* said he. Only then did the Holy Prophet ﷺ give instructions for Mâ'iz to be stoned to death.[14]

In some narrations it is even mentioned that when Mâ'iz ؓ came to confess for the fourth time the Prophet ﷺ asked him: *'Are you married?'* Mâ'iz replied, *'Yes'*. Then the Prophet ﷺ suggested, *'Perhaps you have just kissed the woman's mouth or touched her body or stared passionately at her'*. He replied, *'O Messenger of Allâh it was none of these things.'* The Prophet ﷺ then asked him: *'Did you have sexual intercourse with her?'* He replied: *'Yes, I have done so.'* He then asked: *'Just as a bodkin enters into a pot of collyrium or a bucket into a well?'* *'Yes'* said he. The Prophet ﷺ enquired: *'Do you know what is zinâ?'* *'Yes'* said he, *'I have committed an unlawful act with her – that which a husband lawfully engages with his legal wife.'* [15]

It is said that when a stone struck him, he began fleeing until he was overtaken by a person wielding a large camel bone. He was beaten therewith and others joined in until he met his death. This incident was mentioned to the Prophet ﷺ who remarked: *'Why did you not let him off so that he might have turned to Allâh repentently and Allâh would have also looked at him forgivingly.'*

It appears from this that in case of retraction of confession about adultery, the prescribed punishment of stoning to death cannot be administered. This extreme penalty only depends upon continued confession. This tradition also illustrates that the Prophet's ﷺ heart was full of compassion and kindness but he was bound by the laws of Sharî'ah to implement justice in cleansing society of this evil. The Prophet ﷺ also encouraged that pardon should be extended by mutual compromise without the knowledge of judges. But when any crime is brought to their notice, it becomes unlawful to pardon the guilty and criminals. The mere fact that the Prophet ﷺ turned his attention from Mâ'iz during his initial confessions and enquired about his sanity or him being intoxicated, since such confessions are void, reflects the extreme caution he exercised before pronouncing such a punishment, so that Mâ'iz could not be denied an opportunity to repent. Nevertheless, this extreme punishment was necessary in order to establish the kingdom of morality for which the Prophet 鸞 stood.

Another example is that of a female who made such a confession:

"A woman from Ghâmid came to the Prophet 鸞 and said, 'O Prophet 鸞 of Allâh I have committed adultery so purify me.' The Prophet 鸞 sent her away. The following day she returned and said, 'O Prophet 鸞 of Allâh, why do you turn me away? Perhaps you turn me away as you turned away Mâ'iz. By Allâh I have become pregnant.' He said, 'Well, if you insist upon it, then go away until you give birth to the child,'" When she delivered she came with the child wrapped in a rag and said, *'Here is the child whom I have given birth to.'* He said, *'Return and suckle him until you wean him.'* When she had weaned her child she came to him with the child who was holding a piece of bread in his hand. She said, *'O Prophet 鸞 of Allâh, here he is. I have weaned him and he eats food.'* The Holy Prophet 鸞 entrusted the child to one of the Muslims and thereafter pronounced punishment. While stoning her some blood fell on Khâlid ibn Walîd's face who rebuked and cursed her so loudly that the Prophet 鸞 overheard him. The Prophet 鸞 said:
'Softly O Khâlid, this woman has repented so sincerely that if it were to be divided among seventy people of Medina it would have been sufficient for their salvation.'[16]

Some narrations also mention that if such a repentance was offered by an extortionist, he would have been forgiven. The Messenger of Allâh himself presided over the funeral ceremony (*janâzah*) of this woman.

The Prophet 鸞 presented both Mâ'iz and the Ghâmidite woman an opportune moment of going back and reviewing their situations and secretly repenting. But, alas! The divine influence has made them not to accept it, but to be cleansed and purified in the spirit of true repentance. Since they had openly confessed the punishment had to be administered. Had they secretly repented, then Allâh would have forgiven them. But who can be sure of this forgiveness. Therefore they chose the former method as a guaranteed route to Allâh Ta'âlâ's clemency.

From the above hadîth it is deduced that the confession of *zinâ* should be made four times. Both the parties concerned must be present. If one of them admits and the other denies, the judge is to remind him/her of the punishment of the Hereafter which is extremely severe. He will then pass judgement by instructing punishment for the one who admitted and acquitting the other by giving him/her the benefit of the doubt.

Here the following question may be raised: *"Why is it that a married person who commits zinâ is stoned to death while the unmarried is lashed a hundred stripes? Both of them committed the same act."*

Generally speaking an unmarried person who has not tasted the pleasures of marital bliss is more often than not naive and does not really enjoy the act in the real sense of the word. While, on the other hand, a married person is sexually more mature and experiences tremendous delight in such encounters. If his partner is incompatible then there are other avenues of legally fulfilling his carnal desires in the form of a second marriage. She, on the other hand, cannot afford to adulterate her husband's lineage with illegitimate offsprings. Therefore adultery is an infectious disease which needs to be publicly eradicated to serve as a deterrent to other would be offending criminals.

Abdullâh ibn 'Umar ﷺ narrated that the Jews came to the Messenger of Allâh and stated that a man and a woman from among them had committed adultery. The Prophet ﷺ enquired:
'Did you not find the injunction of stoning to death in your Torâh?'
They replied: *'We merely disgraced them and they are whipped.'*
Abdullâh ibn Salâm (who was still a Jew at that moment but later converted to Islâm) interrupted by proclaiming: *'You have lied. Verily the Torâh mentions stoning to death.'*
Then the Torâh was brought and it was opened. One of them put his hand over the verse of stoning to death and only read what was before and after it. Abdullâh ibn Salâm said: Raise your hand, and when his hand was raised the relevant verse became distinguishable.
They said: *'He has spoken the truth, O Muhammad, therein is the verse*

of stoning to death, but we conceal it amongst us.' Thereafter the Prophet ☙ instructed that both of them be punished in accordance with the law of the Torâh.[17]

It appears from this ḥadîth that the non-Muslim under Muslim rule should be governed by their respective laws and not by Islâmic law. How catholic is the spirit of Islâm and how grand is the pronouncement! It cannot be dreamt even by the rulers of the 21st century who are introducing their own laws of crimes. Had there been administration according to this principle, much of communal jealousies and blood-shed would have been averted. It is also clear that non-Muslims trusted the Prophet ☙ in matters secular and this publicly demonstrates the integrity and justice of the Prophet ☙. It also illustrates that the Jews were trying to conceal and obliterate the laws which were not pleasing or appealing to them.

4.2.1.3 CIRCUMSTANTIAL EVIDENCE

If an unmarried woman is found to be pregnant, then the authorities are to investigate and decipher whether she committed *zinâ* voluntarily or forcefully. Similarly, if a woman is married to a person whose reproductive organ has been amputated or to a boy who is sexually not mature, and she is found to be pregnant, they are also to find out the cause of her pregnancy. The same injunction applies to a woman who was married and gave birth to a child within less than six months from the day her husband had sexual intercourse with her.

If after intensive investigation it is found that the pregnant woman, from any of the above quoted cases or any similar cases, was forced or intimidated by someone, or someone slept with her mistakenly thinking that she was his wife as she might have slept in his bed or she was still found to be a virgin since actual penetration did not occur but pregnancy resulted only in ejaculation then she is given the benefit of the doubt if she did not explicitly confess to the act of *zinâ*.

Once *zinâ* has been proven beyond a shadow of doubt then the punishment will be administered irrespective of the status and the prominence of the offender. The glowing example is that of the punishment given to 'Ubaidûllâh, alias Abî Shamhah, the second son of Khalîf 'Umar.[18]

157

One day he passed by the house of a Jew, drank wine and got intoxicated. He saw a sleeping woman and committed *zinâ* with her. She became pregnant. When she got a son, she came to the Prophetic Mosque and placed the child in Khalîf 'Umar's lap saying: *'O Commander of the faithful, take this child as you have greater right over him than myself.'* Then she explained that it was the child of his son Abî Shamhah. Khalîf 'Umar asked her whether it was legitimate. The lady replied: *'From my side it is legitimate but from his side it is illegitimate.'* (Since the lady was not a willing accessory to the crime but was forced into it, therefore the resultant product i.e. the child, was a legitimate action on her behalf because she was the biological mother.) Then she told the whole story. Khalîf 'Umar went home and confirmed that his son had committed the crime although he felt very much ashamed of it. The Khalîf caught him by the collar to take him to the Mosque of the Prophet ﷺ. Abî Shamhah asked him where he was taking him. The Khalîf replied that he was taking him to the Companions of the Prophet ﷺ in the Mosque so that he may take from him the right of Allâh in this world before it is taken from him in the next world. His son requested that he be punished there and then so that the Khalîf may not be put to disgrace in the presence of the Companions. Khalîf 'Umar replied: *'O son you have already disgraced yourself and your father. We must go in their presence.'* 'Umar ordered Maflah to lash him. When he was given seventy stripes his son appealed to the Companions of the Prophet ﷺ to intervene. The Companions requested 'Umar to stop. 'Umar replied: *'O Companions of the Prophet ﷺ, have you not read in the Qur'ân, 'Do not show mercy over them.'* He was given one hundred stripes as a result of which Abî Shamhah passed away. Then Khalîf 'Umar took him to his house, gave him a bath and buried him. Here it must be pointed out that death was not intended, but only the administering of a hundred lashes. If incidentally, as in the present case and which is very rare, the criminal passes away whilst receiving his punishment, then it is not the fault of the administrator. One should not diminish the punishment of the culprit feeling compassion for him for this may obliterate its punitive aspect totally. It should be noted that most of the punishment carried out by the Prophet ﷺ and the four Râshidûn Caliphs were based on confession and not the proof. The woman was acquitted, displaying once more the Islâmic system of ultimate justice.

4.2.1.4 MUTUAL IMPERCATION

Under no circumstances should a husband intentionally deny the fatherhood of his child on flimsy evidence or mere imagination of his enemies. Such a drastic step will prove to be extremely harmful for the future of the child as well as his mother. But if there is concrete proof depicting the dishonesty of his wife and the resultant child being the product of an adulterous affair, then in such cases Sharî'ah does not want to impose the responsibility of the child on the husband of the woman, nor does it want to make him an illegitimate heir to his property. This is where the provision of mutual impercation becomes operational.

It is against human nature for one of the spouses who catches the other committing adultery to be able to co-exist in a tension free environment. The accuser will become miserable being haunted by doubts at every moment of his conscious state. English courts never allow a married couple to give evidence against each other. It is unfair to ask him to produce one eye-witness, let alone four because the accusation partly affects him as well.

First four witnesses shall be demanded of the man who accuses his wife of adultery. If he produces four witnesses then the woman shall be given the punishment of adultery. If he does not produce four witnesses then he shall be told to swear by God four times that he is truthful in the accusation - he did not tell a lie in casting upon his wife the imputation of adultery. In other words these are the four witnesses on oath in place of witnesses of men.

It has been mentioned that one of the companions of the Prophet 鑾, Hilâl ibn Ummaya, came back home at night and found his wife committing adultery with someone. He actually witnessed them on the act and overheard their conversation. Immediately he hurried to the Prophet 鑾 and narrated what he had seen and heard. This was a period when the verse pertaining to the slanderers had already been revealed. The Prophet 鑾 advised him to produce evidence or else he could be lashed eighty stripes since there was no alternative. The Prophet 鑾 was about to order punishment when divine revelation intervened. He recited it to those present with Hilâl and sent for the wife. When the wife presented herself she was told of the accusation and the revelation was read to her. Allâh Ta'âlâ declared:

> *"And for those who launch a charge against their spouses, and have in support no evidence but their own, their solitary evidence can be received if they bear witness four times with an oath by Allâh that they are solemningly telling the truth; and the fifth oath should be that they solemnly invoke the curse of Allâh on themselves if they tell a lie. But it would avert the punishment from the wife, if she bears witness four times with an oath by Allâh Ta'âlâ that her husband is telling a lie; and the fifth oath should be that she solemnly invokes the wrath of Allâh on herself if her accuser is telling the truth."*[19]

They were then told that if the husband is a slanderer he is to confess and face the punishment, a flogging of eighty lashes; or if the wife had really committed adultery she is to admit and face stoning to death. Both Hilâl and his wife had sworn. He swore four times saying that he was telling the truth. Then he was told to curse himself. He swore cursing himself if he was telling a lie.

Then it was the wife's turn. She took the oath four times that he was telling a lie. When she was ordered to invoke the wrath (punishment) of Allâh on herself if her husband was telling the truth, she initially became hesitant. Then she made up her mind saying that she would not be the cause of the shame of her parents. She swore the fifth oath cursing herself if her husband was telling the truth. Thus neither of them was punished by the Prophet 鱀, but were perpetually separated.

If she had confessed her guilt, she would have been given the punishment for *zinâ*. If the husband had hesitated and refused taking the required oaths, he would have been given the punishment for *qadhf* (slander). According to Imâm Abû Hanîfah, if he had refused to take oaths, he should have been imprisoned until he agrees to take the oath or the wife confessed her guilt, or that the husband withdrew the accusation or he divorced his wife. Imâms Mâlik, Shâfi'î and Ahmad ibn Hanbal express a different opinion. If the husband refuses to take the required oaths, he will be given punishment for *qadhf* which equals eighty lashes. If the wife refuses to take oaths of innocence, she will be deemed guilty of *zinâ* and will be given the punishment accordingly. Imâm Abû Hanîfah insists here too she must be detained until she takes oaths.[20]

While the *Qâdî* (Islâmic judge) hears the case, the husband will have two alternatives. He may retract or withdraw the charge before the end of the trials which will immediately bring the case to an end and there will be no need to take any other action nor would there be any embarrassment for the wife. But if he persists in his attitude and takes the oath followed by the oaths of innocence of his wife, as we have described before, the suit of *li'ân* will be deemed complete. There will be no need of pronouncement of divorce by the *qâdî* according to both Imâm Ahmad ibn Hanbal and Imâm Mâlik.[21] But according to Imâm Abu Hanîfah, it will still be incumbent upon the judge to pronounce divorce and dissolve the marriage. Imâm Shafi'î, however, is of the opinion that the moment the husband finishes taking his oaths of *li'ân*, declaring that his wife had committed adultery and invoking the curse of Allâh upon himself if he were a liar, he has shattered the mutual affection and trust that he had in his wife. The moment the husband finishes taking the five oaths, *li'ân* is complete.[22] Therefore these five oaths in its entirety constitutes *li'ân*. After *li'ân*, once the marriage is dissolved by the *qâdî*, it will result in irrevocable divorce according to all the schools of Islâmic Jurisprudence with the exception of Imâm Abû Hanîfah who is of the opinion that if the husband later declares that he had undertaken false oaths and lied, then after the respective punishment is inflicted upon him, he is once more at liberty to remarry her and shoulder the responsibility of the child.[23]

In the context of the permission granted by Islâm to a husband in divorcing his wife, the case of accusation of the wife by the husband takes an entirely different complexion from what it has in the western legal system. In Western countries, the spouse who decides to obtain a divorce has to plead that his or her partner is guilty of adultery and only on the basis of this plea can divorce be granted by a court of law. This was necessarily a potent reason for making false accusations. But in Islâm even if a Muslim catches his wife in an actual act of adultery, which is not generally possible, it is still necessary for him to produce four witnesses who have seen the act itself. In most cases it would be difficult to find witnesses. Therefore, the husband will have to swear in the "Sharî'ah" court four times to the act of his wife's adultery and in addition invoke a curse on himself if he is not telling the truth. It will be a prima facie proof of the wife's guilt. If the wife similarly swears her innocence four times and then she invokes a curse on herself if she is not telling the truth, she will be acquitted of the charge. But if she refuses to take the oath, the charge will be deemed proved against her and she will have to face the punishment. Whatever happens, once the oaths are taken the marriage will be dissolved since it is quite impossible that the spouses would ever be able to live in peace and harmony after such an experience.[24]

4.2.2. ISLÂMIC AND SECULAR LAW

In many societies the scandalous accusations in courts between spouses is regarded as the easiest method of obtaining divorces. Worst still is that majority of these allegations are fabricated cases. In some instances, a lengthy waiting period of almost two years is required before a decree of divorce is given.[25] In the interim period the separated couple are free to satiate their sexual appetite without any restrictions imposed whatsoever with any consenting partners.

The divine ordinance of *rajm* alone is a solution to the recent increase of abductions, fornications, adultery, debauchery and indiscriminate criminal and indecent sexual assaults on females. The measure seems to be the most severe but the evil is also the most heinous, creating chaos and disturbance in society. It has been established that leniency with criminals of this nature merely encourages their immoral pursuits. No measure short of an extreme penalty can stop these offenders. Light punishment displays indeed a very low standard of sexual moral sense of the people. This also illustrates that the Prophet 	ﷺ possessed the greatest moral character in the world and he attached the utmost importance to morality. Let the critics of the Prophet's ﷺ character ponder now over this point in judging the true character of the Prophet. The breach of the greatest trust which is imposed in a man or a woman, the breach which ruins families, destroys household peace, deprives innocent children of their loving mother, a beloved husband of his dear wife, is not looked upon as seriously as the breach of trust of a few rands. This lack of sexual morality gives a sense of great severity according to the Islâmic sentence in the minds of the modern educated man.

The Western law does not hold fornication or adultery by itself as a crime, it becomes a crime only when it is committed forcibly i.e. rape. In contrast to this, the Islâmic law looks upon fornication by itself as a crime, and regards rape or the act of encroachment on the rights of the husband or wife (adultery) as additional crimes. This basic difference between viewpoints of the two systems of law gives rise to the difference in the punishment of the offence. In the case of rape, the Western law rests content with the sentence of imprisonment only; in case of adultery with a married woman it requires the adulterer to pay compensation to the husband. This punishment cannot act as a deterrent, it rather encourages the offenders. That is why fornication and adultery is on the increase in the countries where this law is in force. In contrast to this the Islâmic Law punishes fornication and adultery so severely that the society is automatically cleansed of this crime for a long time. This is why it has never become rampant in the countries where the Islâmic law punishment for it is inflicted, since it so terrifies the whole nation that no one dares commit it. In a way it performs psychological surgery on the minds of those having criminal tendencies, thus instinctively reforming them.

The Western nations abhor the infliction of a hundred lashes or stoning to death. This is not because they dislike the idea of physical torture. It is because their moral sense has not yet fully developed. At first they regarded fornication and adultery as something indecent; now they look upon it as fun, as a pastime which amuses two persons for a little while. Therefore, they want the law to tolerate this act, and not regard it seriously. Obviously, a person who harbours such thoughts would regard a hundred lashes or stoning to death as harsh, but if his rational faculties had developed, he would realize *zinâ*, whether it is committed voluntarily or forcefully, is in each case a social crime that affects the entire society. This will naturally make him modify his view about punishment, so that the society is saved from the hazards of these evils. He would have to admit that it is better to subject one or a few persons to severe physical torture for the salvation of multitudes of people from countless moral and sociological evils than to inflict light punishments on criminals and so jeopardise the well-being of not only the society but also of future generations.

The Western civilization emerged as a result of the urge of favouring the individual against the society, and it has been built on an exaggerated notion of the rights of the individual. Therefore, even if an individual harms the society to his hearts content, the Westerners do not feel ill at ease; they rather put up with it willingly, in most cases. But when the individual is proceeded against with a view to protecting the rights of society, they shudder with horror and all their sympathies go with the individual against society. Moreover, they also have the special characteristic of regarding feelings as more important than reason. Therefore, when they see the individual, as a particular case, being severely dealt with, they feel outraged at the sight of his suffering. But they do not seem to comprehend the far reaching consequences of the damage that is caused to society and the future generations.

Evil men of the modern era contend that if two members of society come together to enjoy each other for a while, society is not harmed. Why should it then interfere with their affair? Of course, society has every right to interfere if one party commits violence or fraud against the other, or becomes a nuisance to the community. But when there is no such apprehension and the matter is confined only to the seeking of pleasure between two persons, society should have no jurisdiction over them. For if the private affairs of individuals be meddled with in this manner, personal freedom will be reduced to nullity.

This concept of personal freedom is one of the absurdities of Western intellect. The social chain in which mankind is bound has not left any individual free from its hold in whatever he does or wherever he is. Whether behind closed doors, or within the protection of walls, he is inextricably linked with society as in the company of others. Therefore, when he is busy squandering his sexual energy aimlessly for temporary pleasure in a secret place, he is in fact sowing the seeds of anarchy and disruption in society and harming it morally, materially and socially. In his selfishness he is striking at the root of all those social institutions by which he benefitted as a member of society, but refused to support their maintenance and survival. When this dishonest person used his sexual energy without any intention of procreating, he in fact, in his personal way, struck a blow at the root of this system. He broke the contract by which he was bound as a human being; and he tried to shift the burden of his responsibility on to the shoulders of others. He is no asset, but in fact a cheat and a thief. To allow him any concession is to commit a crime against humanity.

In societies other than Islâm fornicators and adulterers are not punished at all for their wilful disrespect for chastity. This indeed inflames the passions of young men who disregard the value of sexual morality. The most precious jewel of chastity in a woman's crown of virtue can be compensated for a few coins. Until and unless every government implements the Islâmic code of sentencing every female with the male, there will never be a decrease in fornication, kidnapping and adultery.

Islâm has prescribed punishment in accordance to the nature of the crime. For example, a thief's hand is amputated, since it was the hand which was instrumental in committing the crime. Similarly, since fornication has been classified as a serious offence, an extremely severe punishment has been prescribed for it and a very stern attitude adopted towards those guilty of it. There exists no traces of softness or leniency, and its implementation, by way of compulsory public display, is really admonitory, although it may be a dreadful spectacle. It is also the instruction of the Qur'ân that since the fornicator has stained his modesty with the filth of a disgusting deed, why should there be any more secrecy about his punishment? Rather it must be widely publicised serving as an eye-opener to others. Allâh Ta'âlâ says:

> "And let a party of believers witness their punishment."[26]

The onlookers are also made aware of the presence of an infected individual who may repeat his crime if the opportunity arises. The Qur'ân cautions:

> "Let no man guilty of adultery or

165

fornication marry any but a woman
similarly guilty, or an unbeliever: nor let
any but such a man or an unbeliever marry
such a woman. "[27]

By logical reasoning the punishment for fornication ought to have been amputation of their private parts, thus inflicting pain to those specific organs that are the major role players in this act. But Islâm did not advocate such a policy. The reason for this is that the pleasure derived from fornication is not limited to the sexual organs alone, but every part of the body, every fibre of the nerves partakes of that unique pleasure, and therefore it is considered only justifiable Islâmically to prescribe such a punishment whereby the entire body is enveloped in extreme pain. Amputating the private parts only, would not have been complete since, coupled with pain, the punishment aims at public disgrace and admonition to the criminal. Since the sexual organs are always concealed, no one can witness them being damaged, hence it would not serve as a deterrent to would be offenders.

The second factor is that the punishment would have exceeded the crime, since amputation would have retarded his procreating potential, and could in all probability lead to his death. Therefore, since the risk involved is out of proportion to the purpose of the punishment, Islâm did not advocate it.

If those who are not prejudiced against the laws of Sharî'ah would reflect for a moment, it will become evident that if the Islâmic code of justice is implemented, it will definitely eradicate sexual offences and immorality which have currently reached epidemic proportions.

4.3   THE CARNAL APPETITES

Allâh Ta'âlâ has placed certain appetites and impulses in man so that he is impelled towards the various activities which guarantee the survival of the species. Among the appetites which an individual must satisfy for his personal survival is the consumption of food. The sexual appetite, however, is for the purpose of the survival of mankind. Sex is a strong driving force in the human species which demands satisfaction and fulfilment. Human beings have responded to the demands of the sexual appetite in different forms.

One way is to satisfy one's sexual need freely with whomever is available and whenever one pleases without any restraints of morality, custom or religion. This is the position of the advocates of free sex, for they do not believe in any ethical conduct. This philosophy reduces the human being to the status of an animal, and, if practiced universally, would result in the destruction of the family structure and of all society and is in conflict with the course of natural order.

Islâm duly recognizes the role of the sexual drive, facilitates its satisfaction through lawful channels, and just as it strictly prohibits illicit sex and perverted behaviour, it also accommodates for the regulation of this urge, allowing it to operate within certain limits, neither suppressing nor giving it free rein.

An attempt is now made to discuss the other sexual deviations currently in vogue in modern society.

4.3.1   THE MISTRESS

Society keeps silent over the conduct of the husband who marries one wife but keeps several mistresses and that of the wife who in spite of having a husband has illicit connections with several other men. But the same society will raise slogans of disgrace if someone were to announce a proposal permitting man to legally wed more than one partner. This is where 'western civilization' has made Islâm its target. These are the same westerners to whom the chastity of women has no value and is being plundered openly and is on the market as a trade commodity, but look on as unconcerned spectators. The freedom of sexual conduct and their shocking insensibility to morals has even prompted their thinkers to justify this Islâmic concession, rather than resorting to a few fleeting moments with a mistress.

A 'mistress' was originally a lady who received the romantic and sexual advances of her lover. Just as the word 'lover' has, through the years, come to indicate a definite sexual relationship, so too has the word 'mistress'. And this sexual relationship is by implication illicit, illegal and immoral.

A mistress is to a prostitute as a chauffeur is to a taxicab driver. The taxi driver offers his services for a set fee to anyone who can pay him. The chauffeur is exclusively in the employ of one person. With a prostitute a man undertakes a financial contract; with his wife, a social and legal one; but with his mistress he looks for superficial, emotional as well as sexual intimacy. A man will go to a prostitute simply for a release of sexual tension; he will pay her and he will leave. To his mistress, however, he will expect her to converse and build a relationship through which he could enjoy the excitements of a covert affair.

But what about the mistress herself, of her own feelings and motivations in the affair? There is an underlying immaturity in the character of a mistress or a 'mistress-type', which makes her choose, if she can, the role of the *other* woman. She needs love but prefers not to see the humdrum reality of married life. She enjoys sex but shies away from the obligations of children. She seeks power over her man but without taking the responsibility for his day-to-day needs.

Let us examine the mistress-stereotype. The typical mistress is between 28 and 32 years of age, single and usually in employment. Her job will be one which involves contact with a great many people, for she is very sociable and 'has a knack' with people in general and she aspires for well paid or prestigious posts, with bosses in particular. So she is a receptionist, in advertising or personnel, or she is a model. She may be extremely attractive or at least well-groomed, for she pays a great deal of attention to her looks. When she is in conversation she fiddles continually with her hair or her blouse or her skirt – both to reassure herself that she is presentable and to draw attention to her physical appearance.

She is one of the few women who is able to make friends of her ex-lovers. As for her present lover, she pesters him with questions about his wife – her reactions to their affair or how she behaves in bed. She cannot enjoy herself – by herself – and though she may be vain she has no confidence in her capacity to survive as a human being. She depends on others whom she feels she has to always fool, to disarm and to seduce. Often she enjoys outraging her lovers and her friends and enjoys, too, the delicious feeling that she has 'gotten away with it'. Her looks are her greatest ally, the bait by which she hooks the attention of men and women alike. She flirts at parties; she competes even with her women friends in looks and charm; and she finds nothing so exciting as a new admirer, to boost her morale. She is greedy for other people and extremely competitive, and in some ways it is the competition that excites her. Once she has won she has to move on to make another conquest. The lover, whose attention she has fought for, is discarded as a fool or plaything once he gives in to her. She demands affection, but when she gets it she has nothing to give in return. She does not know how to develop a love relationship though she is an expert at the preliminary encounters. The affair between a man and his mistress may happen for a variety of reasons – it may be the creation of a "love nest" filled with extravagance and luxury or it may be a guilt-ridden affair conducted in sordid hotel rooms. But all such affairs have in common the romance and illicit sexual gratification that accompanies it.

When things go wrong for her, disaster is reflected in illness of some kind – skin diseases, giddiness, tension or distress. When she does in fact suffer physical damage or undergo an operation, her world falls apart. Then there is only one remedy, to go out and find a new admirer, concealing the stench of her filthy past.

Therefore in Islâm it is more dignified for a person to be legally married to a second faithful wife rather than indulging in clandestine liaisons with a mistress who hops in bed with every admirer that showers her with extravagant luxuries. The position of current mistresses can definitely not compare with the position of slave girls in the Prophetic age since Islâm bestowed upon them a legal social status, whereby they did not indulge in sordid and clandestine illicit sexual encounters. The Prophet 鑗 said:

> *"Any man who has a slave girl whom he educates properly, teaches good manners, manumits and marries will get a double reward"* [28]

4.3.2   THE GIGOLO (MALE ESCORT)

Gigolos were essentially dancing partners paid to steer middle-aged women around the dance floor. Gigolo, which was related to the French word for a tall, slim woman was first used to describe professional dancing partners although there is a much earlier English word, "gig", which means "something that whirls". Today, still called a gigolo, the kept man's only dancing may be to the sexual tune of an 'employer' who knows exactly what she wants.[29]

For some men, taking money from women is a way of life. On the French Reviera in the summer, in Hawaii during the divorce season, in London, New York or Paris, wherever women are looking for men, and have the money to pay, the gigolo lies in wait.

At one end of the scale this may be little more than male prostitution. Brothels accommodating women, especially those in their aging years, are scarce. But as more women become executives, university teachers and take up progressively more demanding jobs, they may increasingly find themselves seeking short-term sexual release. In many de luxe hotels a phone call to the hall porter will produce a handsome masseur, whose fee is based on the 'intimacy' of the massage.

Another starting point for the gigolo is in the free atmosphere of a holiday resort. Single woman on vacation may happily dispense money and gifts to the men who please them. And there are always parties, theatres, racecourses, fashion pageants, dances and dinners at which the gigolo can indicate his availability and which may lead to a longer relationship than the massage or the holiday romance. In cases where the relationship is almost entirely sexual and short-term, both gigolo and client may be able to treat it as a businesslike arrangement. She pays and he guarantees satisfaction. The gigolo may simply be after money or position and realize that he can trade on his looks. But more likely there is something in his nature that means he actually prefers the gigolo relationship to any other. He may be passive – instead of seeking a partner he wishes them to choose him and suffer the embarrassment of possible rejection just as the following article appearing in the *"Sunday Times"* under the caption *Widow's expensive 'son'* indicates:

He was 23. She was twice his age. But Johanna Nell and Rudi Smit were the best of friends. The wealthy widow and the handsome bachelor saw each other almost every day. She took him on holiday to Cape Town. They had a ball together at the Carousel and at the Sun City. She paid the R50 000 deposit on his Mercedes-Benz and bought him a cowboy suit for R1500. She made several other payments to him.

The friendship flourished for five months. But then it turned sour...[30]

On her part the woman may be lacking the confidence to believe that a man can love her for herself and prefers to ensure his love with payments. She may, in middle age, like the energetic love-making and vigour of younger men whom, she feels will not normally think of her as a sexual partner. A 'mature' woman may enjoy taking a lover, buying him clothes, giving him jewelry and taking him to expensive restaurants, but she will also want to end the relationship at her convenience. More often the woman is looking for the imitation of love – and the gigolo survives by paying lip service to romance. Sometimes the woman wishes merely to demonstrate her economic power – and her pleasure comes from the humiliation she is able to inflict on a man totally dependent on her.

Therefore the ideal gigolo–client relationship occurs when a woman who happens to have money finds a man who attracts her and who can respond to all the opportunities she offers. She is seeking sexual release and friendship, but has no intention of bending too far; he needs financial support even at the cost of his ultimate rejection. Just as a wife raised to her husband's social position, so is the gigolo raised to his mistress's rank. In return he is her escort and lover.

However, the macho image of the gigolo is dented at the thought of a woman taking control of the relationship, which may lead to quarrels and separations. Even a worm likes to insist that it lays down the rules. Men have been classified as guardians and protectors and not vice-versa as the Qur'ân mentions:

> *"Men are the protectors and maintainers of women, because Allâh has given the one more (strength) than the other and because they support them from their means".*[31]

Justice demands that men are the defenders and protectors of women. They are their maintainers and cherishers. They are the managers of their affairs and therefore should expend of their wealth on their expenses for food, clothing and lodging and other necessities of life. In direct contrast to this male orientated role in society, the gigolo trades his masculinity and survives by the illegal financial support of flirting women.

4.3.3 WIFE SWAPPING

Throughout history, women have been regarded as pawns in the scramble for profit, property, political and social power. Today there's a variation. If you are a married couple you should not be astonished if you are welcomed with 'open arms' by your neighbours, friends or clubs catering exclusively for the wedded. They require your services and are prepared to render theirs in this wife swapping game.

What exactly is meant by 'wife swapping'? Who usually initiates such a relationship and what kind and class of people are most likely to indulge in it?

Any examination of the wife-swapping craze must start from the understanding that it is essentially a problem of the 'highly civilized' West and would appear to have become most widespread in the United States, Britain and some European and Scandinavian countries. However, in some of the more primitive cultures – such as the Eskimos – the "loan" of a mate to a friend who may have travelled hundreds of kilometres between one group of igloos and another is accepted as "natural courtesy". The worship of the Greek god Bacchus also involved wild orgies during which mates were exchanged freely.

Sociologists feel that the involvement in wife swapping exposes basic flaws in the marriage relationship. A couple may be unsuited to each other sexually; their attitude towards each other may have been gradually soured for a number of reasons – disagreements about whether to have children or arguments over money, etc. They may in addition, read and watch just sufficient permissive material which may appear to encourage such filthy practices.

But it is hard to see how a marriage suffering from any such flaws can be helped by wife-swapping, even if the needs for fantasies by the husband and wife are satisfied initially. It is extremely rare for a swapping relationship to last for any length of time and the couple then find themselves together again with all the old problems to face up to and, in all likelihood, some new ones to cope with. Marriage guidance counsellors have reported numerous cases of couples whose already shaky marriage has been finally broken up after indulgence in wife-swapping.

Some of the characteristics of the swapping couple are that they are relatively young (in the 25 to 35 age bracket); they belong to the upper and middle class and generally well off; and, in every case there has been recent tensions within the marriage. The following is the classical example.

Lynne and Jason, both 24, had been married for two years and had no children. Lynne explained how they had first become involved in wife-swapping:

"We went to a party and heard some of the couples talking about wife-swapping quite openly. The next evening we were chatting about it, trying to find out what each other had heard, and he told me that one of the couples we knew – Don and Vicki – had more or less propositioned us . . . That was it. I thought if Jason can do it then he can hardly complain if his wife enjoys herself a bit on the side." [32]

Another method of wife-swapping, most prevalent in the United States is the "organized orgy" where couples answer advertisements and gather with the definite intention of enjoying either "open" intercourse (where

173

all the couples perform in the same room) or "closed" sessions where individual couples retire to different rooms. There is evidence, from the growing number of "personal contact" magazines that are easily available that this practice is also spreading rapidly to our shores.

There is also the "key game". At the party the husbands put their car keys in a jar. Each then picks a key (not their own). For the rest of the weekend the key and the car to which it belongs are his. He gets accessories too. One of them is the owner's wife.

So what does the experience of the wife swappers reveal? More than anything it shows how easily such a situation can develop and how dangerous it can become. In this fourway relationship someone always ends up getting hurt. Even a dog would not tolerate its partner publicly mating with its friend or neighbour. Yet there is every sign that wife-swapping continues unrestricted. On any bookstall, magazine or classified sections of the newspaper may be found *adult amusement* sections with ads such as: "Swinging couple, looking for action and fun. Would like to meet couple similarly inclined. Broad minds (and photographs) essential. Please reply urgently . . . ".

The continued spread of wife-swapping which is the product of the permissive society and the liberated female, really destroys the institution of marriage, since such a sexual experiment creates problems and hazards which is beyond the control of the participants. Islâm abhors such open licentiousness and immorality.

4.3.4   WHY DO AFFAIRS OCCUR?

To many it is rather fashionable to have affairs, and that too, in a way demanding the public's attention. Women and men who do not jump into bed with someone else, and proudly say so, tend to be regarded as old fashioned.

Having affairs, therefore is becoming popular. And those who would not have dreamed of deviating from the straight path a decade ago, are now also beginning to have second thoughts. This is because the factors that lead to unfaithfulness are many but probably the most common denominator for the popularity of affairs is the present permissive social climate.

The Pill has had the blame for an increase in marital infidelity and sexual immorality. No one is going to leap into bed with someone other than their wife or husband simply because they can be sure of no nasty consequences nine months later.

Prior to delving into the reasons as to why there is an increase in extramarital sex it is first important to discover why there is *any* at all. Ask the people who actually do have affairs with other people's wives and husbands and you will get a more precise answer. They were, they will tell you, bored – bored with their mate, and with the sexual relationship they had with their mate – bored with the monotony of married life, be it ever so happy – and bored with the restrictions of that life as well. They longed for some excitement, both sexual and emotional, and some reassurance that they still possessed the ability to inspire that excitement.

But then, we all get bored. All would like the excitement of a little sexual stimulation now and again. So why do we all not turn into sexual adventurers?

Some conservative Westerner may say that the greatest deterrent is fear – fear of getting caught, of throwing away everything, of hurting innocent wives, husbands and children. There is also the fear of getting hurt yourself. Women are more likely to be afraid of starting an affair than men since they are more likely to be caught. It is easy for a married man to have an extramarital love life during office hours, pleading long business appointments. But this is difficult for a woman, for who will take care of her apartment and her baby in the hours that she is illicitly satiating her sexual appetite? She has no secretary to cover up for her – nor any non-existent meetings to attend – unless, of course she is a business woman herself. The married woman with a career is in the same "liberated" position as a man, which is one of the reasons for the increase in extramarital sex. This is why, nowadays, women feel that they are not simply wives or would be wives, but can conduct their own lives and careers more or less as they wish. They feel free to enjoy their own money, their own time, and if they wish the liberty to conduct a passionate affair.

There are, however, certain genuine cases where a family due to financial circumstances, is compelled to send women out to work so that they can make ends meet. Why do the advocates of female emancipation not divert their time, energy and money to creating some sort of home-industries for women ?

If fear does not stop you, they contend, then it is a nobler emotion called loyalty. To the loyal, the crime is not getting caught, it is doing something to be caught at. You do not commit the crime because that in itself would damage the relationship. You would not be the same loving person if you loved someone else – you would have sold out and betrayed the ideal. Such code of conduct is extremely rare and hard to find. Therefore such faithfulness and loyalty is considered less and less important. As long as you do not hurt anybody else, they argue, what harm is done?

Another reason a man engages in extramarital affairs, they say, is to prove himself – again. He has the feeling that life is slipping away, particularly if he is middle aged. He panics and wonders what he has been missing. He feels that however loving and loyal a wife he has she will ultimately fail in creating the thrill and excitement that he craves. Woman also feel this need, but are satisfied more simply. Words of affection or praise coming from a new man in her life can reassure her.

Besides assuming that she is falling in love, a woman will rush into an extramarital bed at once for another reason – revenge. Betrayed and hurt wives are easy targets for seducers. It is an act that says "Anything you can do I can do better." But often revenge is sour, and the bitter taste remains in everybody's mouth.

Often, adultery is a symptom that something is wrong with the marriage. A healthy marriage will never survive a series of secret relationships. An affair can lead from dangerous flirtations to the divorce courts.

But from where did this all start? At a party? In the office? At a crowded public recreation park? The answer is all of the above, and even more. The unrestricted intermingling of the sexes at the working place is by far the biggest breeding ground for such affairs. It is not only the boss's secretary who is capitalising on her charms to climb up the promotion ladder, but it is the woman executive who is by far a greater threat, since there is so much of common ground between the two.

The above-mentioned incidents are directly related to extramarital relations, but what about sex before marriage or 'experimental sex'. The argument advanced is that such a type of sex gives both parties a chance to find out whether or not they are sexually compatible. No insane person, it is said, wants to find himself firmly tied to a partner whose sexual needs are totally different from his own, and exploring each others sexual habits is the best way to prevent this

Those with a strict religious upbringing and who believe in chastity and fidelity before marriage counter attack with the theory that love and sex are inseparable, and that sexual fulfilment is something that develops with time, love and the exclusiveness of one woman / one man relationship.

It is rather interesting to note that many a male, particularly in certain social levels and under the guise of sexual compatibility, is prone to seek sexual enjoyment from every available girl, while insisting that the girl he marries should be a virgin when he first has sex with her. He will defend his 'right' and any other man's right to try to secure coitus from another man's sister or wife, but he may fight or kill the man who attempts to secure sex from his own sister, daughter, wife or fiancee. Therefore pre-marital sex, courting and all the evils that go with it under the guise of sexual compatibility is merely a ploy used by the crazed sexual maniac in sampling the delicacies and charms of every available female.

Islâm has penetrated into the evil designs of the characters of such illicit affairs and not only exposed their perverted tendencies but also sounded a grave warning to would-be offenders.

177

4.3.5   THE NYMPHOMANIAC

Nymphomania is defined as the excessive sexual desire in women. Nymphomania or madness of the womb – is not a modern day occurrence. Basically a hysterical condition, it has revealed itself in a variety of forms throughout the centuries. The frenzied dances of the Middle Ages; rituals to ward off evil spirits; the prancing of the ancient maidens of Greece; and in this era, the wild screams of teenage maidens watching a pop idol are all categories of this craze.

A seventeenth century physician, Philippe Pinel, who made a study of hysteria, made this announcement:

"Nymphomania is most frequently caused by lustful reading, by severe restraint and secluded life, by the habit of masturbation, and extreme sensitivity of the uterus, and a skin eruption upon genital organs .... In the beginning the imagination is constantly obsessed by lustful or obscure matters, (and) conducts a private battle between sentiments of modesty and the impulse towards frantic desires. In the second phase she abandons herself to the voluptuous leanings, she stops fighting them, she forgets all rules of modesty and propriety; her looks and actions are provocative, her gestures indecent; she begins to solicit at the approach of the first man. She makes efforts to throw herself into his arms. She threatens and flares up if the man tries to resist her. In the third phase her mental alienation is complete, her obscenity disgusting, her fury blinded with only the desire to wound and to revile. She is on fire though with fever, and finally she manifests all the different symptoms of a violently maniacal condition." [33]

They are to be found wherever exhibitionism is required and wherever they can display their sexuality. Models, cabaret artists, waitresses, office playgirls, girls in the army, airline stewardesses ... all move in a sphere within which nymphomaniac can flourish. She will display petty jealousies; she will moan about the other girls, she will complain about her food and surroundings. Marriage holds no terror for her and at times she can be an exciting and fascinating woman.

She dresses to 'kill' and stalks her prey favouring red and black at night and short skirts and hunting boots during the day. She is more often fulfilled and reaches orgasm by oral sexuality rather than by vaginal intercourse. Always dissatisfied, the true nymphomaniac will exhaust the most athletic of lovers in an endless quest for the "ultimate orgasm". She will drag any hot blooded creature to bed to quench her appetite. The hunger for material things, jewellery, wealth, property – all are her characteristics. The following is a typical case of a married woman:

"Claudine was a nymphomaniac. Life was a hunt and every man who entered into her vampire greed discovered that she had a voracious and completely insatiable appetite ... She was a hypermarket of sexual wares, as she half stalked, half glided among the guests. No man, other than one totally bereft of sight, could possibly mistake the goods that Claudine offered on her well-stocked shelves. Greedily, frantically, she took all she could from sexual relationships, but it was never enough. The restlessness that drove her from one man to the next was never quelled ... She had succeeded in reducing her husband to total impotence. Physically there was nothing wrong with him; he just could not stand up to the sustained sexual hostility and aggression inherent in his wife's nymphomania." [34]

The following is a description of the unmarried maiden:

"Yvette, the daughter of well-to-do-parents, was 17 when her blatantly promiscuous behaviour so alarmed and offended them – they were themselves extremely religious and considered they had brought up their daughter to the strict moral ethics of the church – that they took her for psychiatric treatment. Yvette's opening gambit was an attempt to seduce the psychiatrist. She discovered a zip undone and asked for his help. She reclined on his couch in such a manner that only a code of practice delivered him from professional misconduct." [35]

Nymphomaniacs, therefore, live in a world of either light or total darkness; and the darkness is most likely to envelop her if she is unable to fulfil her wishes. A failure to make a conquest can prove fatal and sometimes even lead to attempted suicide.

To some 'sceptical and enlightened' modernist the question arises that if a multiple marriage can be contracted as a legitimate outlet for an excessive sexual desire of men, would the same provision be extended to women?

The question of a woman having more than one sexual partner raises a number of problems. One of them is the uncertainty of the paternity of the child, and this is something which will be very disturbing to men, not to be sure that a certain child is their own or that it might be the child of another partner. A society or country abounding with such products would definitely confuse the human genealogy. From a sexo - sociological viewpoint, it is possible for a man to have sexual relations with all his wives, if he has more than one, and impregnate them. But if a female has more than one partner simultaneously, she can, even in that case, be impregnated only by one.

4.3.6 SOLO SEX (MALE AND FEMALE MASTURBATION)

Masturbation is defined as the manual stimulation of the male or female genitals, not by sexual intercourse, designed to produce an orgasm. At some stage and especially during the adolescent years, most people of both sexes find pleasure in touching, pressing, or stroking their own genitals when they are alone and thinking about somebody of the opposite sex.

Most of those who masturbate also reach a climax of excitement and pleasure which is called orgasm. In the male this occurs with the ejaculation of the semen. No such outer sign of the woman's climax is visible. With both sexes the physical feeling is very much the same as that experienced with sexual intercourse.

Masturbation is most common with people who have reached physical maturity, but it is not unknown in children of all ages. Many people are introduced to it through their own venture, whilst some learn it from others.

The earliest reference to it is made in the Old Testament where it is remembered by the *'Sin of Onan'*.[36] *"And it happend when he "went to" the wife of his brother, then he spoilt the seed towards the ground"*. Onan was instructed to have sexual intercourse with the wife of his dead brother. He refused and 'spilled the semen on the ground.' Therefore spilling one's seed is against Jewish and Christian doctrine, and is frequently quoted by clergymen to deter those with an inclination towards masturbation. In contrast to this there is historical evidence that masturbation was greatly prized in some culture. Excavations in the Nile delta have revealed that the ladies of ancient Egypt often had dildoes buried next to them which meant that masturbation was quite dear to them. Girls in some African tribes are actually taught the art of self-abuse. One of the physical results of prolonged female masturbation is an elongation of the labia, which some tribes consider to be extremely attractive sexually.

Women normally refrain from direct manipulation of the clitoris because of its extreme sensitivity. They tend towards a more general stimulation which is maintained during the period of orgasm often extending the time of arousal to three or four orgasms, which is greater in intensity than the one derived through sexual intercourse. Old ladies and widowed or divorced women may return to the masturbatory habit of their teens when sexual pressures become intolerable. Those who respected the code of morality and never masturbated, this is never likely to occur even now. Similarly, pregnant women with previous masturbatory experience may want to also experience it. Some women also masturbate at the beginning of their menstruation, arguing that it eases their menstrual flow and relieve cramps and backaches. Surprisingly enough, those chaste women who do not indulge in such a vile outlet, have no such complaints. The average female will usually be satisfied with three to five manually induced orgasms, whereas mechanical stimulation, as with the electric vibrator, is less tiring and could induce her to go on to long sessions of an hour or more during which she may have 20-25 consecutive orgasms. She will stop only when totally exhausted.

Some women even masturbate by actually watching others do so. This is a typical example:

"Marge and I are apartment neighbours. One morning while she was complaining about her dull sex life with her husband, I blurted out that I had solved a similar situation by masturbating. This broke the ice between us and soon we were discussing the subject quite openly. When she left I hurried into the bedroom and lay down to fantasize about her masturbating herself, in no time I had an orgasm ... I suggested she return so we could do it together ... Never had I experienced anything as erotic or as sexually exciting, and even today it is a constant thrill to watch another woman bring herself to the point of no return ..." [37]

As far as men are concerned, the most popular method is direct manipulation of the penis, though some prefer to move it against a bed or some other object. Most men fantasize during masturbation, while some enjoy observing their genitals. Men are also likely to masturbate more when opportunities for sexual intercourse are not readily available such as in prison or in the army. University–adolescents are the most energetic male masturbators. Although masturbation slows down the advancing years some old men do return to a dependence on masturbation coupled with immoral sexual gratification as this report suggests:

"This man was 63 years old ... He had had homosexual relations with 600 pre-adolescent males, heterosexual relations with 200 pre-adolescent females, intercourse with countless adults of both sexes and with animals of many species ... He had set down a family tree going back to his grandparents, and of 33 family members he had had sexual contacts with 17. His grandmother introduced him to heterosexual intercourse, and his first homosexual experience was with his father ... and (he) had employed elaborate techniques of masturbation ... At one point he said he was able to masturbate to ejaculation in 10 seconds from a flaccid start. Kinsey and I, knowing how much longer it took everyone else, expressed our disbelief, whereupon our subject calmly demonstrated it to us." [38]

Most people masturbate for the first time in adolescence. Kinsey found that masturbation in boys normally began at the age of 14 or 15. Two-thirds of his sample achieved their first orgasm through masturbation, and most of them had heard about it before trying themselves. Girls were more likely to discover masturbation independently and at a later stage than boys. Both in boys and, when it occurs, in girls, this adolescent masturbation paves the way for things to come just as Jeremy describes it:

"I started 'doing it' about three years ago when I was twelve. Some other guys told me about it but I didn't believe them, so I tried it myself. I don't think its right, but I just can't help it – I get the urge and then, before I know it. I'm doing it again. I felt so (terrible) afterwards. Most of the

182

time I just think about different girls like, you know, their bodies and everything. Then I think about the party when this girl let me feel her all over. Every time I think about it I want to do it some more." [39]

Those who achieve insufficient satisfaction from sexual intercourse and return to masturbation, or never give it up, the torments are great. Everywhere they look, their friends are unashamedly enjoying the pleasures of normal sexual relationship. No part of society caters for them and they are even cowardly shy to campaign for "Masturbators Liberation." Sex life for most of them is fairly empty.

One of the most humiliating problems that the constant male masturbator suffers from when he attempts to have sexual relationship is premature ejaculation or the failure to maintain an erection. When he is masturbating, he tends to reach his orgasm as quickly as possible, but in sexual intercourse he normally has to attempt to control his excitement, which can impose a great strain on a person who indulged in self-abuse over a lengthy period.

Therefore people who continuously masturbate, lose out all round. The physical pleasure becomes reduced to a natural act like urinating or excreting, and at the back of their minds there is an awareness that they are missing on the real pleasures of life. No adult can honestly claim to masturbate without a guilty feeling of complete uselessness. Masturbation is merely an exhaustive, rather than constructive undertaking, resulting in nothing but total loss. Once orgasm has been achieved there is nothing else left, except for a feeling of complete emptiness.

The following extracts from the writings of a dignified physician of the Unânî medicine will give one some idea of the damage done through masturbation:

"Most often, students, bachelors or widowers and hypocritical godly persons are its victims. It is such an evil practice that has ruined many families and many more are being ruined today. The lack of manly vigor and decline in the standard of young men's health is evidence enough for this horrible social evil, eating into the vitals of an otherwise healthy nation. If only our young men could foresee the consequences of this evil

183

at their own hands bring on them! It can be said with some certainty that eighty percent of our young men are the victims of masturbation. This accursed practice affects equally the heart, the brain, the liver, the stomach, the kidneys along with the reproductive organs. This practice makes the muscles and the nerves of the reproductive organ sagging and lifeless. Accumulation of fluids in the veins makes it unfit for its normal function. There is extreme feebleness in the power of erection. The heat of the friction between the delicate muscles of the organ and the tough hide of the hand damages the former beyond repair." [40]

Following the excitement which accompanies masturbation, comes the feeling of shame, anger, humiliation, and the sense of futility. This sense of futility and humiliation deepens as the years go on, into a suppressed rage, because of the impossibility to escape. The one thing that it seems impossible to escape from, once the habit is formed, is masturbation. It goes on and on, on into old age, in spite of marriage. And it always carries this secret feeling of futility and humiliation. And this is, perhaps, the deepest and most dangerous cancer of our civilization. Instead of being a comparatively harmless vice, masturbation is certainly the most dangerous sexual vice that a society can be afflicted with, in the long run.

4.3.6.1 MASTURBATION UNDER ISLÂMIC LAW

Islâm strictly forbids the waste of seminal fluid through masturbation. The one who discharges his seminal fluid with his hand is damned. This evil practice removes the normal bright look of a man's face, and he looks melancholy and dejected. He loses his health and quite frequently his vitality and sexual stamina through this disgusting practice.

The Qur'ân declares:

> "The Believers are those who abstain from
> sex except with those joined to them in
> marriage bond, or those whom their right
> hand possess for (in their case) they are free
> from blame, but those who crave something
> beyond that are transgressors." [45]

MASTURBATION UNDER ISLAMIC LAW

Beyond the wife and slave woman all ways and means of sexual satisfaction are unlawful. They include adultery, sodomy, masturbation, etc. From this it can be deduced that masturbation falls under the context 'but those who crave ...' and is therefore immoral and a sin in Islâm.

Views expressed by the Shâfi'î jurists on this matter are clearly illustrated by Imâm Nawawî whose opinion is typical of the Shâfi'î Jurists as a whole. He declared that masturbation was absolutely forbidden. It was only permitted when it was performed by the hand of a man's wife or concubine, for he has a right to the enjoyment of her hand as he has to the rest of her body.[43]

The author of Subul al Salâm according to al Juzairî, states:

> "Some of the Hanbalî and Hanafî Jurists
> are of the opinion that masturbation may
> be permissible in the event that one fears
> (that is, not engaging in it) would lead to
> his committing adultery or fornication. But
> be cautious that such a view is weak and
> is not to be relied upon." [44]

According to Mâlikî school of thought masturbation is deduced to be illegal from the following hadîth narrated by 'Abdullâh ibn Mas'ûd ﷺ:

> "We were with the Prophet ﷺ while we
> were young and had no wealth whatsoever.
> The Prophet ﷺ said: "O assembly of
> youths; whoever amongst you possesses
> the physical and financial resources to
> marry, should do so, because it helps him
> guard his modesty, and whoever is unable
> to marry, should fast, as fasting diminishes
> his sexual power." [45]

Therefore, the jurists of this school are of the opinion that if masturbation was permitted, the Prophet ﷺ would have acknowledged its permissibility because this is much simpler than fasting. Since the Prophet ﷺ did not mention it, demonstrates that it is prohibited.

From all the evidence presented so far, it can be seen that Sharî'at not only classifies this type of unnatural wastage of seminal fluid as illegal, but also advocated strict measures for its prevention.

4.3.7 FANTASIZING

Fantasies and dreams have one basic difference: a dream is predominantly something over which very little conscious control can be exercised, whereas fantasies can be induced and, to some extent, directed. It can therefore be said, that fantasy is that extravagant imagination and fanciful vision by which people tend to escape from the realities of life. Most people fantasize more than they think and it has become the latest craze in this jet set age for a man to imagine that the woman he is making love to is not his faithful wife who was loyal to him for the past ten to fifteen years, but the scantily clad model, revealing more flesh than cloth, who is doing the cat walk on the fashion show parade. It must simultaneously be pointed out that day-dreaming about one's beloved and legal wife cannot be classified in the same category as fantasizing about a strange woman.

It is argued that at the beginning of a love affair, where two people are obsessed with each other, there is clearly no need to explore the world of make-believe. When there is so much to learn about the other's mind and body, there is no need to invent. But what of the man and woman who have lived together for years, who know their partner's mood and convictions almost as well as they know their body? Is it reasonable that they should, if only occasionally, seek extra sexual excitement by pretending that they are having sex with another unknown – and therefore 'charming' person?

This line of argument, however appealing it is, where a spouse is mentally substituted for someone else, can result in devastation and total ruin. It will result in separation or a genuine rift between the couples since, here, pretense is the only method of achieving sexual climax. Many married men try to justify their lustful fantasies by these statements. "Sure I sometimes pretend it's not my wife but the beautiful pinup I saw in the girlie magazine. It may sound a little bad, but at least that way I'm not actually being unfaithful irrespective of what religious men say about lusting in the mind being as bad as committing the actual sins." Some men even express it more explicitly: "Fantasy is the poor man's mistress."

Let us explore the resentment, hurt and ultimate separation of a woman who experienced such a situation. Karen, now a divorcee, spells out the emotional injury her husband inflicted upon her by transforming their sex lives into that of fantasy. "The first two years were OK, but gradually he became more irritable with me. He started to criticize the way I looked, and if we ever went out together he spent his time eyeing other women. I did what I could, tried always to look good for him when he came home ... but none of it worked. Then one night we went out at a friend's house I overheard him talking to another man. 'It's got so boring with Karen that I can only make it if I imagine another bird,' he said.

'I was terribly hurt, but I didn't say anything to him for weeks. Then one night an attractive friend of mine came to visit whom Henry hadn't met before. I could see he liked her and after she'd left he seemed very keen to go to bed. He always kept his eyes closed when making love, and since I had overheard his remark about imagining other women it drove me crazy. This night was just the same, but he had a kind of silly smile on his face as we were having sex and I suddenly said: 'I'm not Jilly, you know, I'm Karen.'

"His reaction was incredible; he opened his eyes, looked at me with a mixture of fear and anger, and stopped immediately. He also coloured up. Of course, he denied it, but you know how there are times when you are sure you have hit the nail on the head, and with that I already knew about his fantasizing, I didn't need proof ... I really will never forgive Henry for making such a horrible dent in my self-esteem." [46]

One of the most common fantasies centres on rape. Many women have admitted that they find the idea of rape, which is regarded as dirty and unwholesome, a compelling one. Another common fantasy involves being watched by an audience while making love. The onlooker may be just one person or a crowd, but either way the stimulation comes from being seen in the depths of the sex act and witnessing the audience's reaction, be it shocked or excited. Of the many fantasies that people indulge in, there is one that commonly causes a lot of worry and guilt in those who experience it: the homosexual fantasy. A person who, on a conscious state, finds the idea horrifying but realizes that he himself has passionate fantasies about other male may be terrified that he is in fact a homosexual, even though his sex life with his wedded partner is healthy and fulfilling. Similarly a happily married woman who occasionally fantasizes about another woman can become very agitated by her unnatural tendencies.

Some fantasies can even destroy. One girl who was forced to live with her husband's obsessional fantasies for years explained:

*"He would ask me about my former life and loves when we were starting to make love. Far from being jealous, inquisitive or concerned, he found my past sexual activities fascinating. In fact, to put it crudely, he could not have successful intercourse unless it was accompanied by my first-hand account of sex with other men...I never want to hear or be involved in any fantasy sex life again. I want to make love to by a man who knows it is **me** he is loving, not some figment of his imagination."*[47]

Fantasy can never be the same as reality. This epidemic could create havoc in an otherwise peaceful and pleasant neighbourhood. Marriages could collapse and homes broken when fantasies solely become instrumental in sexual gratification. Due to the exposure of all kinds of immoral filth and shamelessness in the form of films, videos, TV, plays, magazines, telephone lines and even newspapers, fantasy has become the common trend of modern times. This is completely forbidden and a major sin in Islâm. It resembles adultery of the mind and heart. The Holy Prophet ﷺ has distinctly warned us against this:

"To gaze at a strange woman is the adultery of the eye; to converse with her (without necessity, but merely to derive pleasure) is the zina of the ears; to touch a strange woman is the adultery of the hands; to walk towards a strange woman is adultery of the feet; the heart desires and craves (fantasizes); the sexual organs then either testify to these or deny them".[48]

4.3.8   FETISHISM

A fetish is a peculiar object and activity of sexual desire which is found to be exciting to the relevant person. It may be something like a lock of hair, or some fancy underwear, or rubber or leather articles.

Men are increasingly given in to the temptation to dress up their wives in "exotic" garments designed to stimulate passion. Women may be stimulated to some desire by the sight of a handsome man dressed only in his underwear or even by erotic pictures and films, but only very rarely does their excitement centre upon the objects themselves.

The trade in erotic underwear is booming. We know too well that advertising companies are very much aware of human weakness to sexual stimuli. Automobiles and other products are often publicized less on the basis of their efficiency than on their erotic power to seduce members of the opposite sex. In most of the adverts a scantily dressed model is more often than not used as the bait. Most men whose eyes wander around the lingerie section of departmental stores or husbands, who, slightly shamefaced, present their wives with sexually stimulating underwear are not excited by the items themselves so much as by the thought of a woman wearing it. Wives are often astonished when their husbands request them to wear 'scandalous' garments.

Fetishists can become totally dependent by their own particular obsession so that they are unable to experience sexual excitement except through the fetish object. Ancient societies had no high-heeled shoes, rubber wetsuits, fancy underwear and automobiles or any other objects currently in fashion among fetishists. Therefore this is the disease of modern civilization which tends to legalize such frustrations which it cannot cure. For a man to make love under the stimulation of any kind of fetish is to commit mental rape on females in general.

4.3.9   VOYEURISM (PEEPING TOMS)

A voyeur is one who obtains sexual gratification from looking at others' sexual actions or organs. For most people there can exist a possible sexual response to seeing others in sexual intercourse but for the voyeur, looking is what sex is about. He even goes further by compulsively seeking out situations where he can view the privacy of others, by casually positioning himself so he can glance upwards as women climb a flight of stairs, or an apartment which overlooks the female changing rooms, or a park bench from where he can watch courting couples on the grass.

In the most severe cases he will prowl around buildings at night, trespass in gardens, climb balconies or trees in order to steal a glance through a bedroom window at the couple taking off their clothes or engaging in sex. He normally haunts public places and prefers to operate in darkness. He distances himself from sexual contact and prefers the anonymous role of watcher. Most males even go to the extent of spying through keyholes.

A voyeur is normally classified as a frightened man, usually timid, and violent only when he fears capture. His desire for the forbidden, for overcoming danger, leads him to prowl public parks or trespass in private gardens.

Islâmically, these perverted "peeping Toms" should be severely punished not only for casting their glances in forbidden territory but also for infringing on the privacy of others, especially married couples, whose honour and chastity Islâm has guaranteed. Human curiosity being what it is, cannot allow one to disturb the privacy of other people by watching them undress or having sexual intercourse.

That is why it has been ordained that a visitor seeking permission to enter, will stand to the left or the right of the doorway and not exactly in front of the door. Obtaining permission was necessiated a measure against coming upon the inmates, especially the womenfolk, in their moments of privacy. At the beginning of Islâm, the Arabs could not grasp the real significance of these commands. Therefore they used to peep into the houses from the outside. An incident occurred to the Prophet (P.B.U.H) that once while he was in his cubicle scratching his head with an instrument that he had in his hand, someone came and started peeping through the chinks of the door. When the Prophet became cognizant of it, he was very angry, and said, *"If I had seen him peeping, in time, I would have taken out his eyes...."*[49]

Therefore on coming to somebody's door one should not indulge in the shameful prank of peeping through the lattice or a door partly ajar or even a window without a curtain, since it will defeat the very purpose of taking permission. He would have as well entered right away unannounced. The Prophet 變 has strictly forbidden it. He said:

> *" If somebody tries to peep at you through*
> *a chink without your permission, and you*
> *were to throw a pebble which hits him in*
> *the eye, damaging it completely, you will*
> *not be punishable for the sin".* [50]

The magnitude of this crime can be imagined by the punishment suggested for it by the Prophet 變 who was all compassionate to mankind and was never harsh except in the enforcement of the boundaries prescribed by Allâh in checking moral corruption.

4.3.10   EXHIBITIONISM (STREAKING AND STRIP TEASE)

This refers to a person who indulges in the indecent exposure of his genitals, or rather more simply it means the showing of one's sex organs, the likes of the modern day streaker. A common example is the man, who, quite unasked, displays his private parts to some complete stranger, very often a child or young girl.

Exhibitionism is one of the most common sexually-linked crimes; about a fifth of those charged with a sexual offence are accused of indecent exposure. More often than not, these criminals are males, since very few women expose their private parts in this way, and those that really expose themselves in such ghastly acts of strip-tease where a woman strips to roars of applause, is condoned by the Western laws clearly showing the extent of moral degeneration in the Western world.

The exhibitionist may lurk in parks or deserted streets ready to confront an unsuspecting woman or child or openly draw the attention of a crowd, such as streaking in a packed soccer or cricket stadium. He intends to shock and horrify and also this display could be intended as an invitation to a sexual encounter. The gratification he is after is the victim's reaction of horror, and he may carry this image in his fantasies as he cowardly masturbates later. On the other hand, the encounter can be dangerously frightening for the victim. Although some women may just want to laugh, the majority may become hysterical since the sexual nature of the incident could disturb them.

Outwardly the exhibitionist can be anyone and many are so called 'respectable' men. They vary, too, in age from the young adolescent to the middle-aged or older person. What they do have in common is an immature approach to sex which is linked with a childish need to be noticed. Notoriety can seem desirable to the insecure and immature man who has failed to make his mark in this world. The man who displays himself to a woman sitting near him in a conveyance or crowded area, confronts a group of schoolgirls, or exposes himself to young children in a public park is seeking to achieve the victims horror and reaction coupled with the public attention he would receive by being chased, caught and prosecuted. Therefore, exhibitionism i.e. the desire to expose and display one's genitals is the reverse side of voyeurism, wherein one attains stimulation by watching unsuspecting people undressing or engaging in sexual intercourse.

Islâm has not only condemned such illegal and perverted practices of sexual gratification but has also imposed strict penalties on these immoral criminals.

The Qur'ân forbids all types of exhibitionism in these words:

> *"And play your role by being in your houses and do not keep exhibiting your beauty and decorations like what used to happen in the Jahiliyah period."*[51]

No vulgar worldly display should be made as in the times of Paganism.

During this period the Arabs would strip themselves naked before each other. Men and women performed the ceremony round the K'aba in a state of nakedness. The Prophet (P.B.U.H) said that the following type of women constitute one of the categories of the dwellers of hell:

> *"Those women who seem naked even when dressed ...... thus inviting people's attention, will not enter paradise nor will they smell its fragrance though its fragrance can be smelt from a very long distance."* [52]

Once Miswar ibn Makhrama ؓ was carrying a stone towards the Holy Prophet ﷺ when the garment covering the lower part of his body fell on the way. He did not care and carried on with the load. When the Prophet saw him, he instructed him to go back and cover his body and refrain from moving naked in future.[53] Therefore nudity is such an indecency that can never be tolerated by Islâmic *ḥayâ*.

4.3.11 MASOCHISM AND SADISM

Masochism is the desire to receive pain and the tendency to be stimulated by it, whereas sadism is the word generally used to describe sexual excitement derived from the infliction of pain. The words were invented after de Sade and Sacher-Masoch, two aristocrats whose writings were laden with graphic details of their sexual tastes. It ranged from the hardest of hard-core pornography to mild fantasies in popular magazines. Most people bought them in one form or the other, read them, and were aroused by them. Sometimes they went a step further and acted them out, either in masturbation fantasies or with a sexual partner, some kind of dominant or submissive role.[54]

Most men in modern society have fantasies at some time about the delights of ravishing a beauty who has caught their eye and it is a fact that more erotic literature exists in which women are bound, whipped and beaten and rendered helpless than any other single type of pornography. They claim that many of them enjoy the idea of dominating a woman and having the power to inflict pain on her. But little do they realize that such savagery is a reversion to primeval barbarism when women who were regarded as weak creatures fated only to serve the lusts of men, were flogged, tortured and unmercifully humiliated.

The sado-masochist cannot do without pain, which becomes an addictive drug to him. Thus he tends to degrade human sexuality in the criminality of his behaviour. There is no question of giving pleasure, only of receiving it by whatever means are necessary, either by being excessively aggressive or dependent or both. Sexual partners are thus reduced to the level of mere instruments. Prostitutes armed with an assortment of whips, corsets, chains and minor torture devices, and underground booksellers who specialize in 'bondage and whipping' have made a great fortune in this profession.

Islâm denounces such brutal savagery and advocates love, affection and self-sacrifice and has instructed husbands to be gentle and avoid hurting their wives. Man has been warned against tyranny and oppression to women. The Qur'ân mentions:

> "But do not take them back to injure them,
> (or) to take undue advantage; if any one
> does that, he wrongs his own soul. Do not
> treat God's sign as a jest.[55]

Apparently this verse was revealed to put a stop to taking undue advantage of and tyrannising women in connection with talâq, but a little deeper thought brings to light the fact that it is very comprehensive and through it Almighty has forbidden all types of tyranny to women by their husbands. The Prophet 🕮 in view of the unpredictable state of mind and conduct of women ordained:

> "None of you should beat his wife as he
> would beat his slave, and the very next day
> approach her for the gratification of his
> sexual appetite."[56]

4.3.12 PETTING

In present day society there exists a strong desire to have physical contact with the opposite gender during adolescence. Often a group of boys and girls out together will lose their shyness of the opposite sex and frequently feel strong sexual attraction when enjoying themselves and having fun when jostling and pushing one another. Some, on such an outing, will often pair off, holding hands or cuddling each other.

If a couple feel affection for each other, together with sexual attraction, the next thing they are likely to want to do is to kiss and embrace. Kissing is, of course, also a way of showing affection towards family and relatives, but when a couple is "courting" or "dating" it is more than this, because kissing also arouses sexual desire and gives physical pleasure; simply, kissing is sexual stimulation.

Kissing and cuddling may lead sooner or later to petting. When a boy caresses a girl's body, particularly her sensitive zones and other parts beneath her clothing, he is indulging in petting. In petting the boy usually makes the first move, but a couple will probably soon begin to practise mutual petting when the girl also strokes sensitive organs of the boy's body. Thus petting is physical contact that aims at bringing pleasure and stops short of sexual intercourse. The term "deep petting" is usually reserved for petting that leads to a climax.

It is said that the sexual excitement that a couple feels while petting affects them differently. With girls sexual excitement is experienced widely throughout the body, and it is usual for girls to take longer to be aroused than is the case with boys. Boys find that sexual excitement tends to be localized in the sex organs. There is also an increase in the pulse rate, sometimes with an awareness of the heart "pounding", and rapid or heavier breathing. Finally, there is a feeling of a building up of tension, with a desire for relief of such tension. This accounts for the increasing number of "date-rapes" in the Western world when the female seductress who have been encouraging her partner all the way, ultimately decides to say no. If orgasm is not achieved, sexual excitement gradually subsides, but strong sexual arousal that does not reach a climax is likely to lead to a feeling of dissatisfaction, moodiness and congestion.

Co-education institutions are also the breeding grounds for such vice. Here, the incentives as well as the means of gratification are readily available. Sexual feelings that were awakened in childhood are further aroused here. Boys and girls read dirty sex-inciting literature. The literature which is in great demand in certain universities is so obscene, licentious and indecent that the like of it was never so freely presented before public in history. The information drawn from such literature then becomes the subject of free and frank discussion among young people of both sexes, and thus equipped, they advance towards practical experience. Boys and girls go out for petting parties where they freely drink and smoke. The number of high school girls that become sexually experienced before leaving school is absolutely shocking. This number is even higher than in the later educational stages. Although it must be stated that in schools and colleges there exists some sort of discipline which hinders free interplay of emotional activity, but as the young people leave the educational institution and enter the world, their stirred up emotions and degenerate habits refuse to be bound by any restrictions. They find ever-present situations to excite them emotionally as well as means to gratify their desires. These vices are not only confined to Western society but are also prevalent in some of the Muslim countries such as Turkey and other more secular Islâmic states.

In Islâm, the pleasures of physical contact such as kissing, cuddling, petting, etc., can only be legalized through the institution of marriage. Responsible people do not allow themselves to be carried away by love or affection, or by the strength of their sexual desire that they become involved in unplanned acts of illegitimate sexual gratification.

4.4   THE PERFECT MORAL CHARACTER OF YÛSUF ﷺ

The episode in the Qur'ân regarding Yûsuf ﷺ repelling the passionate
advances of Zulaikhâ demonstrates, besides illustrating the fatal
consequences of fornication, that Islâm compels the preservation of
chastity at all times and under all conditions.

When the chief executive and the then Prime Minister of Egypt, Portiphar,
bought Yûsuf ﷺ at an auction and entrusted him to the care of his wife
Zulaikhâ, she was advised that he should not be treated like a slave, but
should be kept with grace as he may be useful in his grown age, or they
may adopt him because they had no children. But not long after, as Yûsuf
ﷺ emerged from adolescence, and attained the full strength of manhood,
he was of such remarkable appearance that his equal could not be found
in all of Egypt. His master's wife, Zulaikhâ, was fascinated by his manners,
handsome form and face and conceived a passion for him which intensified
daily. Ultimately she tried to seduce him to participate in the gratification
of her sexual appetite by isolating him in her luxurious chambers as the
Qur'ân declares:

> "And the woman in whose house he was,
> solicited him and closed the doors and said,
> "Now come, thou (dear one)!
> He said: "God forbid!
> Verily your husband is my master, he has
> made me a goodly dwelling. No doubt, the
> unjust do not prosper." [57]

Thus we see that Allâh Ta'âlâ was training and directing Yûsuf ﷺ in
attaining the highest standard of moral perfection, while the wife of
Portiphar put him through a dangerously grave test. She was captivated
by his extra-ordinary beauty and tried, presenting all possible fascinating
charms, to win him over and cause his heart to go beyond control. It was
a delicate moment for Yûsuf ﷺ – on the one hand there were all things
luxurious and joyous enjoyment, with freedom to satisfy all sexual
passions, the presence of Yûsuf ﷺ in Zulaikhâ's house and her unusual
loving and admiring behaviour; the expression of earnest desire of a
woman in a lonely hour; the doors shut to stop any alien intrusion; and,

on the other hand there was youth with its power and passions, Yûsuf ﷺ unmarried state – all these factors and motives were so powerful that even the piety of a great holy man could be shattered. But he whom Allâh Ta'âlâ called good-doer and raised to the sublime height of Prophetic innocence, could never be overpowered by Shaiṭân. He cried out: "Allâh forbid!" and all satanic nets were broken because he took refuge in Allâh Ta'âlâ and could not be subdued by any earthly invasion. His spiritual eyes saw something that her eyes, blinded by passion, did not see. She thought no one saw when the doors were closed. He knew that Allâh Ta'âlâ was there and everywhere. That made him strong, and was proof against temptation. Allâh Ta'âlâ mentions:

> *"And with passion did she desire him, and*
> *he would have desired her, but that he saw*
> *the evidence of his Lord: thus (did We*
> *order) that We might turn away from him*
> *(all) evil and shameful deeds."*[58]

Had Yûsuf ﷺ not observed the proof and evidence of his Lord, he would have yielded to his desire or inclination. What was this evidence? It was the sublime conviction of the illegality and horror of adultery, which Allâh had given him.

In spite of this, with Zulaikhâ in her mad passion, the situation became intolerable, and Yûsuf ﷺ ran towards the door. She bolted after him and tugged at him to detain him. As he was retreating, she could only catch hold of the back of his shirt, and in the struggle she tore it. He was determined to open the door and leave as it was useless to argue with her in her mad passion. When the door was opened, it so happened, that her husband was not far off. The woman at once fell back from coaxing to deception. One guilt leads to another. She had to resort to a lie, not only to justify herself but also to have her revenge on the man who had scorned her love. Betrayed love made her ferocious, and she lost all sense of right and wrong. The Qur'ân mentions:

> *"So they both raced each other to the door,*
> *and she tore his shirt from the back and both*
> *encountered her husband by the door. She*

> said: 'What is the fitting punishment for
> one who formed an evil design against thy
> wife, but prison or a grievous
> chastisement?'" [59]

Yûsuf ﷺ bore himself with dignity. He was too noble to indulge in angry bickerings. But he had to disclose the truth. And he did it with quiet simplicity, without argument or bitterness – the woman had desired him and he saved himself by running out. In the nature of things there was no eye-witness to what had happened between them. But as there was a scene with the whole household gathered, wisdom came through one who was not immediately concerned. It is stated that it was a baby of suckling age, who by the miracle of Allâh Ta'âlâ spoke out to prove the innocence of Yûsuf ﷺ and his distinguished position with Allâh Ta'âlâ. Some scholars say that he was not a child but some wise man who said such a prudent word for Yûsuf ﷺ,[60] as declared in the Qur'ân:

> "He said: 'It was she that sought to seduce
> me from my (true) self.' And one of her
> household saw (this) and bore witness,
> (thus):
> 'If it be that his shirt is torn from the front,
> then is her tale true, and he is a liar! But if it
> be that his shirt is torn from the back, then
> she is the liar, and he is telling the truth!'
> So when he saw his shirt, that it was torn
> at the back, (her husband) said· 'Behold!
> It is a snare of you woman! Truly mighty
> is your snare!'" [61]

When the real fact became clear to everyone, Portiphar, as head of the household, had to decide what to do. His own position was difficult, and it was made ridiculous. In fact he was a eunuch and his dignity and rank were advanced by the so-called marriage with a high-born princess. Was he going to proclaim to the world that Zulaikhâ was running after a 'slave'? He was probably fond of her and treated the whole affair as the tricks and snares connected with the madness of love. He also saw the innocence and loyalty of Yûsuf ﷺ . So he requested Yûsuf ﷺ to bury the event into oblivion and should not make it public as it was the cause of much disgrace and humiliation. As was only fair, he apologised to Yûsuf ﷺ and begged him to give no further thought to the injury that had been done to him, firstly by the love-snare of one who was called his wife; secondly, by the utterly false charge made against him; and thirdly, by the scene which must have been painful to a man of such impeccable character as Yûsuf ﷺ. That was not enough. He asked Zulaikhâ humbly to beg pardon for the wrong that she had done to Yûsuf ﷺ as mentioned in the Qur'ân:

> *"O Yûsuf, pass this over! (O wife), ask*
> *forgiveness for thy sin, for truly thou hast*
> *been at fault!"* [62]

Portiphar's wise and discreet conduct would have closed the particular episode of Zulaikhâ's guilty conduct, but the slanderous society gossip by the women of the City began labelling her as such a wretched woman who had fallen so low as to attach herself to her own servant. Their taunting remarks against Zulaikhâ reflected their own cravings and boastings about their own sanctity and purity, whereas the fact was otherwise. The fame of Yûsuf ﷺ's beauty reverberated in the heart of every woman who heard about him. It had created an intense eagerness for just a glimpse of Yûsuf ﷺ by his admirers. So it is not difficult to believe that their discreet discussions were meant as a recourse to Zulaikhâ in order to have a glimpse of Yûsuf ﷺ. Hence they resorted to slandering Zulaikhâ intentionally so that she might become infuriated and do something which might lead to their seeing him; or, in utter desperation, they might have tried to create hatred in her heart against Yûsuf ﷺ; or in the hope of winning Yûsuf ﷺ they might have tried to change her love into hatred through propaganda; or Zulaikhâ might have taken some women into her confidence about her love for Yûsuf ﷺ and her consequent intentions. But those women betrayed her in order to axe their own ends. Regarding this the Qur'ân declares:

> And women in the city said: *"The wife of*
> *the 'Azîz is seeking to seduce her slave*
> *from his true self. Truly he has inflamed*
> *her with love, verily we see she is evidently*
> *going astray."* [63]

When her reputation began to be pulled to pieces with exaggeration and malicious distortions, Zulai<u>kh</u>â invited all the ladies to a banquet. We can imagine their reclining at ease on rich carpets and luxurious cushions. When dessert was served and the talks flowed freely about the gossip and scandal which made their hostess interesting, and when they were just about to cut the fruit with their knives, lo, behold, Yûsuf ﷺ was brought into their midst! When the women saw him they lost their senses as if some electric shock had stunned them. Imagine the excitement his beauty caused, and the havoc it played with their hearts, that instead of cutting the fruit, they cut their fingers, and knew nothing of the accident till their attention was called to the blood upon their garments. This event provides additional proof of his piety and truthfulness. When a little glimpse of Yûsuf ﷺ could amaze those women in a moment, what must have been the state of Zulai<u>kh</u>â during his stay in her household? Naturally she must have solicited him, but he in turn kept pure and innocent like an angel. These women also testified to his purity by calling him a noble angel i.e. a mortal whom they might have taught, could be snared by the women, but an angel could not be defeated by them. On seeing his morality, shame and innocence which were discerned in his manners, they could not but say that he was not a mortal but a noble creature of the heaven which is far away from earthly desires. The Qur'ân states:

> *"When she heard of their malicious talk, she*
> *sent for them and prepared a banquet for*
> *them; she gave each of them a knife, and she*
> *said to Yûsuf* ﷺ, *come out before them."*
> *When they saw him, they were dumbfounded*
> *and (in their amazement) cut their hands;*
> *they said: 'God preserve us! No mortal is*
> *this! This is none other than a noble angel."*[64]

This expression suggests moral dignity and sublimity of character rather than physical beauty or carnal charms. The noble Egyptian ladies were paying tribute to his character as a human being rather than referring to his physical attraction.

Finding encouragement from their passion and their mutual feelings she openly admitted that she had tried to win him, but he had proved inaccessible to her solicitation. And so now Zulai<u>kh</u>â had risen to the height of tragic guilt and had threatened Yûsuf ﷺ. She had forgotten all her finer feeling, her real love and been overpowered by brute passion. After all he was a 'slave' and had to obey his mistress! Or, there was prison, and the company of the vilest, as the Qur'ân mentions:

> "She said: There before you is the man
> about whom you did blame me! I did seek
> to seduce him from (his) true self but he
> did firmly save himself guiltless! And now,
> if he will not do what I say to him, he shall
> certainly be cast in prison and shall be
> doomed to degradation."⁶⁵

When Yûsuf ﷺ saw himself surrounded by not one, but, by now, many lustful women, he supplicated to Allâh Ta'âlâ with prophetic patience and perseverance to save him from their snares. He preferred imprisonment to the sin they were calling him to. He further prayed that if Allâh Ta'âlâ did not help him, he would be yearning towards their cheatings which would be unwise on his part, or if he succumbed to their persuasions he would become ignorant and insane. This demonstrates that the innocence of the Prophets stands with the assistance of the Almighty, and that the Prophets do not become proud of their innocence, but rather acknowledge the source of innocence, which is Allâh Ta'âlâ's help. The Qur'ân mentions:

> He said: "O my Lord! The prison is more
> to my liking than that to which they invite
> me; unless Thou turn away their snare from
> me, I should feel inclined towards them and
> join the ranks of the ignorant."
> So his Lord granted his prayer, then
> removed their guile from him, Verily He is
> All Hearing, All Knowing.⁶⁶

The fact that Yûsuf ﷺ preferred a prison cell rather than gratify the desires of some of the high-placed ladies of society in Egypt, demonstrates the detestation of the crime of fornication and serves as an admonition to those pursuing such a despicable evil. Holding fornication as permissible clearly implies that illicit sexual gratification out of wedlock and prostitution should thrive uncurbed in society.

4.5 PROSTITUTION

A woman's nature is naturally weighed down by the rocks of modesty and it is this natural check which is removed in prostitution, which takes away her bashfulness that did not allow her to talk freely to any stranger, that she now becomes a wanton women. Morality departs from her and she becomes very bold in her advances towards lewdness. Once this practice has taken root in a society, a whole crop of mischief and turbulance sprouts; good deeds and morality find it hard to maintain any place for themselves in this corrupt society and the grandeur and prestige of the nation given to prostitution comes tottering to the ground.

A prostitute is a woman who offers her body for promiscuous sexual intercourse especially for payment. This notorious profession is said to have originated from the so-called 'temple prostitution', a religious practice in certain ancient civilizations where, in what seemed to have been some sort of fertility rite, young women were required to attend the temple and have sexual intercourse with any man who offered her a reward. It was common in ancient Greece where it was tolerated in association with ritual temple prostitution. In ancient Rome prostitution was associated with slavery, and thus acquired the stigma of a degraded occupation. Prostitutes were required to register as such and wear distinctive clothing.[67]

Among Semitic peoples, the Hebrews condemned temple prostitution as sinful and this moral attitude was adopted in the teachings of the early Christian preachers. Their view was that sexual intercourse should only take place within legal heterosexual marriage and that prostitution was sexually immoral. But simultaneously, these clergymen did not voice their opinions for the banning of prostitution. Their argument was that however immoral it was, prostitution was a necessary evil. In the fourth century St Augustine echoed this philosophy in a famous passage:

> *"What can be called more sordid, more void of modesty, more full of shame, than prostitutes, brothels, and every evil of this kind? Yet remove prostitution from human affairs, and you will pollute all things with lust..."* [68]

Some nine centuries later this policy was advocated by St Thomas Aquinas:

> *Prostitution is like the filth in the sea, or a*
> *sewer in a palace. Take away the sewer,*
> *and you will fill the palace with pollution*
> *... Take away prostitutes from the world*
> *and you will fill it with sodomy.*[69]

Some six centuries after this period a European writer, WEH Lecky made this announcement:

> "*The supreme type of vice, she is ultimately*
> *the most efficient guardian of virtue. But*
> *for her, the unchallenged purity of*
> *countless happy homes would be polluted*
> *... On that one degraded form are*
> *concentrated the passions which might*
> *have filled the world with shame. She*
> *remains ... the eternal priestess of*
> *humanity, blasted for the sins of the*
> *people.*"[70]

Therefore the attitude in Europe from the Middle Ages onward was that prostitution, though disapproved of, was tolerated. Prostitutes were identified and localized in licensed brothels, usually located in 'red light' districts. Nevertheless the Protestant Reformers took a much stricter view, condemning prostitution outright as immoral and insisting on its suppression by criminal law. This criminalization was explained on the basis that since prostitution generated crimes in the form of robbery, assault, drug, alcohol abuse and the like, its prohibition would reduce the incidence of crime. And then, since prostitution involves using one's body for the purely commercial purpose of providing another with sexual gratification, which is so ethically wrong, that criminal law had to be implemented to halt this evil practice.

It is morally wrong to provide sex for money since this would treat human beings as objects of commerce. Immanuel Kant, a famous philosopher, mentions that "to allow one's person for profit to be used by another for the satisfaction of sexual desire is to make oneself a thing on which another satisfies his appetite, just as he satisfies his hunger upon a steak. To let one's person out on hire and to surrender it to another for the satisfaction of his sexual desire in return for money is the depth of evil conduct. The underlying moral principle is that man is not his own property and cannot do with his body what he wills. This manner of satisfying sexual desire is, therefore, not permitted by the rules of morality".[71]

The act of prostitution is an oppression to the prostitute herself also, since morality and good deeds go to naught where illicit sexual relations find a place in her life, her money goes down the drain, her vital physical power flows out with the seminal fluid which is the seed of the race and which she wastes so recklessly. Her health is ruined and she earns a bad name. She is constantly wracked by fear, and a deep melancholy comes over her. Her health is always fraught with the danger of succumbing to shameful and dangerous diseases like syphilis, gonorrhoea and the deadly Aids.

Since prostitution is sex outside the marriage relationship it is both non-procreative and devoid of emotional love, and therefore it is contrary to basic social and moral behaviour. It also exposes the prostitutes to various risks to themselves and their health such as Veneral Disease and, in current times, the fatal contraction of AIDS.

Similarly this is an activity that produces disturbances to society. These include, particularly, the public solicitation of trade by prostitutes or their pimps and 'kerb crawling' by customers.

4.5.1 EUROPE, ASIA AND AMERICA : WHERE THE SKIN TRADE FLOURISHES

Few corners of the earth are immune to the flourishing sex trade. When the Iron Curtain disintegrated, few would have guessed that in less than a decade it would lead to an exodus of poverty-stricken East European women, desperate to sell themselves for what rarely turns out to be the good life. From Eastern Europe to the Himalayas, from Tokyo to Beijing, from London to Los Angeles and from Turkey to Dubai, this transaction has created a multibillion-dollar sex trade. Its effect is most devastating on an individual level. Poor women and children are traded as commodities on the street, products bartered, smuggled and sold as pawns against hunger or as an easy access to profits.

On Saturday nights as many as 300 young women line the margins of E55, a Czech highway near the German border. Their costumes vary: light frocks, skimpy red dresses, high heeled boots and glow-in-the-dark pants. They speak a variety of languages: Czech, Romanian, Bulgarian, Hungarian, German. But they have only one thing to sell: sex. For the truckers and migrant workers who travel this route, this particular 12 km stretch of E55 is the "Highway of Cheap Love", the longest brothel in the world. But for the young women, the story is different. Many have been forced into sexual slavery. Some, abducted by conmen, are raped and psychologically intimidated into submission. As they display their wares, their pimps lurk in the shadows, calculating the night's profits. But not all the pimps are gangsters. Often it is Father who sits in the backup car or Mother who negotiates the deal for her daughter. Little Brother may appear with a pail of soapy water to wash a client's car for an extra fee.

Morally, authorities have turned a blind eye at the 'world's oldest profession'. If 100 000 German men annually choose to visit Thailand on package sex tours, who is to object? Only recently has anyone begun to ask how many of Thailand's 2 million prostitutes are minors; or how many have been sold by parents or husbands as indentured servants to brothel owners; and how many have been kidnapped from villages in Burma, Laos and Southern China. A recent conference of Southeast Asian women's organizations estimated that 30 million women had been sold worldwide in the last decade and this is only the tip of the iceberg. In Nepal's Himalayan villages, some 7 000 adolescents are sold each year into the sweat-drenched brothels of Bombay. In Brazil, an estimated 25 000 girls have been forced into prostitution in remote Amazon mining camps. Nigerian street-walkers are flooding into Bologna, while the bright windows of Antwerp's red-light district are filled with Ghanaians in skimpy underwear. Around Miami, massage parlours owned by Cuban immigrants import prostitutes from Colombia, Nicaragua and Canada.[72]

Police say a quarter of Germany's 200 000 prostitutes are now from the former East bloc. Even in the conservative Middle East, charter flights of Russian woman disembark weekly at the airport, ply their trade on 14-day visas and head home, loaded with colour television sets and hi-tech electronics. Even Turkey has not been spared. The women swarm in from Moldovia and Belarus with suitcases of cheap goods to hawk by day. By night they sell their services. The client's wives may not be so lucky. Turkey's Black Sea region has seen its divorce rate jump 20% in the past three years, along with an explosion of gonorrhoea, syphilis and AIDS. Morocco has become a hotbed for Saudi sex tourists. Arabs are even flocking to Bombay, a centre for inexpensive medical treatment, for such common ailments as high blood pressure or skin infections - excuses to stay a week or a month and patronize the brothels that have sprung up around the hospitals. These establishments feature dancing girls in gaudily carpeted and chandeliered halls. Once the 'patient' chooses his girl, they move into a room with a bed decked in flowers, like the nuptial ritual in extravagant Indian weddings. The rate sometimes reaches $1 000 a night. (The average labourer's annual income). In Karachi, human-rights lawyers are expressing resentment against rackets that have kidnapped 200 000 Bangladeshi women into prostitution in Pakistan.

In Tel Aviv the number of brothels has skyrocketed in five years from 30 to 150. Bars in major Chinese cities now offer blond, blue-eyed Russian "hostesses".

Women from the old East bloc are not the only ones enticed into Western Europe. Just recently, Spanish police have dismantled more than a dozen slave-trafficking rings. A Barcelona police inspector was sentenced to seven years in prison for forcing Guatemalan women into prostitution. Dominican flesh traders who are promised top jobs, mortgage their parent's homes on high interest rates to pay for false papers and plane fares. If they refuse to prostitute themselves on arrival, their families are turned into the streets. This is what a young Dominican, transported to Greece, told BBC television, her eyes welling with tears:

> *"I thought I was going to work as a*
> *waitress. Then they said if I didn't have*
> *sex, I'd be sent back to Santo Domingo*

> *without a penny. I was beaten, burned*
> *with cigarettes. I was a virgin. I held out*
> *for five days, crying, with no food.*
> *Eventually I lost my honour and my*
> *virginity for twenty five dollars.* "[73]

Prostitution in Denmark is much more widespread than in Norway and Sweden. In the Scandinavian context, it stands out as the worst example. The sex trade flourishes in Copenhagen's streets and alleys - in massage parlours, restaurants, bars, sex clubs and on the streets themselves. The police estimate that 2 000 women alone work in massage parlours.[74]

The skin trade network operating in Netherlands, Belgium, Switzerland and Germany also lures women from Latin America and Asia. Ring members in Germany recruit poor Philippians in Manila, promising jobs as 'folklore dancers'. After flying to Cyprus they are encouraged into prostitution. When the women, devout Catholics, refuse, they are beaten and mass raped to break their will. Trafficking incidents are also cropping up in the US. In Houston, nude-modelling studios have been supplied by flesh traders from South Korea and Salvadore. In Los Angeles the trade is export-oriented. Americans have been lured to Japan on singing, dancing and modelling contracts and then forced into prostitution.

Females are normally trafficking victims, but men also, whether voluntarily or through poverty, are caught up in the sex marketplace. Recently at Paris' Orly Airport, 15 Algerian transvestites became hysterical when French police tried to deport them without allowing them to change out of their skirts, high heels and wigs. Brought before a judge, the men, now with beards after a week in prison, said they were driven by unemployment to come to Paris every six months in order to feed their wives and children back home. The judge allowed them to change clothes, but it was too late to avoid the shame and embarrassment since French intelligence had already transmitted their photos to Algerian authorities on the day of their arrest.[75]

4.5.2   WHO IS THE PIMP?

Prostitutes are in most cases, the victims of pimps and gangs who defy all form of sexual morality in extracting the services of these ladies for monetary gain. Who is the pimp? What is a pimp? Is the pimp the main villain, the powerful and dangerous man behind the scenes in the prostitution market?

A pimp is a person who allows himself to be supported by a prostituted woman. Sometimes it could be her husband, a boyfriend, a live-in lover, her parents or her little brother. At times it could refer to a network of gangsters who use violence and abuse to force women out onto the street for their economic exploitation. They are evil, manipulative and cunning people from beginning to end.

Sociologists have filled reports and books with labels like home pimps, stable pimps, professional pimps, personals' pimps, club pimps and other profiteers.

Pimps know all the cards and how to play them. The young girl or woman he sets as a target is likely to be naive, lonely and bitter towards the family she has just run away from or the marriage she has just left. She is also likely to be penniless and without job skills. Suddenly a man appears who is friendly, who offers to buy her a meal and, later, a place to spend the night. She hears compliments for the first time in ages, as well as promises to buy her new clothes and have her hair done. The romantic movie scenario is being played out and it may be days, weeks, or even months before she figures out what has happened to her.[76] Therefore the brutal pimp who seduces a woman with love and sweet music and then when she is helplessly entrapped in his charming web, literally kicks her out on the street, is also a criminal accomplice to the prostitute.

But in countries where prostitutes are actively arrested and prosecuted, the pimp automatically plays a different role. In a number of American cities hundreds of prostitutes are regularly hauled into the police station, and the prostitute is totally dependent on having someone on the outside who is prepared to post her bail so that she can be released. This, to her, is where the pimp becomes directly useful in the day-to-day business of prostitution. But the double standard of the American legal system (Europe and Asia not excluded) - where the customer and the pimp go free and the women are imprisoned – serves to promote the flesh trade rather than curb it.

Nevertheless, prostitutes are currently still the victims of pimps and gangs. Almost all the women are abused. The 'Georgian Mafia' is the most violent: rapes, threats with guns and beatings are a daily occurrence. Equally notorious are the so-called Chechen Boys and North Caucasians who deal in weapons, counterfeit money and drugs. Many of the girls have broken teeth. They say they fell down the stairs. But there are so many of them that either this business has the worst - maintained stairs in the world or these girls are being punched, reports a Brussels aid group. In a brothel in Germany, women were beaten with bats and administered electric shocks. In Prague girls in the trade were cut with razors to make them submit.

4.5.3   INFLUENCE OF DRUGS

Drug use is a central element in many prostitutes' everyday life. Getting 'high' and intoxicated are basic stimulants in the street culture where the women often hang out. Drugs are readily discussed: the effect of this or that substance, the quality of what's available, the scarcity in the city, etc. Drugs provide a platform of common experience.

Drug abuse has been extensive by these women. Some of them, for periods of time, use a lot of hard drugs, alcohol, and pills. But this use, they profess, is to some degree tied to social situations, parties, and the hunt for a 'high'. Then there is another group who call themselves 'hooked'. Their drug use is bound up in regular routines of addiction. When this is the case, the obsession for drugs and the hunt for drugs become the primary focus of their lives even at the expense of renting out their vaginas as garbage cans for hordes of anonymous men's ejaculations. It is striking how virtually their entire day is organized around this one object. Most of those that are hooked need three shots a day. After their wake-up shot (fix) they prostitute themselves to finance the midday fix. After that fix they need two more 'customers', one to finance their evening fix and one for the wake-up fix the next day. This can be interpreted as a sign of close connection between drug problems and prostitution.

While the drug problem escalates so does promiscuity among teenagers. Kids, sometimes eleven year olds, get so stoned out of their minds, they end up sleeping with people whose names they don't even know. The following article, *"Agony and ecstasy"*, clearly depicts how local teenagers as young as 12 have become caught up in a vicious circle of sex and drugs:

> *When you enter one of Durban's rave clubs the first thing that strikes you is the number of young girls standing around just waiting for things to hot up. I am told by a regular that many of the girls are under 14. He then points to Melissa and Joanne, who have each popped an illegally obtained ecstasy tablet an hour before the event and already feel 'touchy'. (They have learnt that ecstasy, besides producing the trance-like energy is also a 'love drug' which lets ravers experience sexuality in ways they would not normally do.)* [77]

What they don't know, or possibly choose not to know, is that the drug could kill ... that in some cases the blood can overheat to such an extent that death occurs within hours.

Maybe they haven't read the story of Leah Betts, the British teenager who took her first ecstasy pill at her birthday party. Two hours later she was in a coma. The following morning she was dead.

Another horrifying danger is their addiction to crack – a crytalline mixture of cocaine and baking soda. It is an alarming, attractive and affordable drug. Its dangers and its attractions are the same. It literally makes the user go crack. It is highly addictive – 75 per cent of takers are hooked on it after three goes. It is sold in small packages which are available cheaply. One doesn't have to inject it, or snort it like its parent drug cocaine - one just smokes it. It's very easy to take and it works quickly. It reacts within

8 seconds of inhalation and the user experiences intense pleasure and illusions of the mind before becoming physically tired and paranoid. It is precisely at this moment that drug lords and traffickers pounce upon these defenceless victims for economic sexual exploitation. This is an equal opportunity drug, affecting rich and poor, black and white. No section of the community is safe from it. Drug abuse and trafficking leads to violence and sexual licentiousness through which flesh traders become entwined in this vicious circle.[78]

What is even more disturbing is that many of them don't have enough money to buy drugs, so in order to obtain ecstasy (at about R120 a tablet), younger girls do sexual favours for dealers ... A club patron mentions that even males who were clearly younger than 18 were sometimes taken advantage of by older homosexuals.

> *"I once saw an older homosexual man offer an ecstasy tablet to a young boy. Once the ecstasy had taken effect, the younger person could hardly tell the difference between males and females - this was what the homosexual man hoped for. They then left the club together."*[213]

Therefore female and male prostitution is seen as a dramatic consequence of widespread drug abuse. It is imperative that the disease - drugs - must be fought in combination with the symptom, prostitution, when it surfaces.

4.5.4   CHILD PROSTITUTION

The drug epidemic, poverty and abduction are primarily responsible for an explosion in child prostitution. Kids run away to escape domineering parents or because they are being physically or sexually abused. Some children fall into prostitution through trickery and abduction. Easy prey, they become chattel for the sex merchants. Once victimized by the violent gangsters and pimps who control the sex trade, most children end up addicted to alcohol or drugs. Despair is the norm; suicide is common.

One of the more tragic reasons for the recent upswing in child prostitution is the mistaken belief that young sex partners are less likely to have AIDS. In fact the opposite may be true. Since the girls are small, they are not physically ready for sex yet, and as a result there is rupture and a lot of bleeding that makes them more exposed to HIV infections.

The market for child prostitution has always been strong especially in Asia. In India children command a price three times that of women, partly because of a common belief that sex with a virgin or a child cures veneral disease. Men also find it more thrilling having sex with children and it gives them an added sense of power, they say. To feed the sex market, tens of thousands of girls as young as 12 are recruited in Bombay and other cities, and then with the full knowledge of their parents, are shunted off to brothels.

In Thailand, which has the world's largest child sex industry (co-incidentally 50% of Thai child prostitution are HIV positive – a fact which foreign sex tourists are unaware of or undaunted by), sex mobsters go to great lenghts to find virginal youngsters. Entire villages in northern Thailand along the Burmese border are almost empty of young girls because they have been sold into prostitution. Having exhausted the Thai supply, child traffickers have expanded recruitment into Burma and China. And when the girls are no longer useful, they are tossed away. Prostitutes who returned to Burma from Thailand infected with AIDS are rumored to have been locked in prisons or even killed.

A typical victim of the Thai trade in prepubescent sex is Armine. She was spirited away from her hometown at the age of 12 when child traffickers convinced her parents they would give her a job in a beach resort restaurant. When she reached Phuket, a centre for sex tourism, she was forced into prostitution in conditions of virtual slavery. During her career as a prostitute she entertained two or three customers a night, almost all of them foreigners, until she was rescued by Thai police. But they arrived too late: Armine was tested HIV–positive and died of AIDS.[80]

In recent years Europeans, Australians, Japanese and Americans have flocked to southeast Asia by the thousands to engage in sex acts with Thai, Filipins and Sri Lankan youngsters that would win them a jail term in their home countries. Dozens of tourist agencies cater for this clientele, taking advantage of lax-law enforcement in Third World nations. Another favourite is Pagsanjan in the Philippine, about 65 km off Manila. Many homosexual tourists return there again and again, and have established permanent relationships with not just the boys of the town but also their families. The wealthiest of them buy homes, businesses, automobiles and other expensive items for the boy's parents. Some even "adopt" boys and take them home to Europe or America.

In Moscow alone an estimated 1000 boys and girls of tender age are selling their bodies. A similar rise in child prostitution has occurred in other Russian and East European cities. In Third World countries the numbers are also staggering: an estimated 800 000 underage prostitutes in Thailand, 400 000 in India, 250 000 in Brazil, 60 000 in the Philippines. The newest international sites for child prostitution are: Vietnam, Cambodia, Laos, China and the Dominican Republic. Everywhere, including affluent Europe and the U.S., the pattern is the same. Estimates of the number of U.S. prostitutes under age range from 90 000 to 300 000. Add those who engage in 'survival sex'–earning money for food or drugs–and the number rises to as many as 2,4 million.[81]

Sexual abuse of children is a crime worldwide, and must be prosecuted by criminal law. This problem is just not Bangkok's, Colombo's, Manila's. It's Paris's, Brussel's, Rome's. It's the nice, respectable man who goes down there to molest these children. As long as the man who jets to Thailand to sexually abuse children is not regarded as a criminal, the global agony will continue. These men are worse than vultures. In a selfish desire for gratification, they knowingly feed upon those in our world who most need protection, eroding their dignity, health and hope. The cruel exploitation of our children for profit is a shameful reflection on the state of male morality.

4.5.5 PROSTITUTION IN THE LIGHT OF ISLÂM

In pre-Islâmic Arabia, prostitution was practiced by women who had flags hoisted at their residences. They were regarded as professional prostitutes. Everyone who wished used to visit them. Whenever one of them gave birth to a child, all her visitors used to gather at her place, a physiognomist was called and on the strength of his knowledge, whomsoever he identified the new-born with, it became his, and on no account could he refuse to accept the responsibility, even if in reality he was not the biological father. This was regarded as voluntarily prostitution where the prostitutes themselves benefitted monetarily from servicing their clients.

On the other hand there were men who forcefully subjected their slave-women to prostitution. 'Abdullâh ibn Ubai, the chief of the hypocrites, possessed six slave girls whose bodies he hired for prostitution and consumed their earnings. On one occasion two of them returned after offering their services. One was given a bed-spread as payment and the other a *dinar* (currency in vogue during that period). After this 'Abdullâh ibn Ubai' once more commanded them to prostitute themselves. They refused claiming that they have rejected this unholy profession as they have now embraced Islâm which condemns illicit sexual encounters.[82] On hearing this, this wretched man mercilessly beat and terrorized them into forceful submission. When they presented their case to the Prophet ﷺ, Allâh Ta'âlâ revealed the following verse:

> "And do not force your maids to prostitution when they desire chastity, in order that you may make a gain in the goods of this life. But if anyone compels them, yet, after such compulsion, is Allâh Most Forgiving, Most Merciful."[83]

This is a distinct reprimand to those who compel their subordinates into forceful harlotry for the sake of contemptible worldly gain. It is detestable and is the demonstration of extreme shamelessness and immorality.

Prostitution in and of itself is total abuse of a woman's body. In prostitution, no woman stays whole. It is impossible to use a human body in the way women's bodies are used in prostitution and to have a whole human being at the end of it. Prostitution is not an idea. It is the mouth, the vagina, the rectum, penetrated usually by a penis, sometimes hands, sometimes objects, by one man and then another and then another.... This is 'gang rape' merely punctuated by a money exchange. In most people's minds the money is worth more the woman is. Her so-called sexuality becomes the only thing that matters, her body becomes the only thing that anyone wants to buy. Therefore her sexuality, along with her body, has been turned into a sellable commodity.

When a man uses a woman in prostitution, he is expressing a pure hatred for the female body. He can do anything he wants. She is regarded as dirt and real vaginal slime. Her mouth is a receptacle for semen. She has nowhere to go. There is no police to complain to; he may well be the person who is doing it. The lawyer that she goes to will want payment in kind. When she needs medical help, it turns out that he's also waiting in the queue. Therefore, for a woman in prostitution, this is the experience of life every day, day in and day out. Islâm has not only rescued prostituted women, who were available for the gynocidal kill, but also granted them sanctuary in the blissful union of *"nikâh"* (legal marriage).

Therefore those violating the laws of moral conduct and sexual decency, are not only wreaking havoc in an otherwise stable society but are also inflicted with the terrible dent of degradation and misery.

4.6 PORNOGRAPHY

Pornography is defined as printed or sexually explicit material intended primarily to cause sexual stimulation. Some people use the term to refer to pictorial material that glorifies violence against women by combining sex and the exposure of genitals in a manner that appears to encourage such behaviour.[84]

Degrading sexual objectification of women is common to all pornography. Women are consistently shown naked while men are clothed; women's genitals are displayed but men's are not; they are frequently tied up, gagged, blindfolded and under the physical domination of one or more males. Women are also humiliated and insulted, for example, urinated or defecated upon, ejaculated in her face, treated as sexually inferior or dirty, depicted as slavishly taking orders from men and eager to engage in whatever sex acts men want, or called insulting names while engaging in sex. In violent pornography, they are the recipients of even worse treatment, whereby, women characters are killed, tortured, gang-raped, mutilated and bound as a means of providing sexual stimulation or pleasure to the male characters.[85] Women are even reduced to animals, in sex with animal, and women are often 'anamilised' – and thereby dehumanised – in the language of pornography (as pets, or bunnies, for example.) What does this reflect about the moral value of women in western societies? Susan Brownmiller so eloquently noted that in pornography 'our bodies are being stripped and exposed for the purpose of ridicule to bolster that masculine esteem which gets its kick and sense of power from viewing females as anonymous, panting playthings, adult toys, dehumanized objects to be used, abused, broken and discarded',[86] just as these two examples depict: "I saw a *snuff* movie some years back. After a brutal rape, a young woman was tied to a table, and a hand was amputated with a Black-and-Decker type saw. Then she was raped again, and in the course of it her guts were spilled out by the rapist using a great butcher's knife. I didn't sleep the night I saw the video, and poorly for weeks afterwards. It still fills me with horror."

"I was sitting alone in a friend's home, waiting for this video to begin. What I can tell you is that on that night I watched a man participate in the act of sex with a woman, and during that act he plunged a large hunting knife into her stomach and cut her open from vagina to breast. He then withdrew the knife and stuck it into her left hand, removing the first joints from three fingers, which fell from the bed. The woman's eyes remained open, she looked at the knife and said 'Oh, God not me'. It took her approximately three minutes to die. The camera was left running. The film was then canned and put on the commercial market as entertainment. I have lived in fear ever since, knowing that while the rape and degradation of woman is filmed and sold as entertainment, women's status in society is worthless, and our lives within and outside our homes are also without value".[87]

Some who witnessed this butchery will switch off, some will cry, but some maniac will go out and do it to somebody's wife or daughter.

In recent years videos have revolutionized the availability of pornography and turned video porn into a mainstream entertainment product. Since an increasing number of people own or have access to video cameras, more men are making their own pornographic home movies.

A wave of hardcore computer pornography is also sweeping across the globe. Hard-core computer discs are now easily bought from sources throughout the U.K. and America by mail or telephone. One Los Angeles firm reportedly offered computer porn as a free bonus with bulk purchases of other software.[88] British and American college and university students now have unrestricted access to pornography through computer networks at these institutions and the quality of pornographic images has greatly improved – where once graphics were used to depict a broad range of sexual acts, now near photographic quality images are available.

Telephone pornography is also a relatively new invention, although it is not as lucrative as it was a few years ago. Some controversial issues have forced many telephone companies to shutdown such sources of 'revenue'. For example, in a landmark court case, a family sued Pacific Bell for $10 million because their twelve-year-old son had persuaded a four-year-old girl to orally copulate with him shortly after listening to a $150 worth of dial-a-porn message.[89] Pornography is more often used to try to persuade a child or woman to engage in certain acts, to legitimize the acts and to undermine their resistance, refusal or disclosure of these acts.

In the U.S.A., in one year alone, the pornography industry grossed eight billion dollars, said to be more than the music and movie industry combined. Six of the ten most profitable newstand monthlies were 'male entertainment magazines' and the combined circulation of Playboy and Penthouse was greater than Time and Newsweek. In the U.K., as in the U.S.A., pornography is 'big business'. It was estimated that so-called 'top shelf soft porn' magazines would sell over 20 million copies annually – this being a deflated estimation – since large parts of the industry do not release figures. Statistics indicates that 75 per cent of women involved in pornography are incest survivors.[90] The pattern of repetition of childhood abuse in adulthood, either in the position of abuser or abused, may attract women to pornography. South Africa also faces a wave of pornography as strict apartheid period censorship is lifted. International porn-pedlars are looking for new avenues and see an opening in this country.

Pornography is inherently anti-family and tries to create the impression that real men get satisfaction from secretaries, nymphomaniacs and by ogling girls. The "booby-trapped" husband then expects his wife to perform his exotic fantasies. His wife objects (rightfully so) to behaving like a sex machine. Acutely aware that her figure is unlike the latest pin-up, he is left frustrated and hungry to satisfy the craving which porn has aroused. What does he do? He searches for more explicit porn, more triple X videos and finally ends up in a massage parlour or escort agency. Since he has constantly witnessed the abuse of women in pornography and he cannot engage in that behaviour with his wife, girlfriend or children, he forces a prostitute to do it.

Pornography is addictive. Lust is a powerful addictive drug – it is insatiable, it cannot get enough and it slowly but surely demands greater and greater doses in its relentless but fruitless drive to satisfy its consumer. At the essence of pornography is the image of flesh used as a drug, a way of numbing psychic pain. But this drug lasts only as long as the man stares at the image, before the pain once more reasserts itself. Therefore there is only temporary relief. It is merely a mood-altering agent, i.e. you want more because 'you got relief'. It is this characteristic that leads men to want the experience they have in pornographic fantasy to happen in real life.

Professor F.I.J.van Rensburg mentions: "The plain fact is that this pornography, contrived by photographers and writers who know all the tricks of their trade, is deliberately designed to appeal to youths for whom a great curiosity about the human body is a normal thing. There is a vicious slickness about these publications... There is a horrible fascination in these things. They put in motion all sorts of carnal desires... and it requires no vivid labour of the imagination to perceive a cause-and-effect relationship between the nude magazine, the filthy photograph, the hard-core movie, and the act of adultery or rape." [91]

One of the most infamous serial sexual criminals and killers of all time was Ted Bundy, who believed that his descent into the horrible pit of sexual assault and murder was fuelled by an addiction to violent obscenity. He first discovered 'soft-core' porn in local stores. He also found explicit and violent porn in rubbish dumped in back roads and alleyways. The night before his execution he volunteered a public 'confession' to a religious broadcaster wherein he explained in detail how his addiction to pornography had operated:

> *"It happened in stages, gradually, it didn't necessarily... happen overnight. My experience with pornography that deals on a violent level with sexuality, is once you become addicted to it, you keep looking for more potent, more explicit, more graphic kind of material. Like an addiction you keep craving something which is harder, which gives you a greater sense of excitement. Until you reach a point where you begin to wonder if maybe actually doing it would give you that which is beyond just reading it or looking at it... I've met a lot of men who were motivated to commit violence just like me. And without exception, every one of them was deeply involved in pornography."* [92]

Pornography can therefore be an important link in the chain of sexual addiction and abuse; while it is not the only factor, its influence is often overlooked and underestimated. The addiction to pornography is not fun because underneath all these exhiliration lies desperation and anxiety, shame and fear, loneliness and sadness, that fuel the endless consumption of magazines and strip shows, X-rated films and visits to prostitutes.

The sex functions and the excrementory functions in the human body work so close together, yet they are utterly different in direction. Sex is a creative flow, the excrementory flow is towards dissolution. In the really healthy human being the distinction between the two is instant. But in the degraded human being the deep instincts have gone dead, and then the two flows become identical. *This* is the secret of really vulgar and of pornograhical people: the sex flow and the excrement flow is the same to them. Then sex is dirt and dirt is sex, and sexual excitement becomes a playing with dirt and any sign of sex in a woman becomes a show of her dirt. This is the condition of the common, vulgar human being and this is the source of all pornography.

The portrayal of women as sexual objects enjoying pain or humiliation or rape in a novel or painting cannot be exempted as pornography because the literary establishment call it *art*. Should the law place art above women's lives? Is the loss of a piece of pornographic *art* a greater loss than the loss experienced by a woman who is brutally sexually assaulted as a result of pornography? Surely the answer is 'no'. Labelling such a producer an artist is savagery of the worst kind.

One reason why pornography is incredibly dangerous is that 97 per cent of all the rape stories in pornography end with the woman changing her mind and having orgasms and being represented as enjoying rape. Sex offenders use this type of pornography to justify what they do. It provides them with an excuse and a reason for doing what they do.

One of the harms caused by pornography is that women are forced by partners to mimic the degrading acts and postures they see in videos and magazines. Women and their skin are also being used to advertise every product, cosmetic, dress, perfume and even medication. Every advert displays a model in a bikini advertising for the latest executive cars, or for feminine hygiene products or for nutritious cereal. Also many of the exercise videos use obscene positions to sell those programs. Many of the unnatural sex acts shown in some of the X-rated movies are committed by force and under threat. Many of the tortures which are shown in bondage are against the will of women.

The pornography of to-day, whether it be the pornography of the rubber goods shop or the pornography of the popular novel, film, and play, is an invariable stimulant to the vice of self-abuse and masturbation. Masturbation is the one thoroughly secret act of the human being more secret even than excrementation. It is the one functional result of sex secrecy, and it is stimulated and provoked by our glorious popular literature of pretty pornography, which rubs on the dirty secret without letting one know what is happening. Masturbation is certainly the most dangerous sexual vice that a society can be inflicted with since there is merely the spending away of a certain force, and no return. The body remains, in a sense, a corpse after the act of self-abuse, thanks solely to the mass of the popular pornographic literature and the bulk of the popular amusements which just exists to provoke it.

At every step, liberalists swarm like flies to protect the pornography industries 'free speech', even through - in the case of pornography - a man's speech is a woman's terror. Yet the same liberals would and do limit the freedom of industry to pollute because - in the case of pollution - one man's freedom is another man's hazard.

Watching nudity desensitizes men and women to normal sexual stimulus. People get used to it and therefore this is the most common cause of psychological impotency in the world. Just by becoming accustomed to these in order to get an arousal, they have to perform some more weird acts than plain nudity can provide. Nudity and pornography are also an addiction which leads to other crimes including drugs, murder, rape, abduction, incest and child molestation. It is a perversion and a waste of time. Is it a coincidence that the worldwide increase in rape and paedophilia (child pornography and molestation) has accompanied the increase in easily available pornography?

4.6.1   CHILD PORNOGRAPHERS AND PAEDOPHILES

A child molester is a significantly older person whose conscious sexual interests and unconcealed sexual behaviours are directed either partially or exclusively towards prepubertal children.[93] Such people are often referred to by the term 'paedophile', which means 'child-lover'.

Child pornography and paedophilia has always existed at the margins of society. For centuries those found guilty of it faced stiff punishment and societal disapproval. But a combination of liberalized sexual attitudes, laxer laws and technical advances that facilitate the spread of pornography have planted the seeds of a grim harvest: a hidden epidemic of child pornography that has broken out across the world. Man-child sex isn't something that happens between equals. It's brutal rape, pure and simple.

For years, the sexual abuse of children was thought of as something that took place mainly in Asia, but currently their American and European counterparts have overtaken them in this profession. How big is the problem? Statistics are notoriously tricky for one simple reason: abused children usually don't talk. Children feel ashamed about reliving the experience, and abusers tell them that something bad will happen to them or their relatives if they talk – so the children keep it secret.

Child pornography is closely linked to paedophilia, so its prevalance gives some indication of the magnitude of the problem. In the past three years, London's Scotland Yard seized some 64 000 videos. In one year alone, they secured 200 convictions for pornography involving children. In Germany, where adult pornography is a legal business, police believe that the annual turnover of child pornography is over R1 200 million. Child pornography plays a central role in child molestations by paedophiles, serving to justify their conduct, assist them in seducing their victims and provide a means to blackmail children they've molested. Paedophiles themselves admit the connection. "I had pictures I had taken myself with boys..." says an English paedophile who estimates that he abused 300 boys without being caught. When police finally did get to him they found his "library": a van filled with every kind of child pornography. "It definitely incited me to go further, and reinforced my belief that I was doing no harm," he says. "The kids in the pictures were smiling, you see?" The investigating officer found out that these artificial smiles were forced upon the victims by the adult making the pictures.[94]

The most obvious point about the production of child pornography is that pictures or films depicting adult sexual interactions with children cannot be produced without an act which is defined in law as illegal taking place.

Each piece of child porn involving adults (or in some cases animals) is a document of the sexual abuse of the child.

In the Swedish city of Malmo, police opened a suspicious-looking package from Denmark. It was addressed to M. Lund, a 23 year old bachelor. Out split 60 pornographic photographs of children. When police raided Lund's flat, they found 121 videos of child pornography, and a list of his connections in Sweden, Norway, Holland, Belgium, Germany, Austria and the US. In Epfach, a convicted child abuser was arrested for kidnapping, abusing and killing a seven-year-old child. In Belgium, police arrested M. Dutroux, a convicted rapist; soon afterwards he led them to the bodies of two eight-year-old girls who'd been abducted and imprisoned.[95] A heart-rendering story was told by a father at the recent pornography task force hearings in Durban: His eight-year-old daughter was raped by a 14-year-old boy who had wanted to "practise what he had seen in his dad's porn magazines." [96] The cases are part of a continent-wide web of shame and the images are brutal. A series of prepubescent boys and girls, sometimes babies in nappies, sometimes drugged, usually terrified and in pain are utilized in the preparation of child pornography. Child pornography is a disease which has contributed to 500 000 cases of incest involving father and daughter in the US. Child slave trade for sex involves 5 million children worldwide.

Therefore pornography depicts women as things or commodities enjoying pain or humiliation or rape; being tied up, cut up, mutilated, bruised, or physically hurt, reduced to body parts, penetrated by objects or animals, shown as filthy; bleeding, bruised or hurt in such a manner which makes these conditions sexually exciting. It thereby legitimizes prostitution, rape and child sexual abuse.

The Prophet ﷺ not only prohibited but condemned photography of animate objects. Had mankind only heeded this warning, the filth of pornography and its subsidaries would not have surfaced.[97]

4.7 CHILD SEXUAL ABUSE AND THEIR PERPETRATORS

Child sexual abuse covers a broad range of sexually-oriented activities which involve the child. These range from sexual exposure and fondling, all the way to vaginal or anal penetration. The following are some of the abusive activities:

* An adult showing a child his\her genitals; an adult asking a child to be looked at or fondled; an adult touching a child's genitals; an adult having a child touch his\her genitals; oral genital contact; forced masturbation; digital penetration, or penetration of vagina with foreign objects; anal intercourse; use of children for the production of pornographic materials.

Sexual abuse of children consists of activities which expose children to sexual stimulation inappropriate to their age, psychological development, and role in the family. When such activities occur between family members, the term incest or intrafamilial child sexual abuse is applied. If it is perpetrated by someone outside of the family - a babysitter, family friend, or unknown molester, it is termed as extrafamilial child sexual abuse.[98]

Therefore the perpetrators of child sexual abuse could be fathers, stepfathers, uncles, brothers, cousins and even trusted family friends. It could even be the 'nice' man next door. In at least 95 percent of child sexual abuse cases the culprit is someone the child loves and knows.[99] Sick, sordid and selfish, these perpetrators exploit the innocence and trust of young children for their own sexual gratification. After telling of incestuous experiences as a child, a woman says: "Having been sexually abused by my father for a period of approximately seven years, you can imagine some of the difficulty and confusion that I've experienced throughout my life". Another woman mentions: "When my two oldest girls were in their teens, their grandfather, a faithful (religious) member, was putting his hands where they never should be. He showed the girls pornographic material. He paid another girl to let him 'feel'." [100]

The following are some of the reasons why there is a general reluctance on the part of the abuse victims to share their secret with others:

- loyalty and love for the abuser makes it nearly impossible for them to speak up against people who are supposed to be their protectors, comforters and closest friends

- when they do pluck up enough courage to tell someone, the listener may respond to their revelations with horror, disbelief or denial

- the victim is often passive because of a perception of the abuser's authority; the young child often being told that the sexual activity is acceptable but must be kept secret

- they tell no one simply because no one asks [101]

Damage from early child sexual abuse, from incest, is often enormous. The real horror lies in the fact that sexual activity is a shared experience, and the victim tends to be stained with the guilt of another person's wrongdoing. The discovery of child molestation is a traumatic and stressful event in any family; but the discovery of incest is like stepping into the viper's nest. The mother who has discovered that the abuser is her own husband, or the child's father, stepfather or grandfather, finds her role extremely complicated. Her child becomes the victim; her husband – the betrayer; and she herself – the betrayed; not to mention the rest of the family and society at large.

Islâm has prescribed drastic measures to purify humanity of these bad elements. Not only should these offending criminals be severely punished but also access to their victims should be strictly monitored, if not completely barred. The most disgusting factor is that the great majority of those who are sexually abused experience the abuse from someone they know and trust. And unlike sexual molestation, which is often a sudden and forceful event, intrafamilial child sexual abuse is usually continued over a long period of time. The child's trust has been gained only to be betrayed. Since these types of immoral behaviour can be directly attributed to the flood of licentiousness that is currently wreaking havoc in society, in the form of nudity and pornography, governmental censorship should be duly enforced in completely banning such inciting material.

Society cannot claim to abhor the sexual abuse and exploitation of children and yet allow the portrayal of children as sexualized objects in the popular press and in advertising. It is alarming that we are becoming used to seeing children overly made-up and presented in provocative ways. Turning the pages of a children's clothes catalogue, it is no longer surprising when four-year olds with red painted lips sell blue jeans or underwear. It becomes the norm when 'respectable' magazines and products use children and sex to get their messages across. The implication is that children are available sexually and that youth is the most desirable form of sexuality.

4.8   RAPE

Rape takes place when a man has sexual intercourse with a woman without her consent. Due to the 'sex' part of the act, it is not something people talk about easily, people tend to see rape as a scandal, something to be hushed up, and often do not believe that the woman involved was innocent.

Rape should be seen for what it is. It is an attack upon a woman, and involves coercion, force and violence in varying degrees. It is one of the most common violent crimes in the world. The facts about rape should be considered and understood so that this growing immoral sexual crime problem can be seen in its proper context. Only then can the necessary steps be taken to curb the problem, and to cater properly for the victims.

Rape is an act of aggression in which the victim is denied self-determination. It is an expression of violence which, if not actually followed by beatings or murder, always carries with it the threat of death. It is a form of mass terrorism, for the victims of rape are chosen indiscriminately. Without doubt, forcible rape is one of the most terrifying crimes, since its consequences remain with the victim for many years or perhaps a lifetime, accounting for deep psychological problems. Further, in rape, the stigma usually falls upon the innocent victim, who is hence regarded as unchaste or marred, as if she were more a collaborator than she claims.

But why do men rape? Amongst others, the most contributing factors are the media and pornography, which encourage men to look at women as second class citizens, and as sex objects valued only for their reproductive capacities. It creates an increasingly violent culture that glorifies male domination over women. One convicted rapist volunteered: "You don't want to rape someone for the orgasm. You want to hurt a woman." [102] The use of rape as a weapon to terrorise and subdue women is evident in common threats such as 'if she doesn't watch out, she'll be raped' or 'women ought to be taught a lesson'. These beliefs are reinforced, propagated and legitimized by the media – advertisements, movies, television, pop songs etc. – provocatively dressed models and pornography which unfortunately is very much a part of our culture.

A mere glance at the images of men and women in the media will demonstrate to us their different status, roles and expectations in our society. The role that women play in advertisements is that of the enticing and seductive sex object. Advertisements depicting women as these symbols in various stages of undress accompanying such products as electronic devices, cars, alcohol and cigarettes are obviously directed towards men. They seem to bring women down to the same status as the advertised product, that is, something that can be bought and possessed. Muslims are commanded that the respectable woman is expected to be chaste and jealousy guard her body's 'purity' to award to the winning man. To do otherwise devalues her worth as a human being.

Similarly the current theme in pornography is that women really like being raped and that a lot of ordinary men commit, and get away with rape. Pornography is no safety valve as many people argue. Instead of serving as an outlet for the viewer's sexual and violent urges, it encourages the acting out of violent expression towards women. In the United States alone, more than a million cases of rape were triggered or strongly influenced by pornography.[103] Those areas with large numbers of pornographic outlets tend to have high rape rates. US police reports indicate that rapists are often found with pornographic materials in their possession.[104] Dramatic increases in rape statistics have been noted in countries where pornographic laws have been liberalized, including the US, England, Denmark, Australia and New Zealand. South Africa is said to be on par, and with the extent to which censorship is being relaxed these days, would even supersede these nations.

In an *Asiaweek* report on 'Sex in Asian Moviedom', a police source was quoted as saying "We've had a good number of assault and rape cases linked with pornography of one kind or another'. The report also carried a story of a sex crime committed by a 14-year-old school-boy. He had bound his 10-year-old neighbour's hands, raped her at knife-point and slit her throat. The panel of judges who presided at the boy's trial concluded that he had committed the crime because of the influence of a pornographic film.[105]

In the same way that pornography degrades women, child pornography turns children into sexual playthings. In the US (and its allies), almost half the turnover from the porn industry is from child porn. One and a half million children under 16 are used annually in commercial sex (prostitution or porn). Even advertisements use little girls, who, made up and posing provocatively, have fired men's lust for supple young bodies.[106] Actual cases linking pornography to sexual assaults and rape against children are too numerous to ignore:

* In San Antonia, Texas, a 15-year-old boy who tried to rape a nine-year-old girl told police that his father kept pornographic pictures at home and that 'each time he poured over them, the urge would come over him'.[107]

* In Florida, a nine-year-old boy sexually assaulted an eight-month-old baby girl with a pencil and a coat hanger, imitating acts he had seen in his mother's pornographic magazines. The baby died, and the boy was convicted of first degree murder.[108]

* In California, a nine-year-old girl was raped with a beer bottle by three schoolgirls four days after they saw a TV movie called 'Born Innocent'. The movie had a scene in which several girls used a 'plumbers helper' to rape a girl.[109]

Child pornography has changed the image of children – little human beings to be protected and cared for – into objects of lust and rape. It has made it acceptable for men to violently satisfy their animal appetite on these innocent little girls.

It should also be pointed out that rapists can also be men suffering from some sort of mental disturbance, like chronic depression or schizophrenia (a mental disease marked by disconnection between thoughts, feelings and actions). The rapist (such as a boss, or someone who has power over her), may also get the woman to submit through blackmail, as she could lose her job if she refuses. Although this example is not physically violent, emotional blackmail is used which in itself is a form of sexual violence.

Therefore, to eradicate rape, we have to wipe out pornography and all other vehicles for male oppression, because rape is not the result of uncontrollable sexual energy, but rather it's an expression of violent aggression.

4.8.1   MYTHS ABOUT RAPE

Rape is not a new sexual crime. Throughout the ages women have been raped and sexually abused by men. It is only recently that people have started organizing around the issue of rape, educating the public and giving support to rape victims. A lot of research has been done, and many of the commonly held beliefs about rape have been proved false. Let us look at the myths and facts about rape.

A cloud of myths surround the act of rape, the rapist and the victim because many rape victims seldom speak out about their experiences due to the unfounded shame and social stigma attached to it. Rape is usually seen as a horrible crime that only happens to *other* women.

A common belief about rapists is that he is often a stranger who lurks behind dark isolated alleys and bushes waiting to pounce on unsuspecting women. Although such attacks have occurred, they have been overplayed to the extent that many people are misled into thinking that rapes *always* occur in this manner.

The reality is that women could be raped *anywhere*. Indeed in a New Zealand case which caused a public uproar, a young mother was dragged off a busy Wellington Street, screaming for help, to a nearby school where she was repeatedly raped and sexually abused for five hours.[110] More than one-third of the rapes occur during the daytime (6 am to 6 pm). About one-half occur during evening hours (6 pm to midnight) and one-sixth between midnight and 6 am. About one-fifth of all reported rapes occurred in the victim's home or apartment and an additional 14 percent took place on the street, park, playground or parking lot. More than 6 out of 10 rapes occurred in open, outdoor places.[111]

Rape, at times, is also claimed to be provoked by women who court men's attention by wearing revealing or seductive clothes such as miniskirts, low-cut revealing dresses, skin-tight jeans and denims, bikinis, etc. which sexually arouse men. Flirtatious talking and behaviour with men are also an invitation to sex. Women who socialize and freely intermingle with men, without observing the rules of morality, are considered 'loose', and hence become easy prey to the sexual advances of rapists. The following comment is made by a lady interviewed by one of the newspapers:

> *"Women should avoid dressing in revealing and indecent clothes because these provoke thoughts of lust in the male. It invites rape because after all, she is so dressed in order to attract."* [112]

Girls in their teens are the most vulnerable to rape because they are most interested in securing the attention of the opposite sex, and therefore are most likely to dress and behave provocatively as the following statistics depict: "The rate of reported rape was highest in the 16-19 age group, regardless of the race of the victim. The rate for this age group is nearly three times the aggregate rate." [113]

It is also the issue of consent that usually stimulates questions about the woman's sexual history, or allegations of promiscuity, or suggestions that the women's clothing or behaviour were provocative; these are then the issues to the crime which puts the victim "on trial" as well as accused.

Most people believe that rape is committed by a stranger or a criminal or sex maniac. However, in one study it was revealed that the majority of the accused (67,8 percent) were either related to the victims, friends of the victims or in positions which made the victims trust them. The victim-rapist relationship was mentioned in 93 of the 113 cases studied. [114] These findings reveal that the danger of rape does not come only from strangers. Even men we know and trust may be potential rapists. That's the frightening part. In this very same study of 113 rape cases, violence and force were explicitly stated in 44 cases: victims were robbed, beaten, drugged, threatened (verbally and with weapons such as knives and guns), gagged, punched and pushed to the ground. Seven were killed. The following are just some of the cases:

* A. May, 9, was raped, sodomised and strangled with a piece of wire wound round her neck. A piece of wood was also stuck in the lower part of her body.

231

* S. Hajar, 21, was raped, and strangled with her own brassiere in a man's toilet. There were also burn marks on her body, leading police to believe that her murderer\s had tried to burn her body.

* R. Daud, 15, was raped and murdered and her body tied to a tree. She was believed to have been strangled with her headpiece which was found wrapped round her neck.[115]

Surely, the fact that rape victims are killed shows, beyond any doubt, that rape is an act of violence rather than a mere act of sexual lust. Women and girls of all ages, from pre-puberty to old senile women are open to rape. No girl or woman is immune. For that matter, no young boy is immune either.

4.8.2 ATTITUDES TOWARDS RAPE VICTIMS

Rape leaves permanent psychological scars on the victims that may not heal for a long, long time. It is a terrifying and traumatic experience, and the victim who reports the crime suffers a triple assault. The actual attack is the rape itself. If she survives that, and reports to the police, she suffers a second attack – when she has to submit to repeated interrogation and the re-living of her ordeal, and to medical checks which she might find offensive after what has just happened to her. One victim wrote of her experience when she reported to the police.

"The police officer who took down my report (a man) had no pity for me. He seemed to get his kicks from asking all sorts of personal questions, things like if I was wearing my undergarments. Then I had to wait for a senior police officer – the same thing again! .... While waiting for the senior officer, I was the centre of attraction. Every couple of minutes or so numerous male cops would come into my room with various excuses like to collect files. But I know in my heart, I was the object on display."

"Then I was driven to the hospital for a medical check-up but before my arrival the news had spread like fire. Some guy who had picked up the call from the police station told everyone he knew. Hospital staff were gossiping behind my back and I really felt terrible. I felt I couldn't face the world anymore and the only thing in mind was suicide."[116]

Another interesting point to note is this that in the immediate aftermath and for several days following the assault, rape victims may experience physical pain in areas of the body abused during the attack long after any viable injuries have disappeared: tenderness of the breasts if bitten, discomfort in swallowing if forced to orally copulate, a stinging sensation in the vagina following forced intercourse. Sometimes there are symptoms of this sort without injuries ever having been present.[117]

The third assault the rape victim has to endure is in public – in the courtroom. There her character is torn to shreds. Every bit of her past that could cast doubts on her morals is raked up in front of gawking strangers. And due to the time lag between the hearing and the incident (which can range from a few months to a few years), there is increased chance of inconsistencies and failure to remember details clearly, all of which are pounced upon by the defence. Hence, for much of the time, the victim is subjected to the embarrassment of giving her evidence in front of the extra large crowd that turns up at rape trials expecting juicy 'entertainment'.

It is this fear of public humiliation that has led to the under reporting of rape cases. A victim of a robbery or mugging will almost certainly get unrestrained sympathy from her family and friends. But a woman who has been raped feels 'soiled' and fears the reactions of others towards her. Do people think she was to blame? Will her husband want her anymore? Will her parents be ashamed of her? How can she ever face her friends and colleagues again? These questions will haunt her, adding to her trauma. But then, one might ask: Why should she feel shame, rather than simply anger at the attack?[118] The raped girl is the innocent victim of a brutal aggression, and her defilement should bring no disgrace to her whatsoever, provided she was within the framework of sexual morality.

4.8.3 ANALYSIS OF THE LAW

Rape represents an expression of power and violence to terrorise and humiliate women and forcible penile intercourse is not the only weapon used to assault them. The definition of rape should be widened to include any forcible penetration of the vagina by any means – stick, finger, leg, bottles, knives, etc. Being forcibly penetrated by a foreign object is as violating as being forced into unwanted sexual contact. Similarly forced oral sex and sodomy which often accompany forced intercourse should be included in the definition of rape.

Western laws have made rape difficult to prove. In order to convict a man of rape, the prosecution has to prove that sexual intercourse had taken place; it was without the consent of the women; and it was the accused who had committed the offence.

Sexual intercourse is usually proven through a medical examination of the rape victim and the rapists. In virgins, sexual intercourse is evident by the presence of a lacerated hymen with one or more radial tears, the edges of which are swollen, painful and bleed upon being touched if examined within a day of the rape. The tears usually heal within five or six days, hence the importance of an immediate medical examination to prevent the loss of evidence.

For a women who is not a virgin (married, widowed etc), sexual intercourse can only be inferred from other physical evidence. These include dried seminal stains on the external genital and thighs; recently dried blood on the genital organs; bleeding from the vagina which is not due to menstruation, any injury to the vagina itself, signs of veneral infection in the woman and the presence of the same infection in the accused; seminal and blood stains on clothes. However, many of the above signs are easily lost through washing or delayed examination.

In order to establish the absence of consent both the victim and the rapist are examined for signs of resistance. The victim is examined for tears and rips in clothes as well as blood stains; marks of violence on the body i.e. scratches, abrasions and bruises on the forearms, wrists, face, breasts, chest, lower part of the abdomen, inner aspects of the thigh and back are all indications of a struggle; epidermal cells , fibres and blood on broken nails and debris under the nail; bleeding and injury to the vagina which may also indicate forced penetration and a struggle.

The accused is examined for tears on his clothes or the loss of any portion of his clothes or buttons which will indicate a struggle had taken place; bruises, scratches and teeth bites, especially on his face, hands, thighs and genitals, abrasion or laceration on the head of the penis which may indicate forcible introduction of the organ into the narrow vagina of a child or a virgin.

In order to establish that it is the accused who had committed the crime, he is physically examined (if he is identified and arrested) for the following evidence: presence of blood from the genitals of the victim on the clothes or body of the accused; presence of loose strands of hair on the body of the accused similar to that of the victim. If he has not been circumcised he will be checked for smegma, a thick cheesy secretion found under the foreskin of the penis, which would have been rubbed off during intercourse.[119]

Despite the increasing incidence of rape, not enough is being done to effectively curb the crime and demand justice for the victims. The rape trial is actually the trial of the rape victim.For it is the victim, not the rapist, who has to prove her innocence. The first essential requirement, proof of penetration, is difficult to prove if the victim is not a virgin. Even for a virgin, delayed medical examination would be inconclusive as tears of the hymen heal after a period of five to ten days and become shrunken like the small granular tags of tissue in women who have had frequent intercourse. Lack of consent is also difficult to prove if there are no signs of resistance as in the case of a woman who had submitted to rape under threat of injury or death. In the case of proving the guilt of the accused, it is difficult to do so in most cases. Rape is usually committed when the victim is alone, so there is no witness to confirm the victim's testimony. It is only the victim's word against that of the accused. Therefore the testimony of a rape victim should not be doubted if there is no basic flaw in her evidence. She should also have a right to a closed hearing and a non-publication order so that her identity cannot be revealed in the media.

It is claimed that the requirement for proven evidence in rape cases is to prevent false allegations of rape. A report of rape can be false in three circumstances. First, the report can be made out of malice or mental derangement when no sexual act has occurred. Secondly, a woman who has been raped can make a false identification of the rapist in good faith. Lastly and most problematic are the instances when consensual sexual intercourse has occurred between the defendant and the complainant who later decides to make a complaint of rape. This last possibility is one reason why acquaintance rapes are looked upon with suspicion.[120]

However, the humiliation and trauma suffered by the woman during the medical examination and the trial make it most unlikely that many women will make false reports of rape. And especially in Muslim countries it would take an exceptionally morally corrupt woman to court the stigma that is associated with rape by laying a false charge.

4.8.4   ISLÂM CONDEMNS FORCEFUL COITUS

Islâm has not only withdrawn all its leniency on the rapist but also the wrath against the offender is in full fury. The punishment of the criminal is that it is, but the authority sitting in judgement has also been warned and instructed that here at least he should not grant any concession to the violator to whom Islâm has emphasized the importance of sexual morality and along with it displayed to him the detrimental effect of forceful, violent rape. He should be reminded of the maximum freedom granted to him in satisfying his sexual appetite by approved means, but in spite of this, he wilfully transgressed the limits extended to him by Sharî'ah without any disregard.

The woman who has become the victim of such brutality and is compelled to commit illegal intercourse against her will is exempted from punishment as the Qur'ân declares:

> *"But if anyone compels them, yet after such*
> *compulsion is Allâh Most Forgiving, Most*
> *Merciful."* [121]

In the Days of Ignorance some men subjected their slave-women to forceful harlotry for contemptible worldly gain. Since the element of coercion was utilized on these women who desired chastity, they were therefore 'raped' against their will.

Imâm Bukhârî narrates the following incident wherein a slave raped a slave girl. The culprit was brought before the court of Hadrat 'Umar ⚊, who after investigating the case, sentenced the offender, but acquitted the slave girl who was forcefully raped.

> "*Safiyâ bint 'Ubaid said: "A governmental male slave tried to seduce a slave girl from the khumus of the war booty till he deflowered her by force against her will; therefore 'Umar flogged him according to the law, and exiled him, but he did not flog the female slave because the slave had compelled her to indulge in illegal sexual intercourse without her consent.*"[122]

There is also another incident which occurred during the time of the Prophet ⚊ when a woman came out of her house to join the congregational prayer in the mosque. En-route she was forcefully grabbed by a man who raped her. She screamed and her cries alerted the people who rushed to her rescue and caught the rapist red-handed. He was then produced before the Prophet ⚊. The rapist confessed his guilt and he was punished according to the verdict given by the Prophet ⚊. And to the woman he said: "Go, you have been forgiven by Allâh." [123]

Therefore in forced sexual intercourse such as rape, the innocent party cannot be punished at all. On the contrary he or she is entitled to compensation in some form or the other.

Rape is not the personal private problem of the victim, but a symptom of something that is wrong in society. Even Islâmic countries are not immune to this violation of women's dignity. In a country where a woman's chastity, purity and honour must be preserved at all costs, even to death, women are subject to sexual assault almost daily. In some Muslim states rape is employed as a weapon by political opponents and is utilized as a show of raw power. It is also commonly used for revenge. "It isn't just law enforcers who see rape as a fringe benefit of their positions... And it is an easy crime to commit because punishment for men is so rare".[124] Rape, prostitution and Aids are interlinked.

Therefore, the Islâmic solution to the problem of rape would then be, to expel all forms of sexual excitement and stimulations from the social environment that surrounds us. Besides this, as a deterrent to others, those guilty of such a heinous crime should be publicly punished.

4.8.5 CONCLUSION

Anything that violates the order of the world is a source of evil and anarchy. That is why *zinâ* (fornication and adultery), prostitution, child sexual abuse, rape and all its associates arouses such strong, unanimous condemnation. Islâm remains violently hostile to all other ways of realizing sexual desire, which are regarded as immoral purely and simply because they run counter to the accepted harmony of the sexes and plunge the human species into ambiguity.

Islâm commands its adherents to refrain from all those satanic temptations that encourages a person from unlawful encounters. The Islâmic law looks upon fornication as a crime, and regards rape or the act of encroachment on the rights of the husband or wife (adultery) as additional crimes. Prostitution which is both non-procreative and devoid of emotional love, produces disturbances to society and is contrary to moral behaviour. Nudity and pornography seems to be an addiction which could possibly lead to other crimes such as drugs, murder, rape, abduction, child molestation and incest.

Thus, those violating the parameters of moral conduct by indulging in sexual vice are wreaking chaos in an otherwise harmonious society.

CHAPTER FIVE
Unnatural Sexual Behaviour
MORALITY IN ISLÂM

UNNATURAL SEXUAL BEHAVIOUR

5.1   INTRODUCTION

Homosexuality is one of the most common and most prevalent forms of sexual deviation or unnatural sexual behaviour today. It is generally defined as the preference for sexual relations with a person of the same sex. The term *'homo'* is from Greek, homo – 'same', and not from Latin, homo – 'man'. Homosexuality refers to both emotional attachment and sexual attraction to those of one's own gender. Homosexual people, who are so called *gay* people, may be either men or women. When most people use the term "homosexual", they mean a man who has emotional or sexual preference for other men. Women possessing such preferences are called *lesbians.*[1] Homosexuality as well as other forms of unnatural sexual practices such as lesbianism etc. are not generally considered to be deviant by those who have taken for granted various causative theories for unnatural sex, if the act is not the result of personal preference or attraction but is the consequence of being prescribed, imposed, casual, experimental or the mere need for experiencing momentary sexual gratification. The key word, therefore, in the definition of unnatural sexuality is *'preferred'* However, Islâmically, all unnatural sexual acts are described as sexual deviation and are evil, irrespective of the underlying cause. Homosexuality, therefore, is a crime of aggravated immorality. In addition, much of our society agree with countless other societies throughout the ages in condemning homosexuality. The vast majority of the world's religious denominations take the stance that homosexual acts are sinful. To cite an example of a religious viewpoint, the Roman Catholic Church states:

> *"As in every moral disorder homosexual activity prevents one's own fulfilment and happiness by acting contrary to the creative wisdom of God."*[2]

An indisputable fact about humanity is that everyone owes this existence to the union between his father and mother. This forms the basis for the family, the social unit of society. Although homosexual behaviour has been known to be present in some societies in the past, it is only recently that such behaviour has become increasingly mainstream and open. Due to this vigorous publicity, both sides of the issue, the conservative anti-homosexuals as well as the rejected homosexual elements themselves, have grown louder in voicing their views. Even many of those who do not take a religious stance on the issue find it to be an abnormality and a perversion and have voiced their opposition ever more adamantly against it. Prior to public awareness of the fact that Aids kills and anyone who has sex with others is a potential victim, gay male and female relationships were often casual.

5.2   IS HOMOSEXUALITY A CHOICE ?

Most men are sexually attracted to women, most women to men. To many people, only this is the natural order of things – the appropriate manifestations of biological instinct, reinforced by education, religion and law. Yet a significant minority of men and women are attracted exclusively to members of their own sex. Many others are drawn in varying degrees, to both men and women. How are we to understand such diversity in sexual orientation? Does it derive from variations in our genes or our physiology? Is it, for that matter, a choice rather than a compulsion?

It has been argued through the ages, long before science was ever evolved, that homosexuality is merely a choice. Many people state that gays only have homosexual relations because they choose to do so. Others profess that homosexuality is not a choice and due to the societal stigma which is associated with homosexuality very few would consciously choose a homosexual lifestyle and the discrimination that accompanies it. Socarides (Socrates), who has been successful in reportedly curing gays of their homosexuality, supports the decision that homosexuality is a choice and with proper medical attention there can be a cure. He mentions that homosexuality, the choice of a partner of the same sex for orgiastic satisfaction, is not inborn. There is no connection between sexual instinct and the choice of a sexual object. Such an object is *learned, acquired behaviour*, there is no inevitable genetically inborn tendency toward the choice of a partner of either the same or opposite sex.

Even the American Medical Association Council on Scientific Affairs supported the idea of homosexuality as a choice. In a report distributed by them, it stated,

> *"There are some homosexuals who would like to and probably prefer to change their sexual orientation. Because some homosexual groups maintain contrary to the bulk of scientific evidence that preferential or exclusive homosexuality can never be changed, these people may be discouraged from seeking adequate psychiatric consultation. What is more deplorable is that this myth may also be accepted by some physicians..."* [3]

How true are the predictions of this prestigious Medical Association (AMACSA) for, in direct contrast, the American Psychological Association takes the exact opposite view. In an APA statement on homosexuality, Bryant Welch states, *"The research on homosexuality is very clear. Homosexuality is neither mental illness or moral depravity ... Nor is homosexuality a matter of choice."* [4] He continues that research now indicates that homosexual orientation begins very early in life, perhaps *before* birth. He further states that there should be no reason to discriminate against gays in the slightest way as they are every bit as productive and as much of an asset as any other member of society.

We must be aware that this perverted act is a reversal of the natural order, a corruption of man's sexuality and a crime against the rights of females. The same applies equally in the case of female homosexuality.

The spread of this depraved practice in a society disrupts its natural life pattern and makes those who practice it slaves to their lusts, depriving them of decent taste, decent morals, and a decent manner of living.

5.2.1   THE SCIENTIFIC DEBATE

5.2.1.1   GENETIC THEORIES

Some researchers have turned to genetics in the search for a biological link to sexual orientation. Several recent studies suggest that the brothers of homosexual men are more likely to be homosexual than are men without gay brothers. Of these only one study, *(Baily and Pillard)* included both non-twin biological brothers and adopted (unrelated) brothers in addition to identical and fraternal twins. Their investigation yielded self contradictory and seemingly absurd results; some statistics support a genetic assumption and others refute it.

Identical twins were most likely to both be gay; 52 per cent were in agreement for homosexuality, as compared with 22 per cent of fraternal twins. This result would support a genetic interpretation because identical twins share all of their genes, whereas fraternal twins share only half their genes. Non-twin brothers of homosexuals, however, share the same proportion of genes as fraternal twins; however, only 9 per cent of them were concordant for homosexuality. The genetic assumption predicts that their rates should be equal. Moreover, *Bailey and Pillard* found that the incidence of homosexuality in the adopted brothers of homosexual (11%) was much higher than recent estimates for the rate of homosexuality in the population (1-5%). In fact it was equal to the rate for non-twin biological brothers. This study clearly challenges a simple genetic groundless assumption and strongly suggests amongst others, environment contributes significantly to sexual preference.[5]

Today, people practicing homosexual lifestyles seek tolerance and acceptance from society at large, and have achieved considerable 'success'. By organizing themselves into a political movement, homosexuals vigorously lobby psychiatric, legal and political organizations for changes in discriminatory laws to include sexual preference, and seek such things as the right to adopt children, health, pension and tax benefits enjoyed by legally married heterosexual couples.

The central theme important to their political agenda is the idea that homosexual behaviour is an "inborn" characteristic, perhaps genetic, like race or gender. Hence, according to these homosexual organizations, all moral reservations regarding their behaviour have to be dropped.[6] Many scientists have claimed that homosexuality is rooted in biology, but surprisingly enough, much of the research has been conducted by scientists living a homosexual lifestyle. Before making an analysis of various studies advanced to show a biologic or genetic basis for homosexuality, a few general comments should be made:

When judged, even with the animal world, human beings have been found to be the most genetically unsettled. In the words of Dr Joseph Wortis, Department of Psychiatry: "no complex high-level behaviour of the human species can be reduced to genetic endowment, not house-building and not sexual behaviour."[7]

Preferential and exclusive homosexuality is not naturally found in any human species, and it would be odd for such behaviour in humans to be genetically determined.[8] Homosexuals, needless to say, have reduced reproduction, and should have disappeared long ago if there was a genetic problem.[9]

Another factor, which makes genetic theories unacceptable, are cultural considerations relating to attitudes towards homosexual behaviour. The prevalence of homosexuality increases in cultures indifferent to such perversion, and have a casual attitude towards sex in general. For instance in ancient Graeco-Roman culture, homosexual behaviour was tolerated and was highly prevalent, whereas in cultures in which it was disapproved of, it was much more rare.[10]

Also difficult to reconcile with biologic theories is the fact that ex-homosexuals (people who have given up such behaviour), exist. If homosexual preference is "in the genes" like human racial characteristics like skin colour, change could not be possible. It is therefore clear that sexual preference is not an unchangeable trait. These shifts in sexual tastes of individuals show that homosexuality may be adopted by people who are confused, sexually adventurous, and rebellious, and has nothing to do with biological condition. In an interview with UPI, William Masters and Virginia Johnson stated,

> *"We're born man, woman and sexual*
> *beings. We learn our sexual preferences*
> *and orientations".*[11]

Studies from The Family Research Institute and Kinsey Institute show that the majority of current homosexuals, previously had sexual relations with the opposite sex; are currently sexually attracted to the opposite sex; and one to three percent of heterosexual adults actually considered themselves ex-homosexual.[12] Such studies identify homosexuality as a habit and preference and not an inevitability. Dr R Kronenmeyer stated in the *New York Tribune:*

> *"Homosexuals are made, not born that*
> *way. From my 25 years' experience as a*
> *clinical psychologist, I firmly believe that*
> *homosexuality is a learned response to*
> *early painful experiences and that it can*
> *be unlearned."* [13]

Therefore studies that mark homosexuality as a heritable trait do not say anything about *how* that heritability might operate and influence sexual orientation neither does it make clear *what* is inherited. Genes in themselves specify proteins, not behaviour or psychological occurrence.

5.2.1.2 THE BRAIN AND HORMONES IN HOMOSEXUAL RESEARCH

During past decades, much of the speculation about biology and orientation focused on the role of hormones. Researchers once thought an adult's androgen and estrogen levels determined orientation, but this theory withered for lack of support. Researchers have since pursued the notion that hormones wire the brain for sexual orientation during the prenatal period.

According to this assumption, high prenatal androgen levels during the appropriate critical period cause heterosexuality in men and homosexuality in women. Conversely, low foetal androgen levels lead to homosexuality in men and heterosexuality in women. This theory rested largely on the observation that in rodents early exposure to hormones determined the balance between male and female patterns of mating behaviours displayed by adults, but carefully designed and executed studies, most notably those of L. Gooren of the Free University of Amsterdam disproved those findings.[14] The development of new sensitive hormonal assays now in use fail to show any chemical differences between homosexuals and heterosexuals.[15] Therefore another popular belief which fell into disfavour was the idea that sexual preference is determined by hormone levels.

A group of researchers also recently published a study (neuroanatomic) claiming that a brain structure known as the anterior commissure is larger in women and homosexual men than in heterosexual men.[16] However, many of the subjects died of AIDS and medical information, was scanty, a factor which may have affected the results.

Dr Tâhir I'jâz, M.D. mentions a 1991 published study by Simon Le Vay that claimed that an area of the hypothalamus known as INAH3 is smaller in homosexual men and heterosexual women. The report was the result of the study of the brains from 41 cadavers and stated that there was a similarity in the size of the hypothalamus in gay men and heterosexual women, both smaller than that of the heterosexual men. Dr Tâhir disputes these findings by stating that the study had too many unknown factors to make them valid. For one he states that the sexual histories of the subjects were not absolutely known. Secondly, he states that the 19 homosexual subjects had died of AIDS and studies have shown that brain tissue has been documented to deteriorate in patients with AIDS and many have affected the study's results. Lastly, the hypothalamus was larger in 3 of 19 of the homosexual men than in the mean size of the heterosexual men. Dr Paul Cameron states, "according to Le Vay's theory, 3 of the heterosexuals should have been homosexual, and 3 of the homosexuals should have been heterosexual. When you completely misclassify 6 of 35, you don't have much of a theory." Both agree the study cannot be considered valid.[17]

Indeed, procedures similar to those used by Le Vay have previously led researchers astray. M.Ghar from the Institute of Animal Physiology, Germany, used a cell straining technique similar to Le Vay's to observe the size of the nucleus involved in singing in canaries. Two more specific straining methods, however, revealed that the size of the nucleus did not change.[18]

Given the well-researched, socially and medically destructive effects of homosexual behaviour on individuals, families and communities, compassion should lead us to discourage any cultural promotion of homosexuality as a moral and normal activity. Media reports indicate that homosexual experimentation among scholars has increased considerably in recent years as schools have presented homosexual activity as normal, desirable and even "cool". Sexually vulnerable young people are being steered onto a behavioural path that they and their families will sorely regret and which will even cost some of them their lives at an early age.

Homosexual behaviour, like other destructive vices, can be learned - and unlearned. Under no circumstances should it be promoted, particularly through misrepresentation of scientific studies.

The claim that homosexuality is a biologically predetermined characteristic, and homosexuals are 'born that way' stands on flimsy genetic, hormonal and neuroanatomic evidence. The answer as to the cause of such behaviour and why it appears to be flourishing in today's society is the result of many interacting societal and cultural attitudes and influences. Heterosexuality is the basis for the nuclear family, but this type of family particularly in the West, is disintegrating. Half of all marriages end in divorce and probably 50% of the children no longer grow up in a stable nuclear family. With the conventional family battered from many directions, the conventional pattern of sexual behaviour it required is also battered away. Children and adolescents, growing up without any guidance, are increasingly engaging in sexual experimentation with their own sex (up to a quarter of all adolescents in some countries).[19] Habits and attitudes developed early in life may affect behaviour in adult life. Parents dress their children the way they want to see them. For example, they dress their son like a girl because they wanted a girl and feel satisfied when they see that their child looks like a girl. Or they dress their daughter like a boy and deal with her as if she were a boy. Such relationships between parents and child slowly shift the polarity of a child because the child thinks of himself as having the sex which his clothing suggests. It is advisable that parents dress their boys like males and their girls as females, in the traditional way. Exposure to pornography at young ages and other unusual sexual experiences such as molestation by an older individual is also thought to play a role. A vicious circle is also created; a visible homosexual sub-culture appeals to youth (and older adults) looking for adventure and who are increasingly rebellious and take pride in shocking others. These social factors are a more reasonable explanation than biologic theories and "born that way" explanations.

Perhaps the answers to the salient questions in this debate lie not within the biology of human brains but rather in the culture those brains have created.

5.3   THE MORAL ISSUE

Since their inception, the gay movements are now not only on the brink of overturning the traditional understanding of basic institutions like marriage and family, but they are also dangerously close to gaining a range of additional "advantages" in the form of special minority *protected class status*. Yet under all this confusion, is one basic issue. It is not fundamentally a legal issue, although it has tremendous legal repercussions. It is not really about denying rights to gays. It is not fundamentally a medical issue although it has far-reaching medical implications. It is not really about finding a 'gay-gene' or funding AIDS research or health insurances for 'domestic partners'.

Fundamentally, it is a moral issue which basically, is: Is homosexuality right or wrong? Because what gay activists are pushing for is not just social sympathy or religious tolerance or political participation. They want validation - that is, *complete acceptance* of the homosexual lifestyle as the moral equivalent of heterosexuality. The goal of making it "OK to be gay" is the uniting force behind all gay activism. Sometimes one may be inclined to feel that he is merely trying to meet his need for love just like anyone else, therefore he cannot understand why God, who loves him so much has prohibited men from becoming gay. Moral codes are hard for many people to understand. To many, they seem bigoted and harsh. Try looking at it in this context: do you think theft, lying, murder and adultery are good for a person? Most psychologists agree that a person does harm to himself when he does these things. Because God loves us, He has told us the type of behaviour that will benefit us and which behaviour will harm us. He did not do this arbitrarily (drawing sins out of a hat, etc). He only forbids us to do that which destroys us or our relationship with Him. When we try to break God's natural laws we pay the consequences. In the same way, we harm ourselves when we live in opposition to God's moral laws. Some people differentiate between homosexual orientation and homosexual behaviour, usually viewing only homosexual behaviour as wrongful and sinful. Others, more religiously inclined, feel that both homosexual orientation and behaviour are every bit as illegitimate and disastrous.

5.4   WHAT DOES THE BIBLE SAY?

Religious trends during the past decades have made today's debate over homosexuality almost inevitable. In a growing number of denominations, the Bible's moral statements are increasingly seen as irrelevant to the Christian culture. The latest findings of science and an individual's personal experiences are treated as higher authorities than the Scriptures. Discussions about homosexuality frequently centre around a few isolated Bible passages. Often overlooked is the foundational teaching on human sexuality found in Genesis 1: "So God created mankind... male and female." (Verse 27). Richard Mouw, ethicist and president of the Fuller Theological Seminary, says evangelists want to preserve what they say in the Bible's teaching - that sexual intimacy "only properly occurs within the bounds of a relationship that is heterosexual, lifelong, faithful and confirmed by marriage." [20] The opening chapter of Genesis explains why fornication, adultery and prostitution - as well as "homosexual marriage" - are all distortions in God's original plan for sex. The Church warns that Almighty sternly condemns homosexuality and lesbianism.

> *Because of this Almighty gave them over*
> *to shameful lusts. Even their women*
> *exchanged natural relations for unnatural*
> *ones. And likewise also men, leaving the*
> *natural use of woman, burned in their lust*
> *one toward another. Men committed*
> *indecent acts with other men, and received*

*in themselves the due penalty of their
perversion.*[21]

Some 'scholars' have offered new interpretations for specific Biblical passages that prohibit homosexual acts. In one story of Sodom and Gomorrah (Gen. 19), Lot's (Lût AS.) visitors demand to "know" the angelic visitors. The explanation that they wanted merely "to get acquainted with" the strangers makes Lot's response most puzzling: "Don't do this wicked thing", (Verse 7). The context supports the traditional interpretation of homosexuality, and other biblical passages link Sodom with sexual immorality and perversion (2 Peter 2:7).

In Leviticus 18:22, God clearly commands, "Do not lie with a man as one lies with a woman, that is detestable." Pro-homosexual scholars argue that Christians are no longer under the Mosaic Law. But here, one must carefully distinguish the dietary or ceremonial laws (abolished in the New Testament - Mark 7:19; Heb 10:8-10) from the moral laws (reinforced in the New Testament and still applicable today - Mark 7:20-23; Matt. 5:27-28). Differentiating the two types of laws answers the question, "Why do Christians quote the Old Testament on homosexuality, then ignore the commands that prohibit eating shellfish or wearing clothing of mixed fibres?" The important distinction between these two laws is reflected in the Old Testament penalties for breaking them. Disobedience to ceremonial laws resulted in uncleanness (Lev. 11:24) while breaching the moral law meant death (Lev.20).

The first chapter of Romans is usually considered the most thorough and a clear condemnation of homosexuality in the Bible. It also contains the only specific reference to lesbianism. But some people claim that Paul's statements are "culturally bound", addressed to first-century believers and therefore not applicable today. But God declares that His moral does not change and that His word "stands forever" (Isa. 40:8).

What did Paul mean when he stated that homosexual acts are "unnatural" (Rom. 1:26-27)? Contrary to what a person feels is natural? Not necessarily. Many homosexuals say that they have always felt attracted to others of their own gender. But we live in a fallen world; sin has distorted our perception of truth (Rom. 1:18). So what someone feels is "natural" can still be wrong. Paul was referring to the natural order as God originally created it.

Corinthians 6:9 mentions "homosexual offenders" are included in a long list of people who will not inherit the Kingdom of Almighty (Paradise). This passage seems clear - until the discussions begin about the exact meaning of the original Greek word. Does "arsenokoitai" refer to lustful, uncommitted male prostitution or to a loving, permanent relationship? The literal meaning is "a male who lies with a male". There are no qualifications. *All* homosexual behaviour is forbidden, no matter what degree of love or lust is involved.[22]

What about Jesus's ('Isâ AS.) silence on this issue? There are many sexual behaviours that he did not address (incest, rape, bestiality). That doesn't mean they are permissible. Jesus always upheld the Old Testament law (Matt. 5:17-19), which strictly condemned homosexual acts, and he affirmed abstinence as the only legitimate alternative to pre-heterosexual marriage.

Therefore, those who practice homosexual acts receive in themselves the due penalty for their perversion and reap a bitter harvest of emotional and physical suffering. Though AIDS is not necessarily a direct judgement from God, it certainly is a devastating consequence of sin.

5.5   ARGUMENTS FOR AND AGAINST HOMOSEXUALITY

The following is a question and answer presentation of homosexuality drafted in such a manner where people on both sides of the issue could understand.

5.5.1   PROPONENTS - THOSE ADVOCATING HOMOSEXUALITY

Homosexual extremists have vigorously launched an all out campaign to portray this social evil as a healthy ingredient of man's sexual diet by manipulating scientific data and engaging in heated debates with their opponents. The following statements appearing in the Frequently Asked Questions List exposes the filth with which they are contaminated.

Most of the arguments on homosexuality revolve around these points and their well-known rebuttals:

Being gay is just an abnormal lifestyle
Homosexuals argue that the belief that gayness is a simple lifestyle choice has been researched, and the consensus is that sexual orientation - the sex to which one is attracted - is, in almost all cases, not voluntarily chosen. This seems to be a deliberate concoction. They further proclaim that gayness is not 'abnormal'. Gays are in the minority, but then, so are left-handed people. Gayness is clearly every bit as natural as straightness, and the abnormal label is meaningless, they argue.

The gay rights movement is a social evil
Their concept is that the gay rights movement is a full-fledged part of the civil rights movement. Racism and anti-Semitism (discrimination based on religion) are both intolerable in a democràtic society. Likewise heterosexism (discrimination based on sexual orientation) is intolerable, and for exactly the same reasons. They say, people deserve equal treatment under the law, regardless of race, religion, or sexual orientation. It is apparent that they have equated and confused religious and ethical rights with sexual perversion.

Gays want special rights
The gay rights battles that have been so prominently fought so far have involved efforts to secure laws that would prohibit discrimination based on sexual orientation, just as current laws prohibit discrimination on the basis of race or religion. Sometimes it is asserted that gays will next be attempting to get affirmative action protection for themselves. No gay rights group has ever proposed, or is considering proposing, such legislation, they contend. With homosexuality not only legalized, but also promoted, they are in the process of demanding such 'protection'.

The 'Christian' God says homosexuality is bad
They even declare that some passages in the Bible can be interpreted this way. There are many conflicting interpretations, and in any event, they proclàim that the Bible is not the direct word of God but the words of humans. Many of the cultural implications of the original Hebrew and Greek in the Bible are no longer known. Moreover, there are many other

things that the Bible says that are "bad". Slave owners quoted Colossians 3:22 to prove that God supported slavery. Many doctors resisted providing anaesthesia to women in labour because pain in childbirth was Eve's punishment (Genesis 3:16). And the Bible says that women are forbidden to teach men (1 Timothy 2:12), wear gold or pearls or dress in clothing that 'pertains to a man' (Deuteronomy 22:5). Yet you do not see the fundamentalists complaining about any of these. If an anti-gay poster quotes only the anti-gay parts of his translations of the Bible, and chooses to ignore other interpretations or other parts of the Bible that he does not agree with, it is clear that he is using the Bible to support his anti-gay position, rather than basing that position on the Bible. There are other religions that think poorly of homosexuality. They feel that such religions often also tend to adopt a fundamentalist attitude and are a major threat to the peaceful existence of humanity on this planet.[23]

Accepting gays will lead to social breakdown, like in ancient Rome
There is no reason to believe that the fall of Rome was due to gays any more than that it was due to the rise of the Christian emperors, they contend.

Letting gays into the military will damage military effectiveness
They even say studies have been done on whether homosexuals are in any way less fit for military service than heterosexuals. It was **agreed** (by them naturally), that being gay in no way affects a person's ability to serve with dignity and distinction, and to observe military codes of conduct. Several countries around the world (Israel and Australia, to name two) have no policy against gays in the military and their military capability has not suffered in the least.

Anyone who disagrees about gays is a bigot. 'Bigotry' is defined as "fanatical devotion to one's own group, religion or race, and intolerance of those who differ". They claim that most anti-gay posters who attack gays express their dislike of anyone who is gay; they attack a whole group of people simply because of those people's sexual orientation.

Gays are paedophiles
They claim that studies done of the sexual preferences of paedophiles (people who compulsively abuse non-consenting children sexually) have

shown that the vast majority of paedophiles are straight; that is, there are far fewer gay paedophiles than would be expected given the average number of gays in the general population. It seems that these are merely imaginative statements without any statistical substantiation.

If we accept gays, what next?

Homosexuals exclaim that people who frequently make the above comparison also use the following 'argument': if we accept gayness, why should we not accept sadism, masochism, bestiality, paedophilia, necrophilia? After all, are they not marginalized practices? The argument of why gayness is utterly unrelated to paedophilia has already been elaborated on. No more is it related to sadism etc. Bestiality is morally wrong because animals cannot consent to sex. Therefore, the claim that linking gayness to sadism etc. is simply unjustified, they proclaim.

Gays want to teach kids to be gay

Gays claim that their curriculum contains no advocacy of homosexuality and no sexual content whatsoever. They say that the gay-specific message is simply, "Some kids have gay parents, and some of those families are happy" The gay rights movement wants to educate kids that gays exist. There is no evidence, they say, that children's sexual orientation is shaped by their education in any event - kids can't be taught to be gay. A gay couple that loves each other and the child will certainly make better parents than a straight couple with an unwanted child The most important factor, they contend, in raising a happy and healthy child is whether the parents give the child ample love and support, and not to which sex the parents belong.

AIDS is a gay disease

Gays do not feel that way. They say that AIDS affects gay and straight people and worldwide most people with AIDS are heterosexual. They even go further by emphasizing that the risk of AIDS among the (mostly heterosexual) rural poor is becoming so great that many celebrities have joined a campaign devoted to AIDS education among straight people. The fact that gays were so hard hit by the epidemic says more about the lack of knowledge about the disease in its early days than it says about gay's sexual practices, they assume. Safer sex techniques, many of which were developed by the gay community, they say, have gone a long way towards eliminating the risk of AIDS transmission through sex, and gay women - lesbians - are the group with the lowest risk of contracting AIDS.

Gayness is a genetic defect, since gays cannot reproduce
They feel that the statement, "Gays can't have kids, so they're defective, and they will soon vanish" is clearly absurd, since if it were true, homosexuality would not exist now. Straight people occasionally have gay children and they falsely assume that gayness is a stable part of the human gene pool. They even say that people who argue against gays on the basis that they are defective since they cannot reproduce, clearly do not feel the same way about all the straight people who cannot (or do not want to) have children, therefore their argument is flawed. Moreover, they proclaim that since gays can (and do) adopt, and lesbians can have children through artificial insemination, gays can be parents.

Anal sex is something only gays do and is always unhealthy
Anal sex has been determined by them to be practiced regularly by about 15% of the population which includes gay and straight people of both sexes (men and women). They have not as yet substantiated such a statistic. This, to them, means that only a minority of gay people actually include anal sex of any kind as part of their sex life, which means more straight people enjoy this than gay people. They accept the fact that unprotected anal contact is unhealthy, but then advocate that safer sex techniques can make anal sex extremely safe, and since the anus contains more nerve endings than any other part of the male body (and only the clitoris has more in the female body), many people enjoy anal sex as an integral part of their healthy sex life.[24]
How can one possibly reconcile with such a bestial mentality, where animalistic sexual appetite is satiated via these unnatural channels? This legalized perversion, if not stopped timeously, would ultimately lead mankind to self annihiliation.

5.5.2 OPPONENTS - THOSE OPPOSING HOMOSEXUAL BEHAVIOUR

In order to understand what it means to be gay, you first have to define what gay means? Generally people who hold the view that homosexuality is an alternative lifestyle say that anyone who is primarily attracted to the same sex is gay. To them there is no way out ... in other words, they say you are born gay ... it's in your genetic make up ... etc. They are usually referring to *sexual orientation* when they use the term gay. Others are referring to *sexual practice* when they use the word. The question itself rests on the notion that everyone must have a label of some sort, which is a false assumption.

As far as sexual orientation is concerned, on one end of the spectrum there are people who believe that it is something in a person's genetic make-up that cannot be changed. On the other hand, there are people who prefer the term *sexual preference* and assume that homosexual attractions are entirely a conscious choice of the individual. Both these views have their flaws because they create the assumption that everyone's mind works the same way. The first view also takes extreme liberties with scientific facts relying on recent experiments that have supposedly provided conclusive proof of genetic influence. The fact is, these experiments have not *proven anything*. The latter view fails to acknowledge the fact that there are many people dealing with homosexual feelings who truly desire to lead a heterosexual lifestyle. When one looks at the evidence it is hard to say that most people choose to have homosexual feelings. Practicing homosexuality is where the choice comes into the equation.

People will generally be curious to know that if it is not genetic then where do the homosexual feelings come from? Since each personality is different it is impossible to come up with an equation that would apply to everyone. In most cases gay feelings come from a desire for unconditional love from a person of the same sex. Often this stems from a bad relationship with (or the absence of) the parent of the same sex in the formative years (pre-adolescence). In a few cases they may result from confusion left by sexual abuse in early childhood. But this is not the most important issue because the temptation of attraction is not the sin. Entertaining and acting upon the attraction is where one crosses the line from temptation into sin. It is a fine line that can be avoided by staying away from the edge of it. And *even* if science were to conclude tomorrow that homosexual attraction is influenced by genetic tendencies this would not affect the argument in any way. After all ... studies have shown that many tendencies are genetically influenced, including alcoholism and drug abuse. Yet people are still held responsible for their actions.

One may irrationally assume that why should one be held responsible when one had nothing to do with these attractions? One may have had nothing to do with the initial feelings but one has everything to do with how much control one has over someone else. Because human beings are creatures of habit, the things they do affect the intensity of their feelings. In spite of what some extremists have tried to propagate, human beings are *not* like animals. They have a choice when it comes to all variables in sex: how, when, with whom, etc. ... they are not slaves to instinct.

Adultery is a sin ... so is fornication or even gambling. Why single out homosexual behaviour? No one should single out sins, but at the same time one has to approach the topic with reality by understanding that certain sins have greater earthly consequences than others. Certainly the other sins can be just as damaging as the sin of homosexuality. But today there is a movement to accept homosexuality as an "alternative norm". People who reject this idea are labelled as "intolerant" and are accused of singling out homosexuality, when in reality this is in response to people who say homosexual behaviour is not a sin at all.[25]

5.6   HOMOSEXUAL LINKED BEHAVIOUR PATTERNS

There are behaviour patterns which are not always homosexual, but which are nevertheless *associated with homosexuality*. They include transient, situational, and accidental homosexuality; bisexuality; transsexuality; transvestism; androgyny; and heterosexuality.

5.6.1   TRANSIENT HOMOSEXUALITY

Transient homosexuality means a short period of experimentation, during which the homosexual transaction does not fulfil the emotional and social expectations of the person. Transient homosexuality is usually experienced by some people as part of a general inquisitive enquiry into sexual behaviour.[26]

5.6.2 SITUATIONAL HOMOSEXUALITY

Situational homosexuality is a conventional description, usually applying to a group (or population) of persons who are removed from society, and whose access to opposite gender companionship is denied. Common examples are prison populations, sailors, men under arms, and (in the South African context) the Draconian system of migrant labour, which entails forced compound living where thousands of men are separated from wives and families. It is claimed that situational homosexuality has a direct link with accidental homosexuality in certain circumstances. In Cape Town during and after a series of boycotts in "Coloured' and "African' schools a recognizable increase occurred in male workers. Although there was an even spread of 'Coloured' and white men, some African youths were also involved in commercial sex work.[27]

5.6.3 ACCIDENTAL HOMOSEXUALITY

Accidental homosexuality may be experienced in different forms and in different degrees. Usually it takes place under duress such as rape or coercion, for example, in a prison cell or via group pressure and molestation or seduction by older men.

5.6.4 CHILDHOOD/ADOLESCENT HOMOSEXUALITY

Some form of same-gender experimentation often occurs in boys and adolescents. (For this reason Islâm has discouraged boys and even girls from sleeping in the same bed or under one covering). It is said that for some experimenters this is a way of responding to spontaneous arousal situations.

5.6.5 BISEXUALITY

This refers to those who are sexually attracted by members of both sexes. Bisexual behaviour is sometimes presented as being a period of temporary exploration into either homosexual or heterosexual behaviour. For some it reflects an uncertainty in sexual preference, so that same - and opposite - gender behaviours are both negotiated. Bisexual behaviour may also be reflected as a cult or fringe activity.

5.6.6 TRANSSEXUALITY

This has been defined as those persons having physical characteristics of one sex and psychological characteristics of the other. Transsexuals have also been described as women trapped in men's bodies and some authors have also linked transsexual behaviour with hermaphrodism and deviancy. It is also claimed that transsexuals have a strong desire to be all female, and may or may not have a bodily type to enhance the female status. They are often referred to as 'twilight people', for their ultimate goal is to be heterosexual, yet their sense of acceptance is within the gay framework. A confusing issue arises as to their sexual behaviour. Hence many of them attempt to resolve their sexuality within a circle of transsexuals, and become both homosexual and 'pseudo-lesbian' in their sexual activities. It is not uncommon to see transsexuals with gay partners or being intimate with other transsexuals.

The lifestyles of some of them could even be extremely violent as the following article appearing in the *Sunday Tribune* under the caption *"Trapped in a man's body, she's wanted for serial killing."*

> *Close friends of the man police are hunting in connection with the alleged serial murders of five people say 'he is a woman trapped in a man's body.*
>
> *There is a warrant of arrest for Samuel Coetzee, (more commonly referred to as Kimberley), whom police have linked to the murders of four men and a 15 year-old boy in thePretoria/Johannesburg area over the past three years. The murdered males were all strangled - one was also shot and another had his genitals cut off. (These are some of the crimes of a person who was described as "always like a woman, very feminine and soft, not capable of hurting a fly".)*

> *Being a prostitute he frequented gay bars*
> *and discos like Club 58 in Hillbrow and*
> *had often entered and been placed in drag*
> *queen beauty competitions. After being*
> *found guilty and convicted he committed*
> *suicide in prison.*[28]

5.6.7 TRANSVESTISM

Transvestite behaviour is a mixture of homosexual, bisexual and heterosexual activities. It refers to an urge to dress in clothing of the opposite sex. Cross dressing for them is part of a ritual obsession as well as the creation of an alternative sexual outlet. In Johannesburg, as in Cape Town, one discotheque in particular caters for the sub-culture of 'drag', and beauty competitions are encouraged. Like transsexuals, transvestites are regarded with a certain amount of contempt by many homosexuals. However, there are some gay men who are attracted to the soft, feminine qualities that these transvestites project.

Transvestites are also posing a problem for baffled policemen and magistrates. With the increasing numbers of transvestite prostitutes undergoing sex change operations in Durban, these authorities now face the difficulty of deciding if it is a boy or a girl. Just recently Durban had become the sex change capital of South Africa, with Addington Hospital turning a dozen men into women. But this is creating increasing headaches for police as Brian Boucher, station commissioner for Point Police Station mentions:

> *"At one time, in the '60s Durban had the*
> *largest transvestite population in the*
> *country. A whole suburb of the Cato Manor*
> *settlement was made up of them. Now we*
> *have a number of transvestite prostitutes*
> *and they are becoming a real problem. The*
> *searching process in particular is*
> *extremely difficult. Transvestites want to*
> *be treated as women and as such they want*

261

> *to be searched by women. We obviously*
> *cannot have a woman search the nether*
> *regions so we have now found a*
> *compromise, a man searches below the*
> *waist, a woman police above the waist.* "[29]

Transvestites prostitutes are normally given the option of a fine and literally spend only about five minutes in the cell. Due to such lenient sentences they immediately surface on the streets and once more start plying their trade.

Consequently, societal hatred towards these outcasts has been based in three basic beliefs. The first of these is that these types of homosexual behaviour always manifests itself in sodomy. The second is that it defies the laws of procreation. The third represents these perverts as a subspecies of humankind, characterized by sin.

Homosexuals are seen to be members of a 'third sex', an inversion of the natural process, defying traditional male-female roles. It also involves a man emulating a woman, with the trappings of cross-dressing, effeminate behaviour, and passive psychological responses. Homosexual behaviour represents the activities of paedophiles, including the seduction of young boys. It also reflects self-admiration, a desire to preserve male beauty in a declining male body through the love of younger, sexually attractive males. Homosexuality is also linked to outwardly bizarre behaviour, designed to confuse sexuality with role performance.

5.6.8 HERMAPHRODITE

This refers to a person, an animal or plant having characteristics of both sexes. The Greek derivation of the term androgyny is from *andros* (male) and *gune* (woman). The literal interpretation corresponds to hermaphrodite. It often manifests in people who are clinically confused and secondly, it facilitates imaginative dressing. It is not uncommon to see men in the streets of Hillbrow, Johannesburg, wearing skirts, leather jackets, high heeled shoes and light make-up.

What is a hermaphrodite, a *mukhannath*? A man? A woman? Something else? Is it a malformation of nature? In a world in which the pre-established but divided harmony of the sexes is the rule what exactly is its place and what is its status? Does the hermaphrodite inhertit as a male (double) or as a female (half). Does he\she wear the veil? Where does he\she pray, with the men or with the women? What in fact is he\she?

Al Washtânî defines the hermaphrodite thus: 'He resembles women in his moral qualities, his way of speaking, his way of walking. The name comes from the word *takhannuth*, which is a way of associating gentleness and a break. Indeed the *mukhannath* is gentle of speech and broken of walk. It may be as a result of creation, but it may also be a mode of behaviour deriving from a perversion.' [30] Therefore hermaphroditism is a pole of ambiguity.

The question was already posed even during the lifetime of the Prophet 🐾, who advocated removal to a safe distance. The incident of the Hermaphrodite of Medina is interesting on more than one account. One day, when the Messenger of Allâh was at home Umme Salmâ, one of the Prophet's wives, was visited by a hermaphrodite who said to her: 'If Almighty assures you victory at Tâif tomorrow, I shall take you to the daughter of Ghailân: seen from the front she has four folds on her belly, but seen from behind she has eight! Her mouth? A genuine scarlet flower! When she walks, she folds herself in two! When she speaks, she enchants! The space between her legs is an upturned jar...'. The Messenger of Allah, who was present, then said to her: 'You allowed your eyes to dwell long upon her!' And he decided to exile him. [31]

Ibrâhîm Halbî's *Multaqa al-Abhur* deals with this question and provides a perfect summary of it. [32] The hermaphrodite has two sexes, male and female. He is to be characterized by the sexual organ from which he urinates the most. When there are equal quantities, there is an ambiguity, for the quantity of urine emerging from both sexual organs can no longer serve as a positive criterion. One will then wait until puberty and the appearance of some feature of masculinity. If his beard grows, if he is able to have sexual intercourse, if he has nocturnal emissions, he is a man. If, on the other hand, he menstruates, gets pregnant, has fairly voluminous breasts and can give milk, if one can have coitus with such a person, then she is a woman. But if none of these characters appears, or if, on the contrary, they appear, but in a contradictory way, then there is a definite uncertainty .... and one is dealing with a true hermaphrodite. When the ambiguity is obvious one must be extremely careful to avoid undesired consequences. He will say his prayers veiled, but will take up his position between the men and the women. If ever he says his prayers in the rows reserved for the men, those who were his immediate neighbours on the left, on the right, in front and behind, must perform their prayers again (since their prayer in the company of a woman , may be regarded as null and void). If he has said his prayers in the rows reserved to the women, then *he* must repeat it. (It is his prayer that runs the risk of being null and void, if he later proves to be of the male sex). He must neither wear silk clothes nor jewellery. On his pilgrimage to Mecca he must not wear sewn clothes and he must unveil neither before men nor before woman. He must not travel without a veil. He will be circumsized neither by a man nor by a woman. But a female maid will be hired for him at his own expense or at the expense of the *Bait al-Mâl* (Islâmic Treasury) and she will circumcize him. If he dies before his sex is determined, he will not be washed. But he will be given simply a pulveral lustration (*tayammum*). He will be wrapped in five winding sheets. When he reaches adulthood, he will never attend any ceremony of funeral washing of man or woman. It is advisable to cover his grave with a veil as his body is being lowered into the grave. In the case of an inheritance he must have the smallest share. If his father dies and he has a brother, that brother inherits, according to S͟hâfi'î, two shares and the hermaphrodite only one. According to Abû Yûsuf, he will have the arithmetical average, that is, three-sevenths. If he is found guilty of theft, his hand will be cut off and if ever the law of retaliation is applied to him, he will be treated as a woman, whether he is the victim or the author of the original damage. Due to the fact that a true hermaphrodite cannot be classified as a male or female these measures have been directed to him/her in order to avoid undesired consequences.

This concern to go as far as possible into detail in according importance to extreme cases, shows a genuine attempt to establish as precisely and strictly as possible the limits of the sexes, for these are in fact, limits laid down by Almighty in creating an impenetrable wall between the sexes.

5.7 PHYSICAL ASPECTS OF HOMOSEXUALITY

Modern gay culture has its newest and deepest roots in the homosexual liberation movement that has swept Europe and America in the second half of this century. This movement has attempted to define and legitimize homosexual behaviour (which it has so successfully achieved), and to describe homosexual love in poetry and literature. It exists as a sub-culture within a parent culture. Physical aspects of sexuality may be divided into different categories. These include:

* A focus on genital, oral, anal areas;
* A continual searching for the ideal sexual object - the ecstatic desire to capture the unattainable;
* A continual exploration of the other's sexual features, at the expense of individual and mutual personal growth;
* A constant reinforcement of sexual predating - cruising, camping, etc, as a form of validating a sexual personality;
* Making public, within the parameters of gay meeting places, that sex and sexual encounters are valid. Hence, within the South African context, public cruising (sex-partner hunting) in areas ranging from nude beaches in Cape to Botanical Gardens in Johannesburg, gives the gay person not only the opportunity to seek out sexual partners, but to display a 'public image' as well;
* Dealing with people (or relationships) as transitional objects. The transitional object (the other person) lays the foundation for other kinds of activities ....[33] It also describes the person's searching for aspects that were usually denied during the initial years. These include sexual 'stroking', sexual addiction, cruising (camping) for recreation because of peer group pressure, and multiple sexual partners within an existing relationship.

It is therefore, not uncommon when observing gay men 'camp' one another in bars, clubs, or cruising areas, to note that they might find up to 20 persons desirable, and change their object of desire as frequently as every few minutes or so as a client reported:

> *"I desperately wanted sexual contact. I*
> *spent an evening at the Sea Point wall (a*

well-known venue for gay cruising).
During the course of the evening, I made
contact with seven men. However, each
time, after agreeing to go home with me,
they had a change of mind, and abandoned
me half way home, I repeated this motion
until the seventh person in the space of five
hours accepted my proposals whereby we
negotiated the sex act." [34]

This clearly illustrates the transitional object syndrome. In a period of five hours the client found seven men desirable.

* Dealing with erotica through the medium of pornography, and responding to the sexual stimulus offered by discotheques, steam baths, and public toilets in many well-known shopping centres as well as other brief and secret sexual encounters.

* Active searching for that which is gay. This is reflected in the 'gay compulsory book', **Spartacus - An International Guide for Travellers**, in which South Africa is featured. It contains details of Veneral Disease clinics, police activity, places offering sexual companionship (specifying 'types' of people), and gives ratings for clubs, discotheques, and restaurants catering for sexual types such as 'leather', 'S and M', 'rough sex', and 'sex workers'. In the local context, specific cruising places such as bars, steam rooms, health spas, hotels, and clubs form the nucleus of the sub-culture.

Pursuing erotic reading material, including scholarly overviews of human sexuality generally, or of homosexuality particularly. This includes subscribing to international gay publications such as **Advocate**.

Participating in gay sexual practices. Isaacs and Miller, writing about gay sexuality in the context of AIDS, describe a wide range of homosexual practices. They are:

- auto-stimulation, including masturbation, often accompanied by male erotic-sexual fantasies;
- rubbing together of the body/genital, with ejaculation and/or orgasm occurring without oral, anal, or manual stimulation;
- oral stimulation by one or both partners, one or both

consequently ejaculating with orgasm, with or without ingestion of semen;

- oral penetration with or without ejaculation into the anal canal:

- use of the tongue, not only for kissing, but to insert into and lubricate the posterior private part;

- use of artificial devices, including vibrators, usually applied to sensate erotic zones;

- use of the fingers, often as lubrication for anal intercourse or prostate massage;

- other sex practices, involving three or more people, sadomasochistic ritual, cross dressing, etc; and

- mutual masturbation.[35]

5.7.1   GAY BARS

The gay bar as an institution is perhaps the most conventional and popular meeting place for homosexuals. It offers a 'secure' place, as well as providing access to partners, friendships, gay jargon, news of importance, fashion, outlets for AIDS information through pamphlet drops, and the testing out of particular skills and strategies for the 'beginner' gay.

In a study of public homosexual encounters it was found that one major characteristic was isolated, ie. the virtual absence of verbal utterances:

> *"Individuals ,learn to use the special presentations, bodily posturing, gestural hints, the manners and informal rules unique to the settings ..."* [36]

If a person is 'fancied' by another, a ritual occurs of eye contact, bodily gesture, and mutual smiles or touching of the genitalia. This is usually verified by trips to the toilet, whereby negotiations, approval, or verification will be conducted at the urinal. Drinks will then be bought, and a brief 'getting to know you' dialogue takes place. Thereafter, plans, either immediate or future, are entered into to pursue the contact. The pool area caters not only for those who primarily enjoy swimming, but also for those lesbians who wish to be seen in a 'masculine' context, as well as for those gays who look more 'butch' than normal.

Other gay bars cater for a broad range of gay men and women, and include younger boys and older men who wish to avail themselves of sex worker services, or who like 'a bit of rough trade'. Muggings and/or attacks are known to have occurred at these bars, and as a result they are not always popular with many gay people.

5.7.2   GAY CLUBS AND OTHER VENUES

The gay club is primarily a place or venue where gay people are able to express their sexuality and their varied forms of intimacy without 'fear'. Such clubs are usually hidden away in the dark recesses of downtown areas, and without open advertisement of the venue as gay.[37] South African gay clubs have had a history of being situated in dungeon-like rooms, cellars, or on the tops of buildings, thereby symbolically attesting to the fact that they are separate from mainstream entertainment. This has recently changed. With the mushrooming of clubs in Johannesburg, Pretoria, Durban and Cape Town, coupled with the legalization of homosexuality and the relaxation of police activity (police presence is only prompted by the illegal sale of alcohol and by drug traffic, rather than by homosexual activities), such venues have become not only publicly visible but also easily accessible. One Johannesburg club, known as "After Dark',was the first in elevating gay discotheques to a so-called "respectable status". It opened in an exclusive shopping centre in the northern suburbs of the city. Gays no longer had to negotiate iron doors and ascend or descend stairs to gain entrance. The club was exposed, as it were, to all and sundry. The gay club has the following characteristics:

* It is a meeting place where people of the same gender can enjoy dancing and loud music, and revel in the ethos of the discotheque.
* It is a 'comfortable' venue where degrees of intimacy, such as dancing, kissing, touching, and holding hands can be experienced without fear of 'heterosexual censure'.
* It is a place where sexuality, at its most powerful in terms of image, body language, and fantasy, can be negotiated.
* It is a venue where symbolic or ritual ownership of homosexuality is in process. Within the confines of a building, a person thrillingly

becomes gay, even if this is only temporary.[38]
* The club becomes the 'territory of ownership' for the gay person.
* The club provides access to sexual partners, and becomes the platform for cruising and camping.

Gays feel that these clubs are a response to societal rejection which has caused gays to create a social world of their own. Bronski writes:

> *"It should come as no surprise that gay men, finding that they are not welcome in this world, invent in their imaginations, safer places. One of the most common themes in gay writing is the creation of (delightful) situations free from the world's hostility"* [39]

5.7.3 GAY CAMPING AND CRUISING SPOTS

Camping or cruising is the term used in the gay world for going to a bar, bathhouse or party to pick up a sexual partner. Because camping or cruising cannot be isolated from the sub-culture in most cases, the camping venue becomes paramount to gay existence. Besides the conventional meeting places, a variety of other places exists, such as railway stations, (harbours), shopping centres, youth hostels and hotels.[40]

Cape Town, specifically, is well-known for its relatively 'open and public' aspects of camping. Sandy Bay, a popular nudist beach of international fame, is accessible daily throughout the year for those people wishing to engage in homosexual sex activities. Certain railway stations, department stores (cloakrooms) and streets in the city centre at night offer 'gay tourists' the chance to make contact. Perhaps most camping takes place in a particular Sea Point area known as Graaf's Pool. It is an area concreted off from the beach and adjacent to an enormous rock pool, where men are permitted within the confines of the walled area to sunbathe in the nude. There is a concrete pathway, floodlit at night, leading over the beach and rocks to the enclosure. At night men walk along the public pathway in bright floodlight. Once within the enclosure, their heads appear over the concrete wall while they indulge in sexual behaviour.

Styles of camping include driving around in a motor car, and cruising a particular person or people, with the hope of making contact. Such contact is often dependent on signals, which include nods or gestures from the other party, or 'cat and mouse' chasing in the car to seek out mutual confirmation. Some persons will camp up to 20 people in one session, until they receive some form of sexual gratification. It is not the sense of sexual orgasm that becomes the ultimate desire, but rather the fact that a feeling of acknowledgement (called 'stroked') has occurred.[41]

Some pro gay writers even regard camping as a legitimate form of sexual expression. Plummer concludes:

> *Gay casual sex (pick-ups, cruising) can be seen as a rejection of this narrow (monogamous) definition of legitimate sex, as it expands its range of possible meanings. It includes seeing sex as a form of recreation, simply as game or hobby or fun.*[42]

Seen from a homosexual angle there seems to be a significant drive towards their becoming accepted. Therefore it is extremely outrageous and distasteful to the human conscience, that such immoral and repulsive perverted sexual behaviour which offend both the law of nature and the morals and religious beliefs supported by our society, should have any advocates in our midst.

5.8   GAY MARRIAGE

The institution of marriage as a union of man and woman involving the procreating and rearing of children within the family exists from the time of Âdam ﷺ. Society can get along well – in fact, better – without same sex sexual relationships, but no society can survive without marriages and families. "Gay marriage" is an ideological invention designed to appropriate the moral capital of marriage and family toward the goal of government-enforced acceptance of homosexuality. As such, the term, 'gay marriage' is a counterfeit and a fraud. It would undermine support for marriage by ending marriage's unique spiritual, social and legal status. It would also undermine support for natural families whose foundation is marriage.

Same sex 'marriage' threatens not only the integrity of the marital definition but also religious freedom. Although homosexual activists merely recommend that religious institutions not be forced to perform same-sex ceremonies, it offers no defence for the conscientious Muslim, Christian, or Jew who will not legally recognize same-sex 'marriage'. The law carries the potential use of force against those who will not abide by it. If the commercial industry declines to extend marital benefits to same-sex couples, the law would open them to lawsuits and state compulsion. Schools would be forced to teach the acceptability of gay 'marriage' in family life courses as is illustrated in *The New York Times*: "Once homosexual marriage or domestic partnership is permitted, the schools are going to have to teach that it's equivalent." [43] Homosexuals, efforts to adopt children would be made easier if marriage is stripped of its unique status. All institutions, except specifically religious ones, would be subjected to state enforcement. And religious institutions themselves may enjoy immunity only for a short time. "Religious exemption" implies that the policy itself is at odds with the moral order, but when things get pushy, the state often prevails. Religious freedom can be curtailed anytime a court decides the state wants to do so for "compelling" reasons. Religious exemptions, therefore, are most likely a temporary measure on the way to total acceptance of homosexuality just as the following case proves:

> *"In May, the Hawaiian Supreme Court*
> *ruled 3-1 in Baehr v. Lewin that the state's*
> *exclusion of same-sex couples from*

marital status may be unconstitutional because it amounts to discrimination. Two homosexual men had applied for a marriage license, were denied, and then sued the state. The case eventually made its way to the State Supreme Court, which remanded it to a lower court with instructions to the state to prove "compelling state interests" for limiting marriage to opposite-sex couples" [44]

Homosexuals cannot call a same-sex relationship "marriage" since it lacks a basic ingredient - an entire sex. The joining of the opposite sexes in permanence is the very essence of marriage. Once this is abandoned, there is no logical reason for limiting "marriage" to two people or even to people. Why not have three partners? Or why not a man and his daughter or his dog ...? The logical reason to extend "marriage" to homosexual couples has nothing to do with marital integrity, but only reflects the fact that homosexuals want the same status regardless of its meaning. Anything less, they say, is a denial of human rights. If so, then a threesome or foursome seeking marital status can similarly claim that their sexual tendency must be recognised by society and the law as the equal of marriage or they are facing discrimination. Thus all these types of unnatural practices cannot be sanctioned as being a version of "their" sexual morality.

No society has loosened sexual morality outside marriage and survived as the research of the late Harvard sociologist Pitirim Sorokin reveals. He found that virtually all political revolutions that brought about societal collapse were preceded by sexual revolutions in which marriage and family were no longer accorded premiere status. [45]

The majority of the Hawaii Commission on Sexual Orientation concluded that denial of marriage licences to same-sex couples deprived applicants of legal and economic benefits, including:

1.   joint parental custody;
2.   insurance and health benefits;

3. the ability to file joint tax returns;
4. alimony and child support; and
5. inheritance of property and visitation of a partner or child in the hospital.

The majority also concluded that legalization of same-sex 'marriage' would be an economic boon to Hawaii, as homosexuals would flock there to get married. Apparently, they ignored the possibility that traditional honeymooners may choose another destination and that more than 97 percent of the population of the world is heterosexual.[46]

Hawaii has earned a reputation for being on the "cutting edge" of social experimentation. It was the first to legalize abortion (1970), the first to accept the Equal Rights Amendment (1972) and the fifth to offer special employment protection to homosexuals (1991).

Making gay 'marriage' legal would impose it on all the citizens of Hawaii, and perhaps even on people in the rest of the United States, as the following article appearing in **The Daily News** *(Natal) illustrates, under the caption "Wedding bells for gays".*

San Francisco: James Mays leaned smilingly from the side of a motorised imitation of a San Francisco cable car, as it pulled away with the last of the gay and lesbian couples united in a historic mass wedding ceremony here yesterday.

A cardboard sign affixed to the rear of the red and gold, open-sided car read **"Jest Married"**. *But to the 200 couples legally united in the first public same-sex ceremonies, the occasion marked serious personal commitments in their lives. San Francisco mayor, Willie Brown, and city supervisor, Carole Migden, started the ceremony by supervising the exchanging of vows.*

"It's a testimonial to what we hope will be happening in the 21st century," Mays said.

There were 'brides' adorned in crisply pressed tuxedos. Beaming grooms sported rouge and white gowns.[47]

State sanction of homosexuality in any form is an invitation to the young to experiment with something that may prove deadly. The more homosexuality is encouraged, the more damage will be wreaked among individuals, families and society. This epidemic is not only confined to America, but its poisonous tentacles has been injected globally just as this article describes it under the heading: ***Dutch are all set to give gay marriages the green light.***

Queen Beatrix of the Netherlands is not amused. The Dutch Parliament has backed legislation to grant homosexuals legal and civic marital rights. She normally embraces her country's liberal tendencies and even appointed a gay tutor for her eldest son. The gay community boasts that she is everyone's queen. Homosexual couples can already register their partnerships for social housing and other forms of "common" living. This could be extended to include social benefits and tax status.[48]

What has not been said often enough is that children really do need a mother and father. In a gay household, these same-sex households that are now adopting children, the child immediately doesn't have a father or a mother, so the child is already at a disadvantage. Then the child sees a distorted view of sexuality because of the homosexuality going on around him/her and then that child is intensely curious about what men and women do together or what relationships they have.

Here is an incident of a person who tragically entered prison because he grew up in a lesbian household. He still loves his mother, but he said, "You know, as a boy in a lesbian environment where it was intensely anti-male" - that's all he heard, this bitterness toward men - he said he began having sexual problems. He eventually became a voyeur, and he is on a peeping Tom charge. He was too curious about how normal people have sex. There are hundreds of people like this.[49]

Also the issue of gay adoption crystallises the old, uncomfortable arguments about whether gay unions are natural, valid and truly equal to heterosexual unions. All sides in the debate claim to accept that the child's interest are paramount; it's the way in which these interests are to be protected that inflames furious debate. Adoption can prompt traumatic issues as children grow up. Should the child be of a different race or culture from its parents, the difficulties would be compounded. And having to deal with gay parents in a straight social environment is yet another issue to cope with.

There is no society on earth that has functioned without marriage, and there are many that have gone into the dust bin of history as soon as they cheapened marriage - Rome, Greece and some of the middle Chinese dynasties. When marriage became cheapened, the social fabric began to unravel. This is also evident in this country. We have already cheapened marriage with excessive divorce. We have prenuptial agreements; we have people living together. It has already hurt marriage. But this would be the final blow, to say that it doesn't even have to be a man and a woman. It could be two males, or two females. If humanity doesn't wise up to this, then evil will thrive when good men and women do nothing.

5.9   PRISONS

Many prisoners are forcefully intimidated into entering into homosexual liasons with fellow inmates, sometimes even at the expense of being brutally attacked if initially refusing to comply.

Most prison officers have confirmed that homosexuals operate largely in criminal circles, and it is not difficult to see why they make these assumptions. They say that it was very unlikely that these men were capable of a long-term emotional relationship.

Undoubtedly the insecurity of the homosexual's social situation contributes to promiscuity and hardened behaviour even towards a long-standing sexual partner - in ways that only the most brutal heterosexual man would practice on his wife. It has also been believed that a homosexual is on a calculated path of evil and destruction. Probably the majority of the knowledge of homosexual practices and relationships is based either on spectacular newspaper accounts of criminal cases or on the study of homosexuals in prison. None of these reflects the attitudes or experiences of most homosexuals.

Shortly after arrest, many homosexuals will declare themselves eager for therapeutic treatment - sometimes because they have suddenly become aware of the social consequences of their actions and feel a desire to be 'cured'; sometimes because they feel such a declaration will be in their favour in court or prison. Indeed some disturbed homosexuals who need treatment may resist therapy because they are under the false illusion that all psychology is bent on changing their sexual preference.

5.10   THE MILITARY

The homosexual subculture is recognised as 'liberated' or, in a manner of speaking, undisciplined. This is definitely at odds with the 24 hour discipline system within which soldiers must live and work. Homosexuals are distinguished from others by their behaviour (sodomy). Another group behavioural characteristic is a very high rate of promiscuity. Military records indicate that homosexuals are statistically more likely to engage in misconduct than heterosexuals. They have a higher incidence of drug and alcohol abuse than heterosexuals.

The voice of experience also indicates that homosexuals jeopardize military morale. For example, a survey of active duty officers conducted for the American Security Council Foundation found that 99,03 percent said homosexuals would undermine the unity and readiness of combat units.[50] The Defense Readiness Council compiled a survey of 2 800 retired flag and general officers. Nearly 90 percent said they believe homosexuals undermine morale.[51]

Admitting open homosexuals into the military violates the legal principle of the assumption of risk. This principle states that if you know there is a risk and you assume it, then don't complain when the risk materializes. A recent report from the University of Michigan found that people with HIV are more capable of spreading the virus during the first 60 days of infection, but that blood tests during this period do not find HIV.[52] This means that the military assumes the risk, even though all personnel are initially tested, that soldiers will not be affected. Unfortunately, the current Administration no longer screens out homosexuals, the highest-risk group for contracting HIV. A male homosexual soldier is significantly more likely than a heterosexual soldier to be non-deployable for medical reasons related to HIV infection. If HIV infected, the soldier will be permanently non-deployable. Male homosexuals are more likely to acquire sexually transmitted diseases which can render them non-deployable, such as gonorrhoea, syphilis, and hepatitis B.[53]

The military's homosexual policy dates back to the British Articles of War in 1775. An individual was drummed out of the Continental Army for attempted sodomy in 1778. This case involved an officer (lieutenant) and an enlisted man.[54] Prior to World War II homosexual misconduct was prosecuted under the categories of "conduct unbecoming an officer". After 1900, individuals were punished for committing homosexual acts, which were classified as sodomy.[55] A World War I War Department circular, listed homosexuality as cause for rejection under the category, "psychopathic" characteristics.[56] The War Department's 1941 policy, which was harsher than previous ones, emphasized that homosexual "sodomists" would not be discharged but court martialled. Despite this increased penalty, during the war there was an unofficial toleration of some homosexuals because replacements were not guaranteed. In 1949 this policy was enforced that 'homosexual personnel, irrespective of sex, should not be permitted in any branch of the Armed Forces in any capacity, and prompt separation of known homosexuals from the Armed Forces is compulsory.'[57] In 1958, Class III homosexuals (those who had committed no homosexual act while in the military service) were given general discharges.[58] In the late 1970s, it was recommended that the military remove this ban (it was more than 200 years old, they argued), and replace this phrase 'homosexuality is incompatible with military services'.[59] Current legislation, introduced in 1994, recommends amongst others, that the presence of homosexuals in the military is not a security and health risk, would not contribute to poor morale and claims that the public will soon favour homosexual military service.

A study done by the Freedom of Information Act analyzed 100 army cases from 1989 to 1992. Forty-nine percent of those cases involved children as victims. Eighty-five percent involved victims who had not consented, and five percent of the offenders were HIV-positive.[60] The same report summarized a 1992 incident at Fort Hood, Texas, where 60 homosexual men (soldiers and civilians) met in a public toilet next to a child care centre. The men cut holes in the walls to permit sex between men in adjacent stalls. The men also installed a mirror to allow them to see the approach of intruders. These homosexuals were indiscriminate in their choice of partners and often engaged in sex within moments of entering the bathroom. Sexual acts included oral and anal sodomy, mutual masturbation, and fondling of the buttocks.

A national poll found that a decisive majority of voters disagreed that the President should overrule military leaders and require the military to accept homosexuals.[61]

5.11 LESBIANISM

Female homosexuality, referred to as lesbianism *(musâhaqa)*, is derived from the Greek word *lesbos*. The term lesbian refers to a woman who has an emotional and sexual preference for other women. Some gay women have transitory sexual encounters, but this is unusual. Although gay female relationships normally last longer than gay male relationships, extremely long term relationships (20 years or more) are rare. Serial monogamy (one relationship at a time) seems to be the dominant lesbian life pattern. Loss of romantic love or the inability to sustain feelings across time seem to be major reasons for the breakup of gay female relationships. Gay women also are typically left out in the experience of rearing children, which (being parents) can have a stabilizing effect on relationships.

Women who are lesbian come from all backgrounds and may have any kind of personality. The exaggeratedly masculine 'butch' lesbian or over-feminine 'fem' lend a false image to others who are less showy. Statistically, there are fewer female than male homosexuals who have absolutely no sexual relations with the opposite sex. It can be easier for a lesbian than for a man to maintain a heterosexual front and so contribute to the fact that lesbianism is not always noticed.

During adolescence the lesbian's fantasies are mainly homosexual - and many have their first experience of homosexual love-making in this early stage. Many girls who find themselves attracted to women continue to go out with boys and this is sometimes because they hope to camouflage from their western parents forms of sexual involvement that may cause dismay. As the lesbian grows into her twenties and thirties she may move into the gay world openly acknowledging her sexual tastes and sharing her life with other like minded perverts. Some move in groups, organizing outings and parties that are a forum for promiscuously seeking new partners. It is also irrationally argued that lesbianism, in some cases, happens just because there are no men available eg. in a closed female community such as a prison, army unit, or convent, where it is said that the emotional ties can lead to sexual exploration.

Many lesbians prefer to lead a 'secret' life rather than confront the querying glances of colleagues and acquaintances or the rejection of parents and friends. The lesbian woman faces two main problems: the first is accepting her own deviation, and the second is persuading others to accept. She may, for example, experience doubt and guilt because she feels sexual urges which are abnormal. These conflicting forces can be detrimental as the following case proves:

> *"I was close to suicide," confessed*
> *Elizabeth. "There I was, single, 24, no*
> *prospect of marriage and attracted to the*
> *students I was meant to be instructing.*
> *Classes were torture as I couldn't give any*
> *indication of how I felt for fear of losing*
> *my job. I'd go home in the evening and*
> *cry with tension and worry - all the time*
> *with a picture of one of the girls in my*
> *head."* [62]

Lesbians argue that some of them feel more 'comfortable' with women than with men. Others react strongly against men. Sometimes this stems, they say, from worries about pregnancy and abortion, and men are blamed as the instruments of these calamities. Yet, others express their distaste for being used as a sex object or even from fear of rape. They even say that this hate can twist a lesbian's mind to such an extent that it provides a justification for prostitution. The lesbian prostitute, and there are hundreds of them, takes money from men she 'uses' and despises for their inability to arouse her. She even becomes hysterical at the thought of her own 'girlfriend' being hired away by these despised males. This vicious circle could only terminate if lesbians direct their sexual energy in the proper channels, rather than publicly promoting and satisfying these beastly instincts of theirs.

Love-making for lesbians expresses itself through sexual stimulation and release. The partners' sexual activity may range from kisses and cuddles to mutual masturbation, oral stimulation and pressing their bodies against each other. They are also heavily dependent on dildoes and vibrators.

In modern society the majority of teenage girls have a best friend with whom they share their feelings, experiences and plans for the future. Some even go all the way of sharing a physical sexual relationship as the following incident illustrates:

> *"My girlfriend, best friend, is blond with*
> *beautiful eyes, very sweet and gentle. She*
> *can make me laugh when I am down, and*
> *she kisses me. I like our airy, gay, chattery*
> *times. It's the most important relationship*
> *I have had with a woman in my life: being*
> *in love, making love to her."* [63]

While the above relationship expresses acceptance there are also others that express remorse and regret as the following case proves.

> *"My first mature sexual experience*
> *occurred at sixteen, and I felt very*
> *ashamed... It was with a woman. Nobody*
> *knew it had happened."* [64]

Mothers' sins (and even punishment) are sometimes passed down to their daughters as this case indicates:

> *"Mother's premise has always been that*
> *women friends are significant and true. I*
> *know she loves her woman friends, hugs*
> *and kisses them, takes walks with them*
> *even arm in arm. However, when I told her*
> *(in my teens) I had taken a woman lover,*
> *she fell apart. 'Why do you have to have*

> *... sex ... with a friend?' she sobbed.*[65]

Islâm not only denounces such promiscuous behaviour but also warns of severe chastisement for those indulging in such lewd and unnatural acts relenting not in the least in making it a deterrent. Modern society ignores and disregards inculcating children with good moral conduct and therefore have to bear the brunt of their aggression. The following is a classical example:

> *"The greatest emotional trauma I've met to date was when my parents confronted me about my sexuality and my relationship with my girlfriend. They went wild. They 'battered' me psychologically with all they could. They threatened to commit me to an insane asylum and to kill me."* [66]

Lesbians have even split families apart and left the custody of their children to the discretion of the courts as is evident in the case of Judy, a lesbian parent, living with another woman. An article under the caption, ***Child Abuse Pitted against Lesbianism in Wyoming***, states:

> *Until now, only one custody dispute involving a lesbian parent has ever been heard in the history of the Wyoming court system. (This is only the tip of the iceberg). On December 16, the judge in that case ruled that the mother was unfit because her "open homosexuality has and is likely to create confusion and difficulty for the children" and will "negatively affect development of the children's moral values" (But at the same time), the judge also concluded that "the state has an interest in supporting conventional marriages and families."* [67]

Statements of this nature, made by the highest law enforcing authority, tend to be very ambiguous. On the one hand homosexuality is said to create confusion and negatively effect development of the children's moral values. In spite of this the state is willing to support 'conventional marriages'. This, then reflects the double standards of those who were supposed to be protecting the decline of human moral values.

Islâmically speaking, lesbianism *(musâḥaqa)*, is equally condemned as homosexuality, and those who indulge in it incur the same reprimand as those condemned for bestability and sexual attraction to corpses.[68]

5.12   GLOBAL VIEW REGARDING GAYS

While the majority of Western countries have not only accepted gays in their society, but also granted them special privileges, there are some that still regard this perversion as illegal, and rightly so.

The co-secretary general of the International Lesbian and Gay Association, Spain's Jordi Petit, is demanding that the European Union suspend commercial agreements with the Latin American nations that ban homosexuality - Chile, Ecuador and Nicaragua. Speaking to Spain's national news agency, Petit also criticized Costa Rica and Honduras for refusing to register AIDS groups, and Argentina, Bolivia and Venezuela for tolerating raids on gay bars. And he noted that in Brazil, 1 200 gays have reportedly been murdered in recent years with very few cases solved by police. The European Union which has agreed to recognize the 'rights' of homosexuals not only deserves condemnation, but also has to share responsibility for all those offshoots of vice which have resulted in legalizing homosexuality.

In the Middle East, Israeli gays say the assassination of Prime Minister Yitzhak Rabin was a blow also to the gay cause because Rabin was actively pro gay. Rabin reportedly helped change regulations that barred gays from high-security jobs in the military, and once assisted a reserve officer, Uzi Even, who had lost his security clearance because of his sexual orientation. In addition, the Nov. 6 issue of the newspaper *Yediot Aharonot* noted that Rabin had helped a foreign gay national achieve permanent resident status in Israel so he could live with his lover. The French gay group Homosexualities and Socialism sent a letter to the Acting Prime Minister for that move, calling it "a simple and grand gesture ... showing his respect for life and love, this force that brings people together without any nationalities, borders, religions or conflicts." [69]

It is very puzzling to understand that it demands unnatural tendencies and human deviations to cement peace and goodwill between two hostile countries, and that too sanctioned by the highest authority of the country. Or is this another ploy to entice morally dignified people to their self destruction as we witness from this startling report under the caption *'Turkish gay journalists seek help'*:

> *The Istanbul, Turkey, gay group, Lambda is seeking help producing the weekly gay page donated to it by the newspaper EKSPRES ... Send news items or free subscriptions to gay publications to Yûsuf Kribac.* [70]

Turkey, once regarded as the cradle of human civilization and the fortress of Islâmic culture, is now also being converted into a springboard through which immoral men can spew their poisonous venom to the masses around the globe.

The New National Family Health Survey has found that on the Indian sub-continent the majority of women in 11 of India's 13 states have never heard of AIDS. Only eight percent of respondents in the state of Assam were familiar with the disease. This and other factors lead Indian health officials to predict five million HIV infections by the turn of the century, up from the current 1,5 million. These officials may be extremely elated if their predictions materialize, since it would be a reflection of their intellectual 'fore-sightedness'. Real academic achievement is not in foretelling a global catastrophe, but in preventing it.

The country that vigorously protested against homosexuality and lesbianism was Zimbabwe, which dutifully usurped the voices of the Muslims. Here's MP T Mudariki speaking recently on the floor of Parliament:

"*I move that this House unreservedly condemns the evil and iniquitous practice of homosexuality and lesbianism. We cannot be blackmailed because of the pink dollar or the pink pound. Seventy American homosexual congressmen wrote a letter to our president condemning his patriotic stance against this evil system. In my view, it is a misdirection of efforts ... I just want to warn our heroic people that if we allow or condone such (evil) acts under the so-called human rights banners, if we are not careful, we shall also have rapists, murderers, criminals and those sodomists who are militating to have sex with four-year olds claiming their human rights.*"

MP Border Gezi added:

"*From the way I see it, these people who engage in such activities are sick in mind. It is disgusting to find that a man needs a man instead of a woman. I would like to ask ... that the police should be on the lookout ... for homosexuals and lesbians. They should take them and put them somewhere where they can never be seen because we cannot mix with such people. They will tarnish our image. We should look at ways of keeping these people separate from those who are normal. The problem is that if we take them to jails ... they will start engaging in these homosexual and lesbian practices. If we let them free, you will find them in the night going for other men instead of women to have sex with ... These do not belong to our culture. If they want to fall with their*

> *male or female counterparts, then they*
> *should live somewhere where they do not*
> *mix with us.* "[71]

Let's hear what the president himself announced:

> *Homosexuality is sub-animal behaviour*
> *and we will never ever allow it here. If you*
> *see people in your areas parading*
> *themselves as lesbians and gays, arrest*
> *them and hand them over to the police ... I*
> *find it extremely outrageous and distasteful*
> *to my human conscience that such immoral*
> *and repulsive organizations, like those of*
> *homosexuals who offend both against the*
> *law of nature and the morals and religious*
> *beliefs supported by our society, should*
> *have any advocates in our midst ... I don't*
> *believe homosexuals have any right at*
> *all.* "[72]

5.13 HOMOSEXUALITY IN THE LIGHT OF ISLÂM

The aim of natural sexuality is procreation. Lawful and natural sexual relations between man and woman has been designed by Allâh to preserve the human race here on earth. Homosexuality is negatory of the natural role and aim of sexual activity.

The experts on homosexuality and other forms of sexual deviation advance a series of groundless assumptions in their discussion on the causes of such unnatural sexuality. They attribute it to hereditary taints, genetic causes, environmental influences, animal instincts in man, etc. In certain cases, eg. 'transient homosexuality' where men are separated from women such as in prisons, same sex institutions etc, they argue that the criminal's blame will be considered as diminished in view of his circumstances.

Islâm does not accept any type of justification for the unnatural sin of homosexuality regardless of any biological, psychological or environmental factors which may influence a man to indulge in this type of grossly unnatural immorality. This should not be interpreted to mean that Islâm does not recognize the reality or validity or the existence of the various factors which influence man to commit homosexuality. However, the presence of any destructive influences which lead man towards this unnatural and bestial act of immorality does not constitute a valid excuse for indulgence in acts of deviation and inhumanity. Just as fornication, rape and other criminal acts of immorality cannot be condoned because of biological, psychological, environmental, factors, etc, which may be the causes which occasion the crime, so too, can these factors not be cited in favour of diminished blame for the act of homosexuality. In spite of the existence of the factors (described as causes) of adultery, human culture does not permit man and woman to indulge in this crime notwithstanding the naturalness of heterosexuality. They are required to restrain themselves and behave within the bounds of chastity and morality.

In like manner, man is required to exercise restraint and overcome his emotional, biological demands, etc. and manage the disturbances within him. He, as a member of the highest species of Allâh's creation, is under moral obligation to control the dictates of his lust - whether such lust directs him towards unnatural or natural avenues - and refrain from smearing his soul and intellect in such loathsome indulgence.

Modern studies and the many consequent theories regarding the crime of homosexuality tend to convey a blurred conception of the homosexual. Biological disturbances as well as some environmental factors are even tendered as mitigating circumstances to reduce the stigma and the blame from the homosexual. This idea has made homosexuals daring and revengeful of their unnatural crimes. They have come to regard their misdirected lust as morally acceptable. They, as well as the 'experts' who have undertaken research in homosexuality, have deceived themselves into believing in the idea of diminished blame and moral acceptance of this unnatural act. As long as man's intelligence is not inflicted with insanity, he is held responsible for his actions and he is Islâmically under compulsion to restrain his perverted cravings so that he does not descend into a sub-human level of existence.

Man's gratification of his sexual appetite with another man has a long history of its own. The Qur'ân bears testimony to the fact that the people of the prophet Lût ﷺ (- the nephew of Ibrâhîm ﷺ) sent as a warning to the people of Sodom and Gomorrah, were those who initiated this heinous practice. Before them it was unknown. In this connection the Qur'ân mentions:

> *"We also sent Lût. He said to his people:*
> *'Do you commit indecency such as no*
> *people in creation (ever) committed before*
> *you? For you practise your lusts on men*
> *in preference to women; you are indeed a*
> *people transgressing beyond bounds."* [73]

These Sodomites even indulged in their homosexual orgies publicly. Their wickedness had attained the level where the mere sight of a handsome young man made them so agitated that they pounced upon him as famished people would fall on food. Even honoured guests did not enjoy immunity or any privileged position. They did not hesitate in even resorting to violence in achieving their lustful objects.

The Qur'ân has depicted the scene when the angels of punishment visited Lût ﷺ as his guests in the guise of handsome young men. Hadrat Lût ﷺ did not recognize them in the first instance. But he knew the shameless habit of his people. He was extremely distressed and he apprehended that his people would certainly demand unnatural and shameful sexual activity. His apprehension was correct. They could not sit silent at the news of such "boys" of excellent beauty. These sodomites recklessly rushed to the home of Lût ﷺ to gratify their unnatural desires. Lût ﷺ found himself in a difficult situation. He prompted them to legally satisfy their sexual appetite with women even offering his daughter in lawful marriage to the most gentle of them, and not insisting on this unnatural outlet. Then he very effectively appealed to them, in the name of Almighty, that they should abstain from disgracing him by dishonouring his guests.

The Qur'ân states:

> *And his people came rushing towards him,*
> *and they had been long in the habit of*

*practising abominations. He said: "O my
people! Here are my daughters: they are
purer for you (if you marry)! Now fear
Allâh Ta'âlâ, and cover me not with shame
about my guests! Is there not among you a
single right-handed man?"* [74]

But the accursed people inflamed with evil passions turned a deaf ear to all his reasoning with them. They had lost all sense of morality and were blind in their voluptous sentiments. On this occasion they even taunted him for his frequent protests in the past against their sins. Hazrat Lût ﷺ seemed helpless in the situation in which he found himself,- alone against a rabble of people inflamed with lustful passions. He wished he had the strength to suppress them himself or had some powerful support to lean on! But the powerful support was there, though he had not realized it till then. It was the support of the Almighty. His guests were not ordinary men, but Angels who had come to test the people before they inflicted punishment. They now declared themselves and gave him directions to get away before the morning, when the punishment would descend on the doomed cities. Even in Lût's ﷺ household was one ie. his wife, who detracted from the harmony of the family. She lagged behind and looked back ie. one whose mental and moral attitude, in spite of association with the righteous was to hark back to the glitter of wickedness and sin. Finally the wrath of Almighty descended upon them, their cities were turned upside down and showers of stone rained on them. Regarding this the Qur'ân mentions:

*"Then when Our decree came to pass, We
turned the cities upside down, and We
rained thereon stones of baked clay, piled
up."* [75]

The punishment of turning upside down given to this people resembles outwardly their shameless deed of homosexuality. The shower of stones was very thick so as to form layers. It is also said that the name of each man was written or engraved on those stones which were the cause of their annihilation. The inversion of cities by way of punishment was the task which was assigned to Jibrâ'îl ﷺ. Homosexuality is also a form of

288

sexual inversion, hence the type of punishment was most befitting in that it also symbolized their unnatural acts of immorality. Showers of stones (not hail-stones, but real stones) are not a normal occurrence. So too, the punishment of the inversion of the cities (was quite rightly justified). Thus, unnatural forms of punishment were prescribed by Allâh for the unnatural sins of the homosexual community.

The community of Lût ﷺ was a prosperous nation materially and they inhabited five cities: Sodom, Gamûrah, Udmah, Laboobem and Sûghar. The Qur'ân refers collectively to these five cities with the term *Mu 'tafikât* (the inverted cities). The cities are so designated because of the perverted crimes of sexual inversion of their inhabitants and because they were physically inverted and eliminated by the command of Allâh Ta'âlâ.

Before the people of Sodom, never did this evil even enter the mind of the worst of mankind, let alone practising it. The Ummayad K͟halîfah 'Abdul Malik said that if this episode of the homosexuals was not mentioned in the Qur'ân, he would not have conceded the reality of this crime since it was unthinkable that man will descend to such a degenerate level and debase himself in a type of act which is not indulged in by even the overwhelming majority of lowly beasts.[76]

Nevertheless, even after the community to which prophet Lût ﷺ was sent as a cautioner, met their catastrophic end, sodomy continued and even sometimes flourished. It is now known that homosexuality existed before the pre-Christian era among the so-called 'civilized' nations of the world especially the Greeks and Romans. It was not only confined to the common masses, but even legendary and prominent figures such as Socrates, Aristotle, Julius Caesar and many others practiced it.[77]

In thirteenth century France, homosexuality was the great craze of the day and the government of the country had to enact a law that those found guilty of this unnatural crime will be put to death. And Germany was not far behind in the pursuit of this craze. Before Nazi Germany there was a famous person, Dr Magnus Herschfield, (who had been the president of the society for the Reformation of Sexual behaviour), who launched powerful propaganda in favour of sodomy for six years. Finally 'democracy' acceded to this demand and the strictly forbidden became approved. It was decided by majority vote that homosexuality among the males was no longer an offence provided it was indulged in with mutual consent of the parties involved and in case of the object of the unnatural love being a minor, his guardian had to give his consent.[78] In the Orient, Iran has been notorious and Persian poetry amply supports it. Karachi has also been named in this regard. It is said there were three centres there, where eunuchs carried on their unnatural business. Afghanistan (then under Communist influence), has also been mentioned. India, too, is not so clean in her records in this field, although the common people are involved in it to a limited extent. It is the educated and the sophisticated people who take to it as a diversion. The educational institutions, schools, colleges, and centres of oriental studies too are not free from this curse.[79]

Islâm strictly forbade this detestable deed and prescribed the severest punishment, relenting not in the least in making it a deterrent. The Qur'ân cautions that once people take to homosexuality, they sink to the depths of moral degradation. The admonitory punishment meted out to these transgressors was described in such a moving way that those reciting the Qur'ân may learn the harsh consequences of this evil, and may protect themselves from this outrageous crime. To deter the Muslims from this evil, the Qur'ân initially declared to those participating in this perversion:

> "If two men among you are guilty of
> indecency, punish them both." [80]

Once Prophet Muhammed ﷺ expressed his anticipated fear by stating that among the evils that his *ummah* can take to, he feared sodomy most. In fact, this was a forewarning measure that the *ummah* may guard against, realizing that the Prophet himself had forbidden it. On one occasion the Prophet ﷺ declared:

> "Whoever gratifies his sexual urge with
> another (individual) of his own sex,
> Almighty will not so much as look at
> him." [81]

Undoubtedly sodomy is one of the worst of the most repulsive acts, not even observed among beasts. Therefore the sight of a homosexual will be so disgusting to Allâh that it will intensify His anger to heights where He will not even consider glancing at a sodomist. Through this act man degrades his humanity and announces extermination as his policy. Moreover, it implies wretchedness and misery of the womenfolk and he himself is prone to so many diseases; the basic organs of his body, brain, heart, liver and kidneys become deficiently immune (AIDS), his face lacks the sparkle of health and he looks off-colour and melancholy, with the result that such an incapacitated criminal becomes worthless to women. This wretched outcast deprives himself of the bounty of procreation and the priceless jewel of morality.

5.13.1 MISINTERPRETATION OF QUR'ÂNIC VERSE

Islâm has strictly forbidden sodomy irrespective of it taking place with one's wife or any man or woman. This is the unanimous opinion of all the theologians and jurists of Islâm. However, there are certain people of the Shî'ah sect who classify it as being permissible, wrongfully citing the following Qur'ânic text:

> *"Your wives are as a tilth unto you; so approach your tilth when or how you will."*[82]

It is really mind boggling that these misdirected miscreants quote the above verse in support of their proclamation. In reality, it actually negates their claim, since the word 'tilth' denotes a place where the seed can be planted and harvest achieved, which in a woman is the external reproductive organ or the vagina. Is there any possibility of obtaining offspring through the rear excretory canal? When this is definitely not possible, how can any sane individual produce this verse in support of sodomy even with one's wife. Again, this fact should also be explored that if sodomy with wives were permitted what would become of the aims and institution of *nikâh* (legal marriage)? Assuming a perverted man of unnatural tastes gratifies his sexual passion through sodomy with his wife, then the question arises as to what would the woman do to achieve her matrimonial pleasures. This is injustice in its extremity.

The Qur'ân distinctly clarified this verse:

> *"You may approach them in any manner,*
> *time or place ordained for you by Allâh."*[83]

Carnal minded men ignore this natural path and pursue deviated patterns of fulfilment. In sex morality, manner, time and place are all important. Prophet Muḥammad ﷺ strictly warned against sodomy with women and termed it as an act of disbelief. The tradition which permits a person to approach a woman from the rear implies that he is also at liberty to utilize this 'position' if he so wishes, on condition he deposits his semen in the vagina and not via the rectum. Allâmah Nawawî sums it up:

> *"In view of the so many famous traditions,*
> *the consensus of opinion of the reliable*
> *'ulamâ is that sodomy with a woman,*
> *irrespective of whether she is menstruating*
> *or not is strictly prohibited."* [84]

Sodomists are those accursed groups of men who contribute to their own destruction. They witness the horrible consequences of their evil deeds in this life, which gives them an idea and a taste of the far worse punishments in the Hereafter. Therefore those who seek gratification through unlawful channels, the law of retribution must make them shudder.

5.13.2   PUNISHMENT FOR HOMOSEXUALITY

The people of Lût ﷺ suffered from a national malady of sodomy. They did not refrain from this in spite of numerous stern warnings. This malpractice was never committed by any nation before them. Prophet Lût ﷺ even clearly warned them:

> *"Would you really approach men in your*
> *lusts rather than women? Nay, you are a*
> *people grossly ignorant."* [85]

The people of Lût ﷺ even refused his daughters which were offered to them, in legal marriage, saying they desired men. The *mufassirûn* (experts on commentary of the Holy Qur'ân) reveal that just as men had indulged with other men, so too were women engaged in illicit relationships with other women (lesbianism). Prophet Lût 🕮, by divine inspiration, had migrated with his family from the accursed area, whilst his wife who was a sympathiser was destroyed with the transgressors. Their punishment was in the form of a storm of stones and earthen clusters whilst their cities were being inverted.

Prophet Muhammad 🕮 advised that a person's faith is literally snatched away from him whilst he is engaging in such vile deeds (an adulterer does not commit zinâ whilst his *îmân* is intact), for verily the *îmân* of a person is more precious and dignified in the eyes of Allâh than being in such a shallow and degrading situation.

The Prophet 🕮 sternly warned those engaging in such a heinous crime by prescribing the severest of measures in the form of Capital punishment. He declared:

> "Whoever is found involved in sodomy, put
> him to death, both the active and passive
> one." [86]

From this it is apparent that both participants act in violation of the natural laws of Allâh. The one partner acts bestially by seeking sexual gratification from a man. The passive partner in this vile deed allows himself to be manipulated like a female. This effeminacy is unnatural since he has stooped so low in shamelessness that he is better dead than alive. When sodomy was committed on him with his own consent, there was no trace of life left in him. He is a corpse walking on the surface of the earth polluting it with his stench. After this gruesome crime there is no sympathy, no clemency for both of them anywhere, neither in the society nor in the sight of Islâm. Even a murderer can be saved by the intervention of the family of the deceased, but who is going to give refuge to a sodomist who is causing his own self destruction?

On the strength of the above mentioned *Ahâdîth* the consensus of opinion of majority of the *ummah* is that the sodomist, irrespective of whether he is married or not, should be put to death. This is a crime where remission of clemency finds no place, since this unnatural act has been regarded as being worse than fornication.[87] Another group is of the opinion that the punishment prescribed for the fornicator under the Sharî'ah is also meant for the homosexual, there being no difference between them.[88] As against this, the first group says that there is much difference between fornication and sodomy. For fornication there is a *ḥud* or penalty prescribed by Allâh Ta'âlâ, while there is no such punishment for a homosexual. However, the *Qâdî* (the presiding authority) has the power to prescribe a much more severe and horrible punishment to the culprit. He may be thrown over a hill-top or burnt in fire (Imâm 'Azam and Ḥâkim are of this opinion.) Some even say that he should be slain by sword.

Definite pronouncement is not made by the Qur'ân perhaps because the crime is extremely unnatural and most shameful and cannot be expected of a good society. But now definite legislation is required against sodomy in the light of Islâmic jurisprudence, since not only Britain and America has legalized this filthy practice, but the majority of the Western countries have also adopted this stance. The opinions expressed by both the groups regarding punishment leaves a clear indication that capital punishment in whatever form should be adopted in taking the homosexual's life, especially in Muslim countries where Islâmic law has been constitutionally recognized.

An incident during the time of the Companions of the Prophet is worth noting. Khâlid ibn Walîd ﷺ was informed that there was a person who offered himself for sodomy to people. He wrote about it to Abû Bakr ﷺ, the then Khalîph, then in saddle, and asked for his opinion. Since this was something strange, he called his advisory council and presented the case to them for consideration. 'Alî ﷺ expressed his opinion that since it concerned the unnatural act of the people of the Prophet Lût ﷺ, the punishment for the culprit should also correspond to theirs, and he should be consigned to the flames. Abû Bakr ﷺ liked and accepted this opinion and he wrote back to Khâlid ibn Walîd ﷺ prescribing this punishment. On receiving this instruction from the Khalîph, Khâlid ibn Walîd had the notorious criminal arrested and consigned him to flames.[89]

Allâh has cursed those who alter the frontiers of the earth and four categories of person incur His anger: 'Men who dress themselves as women and women who dress themselves as men, those who sleep with

animals and those who sleep with men'.[90] Homosexuality *(liwât)* incurs
the strongest condemnation. It is identified with *zinâ* and it is advocated
that the most horrible punishment should be inflicted to those who indulge
in it.

5.13.3 PRECAUTIONARY PRE-REQUISITES
5.13.3.1 ABSTAIN FROM EFFEMINATE COMPANIONSHIP

The solution to safeguarding oneself from this abominable liaison, which
will effectively guarantee sexual morality is to keep far away from the
company of handsome boys and other factors influencing this social evil.
Ibn Hajar mentions:

> *"One should refrain from mixing with the*
> *young boys of wealthy persons, since they*
> *are by their looks and their attire, a great*
> *trial, at times greater than that of the finer*
> *sex."*

Then he has narrated the incident of Sufyân Thaurî that on one occasion
he entered his bathroom. Co-incidentally a young boy wanted to use the
bathroom at the same time. When Sufyân noticed him he said, 'Get out
from here and at once'. And then he gave the reason for it:

> *"With a woman there is only one shaitân*
> *that I can see, but with an effeminate*
> *person there are more than ten."* [91]

The jurists have declared that the sight of effeminate persons is forbidden
for fear of their arousing lustful passion in man. In Durr Mukhtâr it is
stated:

> *"The danger of their arousing lust in man,*
> *looking at the face of a woman and an*
> *effeminate person is strictly forbidden."* [92]

An effeminate person *(amrad)* is one who has not yet grown a beard,
though his moustache may just be appearing. Some of the 'ulamâ are of

the opinion that such a young boy, if he is very handsome, then as in the case of women, his whole body is worth covering, and no part to be looked at. Abul Qâsim is of the opinion that looking at his body with lust is forbidden. But if this fear does not arise, then there is no harm in looking at his body or his face. Ibn al-Qattân mentions that to look at beardless boys with lust and with the intention of deriving pleasure in their handsome looks is forbidden, as is the unanimous verdict of the 'ulamâ. Nevertheless, if seeking pleasure is not the object and there is no danger of temptation for the onlooker, then it is unanimously agreed that this is permissible.[93]

Although there is absolutely nothing wrong with a young handsome lad accompanying his uncle on journeys, but the standard of Islâmic morality would rather safeguard them from unwarranted suspicions by strangers unaware of their degree of kinship.

An incident has been reported about Imâm Aḥmad ibn Ḥanbal when once a person came to the Imâm for some business. He was accompanied by a young boy. On noticing him the Imâm inquired about the boy's identity. He told the Imâm that the boy was his nephew. On hearing this, the Imâm advised him that in order for the people not to harbour any doubts regarding the validity of their mutual relations, he should avoid taking him around in public places.[94]

This is the sterling advice of those pious personalities who were notorious for their righteousness, abstinence and deep-rooted knowledge of *dîn*. Are we going to ignore and sideline their opinions by treading to our impending doom?

This is also a stern warning to those deviant elements of present times who utilize the services of young handsome boys in the massage parlours and in the privacy of their bedrooms, and live with them on terms of intimacy. Shâh Walîullâh points out that the adoption of homosexuality and the act of anal intercourse with women are interference in the creation of Allâh since sexual activities is diverted from its purpose. Furthermore, the effeminacy of males is the most abominable of traits.

Islâm strictly abhors men who imitate women and women who imitate men. The evil of such conduct, which affects both the life of the individual and of society, is that it constitutes a rebellion against the natural order of things. According to this natural order, each of the two sexes has its own distinctive characteristics. However, if man becomes effeminate (by allowing himself to be manipulated like a female in the act of homosexuality), and woman become masculinized (by assuming active male role in the act of lesbianism), this natural order will be reversed and will disintegrate.

5.13.3.2 PROHIBITION OF TWO OR MORE PERSONS SLEEPING UNDER THE SAME COVER

It must be emphasized here that with the intention of protecting us from developing homosexual tendency, which could ultimately destroy the moral fabric of society, the Prophet (P.B.U.H.) instructed that no two males, or even two females, should sleep under the same sheet or cloth. Lying together or sleeping under the same sheet, blanket, etc, has been forbidden since it intensifies the passions which sometime create a desire for the act of sodomy. Imâm Râzî declares:

> *"Sleeping together of two men is not permitted under the Sharî'ah, no matter if they both stick to either side (extreme end) of the bed."* [95]

Two persons sleeping together could be detrimental and could lead to dangerous situations. Indulgence in this practice could create avenues for stimulating passions which may at times result in desires for homosexual practices, deriving pleasure from mere friction (two females), or through sodomy (males), both of which are extremely disgusting. It is for this reason, amongst others, that the Prophet instructed parents to separate the beds of even their children at an early age:

> *"When your children attain the age of seven years, order them to pray, at the age of ten years, chastise them for not attending to prayers, and provide separate beds for each one of them to sleep in, at this age."* [96]

From this age sex consciousness develops in a boy and there is a suppressed type, of inclination towards sexual gratification. Separating their beds at this age will create a psychological advantage and children will also benefit tremendously as far as health reasons are concerned.

We should also clearly be reminded that as it is illegal for a man to look at another male's *satar* (that part of the body which is to be hidden), similarly it is also forbidden that the bodies of two men come in such close contact that there is nothing intervening between them. However, a handshake, a simple cordial embrace and such other harmless direct contacts are exceptions. Hâfiz ibn Hajar states:

> *"To touch with the hand the part of the body of a stranger (male) which is satar is forbidden; no matter with which other part of the body his satar is touched, it is equally prohibited."* [97]

All these forbidden postures and activities currently form the basic ingredients of a homosexual's lifestyle. In present times, this injunction must be all the more strictly enforced since there are so many things that excite and agitate the sexual appetite, the atmosphere is well stocked with them, and more or less everyone is affected by them.

5.14   AIDS

When man chooses to blemish the fair face of morality and wilfully violates the limits of the _Sharî'ah_ in his stride, not caring for the prohibited or the approved, the whole nation is put on trial. The downfall of people from a life of dignity to that of disgrace and misery follows in the wake of their unnatural sexual tendencies. As soon as the humanity of a people becomes degenerate the oppressed is sick of life, the standard of the national health falls, and veneral and other common debilitating diseases are rife among the people in general and the younger generation in particular. Aids which is one such disease, is a short comprehensive word but the circle of its evil is so vast it encompasses, not families, tribes and communities but entire countries.

Aids represents the appearance in previously healthy individuals of various aggressive infections and malignancies. It was first seen among homosexual and bisexual males with multiple sex partners (still the predominant victims), hemophiliacs and intravenous drug users.

In the summer of 1981, the Center for Disease Control in Atlanta alerted the medical world to an unexpected outbreak of PC Pneumonia and Kaposi's Sarcoma (a type of skin cancer which causes death by invading other body organs such as the lungs and intestines) in young homosexual men who had no known reason to contract these uncommon diseases.[98] The diseases were apparently connected to a strange form of gradual collapse of the immune system. Now known as the Acquired Immune Deficiency Syndrome, or AIDS, the phenomenon has become widely recognized within the past few decades, leading to growing international alarm.

Heterosexual women and men may now transmit the virus. Fresh blood, semen, preseminal fluid, tears, and infected saliva, must enter the bloodstream for the virus to be transmitted from one person to another. The Aids virus is not superficially transmitted. Transmission can only occur if a critical amount of an infected body fluid gains access to an individual's bloodstream through tissue capable of absorbing it. Rectal and vaginal linings are in this group.

In the developed countries, most of the infected people have been homosexually active men (including bisexuals), intravenous drug abusers, and the recipients of contaminated blood products, particularly people with haemophilia (hereditary tendency to severe bleeding from even slight cuts through failure of blood to clot quickly). Incidence of the disease has been reported worldwide, and it is evident in both males and females. The occurrence of AIDS has also been increasingly noted in heterosexual partners and also in infants born to women in the 'at risk' groupings.[99]

Initially, AIDS is caused by a concealed slow acting virus called 'Human Immunio-deficiency Virus' (HIV). This is whilst the virus remains undetected, without obvious symptoms. When the development and apparent advancement of HIV causes deteriorating health symptoms, this disease is referred to as 'full blown AIDS'. The AIDS virus attacks and destroys the immune system of the body. This destruction prevents the body's defence mechanism from producing the antibodies which counteract all infections. The body therefore cannot fight off common diseases, infections and certain cancers, even with the assistance of antibiotic medication. It is these infections which cause a rare form of pneumonia and a type of skin cancer. HIV infection is believed to be lifelong.

An AIDS carrier is a person who has been infected by HIV, but shows no symptoms and suffers no obvious disease. Such a person is labelled HIV anti-body positive, and can transmit the AIDS virus to other people. HIV is transmitted by the following methods:

a)   *Sexual contact*. Because HIV is found in semen and vaginal fluids, transmission can occur from man to woman, woman to man, or man to man. The highest risk groups for sexual transmission are clearly those men and women (homosexual or heterosexual) who have many sexual partners.

b)   *Mother to child*. The AIDS virus is passed from mother to child in utero, during birth, and possibly, through breastfeeding. A woman infected with HIV may spread the disease to her child during pregnancy, during birth or shortly after birth. It is also possible that an infected mother could transmit the virus through breast feeding. Tragically for pregnant women who are carrying the virus, they stand a 60-70 per cent chance of passing it on to their unborn child. Babies infected with the virus normally die within one to two years.

c) **Blood and blood products.** Transfusion of HIV-contaminated blood can affect the recipient. However, an increasing number of countries systematically screen and reject blood containing this virus. Blood clotting products for disorders such as haemophilia are treated to kill HIV.

d) **Shared needles.** Users of intravenous drugs are a major risk group because many of them share needles and syringes without proper cleaning. But any unsterilized, skin-piercing instrument (including ear-piercing or tattooing needles) can spread the disease from one person to another.

The question arises as to how the AIDS (HIV) virus can be detected when a carrier shows no initial symptoms of the infection? Since a carrier may look and feel healthy the only way this could be detected is through blood tests which will show the presence of the infection. After having become infected with HIV, full blown AIDS could take any time from five years to fifteen years to develop. The *Star* reports, "Of these, almost all will eventually get full blown AIDS for which there is no cure in sight. AIDS takes eight months to two years to kill.[100]

Early symptoms of full blown AIDS often suggest a diagnosis of the disease. Some of the signs and symptoms include:

1) Recurring night sweats, fever and interrupted sleep patterns.
2) Common cold-like symptoms, coughing, short breath.
3) Severe unexplained weight loss and fatigue.
4) Skin rashes, sores, and bruise-like mulberry eruptions on legs.
5) Swollen lymphatic glands.
6) Persistent diarrhoea.
7) Bleeding and discharge from the rectum.

However, in the presence of these signs and symptoms a definite diagnosis cannot be made without a blood test. To what extent these co-factors increase susceptibility to AIDS is not well understood, but they all affect the body's immune system to some degree. Infectious diseases such as tuberculosis and malaria, as well as malnutrition, are also suspected of playing a role.[101]

Once a person has been positively diagnosed with AIDS he could be inflicted with the following crisis:

Shock:
* about the diagnosis and possible death; and about loss of hope for good news (particularly in respect of a cure).

Anxiety and Fear:
* of the uncertain prediction and course of the illness (this is specially related to the complex set of symptoms experienced by AIDS sufferers);
* of the prospect of disfigurement and disability;
* of the effects of medication and treatment;
* of isolation, abandonment, and social/sexual rejection;
* of infecting others and being infected by them;
* of the lover's ability to cope; and
* of loss of competence, physical, social and work abilities.

Depression:
* over the 'inevitability' of physical decline, and loss of body image;
* over the absence of a cure;
* over the prospect of the virus controlling future life;
* over limits imposed by ill-health, and possible social, occupational, emotional, and sexual rejection; and
* because of self-blame and accusation for having been exposed to infection in the first place.

Anger and frustration:
* over the inability to overcome the virus;
* over new and involuntary health and lifestyle restrictions; and
* at being 'caught out' over the uncertainty of the future.

Guilt:
* about past indictable offences and misdeeds resulting in 'illness punishment';
* about the possibility of having spread the infection to others; and
* about being homosexual, promiscuous or a drug abuser.

Obsessive disorders:
* continuous searching for new diagnostic evidence and for bodily symptoms;
* craze over health and diet; and
* preoccupation with death and decline, and with the avoidance of new infections.[102]

It should also be pointed out that HIV cannot spread through casual contact at school, at work, or in the shopping centres. It also cannot be contacted by using the same toilets, by handshakes, hugs, casual, simple light kisses (of reverence, honour or mercy), eating from the same dish, drinking from the same glass, or by food handlers in eating places and restaurants. Yes, of course, AIDS can be contacted from having sex with a HIV carrier. Other high risk sexual activities include the following:

A female having sex with a bisexual man : A man who has contracted Aids from another man can pass it on to a woman by means of sexual intercourse, and possibly through the woman practicing *fellatio* (ie. stimulating his penis with her mouth, either by sucking or kissing it). Anal sex is also said to be the major factor in the transmission of the Aids virus between homosexual men, and possibly an important factor in the passing of the virus between some heterosexuals. When the anus is penetrated, the tissues of the rectum which are very delicate, are damaged and bleeding easily occurs. If the Aids virus is present in the partner's semen, abrasions of the anus will form an important point for the virus to enter the bloodstream.

Sex with prostitutes: prostitutes who stand the greatest chance of being infected with the Aids virus are those who have sex with bisexual men, and those who are intravenous drug addicts who share their unsterilized syringes and needles with other drug users. This is evident from the scarring, bruising or puncture marks on their arms or on the inside of their legs. Indulging in *cunnilingus* with a prostitute (ie. putting the lips and mouth in contact with her vulva) can also be responsible for the transmission of the Aids virus. This applies both to the person doing the 'mouthwork' and the person at the receiving end. There may be traces of menstrual blood in her vaginal fluids, and if the woman is an Aids carrier - these fluids will be contaminated with the virus. The vaginal fluid itself contains small amounts of the virus. Besides, the woman concerned may be carrying other veneral diseases, some of which are easily transmitted via oral sex. If the possibility of contracting Aids from a prostitute does not freeze one's sexual urges then one should be prepared for the tragic and terrifying possibility of unwittingly giving this killer disease to one's spouse. No matter how strong one's sexual urges, sex is simply not worth dying (and killing) for. A sobering thought for anyone having sex with a new partner is that you are (in terms of possible contamination by Aids) having sex with every individual that this person has ever had sex with. It is sobering to note that in Miami, for example, 40 per cent of the street prostitutes are believed to be infected with the Aids virus, while in Nairobi, at least 60 per cent of the female prostitutes population are carriers.[103] One thing is certain - no matter what the infection level of female prostitutes is at the moment in South Africa, it is undoubtedly on the rise if the experience of other countries is anything to go by.

If you are raped by an Aids carrier: As Aids spreads, there are inevitably going to be incidents in which people are infected, and subsequently die, following an act of homosexual or heterosexual rape – a particularly horrifying prospect especially following the mental and physical trauma of the rape itself. The chances of one's finding out for certain that the rapist is an Aids carrier during the immediate period following intercourse is of course extremely unlikely. However, some victims may choose to adopt a 'just-in-case' approach, and wash or douche the area that has been penetrated. Although doing so might conceivably reduce the chances of infection (should the rapist be an Aids carrier) there is a strong legal argument for not doing so: rape victims should not wash away any evidence of rape having been committed (ie. the presence of semen) prior to being examined by a doctor. His evidence that semen was present is often vital in bringing about a successful conviction.

The following could be classified as non-sexual, high risk activities:

Contact with needles and blood contaminated with the Aids virus: If you are involved in taking blood samples; the medical care of an Aids patient; or you share accommodation with a potential Aids carrier who uses intravenous drug equipment - there is always the possibility you could prick yourself with a needle contaminated with blood containing the Aids virus. If this occurs, immediately squeeze the punctured area as quickly as possible and hold for five minutes under running water encouraging the puncture to bleed as profusely as possible. Then wash the area with soap and apply a suitable solution such as Betadine or Mercurochrome.

Sharing of intravenous drug equipment: After homosexuals, intravenous drug users are the next group most prone to infection by the Aids virus. In New York, at least half the city's heroin addicts are contaminated with the virus. Even in Edinburgh, the Scottish capital, the inspection figure is around 30 per cent.[104]

Tattooing: This is a common practice in many of the country's jails; it is especially popular amongst members of gangs (especially in the Western Cape); and it is fairly popular amongst a minority of members of the armed forces. Considering the high incidence of homosexuality in prisons - and the common practice of tattooing with dirty blades and knives - the threat of prisoners passing on Aids to one another is becoming a serious problem. Recently, in Germany, the prison population of a detention centre in Bavaria mutinied when five inmates were found to have Aids. The inmates demanded the punishing of the tattooist, who it was felt had helped spread the infection by using unsterile equipment.[105]

Ritual Sacrifice: This practice is quite common amongst some rural black tribes which may include: deliberate scarring of the face, often a group of people being cut at one time and with the same instrument; sacrification of the penis (supposedly to heighten the men's sensitivity to sexual intercourse), and female circumcision. The actual sacrification holds dangers when the same instruments are used by more than one person without being cleaned. Some researchers believe that the above practices could be playing a role in the horrific rate at which Aids is spreading throughout Central Africa.

How Risky Are The Following Activities:

Going to the Dentist: The large majority of dentists, their assistants, and dental hygienists are highly-professional people who are extremely aware of the dangers of not using clean, sterile equipment on individual patients. By and large, the choices of your picking up Aids from a responsible dentist is very very rare. However, it must also be acknowledged that given a particular chain of unfortunate circumstances - namely a deposit of blood from an Aids carrier being left on an instrument such as a syringe, needle or drill bit, and this instrument then being used in your mouth without first being sterilized - then there is definitely a danger of infection. But while "you" are worrying about getting Aids, your dentist is probably more worried - and with greater justification - about the possibility of picking it up from one of his patients. Of all the people involved in health-care services, dentists and oral hygienists are probably amongst the greatest at risk. Overseas and in South Africa, growing numbers of dentists are wearing masks, goggles and gloves to protect themselves from possible infection by the Aids virus.

An interesting study was undertaken overseas in which the water reservoir of a dentist's high-speed drill was filled with red dye. When a session involving the drilling of a patients tooth was over, the white gowns worn by the dentist and his nurse were examined - and found to be finely impregnated all over with the dye. Doubtlessly they had also inhaled much of the vapour.[106] Needless to say, vapourised, blood-containing saliva is very likely to be a threat if the patient has Aids.

Giving artificial respiration: If one has reason to believe that a person requiring artificial respiration is an Aids carrier, one would probably be well advised to try and form an airtight barrier by placing one's hands between his/her mouth and that of the patient's - especially if the person is bleeding from the mouth or has injuries to the face. If the person is an Aids carrier, his blood will carry the virus, making him potentially infectious.

Health Club spa baths: The combination of specific factors could offer the possibility of being infected, such as: poorly chlorinated water, the presence of fresh blood or semen from an Aids carrier in the water just prior to someone getting in, and having an open cut on one's body through which the virus could enter one's system.

Massage Parlours: It is generally acknowledged that a significant proportion of the women who work for escourt services and massage parlours around the country do in fact perform a variety of sexual services for their clients for an extra fee or *tip*. Hygiene in some massage parlours is questionable. The towel covering the couch on which one is massaged could possibly contain specks of semen from someone who had earlier been given a 'pelvic massage' (manual masturbation by the masseuse). If these specks are fresh, come from an Aids carrier, and a cut or abrasion on one's body comes into contact with any of them, then there is the possibility of infection. Therefore Muslims in particular, and mankind in general should be well advised in abstaining from frequenting such vile places masquerading as health promotion centres, whereas in fact these are the very spots where morality is unashamedly butchered.

5.14.1 AIDS IN AMERICA AND EUROPE

In Europe and America AIDS has been confined primarily to homosexuals and intravenous drug abusers, although promiscuous heterosexuals are also caught in its web. So many men, women and children are presumed to be affected that the disease is being compared to the black death, the plague that swept Europe in the Middle Ages, which killed a quarter of Europe's population in the fourteenth century. Medical experts consider this epidemic an accelerating disaster that 'makes the Ethiopian famine look like a picnic'. The reason for the disease having spread with such speed through the American homosexual community is due largely to the promiscuous behaviour of a large number of the country's gays and the resultant veneral diseases they pick up. Many gays suffering from Aids have reported having had between 25-60 sexual partners a year, while some had several hundred. The greater the number of men that a homosexual man has sex with, the greater his chances of contracting the disease, and if he becomes infected the greater the chances of spreading it further. Most Aids patients in the the U.S.A have had gonorrhoea several times and almost without exception the Aids patients examined were infected with the herpes virus. Ninety per cent showed the presence of syphillis.[107] These diseases had doubtlessly weakened the system and in the case of herpes, provided - via broken blisters an easy point for entry of the virus.

The spread of the Aids virus in the West started in the United States, probably during the late 1970's, with the first victims becoming apparent in 1981 in San Francisco, Los Angeles and New York - all of which have large homosexual populations. Within the space of only six years (up to early 1987) 17 542 Americans have died of the disease and more than 30 000 had contracted the disease (1 870 of them being women). Between one and two million Americans are thought to be infected with the virus, with about 90 per cent of them being unaware that they are carriers and thus continuing to infect others. Three quarters of the entire homosexual population of Los Angeles and San Francisco are believed to be infected with the virus. Aids had been reported in nearly 90 countries ten years ago, and WHO officials then estimated that as many as 100 million will become infected in the next decade.[108]

In the broader context, transmission of AIDS is also facilitated by a high tolerance of extramarital affairs by men, as well as wide acceptance of unmarried men and women having many sexual partners. This promiscuous lifestyle is reflected in the higher incidence of sexually transmitted diseases among people who ignore standard ethical behaviour towards regulating their sexual patterns.

Homosexuals account for a disproportionate number of America's most serious STD's, including syphilis, gonorrhoea, genital warps, and hepatitis A and B. Gay men are one of the top risk groups for being exposed to hepatitis B.[109] A homosexual sex survey in *The Advocate*, a leading homosexual magazine, found that homosexuals who participate in unsafe sex practices with multiple partners and without taking precautions are at great risk of contracting STD's. It revealed that 72 percent of homosexual respondents engage in insertive oral intercourse, 46 percent insertive anal intercourse, 45 percent receptive anal-oral sex, 48 percent in three-way sex, 24 percent in group sex (4 or more), and 10 percent in sadomasochism. Most of the homosexuals in the survey admitted to having had more than 30 sex partners over their lifetime, and about a third (35 percent) report more than 100 partners. The survey also found that homosexual men use condoms only once in 4 times.[110]

According to the Centers for Disease Control and Prevention, homosexuals are especially exposed to contracting HIV. They are a high risk group because of co-factors associated with their lifestyle. These include recreational drug use, homosexual sex, malnutrition, prior incidents of STD's, and, most significantly, sexual promiscuity.[111]

According to the CDC in Atlanta, Aids is now the fourth leading cause of death among women between the ages of 25 and 44 in the United States. The proportion of women with Aids rose from 7 percent to 18 percent. Women are generally more susceptible to contracting the disease through sexual intercourse than their male partners, because the virus is more concentrated in semen than in vaginal fluid and because the sensitive cells of the vagina are exposed to the semen for a prolonged period of time. Women can also pass on the virus to their new-borns through pregnancy, birth or breast-feeding; 20 to 30 percent of infants born to HIV-infected mothers become infected themselves. Women have also been ignored when it comes to comprehensive medical studies on Aids, because until the early nineties, women were considered a low-risk group.

Heterosexuals, it is claimed, have 'fewer' sex partners than homosexuals. A General Social Survey found that 91 percent of men 24 to 29 years of age are heterosexually active. Nineteen percent of these men have had only one lifetime sex partner, 55 percent have had 2 to 19 lifetime partners, and 25 percent have had 20 or more lifetime partners.[113]

Homosexuality also increases medical costs. The US Department of Health and Human Services indicates that the lifetime cost of treating a patient with AIDS - from diagnosis until death - is $102,000. The American Medical Association estimated the per person AIDS patient cost would rise to $639,000 by the year 2008.[114]

To date, "the biggest step forward" in 'combating' the disease has been the discovery in 1983 - by Dr Luc Montagnier of the Pasteur Institute in Paris - of the virus responsible for the disease, and the subsequent development of an antibody test to determine the presence of the virus in the bloodstream.[115] Without such a test, blood banks throughout the world would have been unable to determine which blood had been contaminated with the virus, and this would have resulted in greater infection of the general population.

Homosexuals also have a much shorter life expectancy than heterosexuals, as indicated by a study of more than 6 400 obituaries in 16 homosexual newspapers. The average age of homosexuals who died from AIDS is 39.[116]

5.14.2 AIDS IN AFRICA

There is still intense speculation as to where the Aids virus originated, the most popular theory at present being that it came from somewhere in central Africa. It is thought that an Aids epidemic existed in Zaire for an unknown but presumably lengthy period of time prior to it becoming an uncontrollable pandemic throughout central Africa, infecting Africans in excessive numbers as early as the mid-to late 1980's. Central Africa's AIDS plague appears to have originated around East Africa's Lake Victoria, bordered by Uganda. Countries hardest hit were Uganda, Zaire, Rwanda, Zambia and Kenya. Statistics on the world-wide spread of Aids have always been horrifying. But even the doomsayers may have been too optimistic. Medical researchers working for the U.N. released new data that shows they have been miscalculating the virus's conquest in the developing world. Each day 16 000 people contract HIV, nearly double the previous estimate of the infection. That means that 30,6 million are now living with the virus and it is Africa that accounts for the largest chunk of where the bulk of the infections have been concentrated.[117]

A study of Nairobi, Kenyan prostitutes revealed that four percent were HIV positive in 1981. But by 1985, fifty-nine percent were infected. In Nairobi, street prostitutes tested in 1987 showed sixty-seven percent positive. A tall, dignified woman in her late thirties walked into the University Hospital in Kinshasa, assisted by her grown son. A school teacher and a mother of six, she appeared gaunt and weary. At times it was difficult for her to breathe. She told the doctor about her symptoms in detail. Twenty months earlier she had developed a fever that would not go away. It was followed by prolonged fatigue, then pain in her joints, and finally diarrhoea. She had weighed 75 kilograms before her illness began, she now weighed less than 36. Blood tests and clinical examinations showed that the woman had AIDS. Because the virus was destroying her immune system, she suffered from opportunistic infections, for which she was treated. But it was only a matter of time before she would die.

> *"The plight of this intelligent, educated*
> *woman summarizes one of the cruellest*
> *twists of the African epidemic,' explained*
> *the Western doctor who related her story.*
> *'AIDS is taking away the very people on*
> *whom Africa depends."* [118]

Unlike the developed world, Africa does not have a large reservoir of trained people to run its schools, banks, hospitals, businesses and government. So each loss strikes a severe dent in its national strength.

Consider this: In Uganda, where there is only one doctor per 22 000 people, a 40 year old doctor who administered a clinic serving a large section of the country's south-western region, died last July of AIDS. In Kinshasa, a neurosurgeon - a specialist in acutely short supply in Africa - recently died of AIDS. In the Zambian copperbelt, two-thirds of the men who tested HIV-positive are skilled professionals. Another Zambian study found over eight percent of mostly 'middle-class or well-to-do' expectant mothers to be HIV-positive. High government officials, teachers, military leaders and professionals in many African countries have also been infected. A Zairian doctor told the story of a young widow who worked as an executive secretary. She became romantically involved with a married bank manager, who was also seeing two other girlfriends. Soon the widow became ill, and despite the doctor's best efforts, she died. Then the banker developed similar symptoms and he, too, died. Finally, his two girlfriends also died. All four deaths, the doctor came to realize, were caused by AIDS. Only the banker's wife was spared. [119]

Due to the extremely high incidence of Aids in Central African communities, the possibility of the disease being transmitted by means of blood-sucking insects moving directly from an Aids carrier to a potential victim has been claimed. In the British Medical journal *Lancet*, virologists from Johannesburg pointed out that 15-22 per cent of the Aids cases in Africa have occured in children - who were very unlikely to be contracting the virus via sexual intercourse. Noting that African children are

311

continually being bitten by bedbugs, the researchers concluded: "Bedbugs would probably transmit low levels of infection, but a combination of factors could enhance the possibility of infection by African children. Other factors leading to increased exposure to the disease could be repeated insect bites, and decreased immunity due to malnutrition and tropical diseases - such as malaria.[120]"

The young elite who represent Africa's power are already heavily infected and will die in increasing numbers. If this gloomy scenario consistently accelerates, then AIDS may not only crush Africa's development, returning her to subsistence farming, but also could cause tremendous socio-political changes as did the plagues of old.

5.14.3 AIDS IN SOUTH AFRICA

The first semblance of a formal gay movement emerged in South Africa in January 1966. The police raided a large party hosted in a private home in Johannesburg. Prominent white business people, advocates, doctors, artists and people who had political connections were present. When the raid took place, nine arrests were made and charges were levelled against many people ' because of one or other (alleged) homosexual deed'.[121]

Medical experts believe that AIDS was definitely imported from America initially by homosexual airline stewards, later by haemophiliacs (those to whom even a slight cut induces severe bleeding through failure of blood to clot quickly) who were given blood imported from America and then from mine workers from the north. *The Star* reported that the Deputy President of the Medical Research Council, Dr Walter Prozesky, describing how he had detected South Africa's first AIDS case, mentions:

> *"I was at home on Saturday morning in December 1982, and read an article in Time Magazine about AIDS in the gay San Francisco community. The following Monday a physician phoned me. He had a Johannesburg patient with four different infections from different bacteria, yeast and fungi. We then asked the patient if he*

*was homosexual and if he had recently
been to the States, and it all fell in place.
The patient was an airline steward who
had contracted the disease in the United
States. He and his lover died a few months
later', said Dr Prozesky.*[122]

In a recently released Pinetown (Kwa Zulu Natal) survey the shocking
results depicted the extreme extent to which many young people of all
races in the area are sexually active - one HIV-positive girl had 80 different
partners in one month - and how they discard disease prevention methods,
thus leading to an aggressive spread of AIDS. The survey was conducted
among 1 142 patients who attended the STD clinic at the Pinetown City
Health Department.

The girl who had the 80 sexual partners in one month does not take
precautions and is still sexually active and infecting others, the survey
has shown. This person is not alone in her behaviour but represents part
of a sexually active group of youths (not necessarily prostitutes), said the
Medical Officer of Health for Pinetown, Dr Raymond Will.[123]

The latest figure on HIV infection rates show that the Aids crisis is upon
South Africa. And as for KwaZulu Natal, where the figures are highest,
the impact will be disastrous. A 1997 survey of woman attending state
ante-natal clinics showed that almost 27% were HIV positive, suggesting
an infection rate of about 20 per cent in the broader adult population in
the Province - about one in every five adults. Projections based on the
current trends show that HIV is already having a profound impact - and
the crisis will now accelerate very rapidly. The projections show: [124]

Some two million people in KwaZulu-Natal will die from Aids over the
next 20 years, with death rates peaking at around 130 000 a year by 2006.

Already medical wards in the provinces state hospitals are clogged with
patients suffering from secondary infections caused by full blown Aids.
Due to Aids the population in the province has almost stopped growing.

Over the next 10 years, the number of children aged up to 15 who have lost their mothers to Aids will increase from around 125 000 to around 600 000. According to Professor Alan Whiteside, director of the Health Economics and HIV Aids Research division at the University of Natal, the impact of the epidemic will hit the family unit hardest with important implications for poverty relief. The epidemic is already having a serious effect on hospital and health care resources.

In spite of this alarming revelation regarding the AIDS menace, some homosexuals are still continually seeking outlets for their perverted activities. The following is a clear indication:

> *A steam bath, located in the centre of Johannesburg and catering exclusively for the gay collective, operates daily. Upon admission each customer is supplied with a towel, a clothes-locker key, and a free condom. Issuing the contraceptive is an attempt to prevent unsafe sex practices, but it is regarded by many as an 'invitation to participate in anal sex'.*[125]

The architecture of the steam bath is such that private cubicles afford patrons the opportunity of selecting a partner for sexual interaction in relative privacy. There are community rooms (described as TV or relaxation rooms) as well, where groups of people can participate in group sex. Of note are the number of people who participate in mutual receptive anal intercourse without the use of the condom.

Either the serious implications of these unnatural sexual gratification have not reached the South African homosexual population, or disregard of the situation is prevalent, or both.

Nevertheless, it should also be pointed out that although many countries have legalized homosexual behaviour between consenting adults, a recent study conducted in South Africa, under the auspices of the Human Sciences Research Council, revealed an overwhelming negative attitude in respondents. Over 70 percent thought that homosexuality between consenting adults should not be legalized.[126]

5.15   AIDS AND ISLÂM

Islâm has structured detailed rules of good conduct in the Muslim home, family and society. Promiscuous sexual behaviour has never been condoned in Islâm. The women folk have also been warned about safeguarding their modesty which saves them from falling prey to sexual abuse. The illicit wanderings of men and women for heterosexual indulgence is disastrous. Anyone caught in such an act, which has been established and proven, then public punishment is to be instituted. The critics of such divine code who protest against this by claiming that 'such corporal punishment is barbaric' today cannot save society from self-inflicted destruction and the wrath of Allâh Ta'âlâ.

In this case, it is an 'incurable' disease, the carrier of which is plagued with loss of life in agony, namely the deadly AIDS. Some authorities record and believe an unknown virus was responsible for the downfall of the Roman Empire since a large proportion of the population had been wiped out. In the Middle Ages the bubonic plague irrevocably changed the course of history by causing the death of millions of people. The AIDS pandemic seems to be our modern-day equivalent.

Although AIDS is contracted via sexual intimacy, contaminated blood products, shared needles and mother to child, HIV-AIDS is predominantly spread through secretions of the sexual organs which normally occur in cases of illicit sexual practices out of wedlock. Muslims particularly, and mankind in general, are required to take heed and undertake firm resolutions of abstaining from such unethical and immoral behaviour. The dangers and hazards which are imminent from full blown AIDS should be impressed upon the present day teenagers in particular.

5.16 CONCLUSION

What has been discussed thus far makes it crystal clear that all the unnatural methods of gratifying the sexual urge have been condemned and strict measures adopted for their prevention, since they open avenues of detriment, personal, familial and those affecting the whole of humanity. These vices have contributed to the annihilation of races and nations.

Currently, the Islâmic injunctions in eradicating these unnatural evil tendencies must be all the more strictly enforced since there are so many things that excite and agitate the sexual appetite, the atmosphere is well stocked with them, and most people are affected by them.

CHAPTER SIX
Sex Education
MORALITY IN ISLÂM

SEX EDUCATION

6.1 INTRODUCTION

Sexuality is an integral part of life and it influences personality. It may be denied, repressed or used effectively, but it is part of our lives. Sexuality is a process commencing at birth and ending only with death. For every person there are significant events which highlight sexuality. These include puberty, choosing a partner, childbirth, menopause. Sex education is only one of the many social changes in Western societies, which include legalization of other social evils, that has transformed long established principles and moral values.

In spite of the fact that Islâm has greatly emphasized the acquiring of knowledge, and during the Prophet's time, Muslim men and women were never too shy to ask questions, including those related to private affairs such as sexual life, for Muslim parents of today, sex is a dirty word. They feel uncomfortable in discussing sex education with their children, but do not mind it being taught at their children's school by secular teachers of even the opposite sex, by their peers of either sex, and by the media. The problem with this is that it does not cover the aspect of morality associated with sex, sexual dysfunctions and deviations and the institution of marriage. It is rather alarming that the average child is exposed to more than 10 000 sexual scenarios per year.

These parents should be informed that sex is not always a dirty word. It is an important sphere of our life and Allâh Who cares for all the aspects of our life, and not only just the manner in which we worship Him, discusses creation, reproduction, family life, menstruation and even ejaculation in the Qur'ân. Prophet Muhammad (P.B.U.H.), who was sent to us as a perfect example, discussed and explained many aspects of sexual life with his companions. The main reason why Muslim parents do not or cannot discuss sex education with their children is because of their cultural upbringing, not their religious training. The feeling of shyness or the fear of being ridiculed creates a barrier. They are often brought up in a state of ignorance in regard to sexual issues. Such ignorance and unresolved curiosity are harmful and even sometimes dangerous. They leave Islâmic education to the *madrasahs* and sex education to the public schools and the media. Parents failure to tell their children what they want and need to know would encourage them from receiving and believing unwholesome and inaccurate information from their peers, which is one of the reasons why sexual chastity has been disregarded and presently the world is experiencing the highest rates of out-of-wedlock teenage pregnancy and abortion. Therefore avoiding social contact and simultaneously persevering to keep the youth informed would be wishful thinking on the part of the conservative parent.

6.2   WHAT IS SEX EDUCATION?

Is sex education about knowing the anatomy of the human body or about the act of sex or about reproduction and family life or about prevention of sexually transmitted diseases and unwanted pregnancy? Is giving sex education equivalent to permission in engaging in sex? One sex educator told parents, "I am not planning to tell your children whether or not they should engage in sex or how to do it, but in case they decide to do it, they should know how to prevent sexually transmitted diseases (STD), venereal diseases (VD), acquired immune deficiency syndrome (AIDS) and pregnancy." Therefore standard sex education today tends to be morally bankrupt. It begins with a biological description of sexual function and ends with indoctrination in conception, abortion and venereal diseases.

One of the basic questions is, "Do children need sex education?" Do you teach a tadpole how to swim or just leave it in the water and let it swim? After all, for thousands of years men and women have been having sex without any formal education. In many traditional civilizations, sex education starts after marriage and with trial and error. Some couple learn it faster and better than others due to difference in sexual expression.

Parents have to assume a more responsible role, otherwise children will probably gain information from wrong sources. A father has a duty to be able to answer his son's questions and a mother has the same duty to her daughter. Within a family, the older brother or sister has a duty towards his or her younger brothers or sisters. Apart from these, some meaningful role can be played by the *'ulamâs* and religious leaders.

Sex education, as promoted by some educators is devoid of morality and is, in many ways, unacceptable to our value system. The examples of the teaching of one such educator are:

a)   Nudity in homes (in shower or bedroom) is a good and healthy way to introduce sexuality to smaller (under 5) children, giving them an opportunity to ask questions. At the same time, in the same book, he also states that 75% of all child molestation and incest, half a million per year, occur by a close relative (parent, step-parent or another family member).

b)   A child's playing with genitals of another is a permissible – 'naive exploration' – and not a reason for scolding or punishment. He is also aware that boys as young as 12 have raped girls as young as 8. We don't know when this 'naive exploration' becomes a sex act.

c)   Children caught reading dirty magazines should not be made to feel guilty, but parents should use it as a chance to get some useful points across to him or her about sexual attitudes, values and sex exploration. Like charity, pornography should begin at home!

d)   If your daughter or son is sexually active, instead of telling them to stop, the parent's 'moral duty' is to protect their health and career by providing them information and means for contraception and avoiding VD. Maybe this is true for rebellious teens and their submissive parents.[1]

Educators like these do not believe that giving sexual information means giving the consent for sex. It is no wonder then that some people, after being told the shape, colour, smell and taste of a new fruit, and pleasures derived from eating it, would not like to try it.

Sex education is given in every American school, public or private from grades 2 to 12. The projected cost to the nation was two billion dollars per year. Teachers are told to give technical aspects without telling the students about moral values or how to make the right decision. After describing the male and female anatomy and reproduction, the main emphasis is on the prevention of venereal diseases and teenage pregnancy. With the rise of AIDS, the focus is on 'safe sex' which means having condoms available each time one decides to have sex with a stranger. Currently 76 American schools have started dispensing free condoms and contraceptives to those who go to school health clinics. Very soon there will be vending machines in school hallways where 'children' can get a condom each time they feel like having sex. Therefore sex education invariably includes a study of contraceptive devices and methods. Contraception is seen by many as being the best way to allow young people to experiment with sexuality without the fear of unwanted pregnancy: *'Limit the damage and increase the enjoyment'* is one way that this concept has been described.

Sex education in American schools has not helped decrease the teenager incidence of VD or teenage pregnancy. This is because it has not changed their sex habits. According to the President of the Children's Defense Fund, M.W. Elderman, in a recent report, out of every twenty teens, ten are sexually active but only four use contraceptions, two get pregnant and one gives birth. A John Hopkins study found out of every five 15 year olds, and one in three 16 year olds are sexually active. The incidence increased to 43% in 17 year olds. The Louis Harris poll found that 57% of the nation's 17 year olds, 46% of 16 year olds, 29% 15 year olds were sexually active. Now it is estimated that 80% of girls entering college had sexual intercourse at least once.[2]

South African parents have also been jolted by the electrifying shock of this statistic released by the *Eastern Province Herald.*

More than 30% of matric boys and 25% of Standard 10 girls in Cape Town have had sex, a new study has found. However, 19,8% of boys and 10,2% of girls in the Cape Peninsula have already lost their virginity by Standard 7. The study also found that among 18 year old school pupils in Cape Town, 21% of boys and 8,1% of girls had smoked dagga, while 30,7% and 18,5% of girls smoked one or more cigarettes a day.

The percentage of pupils engaging in heterosexual intercourse were: Std. 6 14,1% boys, 6,8% girls; Std 7 19,8%, 10,2%; Std 8 25,1%, 15,8%; Std

9 27,0%, 18,6% and Std 10 31,6%, 25%.

The study notes that "the results are consistent with the conclusion that it is the students in more junior standards who are particularly at risk." [3]

6.3   HAZARDS OF EARLY SEX

The health hazards of early sex includes sexual trauma, increase in incidence of cervical cancer, sexually transmitted disease and teenage pregnancy. A variety of injuries are possible and do not happen when sex organs are not ready for sex in terms of full masturbation. Some of these injuries have a long lasting effect. Cervical cancer has been thought to be related to sex at an early age and with multiple partners.

About one million or more teenage girls, 80% of whom are unmarried, become pregnant every year, at a rate of 3 000 per day. Of these 1 million, about 500 000 decide to keep their baby; 400 000 resort to abortion and 100 000 decide to give the baby up for adoption. It is a myth that teenage pregnancy is a problem of the black and poor. On the contrary about two third's of the teenagers falling pregnant now are white, suburban and above the poverty income level.

What is the life of pregnant teenagers? Only 50% of them are on welfare. They themselves become child abusers and their children, when grown up, have 82% incidence of teenage pregnancy. 8,6 billion dollars is spent every year for the financial and health care support of teenage mothers.

The sexual revolution of the 60's has affected another dimension of health care. Twenty years ago, 10 million cases of chlamydia, 2 million cases of gonorrhea, 1 million venereal warts, 0,5 million genital herpes and 90 000 cases of syphilis were diagnosed. Currently the statistics are shocking.

AIDS is adding a new twist to our fears. The disease is growing at a rate of one case every minute and so far there is no effective treatment. [4]

6.3.1 PUBLIC SCHOOLS, COLLEGES AND UNIVERSITIES

Since sex education was introduced in British schools more than 20 years ago, school-girl pregnancies have increased from 1 000 to 13 000 a year and the figures are constantly rising. This is one of the points made by the Responsible Society in its report to the Home Office Committee on Obscenity and Film Censorship. They are deeply critical of the expanding "sex education industry" and want tougher laws to protect children from obscenity, indecency and violence. Their report says:

"Some of the visual material associated with these (sex ed) programmes — showing pictures of sexual intercourse, homosexual activity and close-ups of female and male genitalia — would, if displayed to children in a cinema or bookshop, render the exhibitor liable to prosecution. But under the existing law, parents have no redress if their children are exposed to this material in school." [5]

The report claims that sex education breaks down defence mechanisms and natural restraint in children, making them susceptible to instruction in pornography.

In Circular 11/87 issued by the then British Department of Education and Science (now the Department of Education) it was stated that whilst parents have no statutory right to withdraw children from sex education lessons, governors will have the non-statutory "discretion to accept or reject requests from parents for their children to be withdrawn from any sex education to which they object." Subsequent changes to include some sex education concerning HIV and AIDS in the National Curriculum mean, of course, that there can be no withdrawal whatsoever from those particular parts of the sex education programme.

It is probably fair to say that the majority of Muslim parents would only be happy if there was no sex education in schools at all. However, the law thinks otherwise and so sex education is on the curriculum in most schools. Muslims must work towards full recognition of their religious requirements by the government in order to safeguard their children from the undesirable effects of liberal and immoral sex education, by utilizing The 1986 Act (Education No. 2 Act 1986, section 18 (2) (a) (b)).

Parents should be aware that some of the material prepared for sex education lessons is produced by outside agencies who have an agenda far removed from the sort of concerns Muslims have for their children. Anything produced by bodies such as Brook Advisory Centres and Family Planning Association, for example, must be scrutinised by Muslim parents because the underlying philosophy of these organisations is at odds with Islâmic teaching. For example, the Brook publication *Safe Sex for Teenagers* states:

"We must be prepared to challenge our established attitudes that sexual activity in young people is dangerous". Islâm has no objection about young people being sexually active *within marriage* but the Brook concept revolves around the fact that such youngsters are unlikely to be married. Both Brook and the FPA wrongly assume that all teenagers are having sexual intercourse and those who aren't will do so at any moment and so all must have contraceptive protection.[6]

Muslims believe that children should be informed that no contraceptive method – *apart from abstinence* – is 100% safe (e.g. they should be told that out of 733 women who had abortions in one British city from between September and the next March, 334 reported that their partners used condoms for contraceptive 'protection').[7] It is to be regretted that much of the mechanisms of sex including contraceptive devices, are explored in depth whilst the spiritual and emotional impact such details can have on some children is all too often ignored *"No sex before marriage"* is the most effective form of contraception and the *"safest sex"* of all. It appears that those responsible for sex education make no allowances for the fact that children develop physically and psychologically at different ages. Potentially disturbing information is being forced down the throats of children, to even some 7 year olds, regardless of their mental readiness.

British society is, (and this is applicable to most Western societies), to all intents and purposes, secular and materialistic in outlook, and matters such as "the spiritual and moral" aspects of life remain largely ignored or marginalised in terms of the actual curriculum applied in schools. Permissiveness and liberalised social attitudes have led to early sexual experimentation resulting in increasing numbers of abortions, schoolgirl mothers, family tension, illegitimate children and one-parent families. Muslims are strongly convinced that the methodology, content and peer pressure used to teach this sensitive subject contravenes Islâmic teachings. Islâm cannot accommodate countries that have not only legalized homosexuality but have also included it in their sex education curriculum as acceptable behaviour in these words: homosexuality acts (defined as buggery or gross indecency) between males constitute a criminal offence *unless* both parties have attained the age of 21 and the acts are committed with the consent of both in private.

The concept of what constitutes 'acceptable' behaviour needs to be highlighted. It is often said that if you want to know the future, look into the past: history bears testimony that the major civilizations all collapsed once homosexuality was accepted as normal behaviour. There is no place in any school under any circumstances for teaching that which advocates homosexual behaviour, which presents it as the "norm" or which encourages homosexual experimentation by pupils. It must also be recognized that for many people including members of various religious faiths, homosexual practice is abhorred and is morally not acceptable. Tragically, in this very secular world, the guidance given by Allâh is rejected more often than not. It is shocking for Muslim parents to read that *"only 3 percent of young people (aged 16-24) believe that sexual intercourse should be reserved for marriage with nearly half admitting to their first experience before the age of 16..."* [8]

There are many reasons that children get involved in sex. The most common is peer pressure. Their common response is "everyone is doing it". One of the reasons is their desire for sexual competence with adults and a way to get ahead. Sometimes it is due to a lack of other alternatives to divert their sexual energies. Detachment from home can lead to attachment elsewhere. Sexual pressure on them is everywhere, at school, from their peers, from television where about 20 000 sexual scenes are broadcast in advertisement, soap operas, prime time shows and MNET. The hard core rock music nowadays fans the flames of sexual desires. Most parents do not know the type of music their children are listening to. The songs have pornographic lyrics which made Kandy Stroud, a former rock fan, beg parents to stop their children from listening to what she calls 'Pornographic Rock'. [9] This demonstrates that music does in fact excite our sexual mood. It does so by activating melatonin, the hormone from the pineal gland in the brain which is turned on by darkness and turned off by flashing lights. It is the same gland which triggers puberty and affects the sex mood and reproductive cycle.

The schools where Muslims send their children in pursuit of secular education are now being transformed into hives of immorality and dens of vices. Every now and again reports of the filthy goings-on in secular schools appear in the media. These extracts from a *Sunday Times* report bear ample testimony:

"Indian schools have been plagued recently by reports of child abuse and sexual harassment of women teachers. Some alleged school sex pests appeared in court and others were suspended... The department also plans to crack down on affairs between teachers that become common knowledge to.pupils.... The committee said sexual harassment of women teachers was as serious as child abuse in schools. Previously some headmasters squashed sex related incidents. In some cases the headmasters were the offenders..." [10]

The following article appearing in the *Post* under the caption *'Teacher fined for indecent acts'*, highlights the moral character of those who are responsible for supervising our children's secular education:

A House of Delegates primary school teacher who committed indecent acts with eight of his pupils aged between 10 and 12 was fined R3 000 (or nine months) by the Durban Regional Court. The magistrate also sentenced him to two years suspended for five years. The married father of three teenage daughters said he "placed his hands over the boy's pants in an affectionate manner and no force was used". The court heard that he had been a teacher for 28 years and during the period in which the offences occurred he had a "prostrate gland problem" and suffered from hypertension. [11]

The revolting episodes of immorality which have become integrated in college and university life will undoubtedly send shock waves down the spines of Muslims who still have some idea of accountability in the Hereafter. If having become aware of the filthy perpetrations rife on university campuses, a Muslim still finds accommodation in his heart for these immoral dens of vice adorned with external facades of learning, (we are not referring to the exceptions), then he must question his piety. Every rule of the Islâmic Moral Code is violated in these institutions. At schools and universities they are tutored to exhibit themselves to display their *"aurah"*, to fling their arms and expose their legs shamelessly. Recently in a Standerton school, with a predominant Muslim enrolment, mature Muslim girls paraded in a *"zinâ"* display of an exhibition known as "drum-majorettes". Does their Îmân command them to reveal their chastity in this gruesome and immoral display of body revelation?

Among some of the other harâm and immoral events in which young Muslim boys and girls indulge with relish are events such as matric balls, school concerts, end-of-year dances, fetes, etc. Instead of guiding their children and adopting a firm stand against the calamitous participation, parents and guardians shirk their responsibilities and abandon their sacred Islâmic obligations. Some even aid them along the path of moral ruin, by providing financial assistance. "Matric Balls" and other similar exhibitions of carnality in which promiscuous contact with the opposite sex reaches its zenith, are among the surest approaches to *"zinâ"*. How is it possible for Muslim parents to have become so greatly desensitized that they fail to discern the gross evil which is evident in dancing? When even the lustful gaze is severely prohibited by Islâm what can be said of the acts of illegal physical and erotic contact which prevails at the immoral dances? When mingling of the opposite sexes ordinarily is forbidden in Islâm, what then is Islâm's view on the promiscuous physical contact of young boys and girls in such institutions? How can Muslim parents condone such wholesale massacre of Islâmic morality? While parents are vastly to be blamed for this scandalous state of immoral affairs, the youngsters themselves are not absolved of the crime and blame. They have attained maturity and Allâh has endowed them with sufficient intelligence to realize the villainy of their carnal promptings.

Even concerned western leaders and sociologists have come to realize the evil of the dance halls and where this eventually leads society. The practice of dancing is an evil mixture of vulgarity and a crude exhibition of immorality. Even some of the world's greatest authorities have condemned this evil practice. Dr L.L Hollingworth has this to say: *"Dance halls are the modern nurseries of the divorce courts, training shops of prostitutions, the graduating school of infamy and vice".*[12]

Remember the wise words of Dr Sommers who said: *"I attack the modern dance as a reversion towards savagery. As a medical man, I flatly charge that modern social dancing is fundamentally sinful and evil."*[13]

Islâmic law does not permit *"dancing"* and *"healthy social mixing"*. This is a violation of our spiritual law.

Islâm emphasizes self denial, but colleges and universities with their emphasis on liberalism propagate the doctrines of self expression. Girls studying at such institutions are tutored to assert false-independence, to adorn, exhibit and express themselves, to vie and compete in affairs which the Sharî'at has imposed on men. It teaches them to parade their charms and beauty whereas Islâm commands them to conceal their *"aurah"*. Schools and universities teach them that modesty and shame are psychological defects and barriers to progress but Allâh Ta'âlâ tells us that these are virtues of a very high order. The good woman is obedient and harmonious in her husband's presence and in his absence guards his reputation and her own virtue.

> *"Therefore the righteous women are devoutly obedient, and guard in (the husband's) absence what Allah would have them guard."*[14]

The sexual harassment and acts of fornication which females must witness and in which they even participate at these institutions of carnal licentiousness, every Muslim of true faith must concede, are the death knell of the holy and lofty culture of transcendental values for which Islâm stands. These are some of the shocking revelations that the *"Sunday Times"* has exposed under the caption:

Wits hotbed of sex and porn.

Pornography and sex parties are rife on the Wits University campus, according to a shock official report released this week. According to the

Wits Committee of Inquiry into Sexism and Sexual Harassment, students at the Men's Residence:

*   Were asked to donate R5 to procure a prostitute as a birthday present for a house-committee member;

*   Attended strip shows regularly. At one, off campus, the stripper engaged in sexual intercourse with two students in full view of all present;

*   Hired prostitutes to provide live sex for students at the rugby, cricket, hockey, yacht and skydiving clubs.

Many incidents of sexual and physical violence against women students were not reported and disciplinary action was not initiated because of fear of repercussions. Most of the activities were connected to Orientation Week where first year students were initiated into a pornographic culture. A student described how first year students were told the aim for the week was to sleep with as many women as possible. Andre Fouche, 17, a science student said: "I tell you what, they'll never have a fire drill here. They don't know what'll come out of the rooms." [15]

Besides rape and other violent acts, verbal abuse and victimisation, including the vandalising of property of people who opposed such behaviour, and pressure on male students to be involved in the activities demonstrates that these vices are being forcefully dumped down the throats of all and sundry, the Muslims included. Muslim girls even participate in these abominations while their parents believe their daughters are paragons of virtue. Muslims cannot afford to be so naive as to expect that Islâm can subsist in the hearts of their daughters so cruelly exposed to the moral filth and insane stupor of immorality to which they are subjected in these evil educational institutions under the guise of Sex Education. Yet, in spite of hearing and reading of the vile and villainous misdeeds perpetrated at these establishments, Muslims in wanton and total disregard for the commands of Allâh choose to expel their daughters from the sanctuary of the home to intermingle with the criminals of immorality in these libertine institutions.

The following report is also a grim reminder of forced sexual encounters that are prevalent. It appeared under the heading: *Call to curb campus rapes and harassment.* The SA Students Congress (Sasco) today called for extensive campaigns on all university campuses against sexual harassment and rape, and for the expulsion of those students involved in a recent sexual incident at the University of Natal. Referring to the University of Natal's Student Court in which five students were last week found guilty of "physical indecency", it said while the evidence presented amounted to rape, the students were expelled from the residence but not from the university. Women students are reported to be outraged at what they regarded as the lenient sentences imposed on the students.

Results of an investigation into similar events at the University of Cape Town were released a month ago. The report states that nearly a third of female students interviewed said they had been touched in an uninvited and sexual way but none had complained to the authorities because of intimidation.[16]

Yet another article explicitly describes the agency of zinâ under the caption *'Used Condoms Drive Cleaners Bonkers'*

Macho students have been throwing used condoms out of their bedroom windows at residences of the University of Natal in Durban. And it has so annoyed ground staff that a circular has been posted on notice boards asking the "lusty men" to use appropriate refuse bins. Staff of the university's grounds department had to be specially issued with rubber gloves and spades to dispose of the ... condoms.

"It is an extremely positive sign that students are using condoms," said the SRC president. "We are slightly perturbed at their sloppy behaviour, leaving workers with their hands full. We do think it is a serious issue and litter – in any form – is reprehensible." [17]

Note that the university authorities fully sanction these blatant acts of zinâ. Their only concern is the "clean" disposal of the filthy instruments of zinâ!

Among the innumerable examples of the fruits of our labour of Islâmic destruction are the cases of Muslim girls made pregnant by fornicating –

even fornication with *"kufâr"* boys. All shame and modesty has departed from school- going girls. Their shield of *"h.ayâ"* – their divinely given protection – has been ripped off. Similarly, among the many examples of the evil fruits of parental eagerness to 'educate' their daughters along secular lines are the cases of drug taking and alcoholism which have attained alarming proportions. These vices prevail widely among Muslim school-going children.[18]

Muslim parents feel highly satisfied that their daughters are pursuing university education. But what of their modesty and chastity. Is the acquisition of a secular education at the cost of abandoning *"dîn"* and *"Îmân"* worthwhile to you? Are you satisfied with moral and spiritual ruin which you as a parent have engineered by sending them to such establishments? Are you satisfied with your daughters association with undesirable boys and can you tolerate your daughters arm in arm with them? Pursuit of secular education bedevilled by the evil influences is not only unnecessary and futile for Muslim girls, but evil and destructive. When taking into consideration the corruption, immorality, disruption and destruction of Islâmic moral life, which are the consequences of liberalism vigorously propagated in the secular institutions, then without any doubt, it will not be advisable for Muslims to send their daughters in the pursuit of such moral destruction. We must carefully guard not only our own conduct, but also the conduct of our families, and of all who are near and dear to us. The Qur'ân cautions:

> *"O People of Îmân, save yourselves and*
> *your families (wives and children) from the*
> *Fire (of Jahannum) whose fuel is men and*
> *stones..."*[19]

The problems of drugs, alcoholism and immorality rampant in secular schools and universities cannot be wished or washed away. These evils are here, not only to stay, but to increase in leaps and bounds. The latest converts to the immoral cult of western evil are Muslim children. The conversions are taking place rapidly. Soon they will be beyond all control. In the schools of the western world, school-girl pregnancies have soared to tens of thousands every year in spite of the introduction of sex education. Therefore, sex education is in actual fact obscenity and pornography of the worst kind.

6.4   SEX EDUCATION IN ISLÂM

Islâm comprises life in totality where every fragment and facet needs to be seen in the total context. Any aspect of life cannot be isolated. Islâm recognizes the power of sexual need, therefore this cannot be conceived without marital and family life and these are all to be considered in relation to other Islâmic doctrines which control and regulate the behaviour of a Muslim. Before giving education about anatomy and physiology the firm belief in the Creator should be well established. There are many Qur'ânic verses and traditions of the Prophet 靈 depicting the creation of human life, cleanliness and purity, interaction between life spouses and mention of sexual intercourse between the spouses. In the explanation of these verses and Aḥâdîth, issues did arise, questions were asked and both sexes were involved jointly or separately.

A Muslim needs to thoroughly understand all that the Qur'ân has mentioned pertaining to sex and all that the Aḥâdîth included concerning conjugal rights and how spouses should treat each other concerning those conjugal rights. The Qur'ân declares:

> "Now let man but think from what he is
> created! He is created from a gushing fluid
> that proceeds from between the backbone
> and his ribs."[20]

A man's seed is the highly refined extract of his body. It is therefore said metaphorically to proceed from his loins, i.e. from his back between the hipbones and his ribs. His backbone is the source and symbol of his strength and personality. In the spinal cord and in the brain is the directive energy of the central nervous system, and this directs all organs. It is said the semen of man issues from the loin and that of woman from the breast. Some scholars are of the opinion that the loin and breast cover the whole body, i.e. the semen of man and woman is produced in the whole body and then it separates. At this analysis the mention of 'loin' and 'breast' is probably due to this fact that in the production of semen the vital parts (heart, brain, liver) have a special role – of them the heart and the liver have a connection with the breast, and the brain with the loin via the spinal cord.

This theme of creation keeps recurring in the Qur'ân:

> *"Verily We created the human being from a product of extracted clay, then placed him as (a drop of) sperm in a place of rest, firmly fixed. Then We made the sperm into a cloth of congealed blood, then of that cloth We made a (foetus) lump, then We created out of that lump bones and clothed the bones with flesh, then We developed out of it another creature, so blessed be Allâh, the best to create"*[21]

Man was created from earth and his progeny are created from sperm which is the substance of the foods produced from the earth. This sperm is deposited in the ovum and fertilizes it and rests for a time in security in the mother's womb. The first change in the fertilized ovum is the conversion into a sort of clot of congealed blood; the zygote cells grow by segmentation, then the mass gradually assumes shape in its growth as a foetus. The growth in the foetal stage is silent. The foetus is protected in the mother's womb like a king in a castle; it is firmly fixed; and gets the protection of the mother's body. From the lump develop bones, which is garmented with flesh, and various other organs. Thereafter life is injected into it.

Cleanliness (ṭahârah) is one of the basic aspects of Islâm which has been likened by the Prophet ﷺ to half of the faith. The Qur'ân prescribes that particular attention be paid to personal cleanliness after menstruation, post child birth bleeding, wet dreams and intimate sexual contact, with ritual bathing being required in such instances.

Since physical purity and cleanliness is of paramount importance, Islâm has strictly prohibited sexual relations between the spouses during menstruation. Bleeding other than the habitual menses is a sign of disease just like the blood of the wound or vein and does not interfere with the conjugal relationship. During menstruation, a woman is exceptionally sensitive and irritable, so that she may be excited by trifling matters which at other times would arouse no obvious response. There is increased nervous tension, reflex action is more marked and there may be slight twitchings of the legs; also yawning and stiffness in the neck, and sleep is heavier than usual. There is loss of appetite and a certain amount of digestive and intestinal disturbance. It is at this time, that even in perfectly healthy women, fits of ill-temper, moods of depression, impulses of jealousy and outburst of self-confession, are chiefly liable to occur. The statistics of criminality in women show that a very large majority of crimes committed by women are committed during menstruation.

The Jews and the Majûs (Parsees) regarded eating food with the women during menses, and living in the same house as illegal and the then Christians did not even abstain from intercourse. When the Prophet ﷺ was questioned regarding this state, the following verse was revealed wherein it is clearly mentioned that only intercourse is prohibited, but living with women, eating and drinking with them is perfectly all right. The conservative extremism of the Jews and the unrestricted liberalism of the Christians is rejected. In some communities a woman under their code must refrain, during menstruation, from all household duties specially from the preparation of food, and to go near her is an offence. She must, like the leper of ancient times, wear a special garment, or call aloud to all who approach her that she is unclean.

> *"And they ask thee concerning menstruation. Say, 'It is a pollution so keep away from women during menstruation, and do not approach them until they are clean, then when they have thoroughly purified themselves, then go in unto them from where Allâh Ta'âlâ has ordered you. Verily Allâh loves those who repent and loves those who ward off pollution. "*[22]

As a matter of fact, considerations of hygienic cleanliness and of sanitary precaution prohibit the performances of coitus during this period. Severe menorrhagia, perimetritic irritation and inflammations have been observed to follow such indiscretion. Modern technology has also discovered that the menstrual flow contains certain toxic enzymes that could be potentially hazardous if allowed access into the male, or if a clear passage of flow from the body of the female is prevented. This could only result in copulation during menses which is the breeding ground for fatal venereal diseases, and even at times is instrumental in spreading its poisonous tentacles to the unharmed foetus.

Sex is not a thing to be ashamed of, or to be treated lightly, or to be indulged in to excess. It is compared to a husbandman's tilth; it is a serious affair to him; he sows the seed in order to reap the harvest. But he chooses his own time and mode of cultivation. He does not sow out of season nor cultivate in a manner which will injure or exhaust the soil. He is wise and considerate and does not run riot. Thus with human beings, every kind of mutual consideration is required, but above all, we must remember that even in these matters we should not forget the spiritual aspect and our moral responsibility to Allâh.

The Jews prohibited sexual intercourse with the back of the woman towards the man (topsy turvy) and were under the false impression that by doing so the child would be born squint-eyed with proptosis. When the Prophet ﷺ was questioned regarding this, the following verse was revealed signifying that the women are like tillage in which the sperm drop is the seed and the children are just like the products. Consequently one of the main purpose of intercourse is to continue and maintain the generation by the production of children, so you are at liberty in this action whether you go unto them abreast or aback or aside or alying or sitting, but it is important to deposit the seed in the particular place from where production is expected i.e. the vagina. All other forms of unnatural sexuality such as sodomy etc., are strictly prohibited.

Once Hadrat 'Umar ﷺ had sexual relation with his wife through rear entry (not the anal passage). Later he was enveloped by the thought that he had perhaps committed an undesirable act. At once he hurried off to the presence of Prophet Muhammad ﷺ calling out: "I have been destroyed, I have been destroyed...". He was questioned regarding his frantic outbursts, to which he narrated his overwhelming fear of having committed a detestable act. The Prophet remained silent. After some time, the following verses were revealed:

> *"Your wives are as a tilth for you, so*
> *approach your tilth from where you*
> *wish..."*[23]

The most delicate matters are here referred to in the most discreet and yet helpful terms. In sex, morality, manner, time and place are all important and the highest standard are set by social laws, by our own refined instinct of mutual consideration, and above all, by the light shed from the wisdom which we receive from our Creator, Who loves purity and cleanliness in all things.

The human body is naturally inclined towards three postures; i.e. standing, squatting or sitting and laying down. Islâm has granted general permission as far as the sexual positions are concerned provided on condition that no unnatural anal sex is instituted. Medically speaking, sex in the standing posture is undesirable, since it causes harm to the nerves and veins and could result in perpetual tremor. Thus two postures now remain. There are vivid indications in the Qur'ân and Hadîth regarding this. The Qur'ân mentions:

> *"It is He Who created you from a single*
> *soul, and He created therefrom his spouse,*
> *that he might take comfort in her. Then*
> *when he "covered" her, she bore a light*
> *burden and moved with it..."*[24]

This posture is adopted when a woman lies with her face upwards, while the man's body lies over her in such a manner that she is *"covered"* by him. While explaining the method of taking a bath, the following posture of sexual union is indirectly referred to in the traditions, *"When any of you sits between the four portions of a woman and then exerts himself upon her...then bath becomes compulsory"*,[25] which seems to indicate the position in which a woman lifts her knees while the man enters her in a sitting/squatting posture, in which case her thighs and calfs form the "four portions".

337

The Qur'ân also states that sexual relationships within marriage have the aims of procreation, physical enjoyment and achieving peace of mind; husband and wife are described as being 'garments' for each other, each to provide warmth and comfort for their partner. A garment also is both for show and concealment. The question of sex is always delicate to handle:here we are told that even in such matters a clear, open, and honest course is better than fraud or self-deception. The sex instinct is classified with eating and drinking, a carnal desire to be restrained, but not to be ashamed of.

> *"... They are your garments and you are their garments... associate with them, and seek what Allâh has ordained for you..."*[26]

Prophet Muhammad ﷺ also advised his companions that their engaging in sex with their wives, was a rewarded act of charity. In their astonishment the companions exclaimed that how can it be counted as charity since it was done purely out of desire. The Prophet ﷺ then informed them that had it been done with a forbidden woman, it would have been counted as a sin, but since it was done legally, it was regarded as charity.

When intercourse is enjoyed with the proper intentions then not only is it an act of physical pleasure, but also serves as an instrument of attaining great spiritual blessings. During intercourse these intentions could also be made; protection against adultery, safeguarding the gaze from strange woman and also the attainment of pious children who would serve Islâm.

With most creatures on this earth, including man, sex is the means by which the species reproduces itself and so continues to exist. To man, because of his intelligence, sex means more to him than merely reproduction. Sex is very much the basis of all those relationships which are essential for human happiness, friendship and love between the sexes, unselfish affection for the loved one, marriage, family life, love for children, and so on. A man or woman must understand the importance of sex and the pleasure it brings if life is to be spiritually and physically satisfying.

6.4.1 PUBERTY

An attempt is now made to provide a skeleton or framework for a programme of sexual education within Islâmic context commencing with puberty. This is the tumultuous stage in the life of young boys and girls in which sexual appetite is strongest, at times uncontrollable. Although young people have at this stage attained a capacity to think of their future, this is usually subservient to strong passions. If care is not taken of young people in this delicate period of their lives, there is a great apprehension of their going astray. For this reason the Prophet ﷺ has advised parents with this responsibility: " *One who is given by Allâh Ta'âlâ a child, he should give it a beautiful name, should give him education and training and when he or she attains the age of puberty, he should see to it that he or she is married. If the father does not arrange their marriage after puberty and the boy or girl is involved in sin, the responsibility of that sin will be with the father.* " [27]

Puberty is the term used to describe that stage of life when the body gradually changes from its childish state to that of a man or a woman able to have children. When the slow changes of puberty are complete, the young person is physically able to undertake a full sexual life. These teenage years are referred to as adolescence.

The sexual changes of puberty can occur during a wide age range. With boys, puberty usually occurs between the ages of 11 and 17, and with girls between the ages of 9 and 15, although with both sexes it can occur earlier or later. The changes that occur at puberty are quite dramatic but it must be remembered that they happen to everybody so there is no need to be alarmed or ashamed as often happens with those young people who have no knowledge of sex.

6.4.1.1 BOYS AT PUBERTY

The physical changes with boys are:

Hair grows around the genital, or sex organs (this is called pubic hair) and under the arm pits. The genital organs increase in size. The penis grows longer and thicker; the scrotum (the bag holding the testicles) drops down and hangs beneath the penis with the shape of the two testicles – the right usually above the left – quite clearly visible.

The voice "breaks". The high-pitched child's voice disappears and the boy speaks in the deep tones of a man.

The body frame develops. The boy's shoulders grow wider; his height usually increases rapidly; he puts on weight; his muscles become more noticeable; hair grows on the upper lip and face so that he now begins clipping his moustache and allowing his beard to grow. (An important practice of the Prophet 鐐); hair becomes longer and thicker on arms and legs and usually grows on the chest. Boys should remember, however, that being hairy does not mean that a boy is more manly or masculine than a boy whose body hair does not grow very much. And having hair on her face and on other parts of her body does not make a girl less feminine than girls with smooth faces. The development of body hair is very often a matter of ancestry: some families, as well as some races, are more hairy than others.

At puberty seminal fluid (a fairly "thick" liquid) may be discharged from time to time via the penis, generally during the night. This is called nocturnal emission.

6.4.1.2 GIRLS AT PUBERTY

With girls the physical changes are:

The breasts develop in size; the nipples, at first, grow larger and the breasts begin to fill out. With maturing girls, great variations in breast size occur. The size of the breast has no bearing upon a girl's ability to have a full sex life or to feed a baby.

As is the case of boys, hair grows in the genital regions and under the armpits. Puberty is a period of rapid physical change. The girl grows taller and heavier; she becomes broader around the hips; generally she becomes more "rounded" – thus, her arms and legs are now beautifully shaped.

The changes described occur over a period of time, but there is one change at puberty that occurs quite suddenly. This change is menstruation, the beginning of "monthly periods". Menstruation is such an important change – its arrival means that a girl has entered the child-bearing age.

Let us now analyse the shape (anatomy) of each sex and the special characteristics and function that it is designed to perform.

6.4.2.1 MALE SEXUAL CHARACTERISTICS

The chief sexual organ of the male is the penis, situated in the fork between the thighs. Usually it hangs loosely and is approximately 3 to 4 inches in length (sometimes even larger or smaller). When a male becomes sexually excited the penis becomes erect, grows rigid, and increases in length and thickness. The end is covered by the foreskin. The foreskin is removed soon after birth so that the end of the penis (the glans) is uncovered; this is called circumcision, which was the noble practice of all the Prophets (A.S.). Every Muslim male offspring has also been instructed to do so. Besides preventing cancer and various dreadful diseases, circumcision is a great sunnat of Prophet Muḥammad ﷺ who was an apex of purity and cleanliness.

Hanging beneath the penis is the scrotum, a small bag containing the testicles. The testicles are very important for they produce the male sperm which fertilize the female ovum (or egg) and are responsible for such male characteristics as a deep voice and a beard.

Sperms are so small that several millions of them are present in each millilitre of the seminal fluid in which they swim. They are produced continuously in the testicles, and pass up a tube into the body, where they mix into the fluid produced by the prostrate gland which lies at the base of the bladder. This seminal fluid is then stored in a pair of little sacs near by called seminal vesicles, until it is ejaculated through the erect genital.

It should be noted that the sexual organs described here are normal or average, although with most people there are some variations from this "average". Thus, as only one example: The left testicle usually hangs over the right, but it is fairly common to find the right one lower.

When a boy reaches puberty he will find that his body will begin to react differently. Nocturnal emissions (wet dreams) are a means used by the body to get rid of the seminal fluid that has built up. Wet dreams may occur when a boy is having a dream about sex, but this is not always the case. Unexpected erections and wet dreams are natural during the teenage years. It is therefore vitally important to maintain a healthy Islâmic environment especially during this period of adolescence.

6.4.2.2 FEMALE SEX CHARACTERISTICS

The chief female organs of sex are the vagina, the ovaries, the womb (uterus) and the breasts. Apart from the breasts, the only obvious female sex organ is the vulva, the name given to the female external genital organs which lie between the thighs. The vulva consist of the labia, or lips, enclosing the openings to the vagina, the urethra (which leads to the bladder) and the clitoris. The vagina, usually about 4 inches long, is the passage leading to the uterus. During intercourse the penis penetrates the vagina which can easily stretch. The penis cannot enter the uterus. At the top of the vulva (that is, at the front of the labia) is the clitoris, under a very small fold of skin. During intercourse the clitoris, the labia and the walls are stimulated by the regular movements of the male genital.[28] In virgins (girls who have not had sexual intercourse) the entrance to the vagina is usually partly closed by a piece of thin skin (a membrane) called the hymen. When the virgin first has intercourse the hymen is broken or stretched and a few drops of blood may occur (not in all cases), since there are many other reasons for a girl losing her virginity. Jumping excessively, falling, cycling, horse riding, prolonged illness, a heavy menstrual flow or cycle, etc. Therefore it is of vital importance that the husband should not harbour unnecessary suspicions against his wife if for some reason it "seemed" that his newly wed wife was not a virgin. Such suspicion is a grievous crime in Islâm since it could lead to the oppression and harassment of a chaste Muslim woman on unfounded and baseless doubts. The Qur'ân cautions us thus:

> *"O those who believe, avoid suspicion as*
> *much (as possible): for suspicion in some*
> *cases is a sin..."*[29]

A girl's awareness of her physical changes is accompanied by a new awareness of sex by different feelings towards sexual matters. The woman's reproductive organs for the birth of a child are within the body. They are the ovaries, the tubes, and the uterus.

6.4.3 MENSTRUATION

A very important part of a girl's feminity is menstruation or, to use a common term, monthly periods. At the end of puberty the attaining of sexual maturity by the girl is revealed by a "flow" (sometimes an oozing, sometimes a small gushing) of blood from the uterus through the vagina. Blood may flow for some days (to absorb the menstrual flow a woman wears a sanitary pad) and the flow will be repeated at intervals of approximately 28 days, during the entire period of a woman's child-bearing life, that is until she is about 45 to 50 and undergoes change of life (the menopause).

Simply, the beginning of menstruation means that a girl is capable of bearing children. Each month an ovum, or egg, is produced by one or other ovary (ovulation) and moves along the fallopian tube to the uterus. If the ovum is not fertillized by the male sperm, it is washed away by the menstrual flow which occurs about a fortnight after ovulation. Thus, a girl or woman will menstruate about once a month unless she is pregnant or has recently had a baby. If the mentrual flow does not occur, it generally means that conception has taken place, that is, the woman is pregnant.

However, in the first few years after puberty there are often long stages without "periods", extending from a few months to a year. The length of the menstrual period itself varies from around three to ten days; the third day is usually the time when most blood is released.

During menstruation the following changes take place in the female organism:

The power of resistance in the body decreases with the result that heat is lost unduly. resulting in a fall of temperature.

Pulse weakens, blood pressure falls below normal and compuscles decrease.

Endocrines, tonsils and lymphatic glands undergo changes.

The process of protein metabolism suffers a setback. The release of phosphates and chlorides slows down and the process of gaseous metabolism deteriorates. Digestion becomes difficult, and proteins and fats are not easily assimilated by the body. Respiration slows down and the vocal organs suffer changes. Muscles become lethargic and feels cold. The ability to concentrate weakens.

Menstruation normally commences a year or so after the beginning of puberty between the ages of 10 and 16, although some girl's menstruate earlier and some later. Usually, it occurs every 28 days but there are many exceptions: with some it may come as often as every 21 days; with others it may be as long as 35 days between "periods" whilst with many there will be continually varying times between "periods". During menstruation many girls become depressed or agitated a week before or during their periods. Menstrual periods may be uncomfortable or painful for some girls whilst with others no discomfort at all is felt. During this period Muslim women are exempted from *"salât"* (prayers) and are instructed to postpone their fasting until such time that they are once more clean. They cannot touch or recite the Holy Qur'ân neither is *tawâf* of the *K'aba* permitted.

Thus, the woman is provided with the means of producing an ovum which, if fertilized by the male, will grow in the womb (uterus) for nine months until it is ready to be born. Everyone of us was born because his father's sperm fertilized his mother's egg, and so each of us has inherited physical characteristics from his father and his mother. The process by which each of us come into this world can be summed up in these words:intercourse, conception, pregnancy, birth. Each one will now be individually analyzed.

6.4.4 COPULATION

Sexual relations, in physical terms, is the placement of the man's penis in the woman's vagina. When a husband and wife become sexually attracted to each other they feel that sexual intercourse is the crowning point of their relationship for this act gives a very special pleasure.

Although after puberty girls certainly do get sexually aroused, their physical reactions are not so obvious as the boy's. The most noticeable are a tingling in the breasts and secretion of a fluid in the vagina. Whereas it is necessary for the male to be stimulated before he can have an erection and so perform the sex act, the female can have sexual intercourse without being sexually stimulated though it is more enjoyable for her and better for both partners.

Where sexual attraction occurs there is generally a conscious effort to arouse and stimulate the partner by kissing, caressing and general love-play which is both pleasureable and gratifying in itself and a preparation for intercourse as a final act. This is referred to as foreplay. Thus it is extremely selfish for a person not to sexually arouse his wife via foreplay and fufill his carnal instincts like an animal whilst his spouse experiences (no sensation) whatsoever. It is extremely demoralizing for the woman and could later result in drifts in the married couples future life. Therefore no effort should be spared in exploring those regions of a wife's anatomy that will arouse her desires and increase her pleasures. These sensitive areas are commonly known as the "erogenous zones". Although varying in different people they are generally concentrated in the upper abdomen and the area below the navel, behind the knees, the lips etc. If stroked tenderly, these areas flare with passion.

Muslim husbands are even encouraged by none less than the Prophet ﷺ to engage in foreplay with the wife before actual relations. He was once informed that one of his companions, Ḥaḍrat Jâbir ؓ, had married a widowed woman. He exclaimed: *"Why did you not contract your nikâh to a virgin with whom you could play and she in turn could respond in the same manner."* [30]

It is also advisable that no one should fall upon his wife like a beast does.

It is more appropriate that a signal is sent before the actual act.

Nevertheless, one should be extremely vigilant, that during this foreplay milk does not enter the throat since it is extremely destestable for the husband to drink his wife's milk.However, it does not annul the bond of marriage between the spouses.

The whole process of love-making, requires, for its deep satisfaction, sensitivity and affection. There should be an appreciation of the partner's needs as in no other area of life is it gratifying to give as to receive. Tenderness and gentleness, especially during the first sexual encounter is extremely important. Many are under the false illusion that tenderness is against masculinity and the irreparable damage done on the first night creates a gruesome impact on the marriage and sometimes even carry a lifelong stigma.

It is also recommended to mentally and physically prepare oneself before the actual act itself. Any distasteful or distracting factor should be avoided since this could act as a phsychological barrier and turn the opposite partner *"off"* with detrimental repercussions for the married couple. Uncivilized behaviour, dirt, filth and bad odours especially from the mouth or body is very unpleasant. Smokers should be cautioned that if the mouth is not thoroughly cleansed, then besides killing the passion, it could also cause abhorrence and kindle the flames of hatred in his partner. The Holy Prophet 鸞 was extremely particular to apply *halâl* scent ('itr) and to use the miswâk (cleansing of the teeth and mouth) before sexual relations.

Married couples should fix a certain portion of the night or day and husbands should preferably inform their spouses of their intentions in advance so that both could be physically and mentally prepared without being 'caught' unaware. It was the noble practice of the Prophet 鸞 that whenever he returned from an expedition or lengthy journey, he and his Companions would not enter their homes at night, but would rather do so in the morning, so that their womenfolk could be adequately prepared to receive their returning husbands. Those dishevelled and unkempt women could comb their hair, shave and appear presentable. The Prophet 鸞 said: *"If you enter your town at night after coming from a journey, do not enter upon your family till the woman whose husband was absent (for a long period) shaves her pubic hair and the woman with unkempt hair combs her hair."* [31] Therefore, it is of vital importance that a husband announces his anticipated arrival telephonically or by whatever message possible, so that his spouse could be sufficiently prepared.

Besides the physical preparedness, both the participants should be relaxed and free from any mental blemishes in the form of tension, depression, anger, illness and hunger or thirst, which could inevitably destroy the pleasure.

Medically, it is also preferable to cohabit during the latter portion of the night, since the stomach is normally full during the earlier part, and sexual relations during this period could result in health hazards such as exhausting the vital organs of the body nerves, and other vessels. Imâm Ghazâlî also advises that early intercourse could result in a longer period of the night being spent in a state of impurity before the customary ritual cleansing *(ghusal)*.

Complete nudity should be shunned during intercourse. The Holy Prophet 🕮 greatly abhorred such a shameless action to such an extent that he likened this act to the practice of donkeys publicly cohabiting. *"When one of you goes to his wife, he should cover his nakedness even at that time. He should not make himself naked like donkeys".* [32] There's a possibility that children born out of such a marriage could become morally corrupt. Besides nudity it is also disrepectful to face towards the *"qiblah"* (direction towards Mecca) while engaged in sex.

Excessive talking during intercourse is also despicable and not recommended. Similarly gazing at the partners genitals is undesirable. Faqîh Abul-Laith Samarqandî is of the opinion that the former (excessive talking) could result in dumb offspring and the author of Shuratul Islâm mentions that the latter (habitually gazing) could result in blind offspring. The Holy Prophet 🕮 never gazed at the private parts of his wife 'Âishah, neither did she. *Hadrat 'Âishah (R.A.) reported that she never saw the Holy Prophet 🕮 naked (and neither did he).* [33] Technically, although it is permissible, such an act shatters the fragile fibres of morality.

Besides sexual gratification, legal sexual relations are spiritually linked to divine commandments. It is for this reason that before one commences one should beseech the assistance of the Supreme Creator. Failure to do so would result in <u>Sh</u>aiṭân participating with him in his act and deriving pleasure from his wife. On commencing, this supplication (du'â) should be read: *"In the name of Allâh; O Allâh! protect us from <u>Sh</u>aiṭân and prevent <u>Sh</u>aiṭân from that which you have granted us."*[34]

Even ejaculation, which is looked upon with contempt and regarded as a debased act, if deposited in the proper womb and channel is greatly meritorious and regarded as an obedient act of worship. Therefore at the time of ejaculation, this du'â should be made (silently, not verbally):

"O Allâh! Do not grant <u>Sh</u>aiṭân any share of that which you have granted me."

Rebellious and disobedient children, which are quite rampant in our society, is one of the products of not reciting such a du'â. <u>Sh</u>âh A.H. Dehlawî strongly feels that if a prayer like this is not made at the time of sexual relations, but only sexual appetite is fulfilled, as in the case of animals, then the resultant child from such a union would not be protected from the clutches of <u>Sh</u>aiṭân. This is one vital contributing factors towards present day moral stagnation.

Immediately after ejaculation, a man should not withdraw until the woman also achieves satisfaction and climax. Disengaging before she reaches satisfaction is rather selfish and besides breeding animosity, it will create the impression that she was merely being 'used', without any consideration on her behalf. Ḥadrat 'Alî ☀ also advised that one should await the completion (climaxing) of the wife before disengaging, otherwise she would become your enemy.

Just as oral and physical hygiene is important prior to intercourse, it is just as necessary after the act, not only to ensure purity but also as a barrier against many ailments and diseases. After the act both the participants should form the habit of urinating, because semen that is not ejaculated and remains in the urinary canal, leads to certain diseases. By passing water, the track is cleared of all such remaining fluids. The sexual organs should also be cleanly washed, not with cold water though, since this could lead to fever, but with warm water. Yes, after some time when the body heat normalizes, then only cold water could be used. At this point it should be remembered that if a woman washes her private parts with cold water "before" sexual intimacy, she will be aroused and would climax faster than normal. Contrary to this, a man's sexual appetite would dwindle and decrease if he does so. The Holy Prophet 鑿 also tutored his Companions in washing their genitals after this act. He said "... *Perform ablution after washing your private parts....* " [35]

Failure to do so could result in a disease which may be difficult to cure. Also it must be remembered that immediately after relations no liquid should be consumed, otherwise it could lead to the sickness of short breath. After sexual relations both the spouses should wipe themselves with separate cloths (or any sanitary agents). Cleansing with the same cloth could result in marital discord and conflict. If the passions are rekindled and the couple intend performing the sexual act once more, then it is best advisable that they take a bath before recommencing. If this is not possible then *wuḍû* should be performed. Imâm Ghazâlî is of the opinion that the minimum requirement before re-engaging is to urinate and cleanly wash their genitals.

Since Islâm advocates moderation, excessive sexual indulgence could result in sexual and health disorders. Artificial sexual desires, usually created at the sight or thought of attractive women in provocative dressing, sexually stimulating conversations, pornographic literature etc; should be resisted. Yes, when there exists a genuine passionate desire, then it should not be ignored. One of the most damaging effects of uncontrolled excessive sex and masturbation is premature ejaculation, which could cause chaos and frustrations in an otherwise stable and harmonious marriage. This self inflicted disease which is presently very common has shattered many marriages by leading them to the divorce courts. Premature ejaculation is normally caused by the semen thinning out and resulting in the flow of a substance called *"mazî"* (a fluid preceeding the flow of semen), and also by the weakness of the nerves in the male genital. Semen could be ejaculated within half a minute or even less after penetration (if it does occur at all), or even before, whereas the average time for ejaculation is much, much more. Proper food and vitamins should be consumed to rectify the thinness of semen, and excessive indulgence should be curbed to avoid the weakening of the nerves. Failure to do so could ultimately result in sexual impotency with many victims speeding off to the virility clinics, which so proudly advertise their services in almost every major newspaper.

Since women are' said to have a higher sexual drive than men, those suffering from sexual impotency could be ridiculed and despised, if precaution is not taken. There are even cases of wives of such people flirting and courting other men. (May Allâh protect us). Proper food and diets which create healthy and well nourished bodies, should be consumed. Even Prophet Muhammad 🌸 mentioned specific foods which contribute towards enhancing the sexual strength such as eggs etc. Once he complained to Jibrail 🌸 regarding his sexual strength and was advised to consume *"harîsa"*, (a thick soup made from pieces of meat, crushed wheat, certain spices, butter etc) since it has the potency equal to forty men.

Another very disturbing practice, which has reached the Muslim world via pornograhic literature from the West, is questions relating to the vile act of oral sex. Many young couples have displayed keen interest to learn the Islâmic ruling on such a despicable act.

Initially it must be accepted that Islâm advocates the highest code of moral conduct and this vile act is in direct contrast to such ethical teachings. Then it must be realized that the mouth is a vital organ in the harmonious function of the human body. It is the pathway for the recitation of the Glorious Qurân and *dhikr* (remembrance of Allâh). For this very reason, cleansing of the mouth with miswâk has been greatly emphasized. How then, can this important vehicle be defiled and abused for the horrible act of oral sex?

Also, ejaculating by rubbing and stroking the male genital against the partners thighs and other sensitive areas have been equated with masturbation in some Islâmic Juridical literature, and hence has been classified as not permissible. The reason behind this is that semen ought to be channelled and deposited into the womb and by spilling its contents anywhere else, a person would be guilty of wastage. Mufti Kifâyatullâh is of the opinion that the above mentioned ejaculation *("tafkhîz")* is *harâm* (forbidden) except in a case of extreme necessity. Hadrat Muftî Shafî' (the former grand muftî of the Indo-Pak sub-continent) comments, that if *"tafkhîz"* is commissioned by dire necessity such as the spouse being in the state of post-natal bleeding or mentruation etc, and it is unlikely for him to subdue his passion, then it would be permissible without any detestability *("makrûh")*. If this condition of necessity does not arise then it would be detestable for him to employ such an act.

6.4.5 DIVULGING THE SECRETS OF INTIMACY

Morality is unashamedly butchered when members of both the sexes revel in exposing the intimate details of their private sexual encounters to companions and associates. This shameless trend destroys the very fibre of *hayâ* (modesty) and strikes at the root of Îmân. Muslims should not only themselves desist from such a contagious disease, but should also condem and prohibit others from this vile exposure.

Prophet Muhammad ﷺ strictly forbade husbands from divulging the secrets of their sex lives with their wives to other people nor to describe their physical features to anyone. He also instructed his Companions not to divulge what goes on, in private, between husband and wife. He equated this to a devil making love to a she-devil. He also instructed women not to describe their female friends to their husbands as though they can actually visualize the woman described. The Prophet ﷺ said: *"A woman should not look at or touch another woman to describe her to her husband in such a way as if he was actually looking at her."*[36] This is to prevent masturbation in fantasy and objects of disgust.

By resorting to such derogatory narrations, outsiders with ulterior motives are afforded an opportunity of participating in one's private sexual life. At the time of such an exposure they may express relish, and as soon as they have digested all this explicit material, then they either secretly fantasize being in sexual contact with the narrator's partner, or they express abhorrence to others, and look upon the narrator in a disgraceful manner. It is for precisely this fact that the Holy Prophet ﷺ severely cautioned his followers in these words: *"Amongst the "worst" of people in Allâh's sight on the Day of Resurrection is the husband who indulges in intimacy with his wife, then reveals her secrets to others."*[37] (And likewise cursed is that wife who reveals her husband's intimate secrets. The Prophet ﷺ

also warned that a woman should not look at or touch another woman and thereafter graphically describe her to her husband in such a way as if he was actually looking at her).

Also besides indecent exposure, the very act of intercourse should be concealed and should be a completely private affair. It is definitely against the moral code of modesty for an intruder to be an eye-witness to such an intimate relationship, which could be mentally disturbing to the married couple. Such importance has been attached to this type of privacy that it is greatly disliked *(makrûh)* for even a baby or an animal to be present during this particular moment. It is also detestable to engage in sexual relations in the presence of a sleeping person, an unconscious person, a child or even an insane person. But modern civilization has progressively deteriorated to such an extent that not only their steamy sex sessions are broadcast live to all humanity but also microscopic devices have been inserted into their genitals to measure the gravity of their pounding orgasms, as an extra bonus to this live coverage.

6.4.6 CONCEPTION

It is in the best interest of the survival and healthy growth of society that indiscriminate indulgence in sexual liaison should be absolutely prohibited. The legal way (through marriage), should be the only channel to satisfy the sexual desire. To permit individuals to indulge in illicit relationships is tantamount to committing a crime against society, since illegitimate impregnation and the resultant conception takes place at a time when both the guilty partners are seized by a fit of purely animal passion. Thus an illegitimate child can inherit only the animal qualities of its parents. Therefore, ejaculation must be regulated and chanelled towards its legal domain.

Conception refers to a fertilized egg that survives through implantation on the uterine wall. The Qur'ân mentions:

> "We have created everyone of you out of
> dust, then out of a drop of semen (nutfah),
> then from something that clings ('alaqah),
> then from a chewed like lump (mudghah)

> *complete in itself (mukhallaqah) and yet*
> *incomplete (ghair mukhallaqah) in order*
> *that We may manifest Our powers to*
> *you.*"[38]

This implies that first your father Âdam ﷺ was created from dust, then you were created from a sperm-drop. Or it means that food was created from dust which developed into sperm-drop crossing different stages, then you were formed from the sperm-drop passing many stages.

In a ḥadîth it is stated:

> *"When forty-two nights have passed over*
> *the sperm drops, Allâh sends an angel to*
> *it, who shapes it and makes its ears, eyes,*
> *skin, flesh and bones. Then, he says, "O*
> *Lord! It is a male or female? And your Lord*
> *decides what He wishes and the angel*
> *records it."*[39]

This is a clear indication that organ differentiation occurs only forty-two days after conception.

Qâdî Pânîpatî in his *"Tafsîr Maẓharî"* mentions the ḥadîth narrated by Ibn Maс‘ûd ؓ wherein the Prophet ﷺ said:

> *"Each of you is constituted in your*
> *mother's womb for forty days as a nutfah*
> *(that is, a drop of sperm), then it becomes*
> *congealed blood for an equal period, then*
> *a chewed lump for another equal period,*
> *thereafter an angel is sent to write four*
> *things, viz, his actions, his lifespan, his*
> *sustenance, and whether he is going to be*
> *a pious or evil person, then he breaths the*
> *soul into it..."*[40]

In this ḥadîth direct reference is made to the ensoulment of the foetus after 120 days from the time of fertililzation.

Medical research has also testified to the fact that after approximately 120 days the foetus reasonably resembles a human being. Fertilization takes place when the female's egg, or ovum, unites with the male's sperm. This may occur through sexual intercourse or artificial insemination, or more recently, through the method of test-tube or in-vetro fertilization and embryo transfer. Islâmically speaking, only the first method is permissible, provided it is legally done. Artificial insemination is only permissible if the wife is unable to become pregnant in the natural way; there must be absolute certainty that the semen which is being used is that of her husband and the semen must not be acquired by self masturbation. All other methods of fertilization are prohibited. At orgasm, the man ejaculates a thick white substance called semen, which contains sperm.

The sexual act leads to deposition of 2 ml to 10 ml of semen (with a concentration of about 80 million sperms per ml) in the vagina. Within minutes some of the sperms have entered the cervical canal of the womb and migrate up the uterus and through the fallopian tubes. If this event coincides with ovulation of the female, sperms encounter the ovum near the finbrial end of the tube and usually only one sperm penetrates the ovum to establish union of female and male sex cells thereby establishing a new life. The size of the human egg has been compared to the head of a small pin. Sperms are so minute that it has been estimated that all the individual sperms which gave rise to the world's population, if put together, will amount to only a few timbles (metal or plastic cup) full. The fertilized ovum is transported through the fallopian tube back to the uterine cavity and about five days later implants in the lining of this cavity. A further division of cells in the ovum occurs and an embryo develops which gradually takes the shape of a human being. At two months of pregnancy the foetus is approximately 4 cm long; at 4 months 16 cm; at 6 months 30 cm etc. Damage to the foetus by a virus (eg. German Measles) or certain medicines like thalidomide, is liable to affect the organs developing at that time. This is why German Measles (Rubella) is most likely to cause damage during the first three months of pregnancy. Thereafter the foetus begins to look reasonably like a human being with arms and legs, hands and feet.[41]

6.4.7   PREGNANCY

If the intention of a couple is to achieve pregnancy, it is important to be patient about doing so, to time intercourse to coincide with ovulation, and to use the most efficient position during intercourse. Medically speaking, a woman in her twenties should allow herself about six months to conceive. A woman in her thirties should allow about a year, with the probability of conception dropping as the woman gets older.

When is the best time to have intercourse to maximize the chance of pregnancy? Since a woman is fertile for only about 48 hours each month, the timing of intercourse is important. In general, 24 hours before ovulation (i.e. when a fertilized or matured egg is released from an ovary into the fallopian tube), is the best time. There are several ways to predict ovulation. Many woman have breast tenderness, and some experience a tingling sensation. Also, a woman may record her basal body temperature and examine her cervical mucus. After menstruation, the vagina in most woman is without noticeable discharge because the mucus is thick. As the time of ovulation nears, the mucus thins to the consistency of egg white which may be experienced by the woman as increased vaginal discharge. Intercourse should occur at this time.

During intercourse, the woman should be on her back and a pillow should be placed under her buttocks after receiving the sperm so a pool of semen will collect near her cervix. She should remain in this position for about 30 minutes to allow the sperm to reach the fallopian tubes.[42]

Approximately for nine months, the baby (at first referred to as the embryo and later the foetus), grows in the mother's uterus, increasing from microscopic size to about 3 kilos in weight before birth. The unborn baby is contained in a bag of fluid to protect it from injury, and is nourished by food and oxygen from its mother through the placenta or *(afterbirth)*, via the umbilical cord which is attached to the baby's navel.

The placenta is like a thick meaty plate forming part of the bag in which the baby floats, and is attached to the inside of the uterus. What happens is that the baby's blood flows along the cord to the placenta, where it goes through many tiny blood vessels so that food and oxygen can pass directly from the mother's bloodstream into that of the baby.

6.4.8 BIRTH

Although childbirth and the labour preceding it are sometimes thought of as a painful ordeal, many woman describe the birthing experience as 'fantastic', 'joyful' and an 'unsurpassed gift' from Almighty. Normally about nine months after conception birth occurs. Although Islâmically speaking, the minimum period required for birth after conception could be as little as six months. Before this period would result in an illegitimate birth.

Couples who give birth to a child have several methods from which to choose, including Lamaze, Dick Read, Bradley, Le Boyer, regional anesthesia, and Cesarean births. The first four methods introduced the theory that it was a woman's fear of childbirth that produced the physical pain during delivery and that pain could be avoided by teaching the woman to relax. It emphasized breathing and relaxation excercises, basic information about the birth event, and the husband's support. These methods emphasize drug-free deliveries.[43]

But not all pregnant woman have the interest or the time to devote to childbirth preparation according to these methods and prefer to rely on more traditional methods of giving birth to their children with the least amount of pain. Two commonly used procedures for administering anesthesia are the caudal and epidural. Both involve introducing drugs into the spinal column, which eliminates the pain typically involved in childbirth. The caudal involves placing a needle at the base of the tailbone; the epidural involves placing the needle further up the backbone. Other women prefer medication, which are usually administered intravenously, to alleviate labour pain at the onset of three to five contractions. These analgesics reduce the pain but allow the woman to be aware of the childbirth process.

Regardless of which method of childbirth a couple choose, most anticipate that the baby will be born by passing through the vaginal canal. As a result they receive little information about cesarean births. In Cesarean section, an incision is made in the woman's abdomen and uterus and the baby is removed. The term does not derive from the Roman Emperor Caesar being delivered in this way but from a law passed during Caesar's reign that made it mandatory for women dying in the advanced stages of pregnancy to have their babies removed by surgical means.

Cesarean deliveries are most often performed when there would be risk to the mother or the baby through normal delivery; as examples, the foetus may be positioned abnormally, the head may be to large for the pelvis or the mother may have diabetes or develop toxaemia (increased blood pressure) during pregnancy. The woman is put to sleep with general anesthesia or given a spinal injection, enabling her to remain awake and be aware of the delivery.

In a normal delivery the uterus, which is made of muscle, undergoes a series of strong contractions and the baby is gradually pushed through the vagina which has become more elastic to provide an easier exit. The new born baby begins to breath with a cry; the umbilical cord is cut; a new life has entered this earth. A little later the sac in which the baby has developed is expelled from the mother. A common term for this is "afterbirth".[44]

A few days after birth the mother begins to produce milk in order to feed the baby. The breasts, now larger than normal as they contain milk, are the means by which the young baby is fed from the nipples. The young human baby is even more dependent upon its mother, whom Allâh has created as a vital source of nourishment, than are other young animals. The strong emotional bond between mother and baby develops early, so that mother and infant resist separation.

6.4.9   THE ROLE OF THE MUSLIM PHYSICIAN

Muslim physicians need to consider several issues: Why is the question of sex education being asked only at this time? Is education such an important issue in Muslim life and Muslim society? Furthermore, who needs sex education? How and when should it be made available? Who should face the problem and provide the service? What are the sources and means of information? What are the problems and dangers of practical application and what are the ethical and moral issues?

This multitude of questions reflect the anxieties of Muslim medical men who put their faith and fear of Allâh before their career and profession. Their fear of committing a sin predates their enthusiasm of doing a successful job.

The question arises because sex education is part of a package being delivered to Muslims by ungodly men in an attempt to dismantle them from their basic roots of Islâmic life. This package comprises abortion, insurance, contraception, liberal attitudes to alcohol and drugs, nudity and other anti-Islâmic behaviour. Unfortunately part of the package has already been delivered, received and well digested. If we are not careful there is worse to come. Nowadays such anti-Islâmic behaviours and concepts are not necessarily delivered by foreign anti-Islâmic agents. Muslims professing to be liberalists, reformists or saviours are doing the job.

Do Muslim doctors really have a role in sex education? The chances are there that once in a lifetime a consultation may involve a sexual problem. What can they do? The first requirement is a combination of medical knowledge and Islâmic orientation. One should know where one stands. The second requirement is setting limits on moral and ethical principles. And the third is a knowledge of the patient and his* or her religious and moral orientation. If these requirements are satisfied then one may be facing one of three situations:

a) Sex education
b) Sexual deviation
c) Sexual dysfunction

If any of these situations arise outside a marriage relationship it is definitely impossible helping somebody continue such a relationship. It is a sin to help objects of disgust. If there is any education for non-marital relationships that would then be to prohibit them or suppress the desire. One cannot help these people at the expense of religious convictions. Islâm cannot be sacrificed for those who move towards moral degradation or try to avoid the legal responsibility for their non-Islâmic sexual behaviour. Within a marital relationship, how much can we indulge in sex education? One can consider situations where spouses come for help but one cannot go out of one's way to preach sex education. Of course, people need to know the dangers of veneral disease, rape, illegitimacy and criminal abortion but this should not by necessity be exclusively for the medical profession to preach.

6.4.9.1 WHAT DO MUSLIM DOCTOR'S HAVE TO TEACH?

The Muslim doctor needs to understand thoroughly all that the Qur'ân has mentioned pertaining to sex and all that the Traditions of the Prophet ﷺ included concerning conjugal rights and how spouses should treat each other concerning those conjugal rights.

The physician can even offer his expertise in cases of sexual dysfunction within a marital relationship. He has still to set limits to how deep and how far he can go. The decency and virtue of marital bondage and privacy of such a relationship need not be obscenely dissected and divulged to a third party, particularly if he or she be of the opposite sex, and here the need for same sex therapists becomes vitally important.[45]

Do Muslim doctors really need to worry that much about sexual problems? Do they have so many problems as to warrant explicit discussions? A more general answer is that in a practicing Muslim society they should not expect to face the same problems. One main reason to believe this assumption is that the Qur'ân and the Sunnah should be the framework for Muslim life and thus shape and fashion the behaviour and attitudes of Muslims. As the children are brought up they will have an Islâmic orientation to marital life and sex education rather than a separate and major issue in isolation. Muslims do not need to take sex as an issue and introduce it into the education of children. We need to introduce to them the Qur'ân and Sunnah in totality. If they can care for their Islâmic character other issues will take care of themselves. Virtue breeds virtue and vice breeds vice.

Let alone Muslims, even concerned Christians are beginning to express their reservations about the present day sex education which is being forcefully dished out in secular institutions.

6.4.10 ROLE OF PARENTS IN SEX EDUCATION

The role of parents in education is of such importance that it is virtually impossible to find an adequate substitute. It is therefore the duty of parents to create a family atmosphere inspired by love and devotion to Allâh which will promote an integrated, personal and social education of their children. The family is therefore the principal element for the inculcation of social virtues which are necessary to every society.

In particular, education in sexuality and true love, is confronted today by a culture guided by positivism. To be convinced that this is the case, one needs only to look at certain sexual education programmes introduced into the schools, often, notwithstanding the disagreement and even the protests of many parents. Sex education which is a basic right and duty of parents, must always be carried out under their attentive guidance and controlled by them. The practice of decency and modesty in speech, action and dress is very important in creating an atmosphere suitable for the growth of chastity, but this must be well motivated by respect for one's own body and the dignity of others. Parents should be watchful so that certain immoral fashions and attitudes do not violate the integrity of the home, especially through the mass media.

The good example set by parents is essential in strengthening the chastity of young people. A mother who values her maternal vocation and her place in the home greatly helps develop the qualities of femininity and motherhood in her daughters, and sets a clear, strong and noble example of womanhood for her sons. A father, whose behaviour is inspired by masculine dignity without macho, will be a perfect model for his sons, and inspire respect, admiration and security in his daughters.[46]

Each child is a unique person and must receive individualized information. Since parents know, understand and love each of their children, they are in the best position to decide what the appropriate time is for providing a variety of information according to their children's spiritual and physical development. No one can take this capacity for discernment away from conscientious parents. The moral values must always be part of their explanations. Parents should stress that Muslims are called to live the gift of sexuality according to the plan of the Almighty ie. in the context of marriage or abstinence before marriage.

In general, the first sexual information to be given to a child does not deal with a genital sexuality, but rather, the miraculous working of the Almighty at the birth of a brother or sister. The child's natural curiosity is stimulated, for example, when he/she sees the signs of pregnancy in his/her mother and awaits the arrival of a baby. Parents can take advantage of this situation in order to communicate some simple facts about pregnancy, but always in the context of wonder at the creative work of Allâh Ta'âlâ, who wants the new life He has given to be cared for in the mother's body, and not deliberately destroyed. The 'years of innocence' must never be disturbed by unnecessary information about sex. Boys and girls of this age are not particularly interested in sexual problems, and prefer to associate with children of their own sex. In this period a boy is at a relatively peaceful stage of his development. This is often the easiest time for him to build a good relationship with his father. At this time, he should learn that, although it must be considered a divine gift, his masculinity is not a sign of aggressiveness or superiority with regard to women, but a call from Almighty to take on certain roles and responsibilities.

Nevertheless, in the context of moral and sexual information, various problems can arise in this stage of childhood. In some societies today, there are planned and determined attempts to impose premature sex information on children. Such information tends to shatter their emotional and educational development and to disturb the natural peacefulness of this period of life. Parents should politely but firmly exclude any attempts to violate children's innocence which compromise spiritual, moral and emotional development. A further problem arises when children receive premature sex information from the mass media or from their peers who have been led astray or who have received premature sex education.

In answering children's questions, parents should not give the false impression that sex is something shameful or dirty, because it is a great gift of Almighty who placed the ability to generate life in the human body. Parents should also avoid the widespread mentality that girls are given every recommendation regarding virtue and the value of virginity, while the same is not applicable to boys.

Parents today should be attentive to ways in which an immoral education can be passed on to their children through various methods promoted by groups with positions and interests contrary to Islâmic morality. In the first place, parents must reject secularized and anti-natalist sex education, which puts the Creator at the margin of life and regards the birth of a child as a threat. This sex education is spread by large organizations and international associations that promote contraception, abortion, and sterilization. These organizations want to impose a false lifestyle against the truth of human sexuality. Working at national or state levels, these organizations try to arouse the fear of the threat of over-population among children and young people to promote the contraceptive mentality.[47] Furthermore, some antinatalist organizations maintain and protect those clinics which, violating the rights of parents, provide abortion and contraception for young people, thus promoting promiscuity and consequently increasing illegal teenage pregnancies. As we look beyond the year 2 000, how can we not think of the young? What is it being held up to them? A society of things and not of persons or the right to do as they will without any restrictions, provided it is *safe*. The unreserved gift of self-control of one's passions, the sense of responsibility - these are notions considered as belonging to another age.

Another abuse occurs whenever sex education is given to children by teaching them all the intimate details of genital relationships, even graphically. Today this is often motivated by wanting to provide education for safe sex, above all in relation to the spread of AIDS. In this situation, parents must also reject the promotion of so-called safe sex or safer sex, a dangerous and immoral policy based on the deluded theory that the condom can provide adequate protection against AIDS. Parents must insist on continence outside marriage and fidelity in marriage as the only true and secure education for the prevention of this contagious disease.

The following article under the caption *"Sex education concern as British schools rocked by gang rapes of young girls"*, is a shocking revelation of the disastrous effects of premature sexual education.

> *London: Three 13 year old members of a schoolboy gang have been questioned by Leicestershire police after being accused of dragging a young girl pupil into a classroom cupboard and sexually assaulting her. In another incident, a boy aged 13 appeared before magistrates at Wolverhampton on Friday accused of raping a 12 year old girl from his school in an attack involving a group of other youths. The two alleged attacks follow a statement made to police by a London girl of nine earlier in the week that*

> *she was raped by five boys, four aged 10*
> *and one nine, at a school in Shepherds*
> *Bush in west London.*
>
> *The incidents have caused concern among*
> *educationists and led to questions about the*
> *adequacy of juvenile sex education. These*
> *incidents were horrific and something no*
> *school or society should tolerate.*[48]

6.4.11   HOW TO TALK TO YOUR TEENAGER ABOUT SEX?

Religiously inclined people are now reclining towards divine direction in regulating the sexual education of their teenagers. The following is a summarized version of an interview, under the above caption, with someone who founded the Crisis Pregnancy Centres in King Country, Washington,[86] and who speaks in classrooms, on radios and in religious institutions about the dangers of sexual activity among teenagers and the critical need for abstinence:

*   *Where do you recommend parents begin in talking to their teenagers*
    about sex? Many parents feel embarrassed or intimidated discussing
    this important but controversial subject.

First of all, parents need to realize they are the "best" teachers of sex education and "stop" giving the job to someone else. A recent Louis Harris poll showed teenagers' number-one choice of where they wanted to learn about sex was from their parents. Second, when parents are involved with teenagers in sexual decisions, then teen sexual activity and pregnancy rates drop significantly. Third, the need for parents to develop their communication skills is emphasized. Begin with good eye contact. Listen carefully to them. Be sensitive to their feelings. Ask questions that draw the teenagers out like what information the child has about Aids or other sexually transmitted diseases.

Teaching your child about sex is a process which begins when he or she is young and continues throughout their youth. It isn't just sitting down for one BIG talk.

* *What are the major issues parents should discuss with their teenager?*

There are six things recommended for parents to share with their teenagers. First, marriage, love and sex all go together. Sex within marriage is part of God's plan for procreation and marital satisfaction. When you're married you have total privacy. If you are both virgins at marriage you avoid the health risks of STD's (sexually transmitted diseases). You also don't feel guilty about illicit affairs.

Second, teenagers need to know that love, and not sex, is the more important factor. Right now teenagers are being taught that sex is everything. Media influences and peer pressure tell kids sex is just normal, to get as much as they can. It needs to be emphasized that commitment is the important issue.

Third, teenagers need to be taught the difference between affection and lust. When teens are involved in deep kissing or touching each other's bodies for the purpose of sexual arousal, they are engaged in lustful behaviour. Teach them that premarital sex is a design for disaster.

Fourth, parents need to teach their teens the importance of self-control. They exercise self-control in many other areas of their lives, they can do so over their sex drives as well. Titus 2:12 says the grace of God "teaches us to say 'No' to ungodliness and worldly passions, and to live self-controlled, upright, and godly lives."

Fifth, it's important for parents to develop strong relationships with their teenagers. As their children get older, parents tend to spend less time with them as their friends become more important.

Sixth, parents should emphasize the destructive nature of datings. When teenagers start dating, sex is on their minds. In fact during a recent survey, 25 % of college freshman boys responded by saying that if they have paid for the food and the girl does not go all the way, they have a right to force her to have sex. Many rapes occur at the end of the date and are not reported. Anything which breaks down sexual inhibition and loss of self-control i.e. alcohol, drugs, parking in darkened alleys, petting or just being together for two members of the opposite sex in a secluded place should not be allowed for teenagers. Kissing and petting is preparing the body for sex. The body can be brought to a point of no return.

* *What influences on teenagers do parents need to be aware of?*

Parents need to be aware there's a tragic, self-fulfilling prophecy being promoted by movies, TV, rock music and many educators. It says to teenagers, "You will be sexually active. It's a natural part of your life, so you need to know how to prevent any problems."

Teens think "Yeah, I'm going to be sexually active. It's normal."

That's a tragedy. What they don't hear about is the devastation. There are so many problems associated with teenage sexual activity. Pregnancy, Aids, STD's, and spiritual and emotional trauma.

* *What are the most important issues facing teens today?*

Unless teenagers become sexually abstinent before marriage, they face a dim future. Abstinence, which is the only foolproof way of preventing STD's and pregnancy, must be taught.

* *Are kids responding when they are told they can be abstinent?*

Yes. There are three studies which show a significant number of teenagers are responding positively when they are taught abstinence in a clearly defined, systematic way for a long time.

* *Where do you recommend parents begin?*

Parents are urged to pray for their children. Let them be informed that you are praying for their health, safety, and moral purity. Teach them what Divine Revelation says about immorality? Married sex, which reflects true love, should be contrasted with premarital sex, which is selfish, exploitive, and only ends in problems. Not only physical problems, but spiritual loneliness and psychological and emotional trauma.[87]

6.4.12   SEXUALITY AND THE ELDERLY PERSON

Islâmic sexual education does not confine one's sexual activity to a specified period or a fixed age. As long as a person directs his sexual energy in the proper channel, he is free to exercise this right without any restrictions as to his age limit. It is difficult for many people to think of men and women late in life as having sexual feelings, sexual needs or sexual relationships. Cultural backwardness usually plays a large part in this misconception, which may be strengthened by the common tendency of the youth to deny the inevitability of ageing. Despite increasing scientific evidence to the contrary, many cultures continue to maintain the belief that by the time one passes the age of sixty, sex is neither necessary nor possible. Most older people try to deny or suppress their sexuality to avoid the ridicule or censure of younger people. Disapproval by children and even grandchildren results in feelings of guilt.

Society owes a great debt to the elderly. People need to know and accept that for the majority of old people, sexual activity plays an important part in their married lives. Furthermore it needs to be stressed again that for all human beings, regardless of age, there is more to sexuality than just the act of sex. For a man, there is the satisfaction of still being masculine; for a woman, still feeling feminine; for both still being wanted and needed. There is the comforting warmth of physical nearness and the pleasure of companionship. The need to be held and to hold; the need to relate to another person, the need to express feelings and be recipient of other's communicated feelings, neither wastes away through lack of use nor ends with ageing. Yet society continues, culturally and psychologically, to oppress the sexuality of the aged.

6.4.13   SUMMARY

In Islâm sex has always been taken seriously and it should remain so. It is not a subject for fun or mere absolute pleasure. It is never discussed obscenely or subjected to scrutiny. Decency and due respect always characterize the subject.

*   Sex is never discussed in isolation for its sake or mere pleasure. It is always related to marital life and family life. It is viewed as a superior human relationship subject to strict regulations. Thus sex within a marital relationship is a worship that is rewarded. Outside a marital relationship sex is a punishable sin and a criminal offence.

*   Sex is a private matter between spouses. What goes on is confidential and should not be divulged to outside parties. The human factor in marital and sexual relationship is superior to mere pleasure.

*   Legislation concerning sex is not subject to change by pressure groups or change in social attitudes.

*   Like the rest of Islâmic teachings, knowledge about those verses and Traditions on the subject is not age-specific and is not meant to start at a certain age. As the Muslim is learning the Qur'ân and Sunnah he or she will come across these teachings.

6.4.14   CONCLUSION

Some people concede that the factors which are being regarded as sex stimulants such as graphic sexual education, and thus required to be eradicated from social life, are indeed the very soul of art and aesthetics. Their eradication, it is contended, will be tantamount to depriving human life of grace and beauty. We do concede that art and aesthetics are valuable things which must be protected and made to flourish, but social and sexual morality and the collective well being of man are even more valuable. It cannot be sacrificed to any art, any aesthetic taste. It is not a private and personal view of ours, it is the demand of both reason and nature. The art and aesthetic taste in the form of sex education currently being dished out leads man to his ruin and downfall rather than to safeguarding his chastity and therefore cannot be allowed to prosper in society.

Anything that is deemed as fatal to man's collective life is not tolerated anywhere for the sake of art. For instance, the literature that causes sedition and chaos and incites man to kill and plunder cannot be endured merely for its literary charms and merit. The pictures that reflect feelings of injustice and iniquity, or in which universal moral principles have been broken cannot be recieved well by any law, no matter how artistic they may happen to be. Man has shown great ingenuity in the arts of forgery and fraud, but no civilized society worth the name was ever prepared to appreciate these arts. Thus it is universally admitted that sexual morality is more valuable than any fine art, any aesthetic taste.

6.4.15 GENERAL CONCLUSION

When the glorious sun of Islâm rose, brightening the world, its powerful rays pierced through the dark clouds of ignorance and narrow-mindedness that had prevailed before. Thus, the once humble and oppressed human race awakened to a brighter and more meaningful existence.

When Islâm dawned in the wayward land of Arabia, the new creed not only galvanised the people in and around the Arabian Peninsula, but it jolted the entire humanity. The heavenly message from the mouth of an unlettered Prophet 靀 had already electrified the corrupt, cruel, unrefined and perverted Arabs and made them Allâh fearing, humane, morally chaste and angelic.

But mankind today is virtually impregnated with an obsession of immorality. Undiluted sex and sexual symbols converge on people from all directions, advertising, movies, television, literature, the arts, even learning at all levels are constantly engaged in the description, treatment and discussion of sex. Clothes, cosmetics, even houses are sold because they are claimed to have sex appeal; children at a relatively tender age are indocrinated with false notions of sex education. The entire movie industry is directed toward sex; if the objective result is not always pornographic, the subjective intention certainly is. It can safely be said that sex is flaunted in every medium of communication, in almost every field of human endeavour, to an extent that was never possible even during times of the most extensive licentiousness in Western civilization.

This is not to say that sex in itself is pornographic or that an attempt should be made to banish it entirely from society: even if it were possible it would definitely not be desirable. The real significance of this sudden onrush of sex is that it creates an awareness of sex where such constant awareness is neither necessary nor even useful. Modern man continues to create and stimulate a need which he then proceeds to prohibit. The need for sex, once stimulated to the breaking point, cannot, however, simply be ignored; it does not go away by itself, but seeks outlets which may at times be far more undesirable than the goal originally sought.

The question that is equally disturbing the mind of the governments as well as religious leaders and moralists is how to arrest the evil of obscenity which is infesting the society in one form or another. It is prevalent in men, women, grown-ups and teenagers in varying degrees and scope. The outburst of indecency, in private and in public, has assumed proportions that have forced even the secular society to cry a halt. Decent people have become horrified, wounded, and disgusted by the unrestrained liberty in sexual anarchy which is currently prevalent. Above all, a totally misplaced sense of social values, resulting in a so called promiscuous society, is adding salt to the wound. It is not surprising therefore, that the order of the day is sex-orientated movies, crime-laden films, erotic fiction, pornographic literature, fast and sensuous music and dance fashion, semi-nude modelling, provocative dressing, and the like, that kindles the flame of animalistic passions. The legalization of prostitution, homosexuality and lesbianism, which is not only encouraged and promoted, but also justified under the guise of 'inborn natural instincts' has left mankind in a consequent whirlwind from where there's no exit. Consequently it can be said that the flood of pornography; adverts demanding your attention and physical presence towards illicit and unnatural liasions; and a host of evils which today can be found in the mail; on the news-stands, on television and even on computer screens is a response to the need created by society itself, a society which permits immorality as long as it is spoken, but frowns upon it when it is enacted.

Thus society, especially in the Western nations, which were sick since long ago have further degenerated. The civilization and culture are both in a mess. In their search for peace of mind they are wondering aimlessly and seeking relief in addictive drugs, freedom from all restrictions and discipline, nudity and unbridled sex. Their matrimonial system has failed. In the beginning husbands and wives suspected each other, but now, unable to prevent it, they shut their eyes and tacitly consent to each others sexual misbehaviour. Marriages are avoided as far as pssible and divorces are the order of the day. Not able to cope with the widespread sexual revolution, many countries in the West have legalized these vices rather than contain them. The new sexual freedom and the cult of nudity are a way of escaping from our responsibilities towards our fellow human beings. The sexual partners are often, strictly speaking, strangers in the night, and very often in broad daylight too. Therefore, sexuality today is no more than a 'commerce' of the body without the participation of the spirit.

369

Today, women in 'civilized' countries are spending the major portion of their own and their husbands' incomes on make up and decoration, and the rising expenditure in this account is becoming more and more unbearable. Muslim women are blindly emulating their western counterparts. Is not this craze the gift of the lustful eyes that eagerly wait to greet decorated ladies in the shopping malls and bazaars, offices and social gatherings? The question is: Why is this craze for beautification among women becoming more and more catching everyday? – Most surely, it is due to the feminine urge to win the approval of men and to fascinate them. But for what purpose? Is it an innocent urge? Does it not spring from the hidden sexual desires which crave for their fulfilment outside their lawful, natural sphere by similar desires on the other side?

Clothing nowadays manage to be both attractive and seductive ... skirts are up, necklines are down, jeans and denims are skin tight, and figures are better than ever, to which there can be few objections... It is symptomatic of an era in which sexual pleasure is increasingly considered an almost constitutional right, in which self-denial is increasingly seen as backwardness rather than virtue. While technological advancement has reduced fear of long-dreaded earthly dangers, such as venereal diseases, illicit conception and AIDS, man's indifference towards accountability has diminished fear of divine punishment.

Let it be enough to say that incest is not very uncommon in certain populous quarters of our famous cities. Parents, educators and the guardians of morality at large do pull themselves together to say "don't", but they usually sound half-hearted. Even the behaviour of certain so called professed Muslims is illustrative of the mentality of "those who neither follow this way nor that...?"

On the one hand, these people claim to cherish the Islâmic standards of morality, culture and nobility of character, and want their women to be chaste and modest, and their homes free from immorality. But, on the other hand, they also crave the charms, lustful pleasures and ill-gotten material gains of the western way of life, trying to remain immune to its abuses. But this attitude is illogical in many ways. Firstly, it is wrong to graft together mutilated parts of two civilizations which are opposed to each other in ideas and structures. Secondly, it is wrong to allow relaxation of the sound moral principles of Islâm, give people the habit of violating the law, and then try to stop them within the "harmless" bounds. All wrong customs have an innocent beginning in the community life, but as they are handed down from one generation to the other they assume unusual dimensions. Therefore, the blend of the Western and Islâmic ways is no solution at all.

Anything that violates the order of the world is a source of evil and anarchy. That is why *zinâ* (fornication and adultery), pornography, prostitution, rape, and all its associates arouses such strong, unanimous condemnation. Islâm remains violently hostile to all other ways of realizing sexual desire, which are regarded as unnatural purely and simply because they run counter to the accepted harmony of the sexes and plunge man into ambiguity. As a result the divine curse embraces both the boyish woman and the effeminate man, male and female homophilia, auto-eroticism, zoophilia, etc. Indeed all these 'deviations' involve the same refusal to accept the sexed body and to assume the female or male condition. Sexual deviation is a revolt against Almighty.

Thus, sexuality and morality, after providing for centuries a sort of happiness, peace and integration, are today being shredded into types of estranged compartments. The exercise of sexuality was a prayer, a gift of oneself, an act of charity, but mankind in general and Muslims in particular, gradually came to attach themselves to the external forms of sexual activity, rather than to the soul that ought to spiritually enkindle it.

There are, of course, laws, censorship and ethical codes to eradicate sexual immorality. It, however, needs more than a mere crime-and-punishment approach. Firstly, the mental outlook needs to be corrected by means of proper education and upbringing. The initiative to curb unlawful sexual appetite should be so great, that the wrongdoer should himself become conscious of the sin inherent in his obscene and indecent behaviour. Secondly, the general public opinion against these violations should be taken to such a pitch that the transgressor will feel that he is being looked down upon by the entire community, and he had, therefore, better mend his ways in order to be a respected citizen of society. Indeed, public opinion is a powerful instrument to eradicate this menace. Besides these, effective hurdles should also be placed in the paths leading to sexual anarchy.

Islâm provides by far the strongest sheet anchor against sexual perversion. Islâm also fully realizes that man possesses not only the spiritual soul but also a physical body. He has not only angelic traits of character but also the potential to become morally corrupt. To satisfy the sensuous instincts of mankind, Almighty has structured well-defined parameters which must be strictly adhered to. For this very reason, the punitive laws of Islâm, on the one hand, compulsorily stamps out all indecencies, and on the other, it protects the righteous elements of society against malicious encroachments. Whereas the moral teachings of Islâm cleanse man from within so that he does not feel inclined towards sin, its punitive laws regulate his external behaviour, so that if his moral training remained defective, his evil inclinations taking practical shape may be forcefully suppressed.

REFERENCES AND FOOTNOTES

CHAPTER ONE

1) al-Bukhârî, Muhammad ibn Isma'îl *Sahîh al Bukhârî* (India: Mukhtâr and Co., 1983) Vol.2:903.
2) Ibid.
3) Qur'ân.
4) Rahmân, Fazlur, *Islâm and Modernity* (Chicago: The University of Chicago Press, 1982) 5-20.

CHAPTER TWO

1) Kittel, Gerhard, *Theological Dictionary of the New Testament* (Michigan, U.S.A.: W.M.B. Eerdmans Publishing Company, 1968) 777-778.
2) Rahmân, Afzalur, ed., "Role of Muslim Women in Society", *Encyclopedia of Seerah* (London: Seerah Foundation, 1987) 4.
3) Maudûdî, S.A.A., *Purdah and the Status of Woman in Islâm* (Pakistân: Islâmic Publications Ltd., 1990) 6.
4) The Age of Greek Gods and Heroes, *Fortnightly Life*, 25 March 1963.
5) Kittel, op.cit., 779-781.
6) Maudûdî, op.cit., 8.
7) The Whispers of Pompeii, *Fortnightly Life*, October 3, 1966.
8) Gibbon, Edward, *The Decline and Fall of the Roman Empire* (U.S.A.: Classics Appreciation Society, 1956) 391, 441.
9) al-Tabarî, J'afar Muhammad ibn Jarîr *Târîkh Tabarî* (Beirut: Dâr al-Kutub al-'Ilmîyah, n.d.) Vol.3, 138.
10) Ibid. Vol.2: 88-89.
11) Walîullâh, Shâh Dehlawî, *Hujat Allâh al-Bâlighah* (India: Mukhtâr and Co., n.d.) Vol.1, 105.
12) Walker, Benjamin, *Hindu World* (Great Britain: George Allen and Unwin Ltd. 1968) 603-606.
13) Majumdar, R.C., *An Advanced History of India* (London, 1948) 822.
14) Nadwî, Abdul Hasan, *Western Civilization, Islâm and Muslims* (New Delhi: Markazî Maktabî Islâmî, n.d.) 31, as quoted from *Tamaddun 'Arab* 318.
15) Saraswati, Dayanand, *Satyarath Prakash* English Translation: *"The Light of Truth"* by Upadhyaya, Gayaprasad (New Delhi: Kala Press, 1956) 117-118; 152-153.
16) *Tamaddun 'Arab*, op.cit., 373-374.

17) *Times of India,* 14 September 1987.

18) Bhattacharya, A.N., *Dharma-Adharma and Morality in Mahabarata* (New Delhi: S.S. Publishers, 1992) 89-107.

19) Ibid., 93-94.

20) Kandam, Bala, *Gnana Surian* (India: Kudi Arasu Press, n.d.) Chapter 14.

21) *Times of India,* November 10 1987.

22) *D.P.A. News,* India, 6 November 1986.

23) *Encyclopaedia Judaica* (Jerusalem, Israel: Keter Publishing House Ltd., 1971) 624-626.

24) Kittel, G., op.cit., vol.1 : 783.

25) *Encyclopaedia Judaica* op.cit., vol.2 : 1028-1032.

26) Ferguson, Everett, *Studies in Early Christianity* (New York: Garland Publishing Inc., 1993) 20-21.

27) Ibid., 134-201.

28) Ibid., 201.

29) Ibid., 288.

30) Ibid., 282.

31) Veyne, Paul, "The Roman Empire", in *A History of Private Life 1: From Pagan Rome to Byzantium* (Cambridge: Harvard University Press, 1987) 35.

32) Lecky, W.E.H. *History of Morality of Europe,* Vol.2.

33) Rahmân, Afzalur, op.cit., Vol.2., 18.

34) Kittel, G., op.cit.

35) Radcliff, A.R., *African Systems of Kinship and Marriage* (London: London Press, 1970) 180.

36) Khân, Majîd 'Alî, *Muhammad The Final Messenger* (Lahore: Sh. Muhammad Ashraf Publishers, 1983) 32.

37) Bahador, Syed Ahmed Khân, *Life of Muhammad* (Lahore: Premier Book House, 1968) 122.

38) Qur'ân, 24:33.

39) al-Bukhârî, op.cit.

40) Ibn Kathîr, Vol.3, 288.

41) Qur'ân, 16:58-59.

42) Nadwî, A.H.A., *Islâm and the World* (New Delhi: Markazî Maktabî Islâmî, n.d.) 31.

43) Qur'ân, 43:17.

44) Qur'ân, 81:8-9.

45) Daryâbâdî, 'Abdul Majîd, *Tafsîr Daryâbâdî* (Pakistan: The Taj Company Ltd., n.d.), Vol.2, 609-A.

CHAPTER THREE

1) Mutahharî, A.M., *Social and Historical Change* (Berkeley: Mîzân Press, 1986) 3:13.
2) Qur'ân, 49:13.
3) Qur'ân, 48:32.
4) Broom, Leonard and Selznick, Philip, *Sociology* (New York: Harper and Row Publishers, 1973) 19.
5) Qur'ân, 5:105.
6) Bensman, J., *"Community"* in Encoclypaedia America, vol. 7. p.449.
7) Tonnies, Ferdinand, *"Community and Society"* East Lausing, Michigan, 1997.
8) Durkheim, Emile, *The Elementary Forms of the Religious Life,* New York, 1965.
9) *Oxford English Dictionary,* second Edition, vol. 3, 1989.
10) *Webster's New Twentieth Century Dictionary* (of the English Language, unabridged, second edition) New York, 1972.
11) 'Alî, Dr Muhammad Mumtâz, *The Concept of Islâmic Ummah and Sharî'ah,* (Malaysia: Pelanduk Publications, 1992) 9-19.
12) Qur'ân, 51:49.
13) Qur'ân, 42:11.
14) Qur'ân, 2:223.
15) Rahmân, Afzalur, op.cit., 28.
16) Ibid. 41.
17) Bureau, Paul, *Towards Moral Bankruptcy* (London: Constable and Co., 1925) 106-108.
18) Ibid. 111-112.
19) Ibid. 115.
20) Qur'ân, 4:1.
21) Qur'ân, 49:13.
22) Qur'ân, 31:14.
23) Qur'ân, 17:23.
24) Qur'ân, 4:11.
25) Qur'ân, 4:7.
26) Qur'ân, 4:11.
27) Qur'ân, 4:12.
28) Qur'ân, 9:71.
29) Qur'ân, 2:30.
30) Qur'ân, 2:34.
31) Qur'ân, 2:228.
32) Qur'ân, 2:282.
33) Qur'ân, 4:34.

34) Qur'ân, 21:7.

35) Qur'ân, 33:33.

36) Qur'ân, 33:59.

37) Qur'ân, 43:18.

38) Sahih al-Bukhârî, op.cit.

39) Ibid. Vol. 1:44

40) Chaudhry, Muhammad Sharîf, *Women's Rights in Islâm* (New Delhi: Adam Publishers and Distributors, 1991) 168-173.

41) Badawî, Dr Jamâl A., *The Status of Women in Islâm* (Saudi Arabia: Wakf Cendoment, 1991) 25.

42) al-'Asqâlânî, Ahmad ibn Hajar, *Fath al-Bârî Sharh Sahih al-Bukhârî* (Beirut: Matba'at al-Bahîyat al Misriyyah, 1982) Vol. 7:82.

43) Haddard, Yvonne Y., *The Contemporary Islâm and the Challenges of History* (New York: State University Press, 1982) 58.

44) 'Abdul Raûf, M., *Marriage in Islâm,* op.cit.

45) Smith, Jane I., "Women in Islâm, Equity, Equality and the Search for the Natural Order" in *Journal of the American Academy of Religion* Dec. 1979, 517-537.

46) Haddard, op.cit., 207-220.

47) Ibid. 221.

48) *Nidâ-e-Haram,* Karachi, Jamâd al-Ûlâ, 1369 A.H.

49) Qur'ân, 17:31.

50) Qur'ân, 81:8-9.

51) Qur'ân, 60:12.

52) Chaudhry, op.cit., 23.

53) al-Nawawî, Abu Zakarıyä ıbn Sharaf, *Riyâd al-Sâlihîn* (Lahore: Pakistan N'umânî Kutub Khânâ, 1977) 186.

54) Ibid. 187.

55) al Hâtimy, Sa'îd 'Abdullâh Seif, *Women in Islâm: A Comparative Study* (Pakistan: Islâmic Publications Ltd. n.d.) 46.

56) *Encyclopedia Britannica Micropedia* Vol. 9 : 585.

57) Siddiqî, Muhammad Iqbâl, *Islâm Forbids Free Mixing of Men and Women in Islâm* (New Delhi: Adam Publishers and Distributors, 1986) 6.

58) Jameelah, Maryam, *Islâm and the Muslim Woman Today* (Lahore: Mahomed Yûsuf Khân, 1976) 33-37.

59) Hole, Judith and Levine, Ellen, "The Rebirth Feminism" in *The New York Times*, New York, 228.

60) Ibid. 240.

61) Cooke, Joanne, *The New Woman; A Motive Anthology on Women's Liberation* (New York, 1970) 79-81.

62) Maudûdi, op.cit., 52-53.

63) Haralambos and Holborn, *Sociology: Themes and Perspectives* (London: Harper Collins Publishers, 1966) 638-9.

64) Velde, Dr Van de, *Sex Hostility in Marriage* (London: George Allan and Unwin n.d.) 69.

65) Maudûdî, op.cit., 111-122.

66) Qur'ân, 30:21.

67) Qur'ân, 16:72.

68) 'Abdul Raûf, Muhammad, *Marriage in Islâm* (New York: Exposition Press Inc. 1977) 15.

69) al-Sijistânî, Abû Dâwûd Sulaimân ibn al-Ash'ath, *Sunan Abî Dâwûd* (Deoband, India: Mukhtâr and Co. 1985) 295.

70) *Sahih al-Bukhârî*, op.cit., 95-96.

71) Rahmân, A, *Encyclopedia of Seerah*, op.cit., 153

72) *Al Ahrâm Daily*, May 29th 1961.

73) Karîm, Fazlul, *Al-Hadîs: Mishkât al-Masâbîh* (Lahore: Pakistan The Book House, n.d.) 678-680.

74) Chaudhry, M.S., op.cit., 95-96.

75) Qur'ân, 4:3.

76) *Sahih al-Bukhârî*, Bâb al-Qasam, op.cit.

77) Qur'ân, 4:129.

78) *Sidq-e-Jadîd*, Pakistan, September 8th 1950.

79) Schopenhauer, Arthur, *Record*, Lagos, 20th April 1901.

80) Zamzan, Lahore, September 15th 1945.

81) Kalachen, *Islâm and Sexual Science*, 287.

82) Lemu, 'Âisha B, *Woman in Islâm* (Leicester, U.K.: The Islâmic Foundation, 1978) 45-46.

83) Heeren, Fâtima, *Family Life in Islâm* (Leicester, U.K.: The Islâmic Foundation, 1978) 45-46.

84) Siddîqî Trust, *Polygamy*, Karachi, n.d. 32.

85) Ibn al-Humâm, Kamâluddîn, *Fath al Qadîr*, (India: 'Uthmâniyyah Oriental Publications Bureau n.d.) Vol.3:155.

86) Abû 'Îsâ, Muhammad ibn 'Îsâ, *Sunan al Tirmidhî* Bâb al-Nikâh (Delhi, India: Kutub Khâna Rashîdiyyah n.d.).

87) Gibbs, H.A.R. and Kramer, J.H., Shorter Encyclopaedia of Islâm (Leiden: J.R. Brill, 1961) 419.

88) Qur'ân, 23:5-6.

89) Qur'ân, 4:24.

90) Qur'ân, 2:236.

91) Qur'ân, 2:236; 9:69; 6:128; 33:28; 33:49; 46:20.

92) Qur'ân, 4:25.

93) Muslehuddîn, Dr Muhammad, *Mutâ* (Lahore: Islâmic Publications Ltd., 1974) 3-9.

94) al-Jaṣṣâs, Abû Bakr Aḥmad ibn 'Alî, *Aḥkâm al-Qur'ân*, (Beirut: Dâr al-Kitâb al 'Arabî 1335 A.H.) Vol. 2:178.

95) al 'Asqalânî, *Fath al Bârî*, Kitâb al-Nikah op.cit., Vol. 9:173.

96) Ibn Taimîyah, Taqî al-Dîn Aḥmad, *Minhâj al-Sunnah al-Nabiwiyya* (Cairo: Maṭba 'at Kurdistân al 'Ilmîyah 1326 A.H.).

97) al Qurtubî, Abû 'Abd Allâh, *al Jâmi'i lî Aḥkâm al-Qur'ân* (Cairo: Dâr al-Ma'ârif, 1967) Vol. 5:130.

98) al-Shawkânî, Muḥammad ibn 'Alî ibn Muhammad, *Nail al-Awtâr* (Cairo: Dâr Matabi' al Sha'b, 1965) Vol. 6:130.

99) *Tafsîr al Ṭabarî; Tafsîr ibn Kathîr; Tafsîr al-Râzî; Tafsîr al-Khâzin; Tafsîr al-Suyûtî; Kanz al-'Ummâl; Ah kâm al-Qur'ân by al-Jaṣṣâs. Ṣaḥiḥ Muslim; Sunan al-Dârmî; Sunan al-Baihaqî.*

100) *Tafsîr al-Ṭabarî*, Vol. 5:9; *Tafsîr al-Râzî*; Vol. 3:200-202; *Tafsîr al-Baghawî*, Vol. 1:423; *Tafsîr Abî Hayyân*, Vol. 3:218; *Tafsîr al-Zamakhsharî*, Vol. 1:360; *Tafsîr al-Baidâwî*, Vol. 1:269; *Tafsîr ibn Kathîr*, Vol. 1:474; *Tafsîr al Qurtubî*, Vol. 5:130; *Tafsîr al-Khâzin*, Vol. 1:357; *Aḥkâm al-Qur'ân*, by al-Jaṣṣâs, Vol. 2:128; *Aḥkâm al-Qur'ân* by Qâdî, Vol. 1:162; *Sharh Ṣaḥiḥ Muslim* by al-Nawawî, Vol. 9:181; *Musnad Ah mad*, Vol. 4:436; *Sunan Baihaqî*, Vol. 7:205.

101) *Tafsîr al Qurtubî*, Vol. 5:130; *Tafsîr al Ṭabarî*, Vol. 5:9; *Aḥkâm al-Qur'ân*, by al-Jaṣṣâs, Vol. 2:178; *Ṣaḥiḥ Muslim*, Vol. 1:395; *al Nihâya* by Ibn Athîr, Vol. 2:249; *al-Mahadarât* by Râghib, Vol. 2:94; *Târîkh al-Khulafâ* by Suyûtî, 93.

102) al Qurtubî, op.cit., Vol. 5:132.

103) al-Râzî, Abû Bakr Muhammad ibn Zakarîyya, *Tafsîr al-Râzî*; (India: 'Uthmâniyyah Oriental Publications Bureau, 1960) Vol. 3:200.

104) *Zâd al-Ma'âd* by Ibn Qayyim, Vol. 1:144; *Tafsîr al-Usûl* by Ibn al-Daiba' Vol. 4:262; *Fath al Bârî* by Ibn Hajar, Vol. 9:141; *Kanz al-'Ummâl*, Vol. 8:294.

105) *Kitâb al-Umm* by Imâm Shafi'î, Vol. 7:219; *Sunan al-Kubrâ* by Baihaqî, Vol. 7:206; *Muwatta* by Imâm Mâlik, Vol. 2:30.

106) *Tafsîr Abî Hayyân*, Vol. 3:218; *Al-Durr al-Manthûr*, Vol. 2:140; *Tafsîr al Ṭabarî*, Vol. 5:9.

107) *Bidâyat al-Mujtahid* by Ibn Rushd, Vol. 2:58; *Al Fayiq* by Zamakhsharî, Vol. 1:331; *Tafsîr al-Suyûtî*, Vol. 2:140.

108) *Kanz al-'Ummâl* op.cit., Vol. 8:294.

109) Mus lih uddîn op.cit., 25.

110) al-Jawziyyah, Muhammad ibn Abî Bakr ibn Qayyim, *Zâd al Ma'âd fî Khair al 'Ibâd* (Cairo: Matba'at al Halabî 1950) Vol. 4:7.

111) Shaltût, Mahmûd, *al-Fatâwâ* (Cairo: Matbû'at al Idârat al Ammat lî al Thaqafah of al Azhar December 1959).

112) al-Nawawî, Abû Zakariyâ Yahyâ ibn Sharaf, *Sharh Sahih Muslim* (Cairo: Dâr Matabi'al Sh'ab n.d.) Vol. 9:181.

113) al Râzî, Muhammad Fakhruddîn ibn Ziâuddîn, *Tafsîr Kabîr* (Cairo: Dâr Matabi'al Sh'ab n.d.) Vol. 2:415.

114) *Tafsîr al-Tabarî*, op.cit., Vol. 8:179.

115) al-Jassâs *Ah kâm al-Qur'ân*, op.cit., Vol. 2:177-188.

116) al-Zamakhsharî, Muhammad ibn 'Umar, *al-Kashâf* (Cairo: Dâr al-Ma'ârif n.d.) Vol. 1:169.

117) al-Qurtubî op.cit., Vol. 5:129-132.

118) Ibn Kathîr, Imâmuddîn Abî al-Fidâ Isma'îl, *Tafsîr al-Qur'ân*, (Damascus: Al-Maktab al-Islâmî n.d.) Vol. 1:474.

119) al-Baidâwî, Qâdî Nasîruddîn, *Tafsîr Baidâwî* (Cairo: Dâr al-Ma'ârif n.d.) Vol. 1:115.

120) al-Âlûsî, Sayad Mahmûd, *Rûh al-Ma'ânî* (Beirut: Dâr al-Kitâb al-'Arabî n.d.) Vol. 5:5.

121) Ibn 'Abbâs, 'Abdullâh, *Tafsîr Abdullâh ibn 'Abbâs*, (India: 'Uthmâniyyah Oriental Publications Bureau, 1280 A.H.) Vol. 1:64.

122) Ibn Taimîyah, *Minhâj al-Sunnah* op.cit., Vol 2:155-157.

123) al-Jawziyyah, *Zâd al Ma'âd* op.cit., Vol. 4:6.

124) al-Shawkânî, *Nail al-Awtâr*, op.cit., Vol. 6:133-138.

125) al-Nawawî, *Sharh Sahih Muslim* op.cit., Vol. 6:133-138.

126) Tûsî, Shaikh Abû J'afar, *Tahdhîb al-Ahkâm* (Tehrân, Irân: Dâr al-Kutub al-Islâmiyyah n.d.) 183.

127) Kulaynî, Muhammad ibn Y'akûb Abû J'afar, *Usûl al-Kâfî* (Tehrân, Irân: Dâr al-Kutub al-Islâmiyyah, 1374 A.H.) Vol. 2:191.

128) Ibid. 189.

129) Kulaynî, Muhammad ibn Y'akûb Abû J'afar, *Furû' al-Kâfî* (Tehran, Irân: Dâr al-Kutub al-Islâmiyyah, 1374 A.H.)

130) Tûsî, op.cit., 187-188.

131) Kulaynî, *Furû' al-Kâfî*, op.cit., 196.

132) Qummî, 'Ali ibn Ibrâhîm, *Tafsîr al-Qummî* (Najaf, Irâq: Matba'ah an-Najaf, 1386) 308.

133) Kashânî, Fathullâh, *Tafsîr Minhâj al Sâdiqîn* (Tehrân, Irân: Dâr al-Kutub al-Islâmiyyah, 1396 A.H.) 356.

134) Ibid. 356.

135) Bâbawaih, Shaikh as-Sâdiq ibn J'afar Muhammad ibn 'Alî, *Man Lâ Yahdhuruhul Faqîh* (Najaf, Irâq: Matba'ah an-Najaf, 1376 A.H.) 150.

136) Kulaynî, *Furû' al-Kâfî*, op.cit., Vol. 2:200.

137) Salâmah, Dr Ahmad 'Abdullâh, *Mut'ah, The Sunnî and Shî'ah Perspectives on Marriage* (Jeddah, Saudi Arabia: Abul-Qâsim Publishing House, 1995) 18-20.

138) Qur'ân, 57:27.

139) al- Dasûqî, Shams al Dîn Muhammad ibn 'Arafah, *Hâshiyah al Dasûqî* (Cairo: Dâr Ihyâ al Kutub al 'Arabiyyah n.d.) Vol. 2:9.

140) al-Jawziyyah, *Zâd al-Ma'ad*, op.cit., Vol. 3:146.

141) al-Nawawî, *Sharh Sahîh Muslim*, op.cit., Vol. 1:450.

142) Walîullah, Shah, *Hujjat-Allâh al-Bâlighah* (India: 'Uthmâniyyah Oriental Publications Bureau n.d.) Vol. 2:122.

143) Qaradâwî, op.cit., 178-179.

144) *Sahîh al-Bukhârî*, op.cit.

145) Qur'ân, 2:221.

146) *Matthew*, 5:31-32.

147) *Matthew*, 19:6.

148) Qaradâwî, op.cit., 209.

149) Commentary on Gospel according to Matthew, Institute of Coptic Catholic Research.

150) Wâfî, 'Abd al Wâhid, As quoted in *Huqûq al-Insân fî al Islâm* (Human Rights in Islâm) 88.

151) Maudûdî, *Purdah*, op.cit., 59.

152) al-Sijistânî, op.cit., Chapter on Talâq.

153) Qur'ân, 4:34-35.

154) Qur'ân, 4:130.

155) Qur'ân, 2:229.

156) Miftâhî, Muftî Zafeeruddîn, *Modesty and Chastity in Islâm* (New Delhi, India: Qâzî Publishers and Distributors, 1993) 186-187.

157) Qur'ân, 2:232.

158) Qur'ân, 4:128.

159) al-Jawziyyah, *Zâd al-Ma'âd*, op.oit., Vol. 4:34.

160) Qur'ân, 4:19.

161) Qur'ân, 58:2.

162) Sâbiq, S., *Fiqh al Sunnah*, op cit. Vol. 7:137.

163) Doi, 'Abdur Rah mân I. *Sharî'ah: The Islâmic Law*, (London, Ta Ha Publishers Ltd., 1984) 187.

164) Qur'ân, 2:226-227.

165) Qur'ân, 24:6-9.

166) Qur'ân, 2:230.

167) Doi, A.R.I. *Women in Sharî'ah*, (London, Ta Ha Publishers Ltd., 1989) 92-93.

168) Abû 'Îsâ, *Sunan al-Tirmidhî*, op.cit., Vol. 9:25.

CHAPTER FOUR

1) Leviticus, 18:6-20.
2) Qur'ân, 17:32.
3) al-Qaradâwî, *The Lawful and the Prohibited in Islâm,* op.cit., 152.
4) Sahîh al-Bukhârî, op.cit., Kitâb al Hudûd.
5) Sahîh al-Bukhârî, op.cit., Kitâb al Hudûd.
6) 'Uthmânî, Shabîr Ahmad, *Tafsîr 'Uthmânî* (Pakistan: Aalameen Publications, 1991) Vol. 2:1285.
7) Qur'ân, 4:15.
8) Qur'ân, 4:16.
9) Qur'ân, 24:2.
10) Sahîh al-Bukhârî, op.cit., Kitâb al Hudûd.
11) Ibid.
12) Qur'ân, 24:4-5.
13) Qur'ân, 24:23-24.
14) Sahîh Muslim, op.cit., Vol. 2:67.
15) al-Sijistânî, *Abû Dâwûd,* op.cit., 608.
16) Sahîh Muslim, op.cit., Vol. 2:68.
17) Ibid.
18) Doi, *Sharîah: The Islamic Lâw,* op.cit., 240-241.
19) Qur'ân, 24:6-9.
20) *Bidâyah al Mujtahid,* op.cit., Vol. 2:120.
21) *H âshiyah al Dasûqî,* op.cit., Vol. 2:467.
22) *Bidâyah al Mujtahid,* op.cit., Vol. 2:121.
23) Ibid.
24) Doi, *Women in Sharî'ah,* op.cit., 127.
25) Al Hâtimy, *Women in Islâm,* op.cit., 143.
26) Qur'ân, 24:2.
27) Qur'ân, 24:3.
28) Sahîh al-Bukhârî, op.cit., 760.
29) Nicolas, op.cit., 135-141.
30) Sunday Times, March 23, 1997.
31) Qur'ân, 4:34.
32) Nicolas, op.cit., 158-160.
33) Ibid., 81-85, 125-129.
34) Ibid., 125-126.
35) Ibid., 128.
36) Genesis, 38.
37) Gathorne-Hardy, Jonathan, *Love, Sex, Marriage and Divorce* (London: Jonathan Cape Ltd. 1981) 62-63.
38) Ibid. 54-55.

39) Nicolas, op. cit., 153-157.
40) Miftâhî, *Modesty and Chastity in Islâm*, op. cit., 64-65.
41) Qur'ân, 23:5-6.
42) *Tafsîr 'Uthmânî*, op.cit., 1526
43) al-Nawawî, Abû Zakariyyâ Yahyâ ibn Sharaf, *Rawdat al-Tâlibîn* (Damascus: al-Maktab al-Islâmî n.d.) vol 7:206.
44) al-Juzairî, 'Abd al-Rahmân, *Kitâb al Fiqh 'alâ al-Madhâhib al-Arba'ah* (Beirut: Dâr al-Fiqh al-'Arabî n.d.) vol 5:137.
45) *Sahîh al-Bukhârî*, op.cit., vol 2:758.
46) Nicolas, op.cit., 108-9.
47) Ibid., 111.
48) *Sahîh al-Bukhârî*, op.cit., vol 2:922-923.
49) *Sahîh al-Bukhârî*, op.cit., vol 4:60.
50) *Tafsîr Ibn Kathîr*, op.cit., vol 2:279.
51) Qur'ân, 33:33.
52) *Sahîh Muslim*, op.cit.
53) Ibid.
54) Nicolas, op.cit., 207-211.
55) Qur'ân, 2:231.
56) *Sahîh al-Bukhârî*, Chapter on the Repugnance of Beating Wives, op.cit.
57) Qur'ân, 12:23.
58) Qur'ân, 12:24.
59) Qur'ân, 12:25.
60) *Tafsîr 'Uthmânî*, Vol. 2:1059.
61) Qur'ân, 12:26-28.
62) Qur'ân, 12:29.
63) Qur'ân, 12:30.
64) Qur'ân, 12:31.
65) Qur'ân, 12:32.
66) Qur'ân, 12:33-34.
67) Jagwanth, S., *Women and the Law* (Pretoria: H.S.R.C. Publishers 1994) 130-145.
68) De Ordine II.4(12).
69) Opuscula XVI.
70) Jagwanth, S., *Women and the Law* (Pretoria: H.S.R.C. Publishers 1994) 137-140.
71) Ibid. 146.
72) *Time*, (Rockfeller Centre, New York : Time Inc. 1977).
73) Ibid. 27-28.
74) Hoigard, Cecilie, *Backstreets Prostitution, Money and Love* (Oxford, U.K.: Blackwell Publishers 1992) 194.
75) *Time*, op. cit., 28.

76) Barry, Kathleen, *Female Sexual Slavery* (New Jersey: Prentice Hall Inc. 1979) 76.

77) *Sunday Tribune,* March, 1997.

78) Tyler, Rodney, *Daily Mail,* Friday, June, 1989.

79) Ibid.

80) *Time,* June 21, 1993, 40.

81) Ibid., 39.

82) Pânîpatî, op. cit., vol 8:359.

83) Qur'ân, 24:33.

84) Longino, Helen, 'What is Pornography?' in Lederer, Laura (Ed.) *Take Back The Night* 1980, 41-44.

85) Ibid., 42-44.

86) Brownmiller, Susan, 'Against Our Will, Men, Women and Rape' in *Women and the Law,* Jagwanth, S (Ed.), (Pretoria: H.S.R.C. Publishers 1994) 291.

87) Itzin, Catherine, *Pornography, Women, Violence and Civil Liberties* (New York: Oxford University Press, 1992) 49-50.

88) Erlich, Reese, 'Computer Porn at the Office', *The World, San Francisco Examiner* August 13, 1987 7.

89) Viets, Jack, *San Francisco Chronicle* October 15, 1987 A23.

90) Essop, Omar, *Pornography, A New Form Of Terrorism* (Denver: A.I.S. n.d.)

91) Van Rensburg, F.I.J., *Pornografie* (Mayville, Durban: Butterworth-Uitgevers (Edms) Bpk 1985) 125 as quoted from Kilpatrick, J.J., *The Smut Peddlers* (London:Elek Books 1961) 240, 289.

92) Jarvis, Charles W., 'Dobson-Bundy Interview' in *Focus on the Family* Colorado, Springs http://www.opendoor.com/Higher.Ground/tb.html.

93) Groth, A., et.al. "The Child Molester: Clinical Observation" in *Social Work and Child Sexual Abuse* (New York: Plenum Publishing Corp., 1982) 129-144.

94) Chelminski, Rudolph and Moussouris, Olivia in 'Europe's Paedophile Plague', *Readers Digest* April 1997 126-127

95) Ibid.

96) *The Daily News,* November 21, 1994.

97) Al-Hadis, op.cit.

98) Hancock, Maxine and Mains, K.B., *Child Sexual Abuse* (Great Britain: Highland Books, 1988) 6-7.

99) Hancock, Maxine and Burton Mains, Karen, *Child Sexual Abuse* (Great Britain: Highland Books, 1988) 5-11.

100) Ibid. 13.

101) Siemers, Mary Ellen, *"Treatment Methods for Adult Female Survivors of Incest: A Review of the Literature",* unpublished Masters Thesis, University of Wisconsin, May, 1986. 11-13.

102) Clark, Lorenne and Lewis, Debra, *Rape: The Price of Coercive Sexuality* (Toronto: Women's Educational Press 1977) 144.

103) *International Coalition Against Violent Entertainment* (ICAVE). Press Release 'Research finds rape common experience for American women. Pornography linked to large number of cases.' September 16, 1985.

104) Ledera, Laura, *Take Back The Night* (New York: Bantam Books 1982)11.

105) Consumers' Association of Penang, *Abuse Of Women In The Media* (Penang: C.A.P. 1983) 30.

106) Ibid. 67.

107) Leedera, L. op. cit. 66.

108) *Buffalo News*, Florida, April 24, 1984.

109) Ledera, L. op. cit. 11.

110) *The Star*, 'Kivis shocked by wave of violence' July 1, 1987.

111) Chappell, Duncan, *Forcible Rape* (New York: Columbia University Press 1977) 94.

112) *The Star*, 'Schoolgirls are in highest rape-prone groups' November 3, 1986.

113) Chappell, D. *Forcible Rape*, op. cit. 91.

114) Consumers' Association of Penang, *Rape in Malaysia* (Malaysia: C.A.P. 1988) 27

115) Ibid. 32.

116) *Sunday Mail*, March 30, 1986.

117) Rowland, Judith, *Rape: The Ultimate Violation* (London. Pluto Press Ltd. 1986) 141.

118) C.A.P. *Rape in Malaysia*, op. cit. 62-5.

119) Modi, *Modi's Textbook of Medical Jurisprudence and Toxicology* (Bombay: N.M. Tripathi Private Ltd. 1977).

120) C.A.P. *Rape in Malaysia*, op. cit. 53, 71-3.

121) Qur'ân 24:33.

122) *Bukhârî*, op. cit. Chapter on "No punishment for the raped girl" vol 2: 1027-8.

123) *Jam'al-Fawâid*, op. cit. vol 1: 287.

124) Goodwin, Jan, *Price of Honour* (U.S.A.: Little Brown and Co., 1994) 52-62.

CHAPTER FIVE

1) Knox, David, *Choices in Relationships* (New York: West Publishing Company, 1988) 48-50.

2) Hubbard, R., Wald, E., *Exploding the Gene Myth* (Boston: Beacon Press 1993) 94.

3) *Is Homosexuality a Choice?* http.www.dallas.net/~ligon/choice.htm

4) Ibid.

5) Byne, William, *"The Biological Evidence Challenged" in Scientific American* (New York: Scientific American, Inc. May 1994) 54-55.

6) Faris, Donald, *The Homosexual Challenge* (Markham, Ontario: Faith Today Publications 1993) 22.

7) Wortis, Joseph, "Homosexual Warriors", *Biologic Psychiatry* (New York: State University of New York 1993) 33:225-226.

8) Gairdner, William, *The War Against The Family* (Toronto: Stoddart Publishing Co. 1992) 367.

9) Baron, M., "Genetic Linkage and Male Homosexual Orientation" in *British Medical Journal* August 7, 1993.

10) Broude, G., Green., "Cross Cultural Codes on Twenty Sexual Attitudes and Practices", *Ethnology* 1976 15:409-430.

11) U.P.I., April 23, 1979.

12) Cameron, P., *"Born What Way?* (Washington: Washington D.C. Research Institute 1993).

13) *New York Tribune*, May 6, 1983.

14) Byne, W., *Scientific American,* op.cit., 52.

15) Ibid.

16) Allen, L., Gorski, R., *Sexual Orientation and the Size of the Anterior Commisure in Human Brain* (U.S.A.: Proc Natl Acad, Sci 1992) 89: 7199-7202.

17) *The Brain and Hormones in Homosexual Research*: http:/w.w.w.dallas.net/~ligon/brain.htm.

18) Byne, W., *Scientific American,* 53.

19) 'Ijâz, Dr Tâhir, *Homosexuality - An Analysis of Biological Theories of Causa-tion*, Winnipeg, Canada http:/w.w.w.utexas.homo0894.html edu/students/amso/rors

20) *The Moral Debate on Homosexuality* http:/www.dallas.net/ ligon/j intro.htm.

21) Romans 1:26-27.

22) Davis, Bob, Homosexuality in America : Exposing the Myths, *Moody Magazine*, May 1994.

23) Jellinghaus, Rob, robj@netcom.com uunet!netcom!robj (alt.politics.homosexuality) The A.P.H. *Frequently Asked Questions List*, Jan 22, 1994.

24) Ibid.

25) Smith, Michael and Bourgeois, Brent, *The Gay Dilemma* crossnet@nando.net.

26) Isaacs, Gordon and McKendrick, Brian, *Male Homosexuality in South Africa* (Cape Town: Oxford University Press 1992) 28.

27) Bundy, C. "Street Sociology and Pavement Politics: Aspects of Youth and Student Resistance in Cape Town 1985" *Journal of South African Studies,* April 1987, 13(3):303-330.

28) *Sunday Tribune,* April 14, 1996.

29) *Saturday Paper,* May 3, 1997.

30) al-Washtânî, commentary by *Sahih Muslim* op. cit., 444.

31) *Sahih Muslim* op. cit., 445.

32) al-Halbî, Ibrâhîm, *Multaqa al-Abhur* (Turkey: Istanbul Press, 1296 A.H.) 224-225.

33) Chescheir, Martha, "Some Implications of Winnicott's Concept for Clinical Practice", *Clinical Social Work Journal* 1985 13(3):228.

34) Isaacs, G., op. cit., 78-81.

35) Isaacs, Gordon and Miller D., "Aids - Its Implications for South African Homosexuals and the Mediating Role of the Practitioner", *South African Medical Journal* 68, 1985 327-330.

36) Blachford, Gregg, "Male Dominance and the Gay World" in Plummer, Kenneth (ed.) *The Making of the Modern Homosexual* (London: Hutchinson 1981) 190-191.

37) Schurink, W.J. *Gayness : A Sociological Perspective.* Paper presented at Mardi Gay : GASA Fourth Convention, Johannesburg.

38) Read, Kenneth, *Other Voices : The Style of a Male Homosexual Tavern* (California: Chandler and Sharp 1980) 69-70.

39) Bronski, Michael, *Culture Clash - The Making of Gay Sensibility* (Boston: South End Press 1984) 53.

40) Stanford, John, *Spartacus Internatinal Gay Guide* (Holland: Spartacus 1981) Eleventh Edition.

41) Isaacs, G., op. cit., 69-107.

42) Plummer, K., "Going Gay : Identities, Life Cycles and Lifestyles in the Male Gay World" in Hart, I. and Richardson, D. (eds) *The Theories and Practice of Homosexuality* (London: Routledge and Kegan Paul 1981) 198.

43) Dunlop, David, "Panel in Hawaii Recommends Legalizing Same-Sex Marriage" *The New York Times,* Dec 11, 1995 A-18.

44) The Constitution of the State of Hawaii states: All persons in Hawaii are entitled to be ... free from illegal discrimination or the denial of basic rights on the basis of gender. 74 Haw. 530 1993.

45) Sorokin, Pitirim, *The American Sex Revolution* (Boston: Porter Sargent Publishers 1956) 77-105.

46) Hawaii Commission on Sexual Orientation "Article 1, sections 2, 3, and 5."

47) *The Daily News*, March 26, 1996.

48) Cranford, Helen, The Telegraph as quoted in *The Sunday Times* April 21, 1996.

49) Straight Talk April 10, 1996 http:/www.townhall.com/townhall/FRC/net/ st96d2.html

50) American Security Council Foundation, "Confidential Survey of 1040 Active Duty U.S. Flag and General Officers" June 7-21, 1993.

51) Defense Readiness Council, "Survey of Retired Flag Officers", June 15, 1993.

52) McCann, Hugh, "HIV Infection Rate Highest at Outset". *The Detroit News*, January 6, 1995 B-3.

53) Department of the Army Memorandum, "Potential Medical Implications of Homosexuality in the Military" Office of the Surgeon General, April 29, 1993.

54) Fitzpatrick, John, *The Writings of George Washington ... 1745-1799* (Washington: G.P.O. 1934) vol. 2:83-84.

55) JAG Reports for 1889 and 1890 state that 670 and 890 soldiers were convicted under Article 62.

56) W.D. OTSG. Circ. "Examinations in Nervous and Mental Disease" in *The Medical Dept. of the United States Army in the World War* (Washington: G.P.O. 1929) vol. 10:66-69.

57) Berube, Allen, *Coming Out Under Fire : The History of Gay Men and Women in World War II* (New York: Free Press 1990) 261.

58) William, Collin and Weinberg, Martin, *Homosexuals and the Military* (New York: Harper and Row 1971) 28.

59) Snyder, William, "Gays and the Military : An Emerging Policy Issue" *Journal of Political and Military Sociology* 1980 vol. 8 no. 1 - 74.

60) Department of the Army Memorandum "Analysis of Punitive Homosexual Separations" prepared by the Office of the Judge Advocate General, May 27, 1993, FY 89-92.

61) National Survey - March 31, 1993, Fabrizio, McLaughlin and Associates, Alexandria. April 2, 1993. This poll was commissioned by the American Security Council Foundation.

62) Nicolas, W., op. cit., 187-190.

63) Hite, Shere, *The Hite Report on the Family* (London: Bloomsbury Publishing Ltd. 1994) 134-135.

64) Ibid. 135.

65) Ibid. 117.

66) Ibid. 118.

67) O'Donnell, David, Wyoming (U.S.A.) *Custody Battle : Abuse v Lesbianism* GLB-NEWS<GLB-NEWS@BROWNVM.BROWN.EDU> March 1995.

68) al-Râzî, Fakhruddîn, *al-Tafsîr al-Kabîr* op.cit.

69) Wockner, Rex, Outlines Chicago, Dec 1995 outlines@suba.com.

70) Ibid.
71) Buckmere, Ron, Zimbabwe Parliament Debate on *Homosexuality and Lesbianism* Nov 1995<ron@aba cus.oxuedu>
72) Ibid.
73) Qur'ân, 7:80-81.
74) Qur'ân, 11:78.
75) Qur'ân, 11:82.
76) Homosexuality, *The Majlis*, op. cit.
77) Miftâhî, op. cit., 255-256.
78) Maudûdî, *Purdah*, op. cit., 59.
79) Miftâhî, op. cit., 258.
80) Qur'ân, 4:16.
81) Abû 'Îsâ, Muhammad ibn 'Îsâ, *Sunan al-Tirmidhî*, (India: Kutub Khânâ Rashîdîyah n.d.) vol. 1 : 148.
82) Qur'ân, 2:223.
83) Qur'ân, 2:222.
84) al Nawawî, *Sharh Sahîh Muslim* op. cit., vol. 1 : 463.
85) Qur'ân, 27:55.
86) Ibid.
87) Ibn Qayyim, *Al-Jawâb al-Kâfî*, op. cit., 229 (Those supporting this view were Abû Bakr, 'Alî, Khâlid ibn Walîd, 'Abdullah ibn 'Abbâs, 'Abdullâh ibn Zubair, Khâlid ibn Zaid, 'Abdullâh ibn Mu'ammar, among the Companions, and then Zahrî Rabi'ah ibn 'Abd al'Rahmân, Imâm Mâlik, Ishâq ibn Rehwaiah and Imâm Ahmad ibn Hanbal among the followers after the Companions, are all unanimous on it. And Imâm Shâfi'î is partly of this opinion.)
88) Ibid. ('Atâ ibn Rabî'ah, Hasan Basrî, Sa'îd Ibn Musaiyeb, Ibrâhîm Nakha'î, Qatâdah, Auza'î, Imâm Abû Yûsuf, Imâm Muhammad and Imâm Shafi'î in his stated opinion. There is a report of Imâm Ahmad too in this behalf.)
89) Ibid.
90) 'Ainî, *'Umdat al-Qârî fî Sharh Sah ih al-Bukhârî* (Istanbul, Turkey, 1289 A.H.) vol. 10:279.
91) al-Asqalânî, Ahmad ibn Hajar, *Miftâhî al-Khitâbah* (Beirut: Matba'at al-Bahîyat al-Misriyyah n.d.) 217.
92) Muhammad 'Alâwuddîn Haskafî, *Durr al-Mukhtâr* (Pâkistân: Maktabah Mâjidiyyah 1399 A.H.) vol. 1:285.
93) Ibn 'Âbidîn, Muhammad Amîn, *Rad al Muhtâr* (Pâkistân: Maktabah Mâjidiyyah 1399 A.H.) vol. 1:285.
94) al-Asqalânî, *Miftâhî al-Khitâbah*, op. cit., 217.
95) al-Râzî, Muhammad Fakhruddîn ibn Ziâuddîn *Tafsîr Kabîr* (Beirut Maba'at al-Bahîyat al-Misriyyah n.d.) vol. 1:259.
96) al Nawawî, Abû Zakarîya Yahyâ ibn Sharaf, *Riyâd al Sâlihîn* (Pâkistân: N'umânî Kutub Khâna n.d.) 159.

97) al Asqalânî, *Fath al Bârî*, op. cit., 21, 48.

98) Gong, Victor, "Preface - Update on Aids Research" in *Understanding Aids - A Comprehensive Guide* (London: Cambridge University Press) xv-xxii.

99) Borland, Mary, "Helping Children with Aids : The Role of the Child Welfare Worker" *Public Welfare*, Winter Issue vol. 2 : 329.

100) Clarke, James, *The Star*, November 3, 1889.

101) Hoff, Lee Ann, *People in Crisis, Understanding and Helping* (California: Addison-Weekly Publishing Company 1978).

102) Miller, David, "Counselling : ABC of AIDS", *British Medical Journal* 1987 vol. 1: 673.

103) Spracklen, Dr Frank, *Avoiding Aids* (Cape Town: Anubis Press, 1987) 18-21.

104) Ibid., 20-21.

105) Ibid., 21-22.

106) Ibid., 18-22.

107) Ibid., 12-13.

108) Ibid., 6-7.

109) Hansfield, H., "Sexually Transmitted Disease in Homosexual Men", *American Journal of Public Health*, 1981 vol. 9 : 989-990. See also Jaffe, H.W. and Keewhan, C., "National Case-Control Study of Kaposi's Sarcoma and Pneumocystis Carinii Pneumonia in Homosexual Men, Part 1, Epidemiological Results", *Annals of Internal Medicine* 1983 vol. 99(2): 145-157.

110) Lever, Janet, "Sexual Revelations : The 1994 Advocate Survey of Sexuality and Relationships : The Men", *The Advocate* August 23, 1994 21-22.

111) Ibid.

112) Wrottesley, Roz, Fairlady (Cape Town: National Magazine Ltd. May 1, 1997) 80.

113) Seidman, Stuart and Rieder, Ronald, "A Review of Sexual Behaviour in the United States', *American Journal of Psychiatry*, March 1994, vol. 151 : 335.

114) *HIV Treatment May Cost $15 Billion by 1995*. Research Activities, U.S. Dept of Health and Human Services, July 1992, no. 155:1, and *HIV and Homosexuals in the Army Versus the Civilian Community*, Dept of the Army Information Paper, Office of the Deputy Chief of Staff of Personal, Jan 27, 1993.

115) Spracklen, F., *Avoiding Aids* op.cit., 6.

116) Cameron, Paul, "The Homosexual Lifespan", *Omega* 1994, vol. 29, no. 3 : 249-272.

117) Zarembo, Alan, "The Aids Gap" in *Newsweek*, December 8, 1997) 40-43.

118) Waterval Islâmic Institute *Islâm and Aids* (Lenasia: Jamî'atul 'Ulamâ 1991).

119) Ibid.

120) Ibid., 25.

121) Joubert, Dian, *Tot Dieselfde Geslag : Debat oor Homoseksualiteit in 1968.* (Cape Town 1974) 2.
122) *The Star* December 10, 1990.
123) *Saturday Star*, Nov 3, 1990.
124) *Sunday Tribune*, March 29, 1989-19.
125) Isaacs, G., op. cit., 123.
126) Glanz, L., *Attitudes of White South Africans Toward Certain Legal Rights of Homosexuals.* Memorandum submitted to the President's Council, Pretoria H.S.R.C. 1987, 1.

CHAPTER SIX

1) Athar, Shâhid, *Sex Education: An Islâmic Perspective* (Chicago:Kâzî Publications 1995) 2-9.
2) Ibid.
3) Desai, Moulânâ A.S., *The Majlis,* vol 10 no.1 Page 6.
4) Athar, S. op. cit., 9-10.
5) Reproduced from the *Eastern Province Herald* and quoted in The Majlis op. cit.
6) Sarwar, Ghulâm, *Sex Education:The Muslim Perspective* (London:Muslim Educational Trust 1989) 2-27.
7) *The British Journal of Family Planning* 1990 15:112-117.
8) *The Independent* 21 July 1992.
9) Athar, S. op. cit., 10-11.
10) *Sunday Times* as quoted in The Majlis op. cit. vol 10 no. 10 Page 7.
11) *Post* as quoted in The Majlis op. cit. Page 12.
12) Majlisul 'Ulamâ of South Africa, *Debs Ball* (Benoni:Young Men's Muslim Association n.d.) 3.
13) Ibid.
14) Qur'ân, 4:34.
15) *Sunday Times* as quoted in The Majlis vol 10 no. 2 Page 8.
16) South African Press Association (Sapa).
17) *Eastern Province Herald* 2 Nov. 1989.
18) Majlisul 'Ulamâ of South Africa, *Alcoholism, Drug Addiction and Immorality in Schools* (Benoni:Y. M.M.A. n.d.) 3-4.

19) Qur'ân, 66:6.
20) Qur'ân, 86:6-7.
21) Qur'ân, 23:12-14.
22) Qur'ân, 2:222.
23) Qur'ân, 2:223.
24) Qur'ân, 7:189.
25) *Ṣaḥîḥ al-Bukhârî*, op.cit. Chapter on "If male and female organs come in close contact", vol 1:43.
26) Qur'ân, 2:187.
27) Miṣhkât, op.cit. 271.
28) Edwards, I.S., *Sex For Modern Teenagers* (Adelaide:Rigby Publishers Ltd 1981) 9-27.
29) Qur'ân, 49:12.
30) *Ṣaḥîḥ al-Bukhârî*, op.cit., vol 2:760.
31) *Ṣaḥîḥ al-Bukhârî*, op.cit., 788.
32) *Ibn Mâjah*, op.cit.
33) *Tirmidhî*, op.cit. 776.
34) *Ṣaḥîḥ al-Bukhârî*, op.cit., 766
35) *Ṣaḥîḥ al-Bukhârî*, op.cit., 42.
36) Ibid., 788.
37) *Ṣaḥîḥ Muslim*, op. cit; *Ṣaḥîḥ al-Bukhârî*, op.cit., vol 2:760.
38) Qur'ân, 22:5.
39) *Ṣaḥîḥ Muslim*, op. cit. Kitâb al-Qadar.
40) Pânîpatî, *Tafsîr Maẓharî* op. cit. vol 11:168-169 See also *Ṣaḥîḥ Muslim*, Kitâb al Qadar 332.
41) Oosthuizen, G.C., *The Great Debate:Abortion in the South African Context* (Cape Town:The Citadel Press 1974) 14-15.
42) Knox, David, *Choices in Relationships* (New York: West Publishing Company, 1985) 466-467.
43) Ibid., 475-477.
44) Edwards, I.S. op.cit. 27-29.
45) Athar, S. ed. *Sex Education:An Islâmic Perspective* Internet http://www.safaar.com/s5.html.
46) Paul II, Cf. John, Apostolic Exhortation, *Familiaris Consorto*, Nov. 22, 1981 - 25.
47) Cf. Pontifical Council for the Family, *Ethical and Pastoral Dimensions of Population Trends* (Vatican: Libreria Editrice Vaticane, March 25, 1994) 28 and 84.
48) *Sunday Tribune*, May 11, 1997.
49) Johnson, Sharon K., *How to talk to your teenager about Sex* (Issaquah, Washington: S.K.Johnson 1989) 21-22.
50) Ibid.

BIBLIOGRAPHY

'Abdul Raûf, Muhammad, *Marriage in Islâm* (New York: Exposition Press Inc. 1977).

Abû 'Îsâ, Muhammad ibn 'Îsâ, *Sunan al Tirmidhî* Bâb al-Nikâh (Delhi, India: Kutub Khâna Rashîdiyyah n.d.).

al-Âlûsî, Sayad Mahmûd, *Rûh al-Ma'ânî* (Beirut: Dâr al-Kitâb al-'Arabî n.d.).

al-'Asqâlânî, Ahmad ibn Hajar, *Fath al-Bârî Sharh Sahîh al-Bukhârî* (Beirut: Matba'at al-Bahîyat al Misriyyah, 1982); *Miftâhî al-Khitâbah* (Beirut: Matba'at al-Bahîyat al-Misriyyah n.d.).

al-Baidâwî, Qâdî Nasîruddîn, *Tafsîr Baidâwî* (Cairo: Dâr al-Ma'ârif n.d.).

al-Bukhârî, Muhammad ibn Isma'îl *Sahîh al Bukhârî* (India: Mukhtâr and Co., 1983).

al-Dasûqî, Shams al Dîn Muhammad ibn 'Arafah, *Hâshiyah al Dasûqî* (Cairo: Dâr Ihyâ al Kutub al 'Arabiyyah n.d.).

al-Hâtimy, Sa'îd 'Abdullâh Seif, *Women in Islâm: A Comparative Study* (Pakistan: Islâmic Publications Ltd. n.d.).

al-Jassâs, Abû Bakr Ahmad ibn 'Alî, *Ahkâm al-Qur'ân*, (Beirut: Dâr al-Kitâb al 'Arabî, 1335 A.H.).

al-Jawziyyah, Muhammad ibn Abî Bakr ibn Qayyim, *Zâd al Ma'âd fî Khair al 'Ibâd* (Cairo: Matba'at al Halabî, 1950).

al-Juzairî, 'Abd al-Rahmân, Kitâb al Fiqh 'alâ al-Madhâhib al-Arba'ah (Beirut: Dâr al-Fiqh al-'Arabî n.d.).

Allen, L., Gorski, R., *Sexual Orientation and the Size of the Anterior Commisure in Human Brain* (U.S.A.: Proc Natl Acad, Sci, 1992).

al-Nawawî, Abû Zakariyyâ Yahyâ ibn Sharaf, *Rawdat al-Tâlibîn* (Damascus: al-Maktab al-Islâmî n.d.), *Riyâd al-Sâlihîn* (Lahore: Pakistan N'umânî Kutub Khânä, 1977); *Sharh Sahih Muslim* (Cairo: Dâr Matabi'al Sh'ab n.d.).

al Qurtubî, Abû 'Abd Allâh, *al Jâmi'i lî Ahkâm al-Qur'ân* (Cairo: Dâr al-Ma'ârif, 1967).

al-Râzî, Abû Bakr Muhammad ibn Zakarîyya, *Tafsîr al-Râzî*; (India: 'Uthmâniyyah Oriental Publications Bureau, 1960)

al-Râzî, Muhammad Fakhruddîn ibn Ziâuddîn, *Tafsîr Kabîr* (Cairo: Dâr Matabi'al Sh'ab, n.d.).

al-Shawkânî, Muhammad ibn 'Alî ibn Muhammad, *Nail al-Awtâr* (Cairo: Dâr Matabi' al Sha'b, 1965).

al-Sijistânî, Abû Dâwûd Sulaimân ibn al-Ash'ath, *Sunan Abî Dâwûd* (Deoband, India: Mukhtâr and Co. 1985).

al-Tabarî, J'afar Muhammad ibn Jarîr *Târîkh Tabarî* (Beirut: Dâr al-Kutub al-'Ilmîyah, n.d.).

al-Zamakhsharî, Muhammad ibn 'Umar, *al-Kashâf* (Cairo: Dâr al-Ma'ârif n.d.).

393

'Alî, Dr Muhammad Mumtaz, *The Concepts of Islâmic Ummah and Sharî'ah*, (Malaysia: Pelanduk Publications, 1992).

Athar, Shâhid, *Sex Education: An Islâmic Perspective* (Chicago:Kâzî Publications, 1995); Internet http://www.safaar.com/s5.html.

American Security Council Foundation, *"Confidential Survey of 1040 Active Duty U.S. Flag and General Officers"* June 7-21, 1993.

Badawî, Dr Jamâl A., *The Status of Women in Islâm* (Saudi Arabia: Wakf Cendoment, 1991).

Bahador, Syed Ahmed Khân, *Life of Muhammad* (Lahore: Premier Book House, 1968).

Baron, M., "Genetic Linkage and Male Homosexual Orientation" in *British Medical Journal* August 7, 1993.

Barry, Kathleen, *Female Sexual Slavery* (New Jersey: Prentice Hall Inc., 1979).

Berube, Allen, *Coming Out Under Fire : The History of Gay Men and Women in World War II* (New York: Free Press, 1990).

Bhattacharya, A.N., *Dharma-Adharma and Morality in Mahabarata* (New Delhi: S.S. Publishers, 1992).

Blachford, Gregg, "Male Dominance and the Gay World" in Plummer, Kenneth (ed.) *The Making of the Modern Homosexual* (London: Hutchinson, 1981).

Borland, Mary, "Helping Children with Aids : The Role of the Child Welfare Worker" *Public Welfare*, Winter Issue.

Bronski, Michael, *Culture Clash - The Making of Gay Sensibility* (Boston: South End Press, 1984).

Broom, Leonard and Selznick, Philip, *Sociology* (New York: Harper and Row Publishers, 1973).

Broude, G., Green., "Cross Cultural Codes on Twenty Sexual Attitudes and Practices", *Ethnology,* 1976.

Brownmiller, Susan, 'Against Our Will, Men, Women and Rape' in *Women and the Law*, Jagwanth, S (Ed.), (Pretoria: H.S.R.C. Publishers, 1994).

Buckmere, Ron, Zimbabwe Parliament Debate on *Homsexuality and Lesbianism* Nov 1995<ron@aba cus.oxuedu>

Buffalo News, Florida, April 24, 1984.

Buhler, G., *The Laws of Manu* (New Delhi: Motilal Banarsidas, 1964).

Bundy, C. "Street Sociology and Pavement Politics: Aspects of Youth and Student Resistance in Cape Town 1985" *Journal of South African Studies*, April 1987.

Bureau, Paul, *Towards Moral Bankruptcy* (London: Constable and Co., 1925).

Butler, A.J.: *Arabs Conquest of Egypt and the Last Thirty Years of the Roman Dominion* (London: T.Werner Laurie, n.d.).

Cameron, P., *"Born What Way?"* (Washington: Washington D.C. Research Institute 1993); "The Homosexual Lifespan", *Omega* 1994.

Cf. Pontifical Council for the Family, *Ethical and Pastoral Dimensions of Population Trends* (Vatican: Libreria Editrice Vaticane, March 25, 1994).

Chappell, Duncan, *Forcible Rape* (New York: Columbia University Press, 1977).

Chaudhry, Muhammad Sharîf, *Women's Rights in Islâm* (New Delhi: Adam Publishers and Distributors, 1991).

Chelminski, Rudolph and Moussouris, Olivia in 'Europe's Paedophile Plague', *Readers Digest* April, 1997.

Chescheir, Martha, "Some Implications of Winnicott's Concept for Clinical Practice", *Clinical Social Work Journal*, 1985.

Clark, Lorenne and Lewis, Debra, *Rape: The Price of Coercive Sexuality* (Toronto: Women's Educational Press, 1977).

Clarke, James, *The Star*, November 3, 1889.

Cooke, Joanne, *The New Woman; A Motive Anthology on Women's Liberation* (New York, 1970).

Cranford, Helen, The Telegraph as quoted in *The Sunday Times* April 21, 1996.

Consumers' Association of Penang, *Abuse Of Women In The Media* (Penang: C.A.P., 1983); *Rape in Malaysia* (Malaysia: C.A.P., 1988).

Daryâbâdî, 'Abdul Majîd, *Tafsîr Daryâbâdî* (Pakistan: The Taj Company Ltd., n.d.).

Davis, Bob, Homosexuality in America : Exposing the Myths, *Moody Magazine*, May 1994.

Davis, William, N., *Holy Anorexia* (Chicago: University of Chicago Press, 1985).

Department of the Army Memorandum, "Potential Medical Implications of Homosexuality in the Military" Office of the Surgeon General, April 29, 1993.

Desai, Moulânâ A.S., *The Majlis* (Port Elizabeth, South Africa: Majlis al 'Ulamâ of South Africa).

Doi, 'Abdur Rahmân I. *Sharî'ah: The Islâmic Law*, (London, Ta Ha Publishers Ltd., 1984); *Women in Sharî'ah*, (London, Ta Ha Publishers Ltd., 1989).

Dunlop, David, "Panel in Hawaii Recommends Legalizing Same-Sex Marriage" *The New York Times*, Dec 11, 1995.

Durkheim, Emile, *The Elementary Forms of the Religious Life,* (New York, 1965).

Edwards, I.S., *Sex For Modern Teenagers* (Adelaide:Rigby Publishers Ltd, 1981).

Encyclopedia Britannica Micropedia.

Erlich, Reese, 'Computer Porn at the Office', *The World, San Francisco Examiner* August 13, 1987.

Essop, Omar, *Pornography, A New Form Of Terrorism* (Denver: A.I.S. n.d.)

Faris, Donald, *The Homosexual Challenge* (Markham, Ontario: Faith Today Publications, 1993).

Ferguson, Everett, *Studies in Early Christianity* (New York: Garland Publishing Inc., 1993).

Fitzpatrick, John, *The Writings of George Washington ... 1745-1799* (Washington: G.P.O., 1934).

Gairdner, William, *The War Against The Family* (Toronto: Stoddart Publishing Co., 1992).

Gathorne-Hardy, Jonathan, *Love, Sex, Marriage and Divorce* (London: Jonathan Cape Ltd., 1981).

Gibbon, Edward, *The Decline and Fall of the Roman Empire* (U.S.A.: Classics Appreciation Society, 1956).

Gibbs, H.A.R. and Kramer, J.H., *Shorter Encyclopaedia of Islâm* (Leiden: J.R. Brill, 1961).

Glanz, L., *Attitudes of White South Africans Toward Certain Legal Rights of Homosexuals*. Memorandum submitted to the President's Council, Pretoria H.S.R.C., 1987.

Gong, Victor, "Preface - Update on Aids Research" in *Understanding Aids - A Comprehensive Guide* (London: Cambridge University Press).

Haddard, Yvonne Y., *The Contemporary Islâm and the Challenges of History* (New York: State University Press, 1982).

Hansfield, H., "Sexually Transmitted Disease in Homosexual Men", *American Journal of Public Health*, 1981.

Haralambos and Holborn, *Sociology: Themes and Perspectives* (London: Harper Collins Publishers, 1996).

Hawkes, J., *The First Great Civilization* (London: London Press, 1973).

Heeren, Fâtima, *Family Life in Islâm* (Leicester, U.K.: The Islâmic Foundation, 1978).

Hencock, Maxine and Burton Mains, Karen, *Child Sexual Abuse* (Highland Books: Great Britain, 1988).

Hite, Shere, *The Hite Report on the Family* (London: Bloomsbury Publishing Ltd., 1994).

Hoff, Lee Ann, *People in Crisis, Understanding and Helping* (California: Addison-Weekly Publishing Company, 1978).

Hoigard, Cecilie, *Backstreets Prostitution, Money and Love* (Oxford, U.K.: Blackwell Publishers, 1992).

Hole, Judith and Levine, Ellen, "The Rebirth Feminism" in *The New York Times*, New York.

Houghton, G.C., *The Institutes of Manu* (New Delhi: Asian Educational Series, 1982).

Hubbard, R., Wald, E., *Exploding the Gene Myth* (Boston: Beacon Press, 1993).

Ibn 'Abbâs, 'Abdullâh, *Tafsîr Abdullâh ibn 'Abbâs*, (India: 'Uthmâniyyah Oriental Publications Bureau, 1280 A.H.).

Ibn 'Âbidîn, Muhammad Amîn, *Rad al Muhtâr* (Pâkistân: Maktabah Mâjidiyyah, 1399 A.H.).

Ibn al-Humâm, Kamâluddîn, *Fath al Qadîr*, (India: 'Uthmâniyyah Oriental Publications Bureau, n.d.).

Ibn Kathîr, Imâmuddîn Abî al-Fidâ Isma'îl, *Tafsîr al-Qur'ân*, (Damascus: Al-Maktab al-Islâmî, n.d.).

Ibn Qayyim, *Al-Jawâb al-Kâfî*, (Cairo: al-Matba'at al Salafiyyah, n.d.).

'Ijâz, Dr Tâhir, *Homosexuality - An Analysis of Biological Theories of Causation*, Winnipeg, Canada http:/w.w.w.utexas.homo0894.html edu/ students/amso/rors.

International Coalition Against Violent Entertainment (ICAVE). Press Release 'Research finds rape common experience for American women. Pornography linked to large number of cases.' September 16, 1985.

Isaacs, Gordon and McKendrick, Brian, *Male Homosexuality in South Africa* (Cape Town: Oxford University Press, 1992).

Isaacs, Gordon and Miller D., "Aids - Its Implications for South African Homosexuals and the Mediating Role of the Practitioner", *South African Medical Journal* 68, 1985.

Jagwanth, S., *Women and the Law* (Pretoria: H.S.R.C. Publishers, 1994).

Jameelah, Maryam, *Islâm and the Muslim Woman Today* (Lahore: Mahomed Yûsuf Khân, 1976).

Jarvis, Charles W., 'Dobson-Bundy Interview' in *Focus on the Family* Colorado, Springs http://www.opendoor.com/Higher.Ground/tb.html

Jellinghaus, Rob, robj@netcom.com uunet!netcom!robj (alt.politics.homosexuality) The A.P.H. *Frequently Asked Questions List*, Jan 22, 1994.

Johnson, Sharon K., *How to talk to your teenager about Sex* (Issaquah, Washington: S.K.Johnson, 1989).

Joubert, Dian, *Tot Dieselfde Geslag : Debat oor Homoseksualiteit in 1968*. (Cape Town, 1974).

Kalachen, *Islâm and Sexual Science*.

Kashânî, Fathullâh, *Tafsîr Minhâj al Sâdiqîn* (Tehrân, Irân: Dâr al-Kutub al-Islâmiyyah, 1396 A.II.).

Khân, Majid 'Alî, *Muhammad The Final Messenger* (Lahore: Sh. Muhammad Ashraf Publishers, 1983).

Kulaynî, Muhammad ibn Y'akûb Abû J'afar, *Usûl al-Kâfî* (Tehrân, Irân: Dâr al-Kutub al-Islâmiyyah, 1374 A.H.); *Furû' al-Kâfî* (Tehran, Irân: Dâr al-Kutub al-Islâmiyyah, 1374 A.H.).

Lecky, W.E.H. *History of Morality of Europe*.

Ledera, Laura, *Take Back The Night* (New York: Bantam Books, 1982).

Lemu, 'Âisha B, *Woman in Islâm* (Leicester, U.K.: The Islâmic Foundation, 1978).

Lever, Janet, "Sexual Revelations : The 1994 Advocate Survey of Sexuality and Relationships : The Men", *The Advocate* August 23, 1994.

Longino, Helen, 'What is Pornography?' in Lederer, Laura (Ed.) *Take Back The Night* 1980.

Majlisul 'Ulamâ of South Africa, *Debs Ball* (Benoni:Young Men's Muslim Association, n.d.).

Maudûdî, S.A.A., *Purdah and the Status of Woman in Islâm* (Pakistân: Islâmic Publications Ltd., 1990).

McCann, Hugh, "HIV Infection Rate Highest at Outset". *The Detroit News*, January 6, 1995.

McLaughlin, Fabrizio and Associates, *National Survey* (Alexandria: March 31, 1993).

Meyer-Bahlburg, H., "Psychoendocrine Research on Sexual Orientation: Current Status and Future Options" *Progressive Brain Research*, 1984.

Miftâhî, Muftî Zafeeruddîn, *Modesty and Chastity in Islâm* (New Delhi, India: Qâzî Publishers and Distributors, 1993).

Miller, David, "Counselling : ABC of AIDS", *British Medical Journal*, 1987.

Modi, *Modi's Textbook of Medical Jurisprudence and Toxicology* (Bombay: N.M. Tripathi Private Ltd., 1977).

Muhammad 'Alâwuddîn Haskafî, *Durr al-Mukhtâr* (Pâkistân: Maktabah Mâjidiyyah, 1399 A.H.).

Mutahharî, A.M., *Social and Historical Change* (Berkeley: Mîzân Press, 1986).

Muslehuddîn, Dr Muhammad, *Mutâ* (Lahore: Islâmic Publications Ltd., 1974).

Nadwî, A.H.A., *Islâm and the World* (New Delhi: Markazî Maktabî Islâmî, n.d.).

Nidâ-e-Haram, Karachi, Jamâd al-Ûlâ, 1369 A.H.

O'Donnell, David, Wyoming (U.S.A.) *Custody Battle : Abuse v Lesbianism* GLB-NEWS<GLB-NEWS@BROWNVM.BROWN.EDU> March 1995.

Oosthuizen, G.C., *The Great Debate:Abortion in the South African Context* (Cape Town:The Citadel Press, 1974).

Pânîpatî, Th, *Tafsîr Mazharî* (Pakistan: H.M. Saeed Co., 1979).

Paul II, Cf. John, Apostolic Exhortation, *Familiaris Consorto*, Nov. 22, 1981.

Plummer, K., "Going Gay : Identities, Life Cycles and Lifestyles in the Male Gay World" in Hart, I. and Richardson, D. (eds) *The Theories and Practice of Homosexuality* (London: Routledge and Kegan Paul, 1981).

Qummî, 'Ali ibn Ibrâhîm, *Tafsîr al-Qummî* (Najaf, Irâq: Matba'ah an-Najaf, 1386).

Radcliff, A.R., *African Systems of Kinship and Marriage* (London: London Press, 1970).

Rahmân, Afzalur, ed., "Role of Muslim Women in Society", *Encyclopedia of Seerah* (London: Seerah Foundation, 1987).

Rahmân, Fazlur, *Islâm and Modernity* (Chicago: The University of Chicago Press, 1982).

Read, Kenneth, *Other Voices : The Style of a Male Homosexual Tavern* (California: Chandler and Sharp, 1980).

Rowland, Judith, *Rape: The Ultimate Violation* (London: Pluto Press Ltd., 1986).

Salâmah, Dr Ahmad 'Abdullâh, *Mut'ah, The Sunnî and Shî'ah Perspectives on Marriage* (Jeddah, Saudi Arabia: Abul-Qâsim Publishing House, 1995).

Saraswati, Dayanand, *Satyarath Prakash* English Translation: "The Light of Truth" by Upadhyaya, Gayaprasad (New Delhi: Kala Press, 1956).

Sarwar, Ghulâm, *Sex Education:The Muslim Perspective* (London:Muslim Educational Trust, 1989).

Schopenhauer, Arthur, *Record*, Lagos, 20th April 1901.

Schurink, W.J. *Gayness : A Sociological Perspective.* Paper presented at Mardi Gay : GASA Fourth Convention, Johannesburg.

Seidman, Stuart and Rieder, Ronald, "A Review of Sexual Behaviour in the United States', *American Journal of Psychiatry*, March 1994.

Shaltût, Mahmûd, *al-Fatâwâ* (Cairo: Matbû'at al Idârat al Ammat lî al Thaqafah of al Azhar, December 1959).

Siddiqî, Muhammad Iqbâl, *Islâm Forbids Free Mixing of Men and Women in Islâm* (New Delhi: Adam Publishers and Distributors, 1986).

Smith, Jane I., "Women in Islâm, Equity, Equality and the Search for the Natural Order" in *Journal of the American Academy of Religion,* Dec. 1979.

Smith, Michael and Bourgeois, Brent, *The Gay Dilemma* crossnet@nando.net.

Snyder, William, "Gays and the Military : An Emerging Policy Issue" *Journal of Political and Military Sociology,* 1980.

Sorokin, Pitirim, *The American Sex Revolution* (Boston: Porter Sargent Publishers, 1956).

Stanford, John, *Spartacus Internatinal Gay Guide* (Holland: Spartacus, 1981) Eleventh Edition.

Straight Talk April 10, 1996 http:/www.townhall.com/townhall/FRC/net/ st96d2.html.

Sunday Times, (Rosebank, Johannesburg: Times Media Ltd. March 23, 1997).

Sunday Tribune, (Durban: Natal Newspaper House, March, 1997).

Tavard, G.H., *Woman in the Christian Tradition* (Notre Dame: University Press, 1973).

The Age of Greek Gods and Heroes, *Fortnightly Life*, 25 March 1963.

The Brain and Hormones in Homosexual Research: http:/w.w.w.dallas.net/ ~ligon/brain.htm.

The British Journal of Family Planning, 1990.

The Daily News, (Durban: Natal Newspaper House, March 26, 1996).

The Moral Debate on Homosexuality http:/www.dallas.net/ ligon/j_intro.htm.

The Whispers of Pompeii, *Fortnightly Life*, October 3, 1966.

Time, (Rockfeller Centre, New York : Time Inc., 1977).

Tûsî, Shaikh Abû J'afar, *Tahdhîb al-Ahkâm* (Tehrân, Irân: Dâr al-Kutub al-Islâmiyyah, n.d.).

'Uthmânî, Shabîr Ahmad, *Tafsîr 'Uthmânî* (Pakistan: Aalameen Publications, 1991).

Van Rensburg, F.I.J., *Pornografie* (Mayville, Durban: Butterworth-Uitgevers (Edms) Bpk, 1985).

Velde, Dr Van de, *Sex Hostility in Marriage* (London: George Allan and Unwin, n.d.).

Veyne, Paul, "The Roman Empire", in *A History of Private Life 1: From Pagan Rome to Byzantium* (Cambridge: Harvard University Press, 1987).

Viets, Jack, *San Francisco Chronicle,* October 15, 1987.

Walîullâh, Shâh Dehlawî, *Hujat Allâh al-Bâlighah* (India: Mukhtâr and Co., n.d.).

Waterval Islâmic Institute *Islâm and Aids* (Lenasia: Jamî'atul 'Ulamâ, 1991).

W.D. OTSG. Circ. "Examinations in Nervous and Mental Disease" in *The Medical Dept. of the United States Army in the World War* (Washington: G.P.O., 1929).

William, Collin and Weinberg, Martin, *Homosexuals and the Military* (New York: Harper and Row, 1971).

Wockner, Rex, *Outlines Chicago*, Dec 1995 outlines@suba.com.

Wortis, Joseph, "Homosexual Warriors", *Biologic Psychiatry* (New York: State University of New York, 1993).